**AIX RS/6000**

## J. Ranade Workstation Series

CHAKRAVARTY • *Power RISC System/6000: Concepts, Facilities, and Architecture,* 0-07-011047-6

CHAKRAVARTY, CANNON • *PowerPC: Concepts, Architecture, and Design,* 0-07-011192-8

HENRY, GRAHAM • *Solaris 2.X System Administrator's Guide,* 0-07-029368-6

JOHNSTON • *OS/2 Connectivity and Networking: A Guide to Communication Manager/2,* 0-07-032696-7

LAMB • *MicroFocus Workbench and Toolset Developer's Guide,* 0-07-036123-3

LEININGER • *UNIX Developer's Tool Kit,* 0-07-911646-9

LOCKHART • *OSF DCE: Guide to Developing Distributed Applications,* 0-07-911481-4

RANADE/ZAMIR • *C++ Primer for C Programmers,* 0-07-051487-9

SANCHEZ, CANTON • *Graphics Programming Solutions,* 0-07-911464-4

SANCHEZ, CANTON • *High Resolution Video Graphics,* 0-07-911646-9

SANCHEZ, CANTON • *PC Programmer's Handbook,* 0-07-054948-6

WALKER, SCHWALLER • *CPI-C Programming in C: An Application Developer's Guide to APPC,* 0-07-911733-3

WIGGINS • *The Internet for Everyone: A Guide for Users and Providers,* 0-07-067019-8

*To order or receive additional information on these or any other McGraw-Hill titles, please call 1-800-822-8158 in the United States. In other countries, contact your local McGraw-Hill representative.* ***BC14BCZ***

# AIX RS/6000

## System and Administration Guide

James W. DeRoest

**McGraw-Hill, Inc.**

New York San Francisco Washington, D.C. Auckland Bogotá
Caracas Lisbon London Madrid Mexico City Milan
Montreal New Delhi San Juan Singapore
Sydney Tokyo Toronto

**Library of Congress Cataloging-in-Publication Data**

DeRoest, James W.
AIX RS/6000 : system and administration guide / James W. DeRoest.
p. cm. — (J. Ranade workstation series)
Includes bibliographical references and index.
ISBN 0-07-036439-7
1. Operating systems (Computers) 2. AIX (Computer file) 3. IBM RS/6000 Workstation. I. Title. II. Series.
QA76.76.063D472 1994
005.4'4—dc20 94-20433
CIP



1 2 3 4 5 6 7 8 9 0 DOC/DOC 9 0 9 8 7 6 5 4

ISBN 0-07-036439-7

*The sponsoring editor for this book was Jerry Papke, the editing supervisor was Joseph Bertuna, and the production supervisor was Pamela A. Pelton. It was set in Century Schoolbook by McGraw-Hill's Professional Book Group composition unit.*

*Printed and bound by R. R. Donnelley & Sons Company.*

*Illustrations and screen images for InfoExplorer and X11 SMIT are reproduced with permission by IBM Corp.*

*This book is dedicated to my wife Meleece. She
has given me five wonderful daughters
and the support it takes to
live with them!*

# Contents

# Preface

*AIX RS/6000: System and Administration Guide* describes the administration and management activities required to install, configure, and operate the AIX Operating System on IBM RISC System/6000 platforms. The text covers many of the tasks common to most UNIX implementations, yet also focuses on the areas where AIX provides different or enhanced functionality. Areas where AIX command personalities represent either or both of its BSD and SYSV counterparts are highlighted.

### Why an AIX Administration Text?

Until very recently, the only information available concerning administering AIX systems resided in the AIX documentation set. Because the AIX manuals are delivered as softcopy with the base product, few sites ordered the hardcopy versions of the manual set. While softcopy manuals work very well for ad hoc queries, they are difficult to read over long periods of time. It's also very inconvenient to pick up your RS/6000 and carry it home to bone up on the operating system after dinner.

The IBM Technical Support Centers have done an excellent job of filling in some of the information gaps with their topical *Red Books*. Periodicals like *AIXtra* and *RS/Magazine* have provided an avenue for disseminating information on vendor products and technologies. Self-support networks like the NetNews `comp.unix.aix` news group have helped to relate product experiences among the user base. What has been lacking is a text that consolidates the data from all these resources for new and experienced system administrators. *AIX RS/6000: System and Administration Guide* is intended to provide this first stepping stone to AIX and RS/6000 management information.

### Who Should Read This Book

The text is intended as a base reference for both new and experienced AIX system administrators. The subject matter is partitioned by function to facilitate quick access. A *keywords* section at the end of most chapters provides pointers into the detailed documentation presented in the IBM hardcopy manuals and InfoExplorer information bases.

The book culminates with a discussion of the emerging *clustering* and *mass storage archiving* technologies. These chapters include examples of these technologies and information on obtaining representative implementations.

## Moving Target

Over the last year, while writing this book, at least three releases of AIX have been announced. Now at the time of this writing, AIX V4 is rumored to be in beta testing. Each release has brought new function to the system. Add to this all the product changes and announcements from both IBM and third-party vendors, and you begin to see the dilemma I find myself in when trying to snapshot the AIX operating system for this text. I have tried to add the new features and information to the existing work as they have been made available. Unfortunately, at some point it was required to close out a chapter. The work includes AIX up to the 3.2.5 release. Future reprints will incorporate the latest version of AIX, as well as new product offerings like DCE.

## Acknowledgments

Like everything in the UNIX world, this text represents the work and experiences of a group of programmers, developers, and administrators whose names are too numerous to mention here. I would like to thank all those who regularly share their experiences and frustrations with the rest of us via the AIX-related news groups and electronic mail discussions. It has been my pleasure to work with many of the IBM AIX development team members and marketing personnel over the years. I can't say enough about the hard work and dedication these folks have done in providing us, the users, with a first-rate technical workstation and operating system. It has been a long and bumpy road from the days of VM/IX, IX/370, PC RT AIX & AOS, AIX/370, AIX/PS2, PAIX to AIX/ESA, and AIX V3. I would also like to thank my colleagues from the Open Systems Group of SHARE, Inc. and the staff at *RS/Magazine* for their continuing support. Many thanks to Martin Timmerman at the University of Waterloo for reviewing the work and keeping me honest in the presentation. Finally, I want to thank my wife Meleece, who is always my first reader and my dearest reader.

*James W. DeRoest*

Part

# 1

# System Administration Tasks and Tools

Chapter

# 1

# Introduction

## 1.1 System Administration

The UNIX operating system hasn't achieved the "drop it in and forget it" simplicity that makes MS-DOS so popular with the masses. Until recently, UNIX primarily inhabited the dusty halls of research institutions and universities. In these environments UNIX was used as a programmer's tool which could be built upon to meet the needs of the research community. It didn't have to be easy, it just had to be low cost and provide standard common interfaces to support research collaboration and tool building. It is the open, standards-based face of UNIX that has brought it to the forefront of the movement toward open systems.

The proliferation of low-cost RISC processors has brought UNIX onto the desktop. The open systems and right-sizing movements have brought UNIX into the commercial glass house. The time has come for UNIX to get a haircut, put on a suit, and go head to head with the legacy operating systems, from desktop to big iron. Vendors and standards groups are scrambling to define and implement UNIX system management and administration tools to satisfy the needs of this diverse user base. Are they succeeding?

We are beginning to see some of the first offerings in the realm of UNIX system management. Many of these tools are taking a good deal of heat from the traditional UNIX system administrator crowd because of the new approaches and protocols being employed to manage stand-alone and distributed UNIX environments. Whether this is good or bad remains to be seen. The Open Software Foundation (OSF) licensed their *Distributed Management Environment* (DME) technology in late 1993. While we wait for the standards to become shrink-wrapped reality, we can test-drive the current vendor solutions and vote on them with our hard-earned cash.

Since you are reading this book, we can safely assume there is still some work to be done. The wealth of services and resources provided also makes it quite complex. Like any multiuser operating system, UNIX requires special care to ensure that resources are distributed equitably among the user base and that these resources are secured from intrusion or failure. Our job as system administrators is to guarantee that these requirements are being met. How do we do it? Read on!

Before we roll up our sleeves and begin hacking on system tables, it might be helpful to those unfamiliar with UNIX history to see how we got to this wonderful piece of software called AIX. The following is an approximate genealogy of UNIX development milestones.

A Brief History of UNIX

| | |
|---|---|
| 1969 | UNIX is born on the DEC PDP-7 |
| 1974 | ACM publishes Thompson and Ritchie's paper on UNIX |
| 1975 | Bell Labs licenses UNIX to universities |
| 1977 | SCO and Interactive Systems founded |
| | BSD 1.0 |
| 1978 | UNIX Version 7 |
| | BSD 2.0 |
| 1979 | Berkeley ARPAnet Contract |
| | BSD 3.0 |
| 1980 | BSD 4.0 |
| 1981 | SUN founded |
| 1982 | AT&T System III |
| | SUN becomes Sun Microsystems |
| 1983 | AT&T System V |
| | BSD 4.2 |
| | Hewlett-Packard HP-UX |
| 1984 | AT&T System V.2 |
| | DEC ULTRIX |
| | X/Open Founded |
| 1985 | Sun NFS |
| | POSIX Founded |
| 1986 | AT&T SYSV.3, Streams, RFS |
| | BSD 4.3 |
| | IBM AIX RT PC |
| 1987 | AT&T SYSV.3.1 |
| | IBM IX/370 |
| 1988 | AT&T SYSV.3.2 |
| | BSD 4.3 Tahoe |
| 1989 | AT&T SYSV.4 |
| | IBM AIX/370 and AIX/PS2 |
| | OSF Founded |
| | OSF Motif |
| | UNIX International Founded |
| | Internet Worm on Nov 2 |
| | Sun SPARCstation |
| 1990 | BSD 4.3Reno |
| | IBM AIX RS/6000 |
| | OSF/1 |
| 1991 | IBM AIX/ESA |

| | |
|---|---|
| | Apple, IBM, Motorola Venture |
| | Sun Solaris 1.0 |
| 1992 | BSD 4.4 |
| 1993 | IBM PowerPC |
| | IBM Scalable POWER Parallel SP/1 |

## 1.2 RISC Architecture

The first *Reduced Instruction Set Computer* (RISC) was developed in 1975 at IBM T. J. Watson Research Center and called the *801* architecture. The IBM PC RT was based on 801 work. Although the 801 used a reduced number of instructions, it executed only one instruction per clock cycle. To improve performance, the 801 group started thinking about executing more than one instruction per cycle. This resulted in a second-generation RISC architecture that was dubbed *AMERICA*. The AMERICA architecture was taken on by the IBM Austin development lab in 1986. Austin development evolved the AMERICA architecture into what we know today as the *Performance Optimized With Enhanced RISC* (POWER) architecture used in the RISC System/6000.

### 1.2.1 Multichip POWER

The POWER architecture uses independent functional units in a superscalar implementation to issue and execute multiple instructions per clock cycle. Separate branch, integer, and floating-point units are fed via a four-word-wide path from the instruction cache, enabling the dispatch of four instructions per clock cycle. The next phase of multichip POWER architecture development will incorporate additional integer and floating-point units, increasing the number of instructions dispatched to six per clock cycle.

### 1.2.2 PowerPC

Back in 1991, IBM, Apple, and Motorola formed a joint development venture that would incorporate the POWER architecture into a single-chip design. This new architecture would come to be known as the *PowerPC* architecture. The PowerPC was designed to be a RISC implementation that could be used in low-cost personal computers, as well as combined in groups for multiprocessor implementations. The group simplified the POWER architecture, improving clock cycle times and the superscalar implementation. In the higher-end chips, 64-bit extensions were incorporated. All models of the chip are multiprocessor-enabled. The PowerPC chip uses three execution units to deliver three instructions per cycle. It is compatible at the application binary interface level with multichip POWER implementations.

At the low end, the PowerPC model 601 is destined for personal

**TABLE 1.1 RISC System/6000 Specifications**

| Model | Clock—MHz | MFLOPS | SPECint | SPECfp |
|---|---|---|---|---|
| 7011/ | | | | |
| 220 | 33 | 6.6 | 20.4 | 29.1 |
| 230 | 33 | 8.8 | 28.5 | 39.9 |
| 250 | 66 (601) | 12.7 | 62.6 | 72.2 |
| 7012/ | | | | |
| 320 | 20 | | | |
| 320H | 25 | | | |
| 340 | 33 | | | |
| 340H | 42 | 18.8 | 48.1 | 83.3 |
| 350 | 42 | | | |
| 355 | 42 | 18.8 | 48.1 | 83.3 |
| 360 | 50 | 22.2 | 57.5 | 99.2 |
| 365 | 50 | 22.2 | 57.5 | 99.2 |
| 370 | 62 | 25.9 | 70.3 | 121.1 |
| 375 | 62 | 25.9 | 70.3 | 121.1 |
| 7013/ | | | | |
| 520 | 20 | 9.2 | 32.8 | |
| 520H | 25 | | | |
| 530 | 20 | 15.4 | 46.1 | |
| 530H | 33 | | | |
| 540 | 30 | 16.5 | 38.7 | |
| 550 | 42 | 18.8 | 48.1 | 83.3 |
| 560 | 50 | | | |
| 570 | 60 | 22.2 | 57.5 | 99.2 |
| 580 | 62 | 38.1 | 73.3 | 134.6 |
| 580H | 55 | 101.1 | 97.6 | 203.9 |
| 590 | 66 | 130.4 | 117.0 | 242.4 |
| 7016/ | | | | |
| 730 | 25 | 15.4 | 46.1 | |
| 7015/ | | | | |
| 930 | 25 | | | |
| 950/950E | 42 | | | |
| 970 | 50 | 36.7 | 117.0 | |
| 970B | 50 | 31.0 | 58.8 | 108.9 |
| 980 | 62 | 42.1 | 126.2 | |
| 980B | 62 | 38.1 | 73.3 | 134.6 |
| 990 | 71 | 140.3 | 126.0 | 260.4 |

*Based on SPEC 92' benchmarks.

computers and technical workstations. The model 604 is intended for midrange systems. A low-power version of the 604 called the 603 is slated for the notebook market. At the high end, the model 620 is designed for numerically intensive and multiprocessor architectures.

## 1.3 AIX and UNIX

Is AIX UNIX? It's certainly different in many respects from what might be coined "legacy UNIX systems." What defines UNIX? Most vendor UNIX offerings, including AIX, pass the SVID tests and are POSIX compliant. Does this make them UNIX? Most of the differences found in AIX are related to system administration. As you might expect, this crowd is the most vocal when it comes to complaining or praising UNIX evolution. AIX offers a very solid mixture of BSD and SYSV features. Users from either environment will find it easy to make themselves at home. The measure of an operating system should be whether or not it provides an environment and tool set that assists rather than hinders your ability to do meaningful work. AIX holds up very well under this definition.

As far as where UNIX is going, one can only hope that the vendor community is serious about maintaining a common UNIX look and feel. The *Common Open Software Environment* (COSE) alliance started by HP, Sun, IBM, SCO, USL, and Univel is a step in the right direction.

## 1.4 AIX and OSF

AIX V3 commands and libraries were accepted by the OSF as the basis for their Application Environment Specification for the OSF/1 operating system. This is good news for the AIX user community in that they can expect to find the face of AIX on OSF/1 offerings from many vendors. Applications developed on AIX should port easily to the OSF/1 environment (grain of salt here).

## 1.5 System Administration Activities

What do system administrators do? They're faster than a speeding bullet and leap tall buildings in a single bound! Seriously, UNIX system management involves a diverse set of tasks that cover the gamut from installation and configuration to end-user support. In large environments, administrative tasks are managed by a group of administrators. Whether you are one or many, each administrator needs a general understanding of administration tasks as a whole.

The text is organized to logically reflect AIX administration themes and components, facilitating rapid location of the subject matter. Chapters comprise detailed subject descriptions, examples, and diagrams. Where appropriate, both *system management interface tool* (SMIT) and command line options are presented. Command examples are flagged with the shell prompt character "#" to distinguish them from other bullets and to remind the user that most configuration activities are performed with `superuser` privileges.

```
# command
```

Each chapter culminates with an *InfoExplorer* topic list for obtaining further information.

This text is intended as a pointer to the more specific information provided in the AIX hard-copy and InfoExplorer documents, as well as to provide some insights based on practical experience with the hardware and operating system.

### 1.5.1 System administration tasks and tools

This section overviews system administration responsibilities and identifies the base reference and management tools. Characteristics of the AIX help system, InfoExplorer, are described. Attention is devoted to using and tailoring the AIX System Management Interface Tool (SMIT), which can be used to manage most aspects of the AIX operating system.

### 1.5.2 System installation

Before you can administer a system, it must be installed. Steps required to install and apply service to AIX in diskfull and diskless environments are discussed. An overview of the RS/6000 architecture and boot process follows.

### 1.5.3 System configuration

Once the operating system is installed, it must be customized. This section describes the *Object Data Manager* (ODM) and how it is used to store and manage configuration data. The steps involved to add disks, printers, terminals, and tape devices to the RS/6000 and AIX are detailed.

### 1.5.4 Network management

This section discusses how to make your system accessible from a number of network architectures and topologies, as well as what tools and protocols are required to centrally manage a network of machines.

### 1.5.5 Services and resources

Now that you have a machine and a network connection, how are you going to make use of it? How do you control resource utilization? This section considers such questions and examines configuring services like electronic mail, Network News, MS-DOS support, and X Windows.

### 1.5.6 Users and security

A great deal of system administrator time and energy is devoted to managing user accounts. This section outlines ways to streamline account management, reporting, and maintaining system security.

### 1.5.7 System recovery and tuning

What do you do when things go bump in the night? Backup strategies and policies are explained. How do you keep your RS/6000 running hot? System monitoring tools and problem analysis techniques are reviewed.

### 1.5.8 Distributed systems

This section looks at tools and techniques that can be employed to build a farm of networked RS/6000s functioning as a loosely coupled multiprocessor. Strategies for providing batch, parallel, and archive services in a clustered environment are described.

Chapter

# 2

# InfoExplorer

## 2.1 AIX Help

Help! It's often the first thing uttered by a new AIX system administrator. You've invoked `man` to access help for a particular command. If you're lucky, a man page will be displayed, but it may be followed by two or three more! Being intrigued rather than put off, you type `man man` and discover the existence of an information marvel called *InfoExplorer* (info). You're still feeling adventurous, so you type `info` and press return. Just when you thought it was safe to go into the water!

One of the first hurdles for new AIX users is mastering the help system. Confusion over documentation location and access mechanisms is the primary problem. The AIX InfoExplorer hypertext documentation system provides a very powerful help search-and-retrieval tool; however, it requires a bit of a learning curve before you get comfortable using the help system. It's too bad that you need so much help to learn help!

## 2.2 InfoExplorer Overview

InfoExplorer provides an extensive GUI for perusing on-line documentation. It is at its friendliest when used from an X11 display, but it may also be used from ASCII tty and pty connections. The documentation *information bases* include AIX and RS/6000 manual text and graphics, reference index, glossary, product-related help files, and add-on databases like the *AIX Technical Library* of HOWTO and closed APAR documents. Hypertext links are used as fast paths between related documents, files, and programs. A public and private note facility supports annotation of documents. The user interface can be individually tailored to specify entry points, search criteria, and printing options. History trails and bookmarks further facilitate moving between documents.

## 2.3 InfoExplorer Installation

InfoExplorer software is delivered as a part of *Classic* AIX. The executables, fonts, `ispath` data and the NLS information bases are located in `/usr/lpp/info` (see Table 2.1). NLS information bases may reside either on CD-ROM or fixed disk. Locating the information bases on fixed disk will provide a snappier response, but requires an additional 250 MB of disk space.

In multilanguage environments, more than one NLS information base set may be installed. Access to a given NLS information base is defined by the `$LANG` environment variable. Separate information bases are provided for each product. A product information base may provide an updated version of the `/usr/lpp/info/data/ispaths` file. The `ispaths` file contains the hypertext paths and links used to cross-reference data in the information bases. Care must be taken to make certain you are using the correct `ispaths` file for the information bases installed on your system.

### 2.3.1 InfoExplorer on CD-ROM

If disk space is at a premium, access the InfoExplorer information bases from the distribution CD-ROM. Note that the CD-ROM distribution of InfoExplorer information bases is a bit different than that of preinstalled versions on disk. Mount the InfoExplorer distribution CD-ROM as a `cdrfs` file system. Copy the `ispaths.full` data file from the CD-ROM onto the fixed disk as `/usr/lpp/info/data/ispaths`.

```
# mount -v cdrfs -r /dev/cd0 /usr/lpp/info/$LANG
# cd /usr/lpp/info/$LANG
# cp ispaths.full ispaths
```

To have the InfoExplorer CD-ROM file system mounted at boot time, add an entry for the `cdrfs` file system to `/etc/filesystems`.

**InfoExplorer CD-ROM `/etc/filesystems`** Entry

```
/usr/lpp/info/En_US:

dev     = /dev/cd0
vfs     = cdrfs
```

**TABLE 2.1 InfoExplorer Paths**

| | |
|---|---|
| `/usr/lpp/info/bin` | Executables for X11 and ASCII displays |
| `/usr/lpp/info/data` | `ispaths` files describing paths and links |
| `/usr/lpp/info/X11fonts` | InfoExp fonts |
| `/usr/lpp/info/notes` | Public notes |
| `/usr/lpp/info/$LANG` | Information databases (CD-ROM mount point) |
| `$HOME/info` | Bookmarks |
| `$HOME/info/notes` | Private notes |

```
mount    = true
options  = ro
account  = false
```

For higher availability, copy selected information bases to fixed disk. These information bases will be available should the CD-ROM `cdrfs` file system not be mounted.

### 2.3.2 InfoExplorer on fixed disk

If you have disk space to spare, InfoExplorer response will be much better if the information bases are stored on fixed disk. To copy selected information bases from CD-ROM to the fixed disk, mount the InfoExplorer distribution CD-ROM as a `cdrfs` file system on the temporary mount point `/mnt`. Copy the selected information bases from the CD-ROM to the corresponding `/usr/lpp/info/$LANG/<name>` directories. Unmount the CD-ROM `cdrfs` file system when copying has been completed.

```
# mount -v cdrfs -r /dev/cd0 /mnt
# ls -al /mnt/$LANG
copy desired databases (Example nav, aix, etc)
# cp /mnt/$LANG/nav/* /usr/lpp/info/$LANG/nav
# cp /mnt/$LANG/aix/* /usr/lpp/info/$LANG/aix
# umount /mnt
```

If you decide to remove an information base from disk at a later date, use the `rm -r` command to erase the information base subdirectory from the `/usr/lpp/info/$LANG` directory.

```
# rm -r /usr/lpp/info/$LANG/pascal       Remove pascal help
```

### 2.3.3 InfoExplorer over NFS

If you want to share InfoExplorer information bases in a networked environment, export the `/usr/lpp/info/$LANG` directory using NFS. Interactive response over NFS to information bases residing on the servers hard disk is a bit better than local CD-ROM response. You may wish to export selected information bases rather than the whole set. Add the information base directories to the NFS server's `/etc/exports` file and an `/etc/filesystems` mount entry on each client.

*NFS Server* `/etc/exports` *InfoExplorer Example:*

```
/usr/lpp/info/En_US -ro,access = daisy.ferris.com
```

*NFS Client* `/etc/filesystems` *InfoExplorer Example:*

```
/usr/lpp/info/En_US:
```

```
dev       = /usr/lpp/info/En_US
vfs       = nfs
nodename  = rigel.ferris.com
mount     = true
type      = nfs
options   = ro,bg,soft,intr
account   = false
```

## 2.4 Using InfoExplorer

To start an InfoExplorer session, invoke the `info` command in X11 based environments, or `info -a` for ASCII devices. InfoExplorer will display the default *task* selection window and an InfoExplorer overview window for first-time users. The initial entry-point window may be customized after you become familiar with the system. Use the `customize` menu bar field to set defaults and preferences. The default menu buttons allow you to select InfoExplorer `Topic & Task Index`, `List of Commands`, `List of Books`, `Programming Reference`, `History`, `List of Bookmarks`, `List of Notes`, `Path`, or `Search`. InfoExplorer look and feel has changed somewhat in AIX 3.2.5, as compared with earlier AIX releases. These differences are minor, thus the information provided will be applicable to earlier versions. (See Figs. 2.1 and 2.2.)

```
# info        Start X11 interface
# info -a     Start ASCII interface
```

Alternate information bases, like the *AIX Technical Library,* are selected using `info -l <name>`.

```
# info -l techlib     Select techlib information base
```

In the X11 environment, menu options and hot links are selected using the mouse point-and-click interface. Scroll bars are used when text or option sets will not fit on one screen. Option boxes are provided to quickly set notes and bookmarks or move back and forth through the screen path.

Accessing InfoExplorer from an ASCII device requires the use of keys to negotiate your way around the system.

### 2.4.1 Hypertext links

Along with menu selections, InfoExplorer allows you to jump between related documents, glossary definitions, and data files, and also enables you to invoke commands through the use of *hypertext links.* Hypertext links are identified within displayed text through highlighting. To activate a link, point and click the mouse button on the highlighted text from an X11 session, or tab to the highlighted text and press the enter key in an ASCII session. Movement between links will be recorded in your session history file.

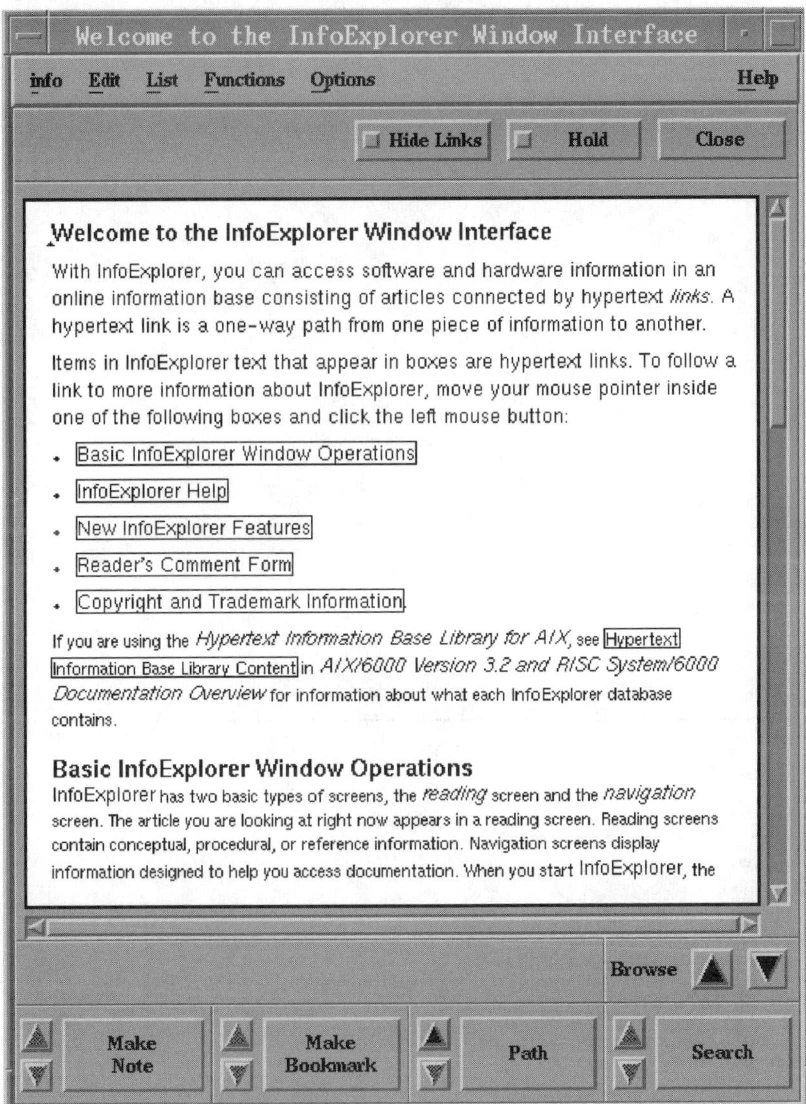


**Figure 2.1** InfoExplorer motif display.

### 2.4.2 Searching

The InfoExplorer search facility helps you find information when you aren't quite certain what you are looking for. Simple and compound text searching are supported with wildcard matching. A simple search involves a single short text string as a search argument (see Fig. 2.3). Compound searching (Fig. 2.4) supports boolean search semantics and defining the scope of the search within the document. You may also limit the information bases included in the search to

```
info    Help    Display    .History    Bookmarks    Notes    Search    Path    Exit

Topic   info Navigation

Topic & Task Index

About the Topic & Task Index

Using

Managing

Programming

Problem Solving

GLOSSARY

Answers to Customer Questions

Licensed Program Specifications (LPS)

README Files

To send a comment to IBM, see InfoExplorer Reader's Comment.
```

**Figure 2.2** InfoExplorer ASCII display.

**TABLE 2.2 InfoExplorer ASCII Key Mapping**

| | |
|---|---|
| Ctrl-N/PgDn | Page down |
| Ctrl-P/PgUp | Page up |
| Ctrl-W | Toggle reading and navigation |
| Ctrl-F/Tab | Move to next hypertext link |
| Ctrl-B | Move to previous hypertext link |
| Ctrl-L | Refresh screen |
| Left arrow | Move cursor one character left |
| Right arrow | Move cursor one character right |
| Up arrow | Move cursor one character up |
| Down arrow | Move cursor one character down |
| < | Move cursor 20 characters left |
| > | Move cursor 20 characters right |
| Ctrl-O | Activate menu bar |
| Esc-Esc/Ctrl-O | Close menu bar and move to text |
| Spacebar | Cycle through options in a ring |
| Enter | Activate a link or selection |

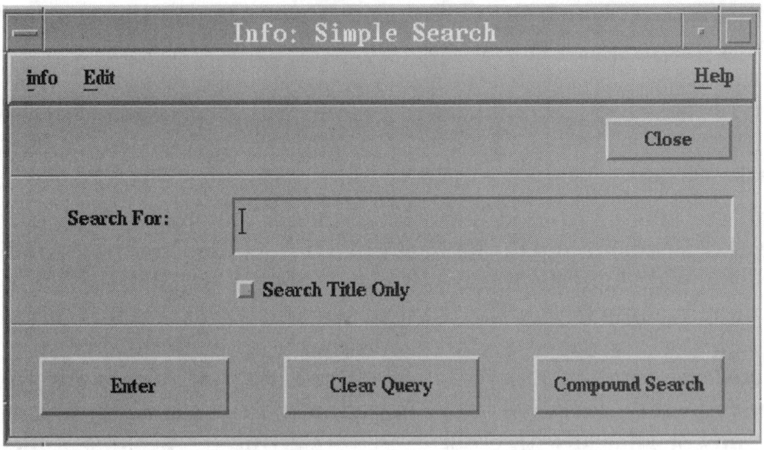

**Figure 2.3** Example simple search menu.

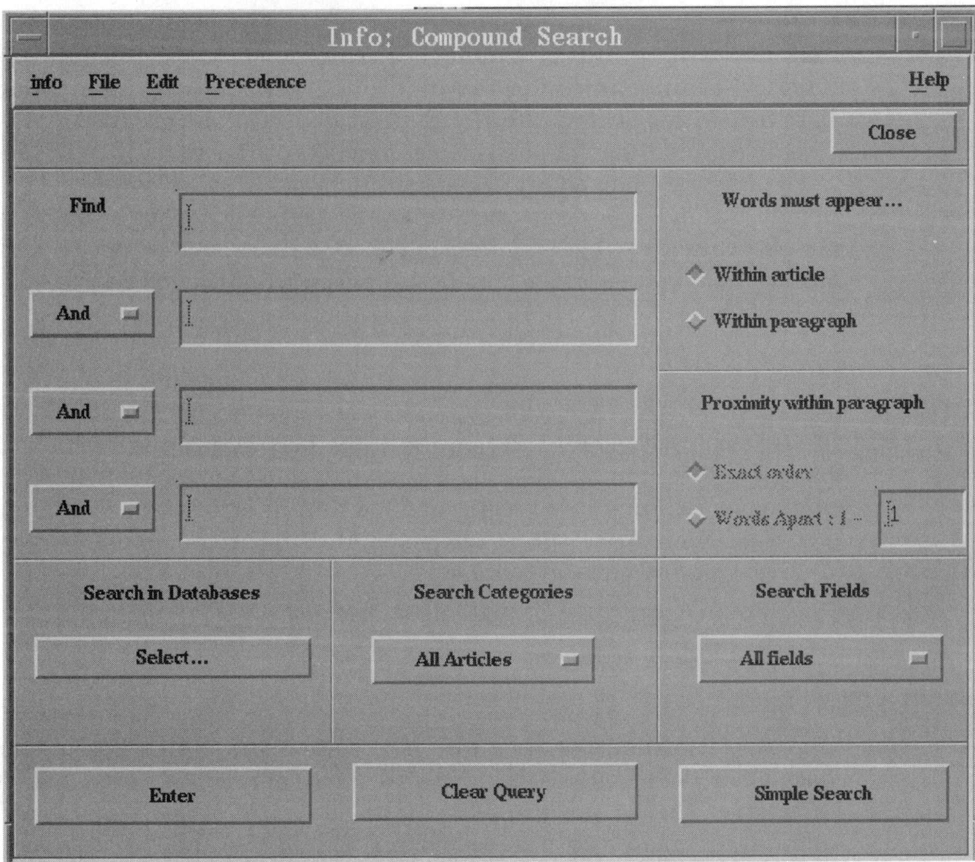


**Figure 2.4** Example compound search menu.

improve response. Quick searches may be invoked from the command line using the `info -h` option.

```
# info -h <searchkey>
```

### 2.4.3 History and bookmarks

To facilitate moving around in an InfoExplorer session, InfoExplorer records the document and display path in a *history* file. New path information is appended to the file as you move about in the system. At any time, you may jump forward or backward by selecting the `path` option. History files may be saved, restored, and shared with other users.

Selected information may be marked for later reference using the *Bookmark* facility. Bookmarks are stored in the `$HOME/info` directory and may be shared with other users by copying the bookmark files to the user's `$HOME/info` directory.

### 2.4.4 Note facility

Just like writing in the margins of hard-copy manuals, InfoExplorer supports an annotation facility. Individual users may tag information base text with *private notes.* Notes are stored in `$HOME/info/notes`. The note format may be customized to individual tastes.

Private notes may added or collected from public notes by the system administrator. Public notes can be grouped together and made available to the entire user base by using the `/usr/lpp/info/bin/mergenote` command. Public notes are stored in the `/usr/lpp/info/notes` directory.

```
# /usr/lpp/info/bin/mergenote <notelist>
```

### 2.4.5 Output

Text from InfoExplorer information bases may be printed or cut and pasted into other documents. Users may customize default print options by defining any valid command and filter stream using shell I/O redirection. Three print selections are supported: *simple printer, pretty print, and artwork printer.*

```
troff -Tpsc | psc | enq -P <PrinterName>
```
Postscript stream

## 2.5 InfoExplorer and `man`

The `man` command has access to information stored in InfoExplorer databases. When invoked, `man` will first search `/usr/man/cat?` directories, then `/usr/man/man?`, and finally InfoExplorer data. `man` and `catman` map man page sections 1, 2, and 8 to InfoExplorer commands documents; sections 2 and 3 to InfoExplorer subroutines documents; and sections 4, 5, and 7 to InfoExplorer files documents. You will need to periodically execute catman -w to keep the database for the apropos and whatis commands up to date.

### 2.5.1 Extracting man pages

A script is provided in the /usr/lpp/bos/bsdadm readme file that can be used to extract the man sections stored in InfoExplorer and store them as flat files in the appropriate /usr/man/cat? subdirectories. There is nothing fancy about the script. Basically it runs the man command on each file and redirects the output to a temp file. The temp file is then moved to /usr/man/cat?.

### 2.5.2 man page format

From time to time you may need to add your own custom man page information. This could be a help file explaining charging policies, backup support, locally developed software, etc. It's a good idea to keep local man pages separate from vendor-supplied help. This keeps it from getting stepped on during installation, maintenance, and upgrade activities. Commonly used location paths for local man pages are /usr/man/manl or /usr/local/man/man?. The $MANPATH environment variable can be set in /etc/environment to include your local man page path. Users may also use $MANPATH to support their own man directories.

```
Local man Page Repositories
/usr/man/manl
/usr/local/man/man?
/usr/local/cat/cat?
```

When creating new man pages, you can use an existing man page as a template. Try to stay within a common style so that your users know what to expect. Each man page should include a NAME section identifying the topic or command, a SYNOPSIS describing the command and argument options and format, a DESCRIPTION section that describes the topic, an OPTIONS section that details parameter and value information, and a section on known BUGS. At the end of the man page, a SEE ALSO section should indicate related information and an optional AUTHOR section should identify the author name and address.

*Example man Page Style:*

```
mycommand(1)

NAME

   mycommand - Does just what I want to do.

SYNOPSIS

   mycommand [will|wont] work

DESCRIPTION
```

```
   mycommand is always used as a last resort. It can be expected
   either to work or fail. mycommand contains no surprises at all.

OPTIONS

   will     Completes the work at hand.

   wont     Take a vacation.

BUGS

   mycommand is always error free!

SEE ALSO

   myprogram(1), myshell(1)

AUTHOR

   Me. Who did you think it was!
```

You can include `nroff` man tags in the man page to control display format (see Table 2.3). After the tags are included, you can test them using `nroff`.

```
# nroff -man mycommand.1 | more
```

*Example man Page with Tags:*

```
.TH mycommand 1

.SH NAME
mycommand \- Does just what I want to do.

.SH SYNOPSIS
mycommand [will|wont] work

.SH DESCRIPTION
.B mycommand
is always used as a last resort. It can
be expected either to work or fail.
.B mycommand
contains no surprises at all.

.SH OPTIONS
.TP 3
will
Completes the work at hand.
.TP 3
wont
Take a vacation.
```

**TABLE 2.3 Sample nroff man Tags**

| | |
|---|---|
| `.TH <name> <num>` | man page name and section number |
| `.SH <section>` | Identifies a subsection |
| `.B <text>` | Bold or highlighted text |
| `.I <test>` | Italics text |
| `.PP` | Block out a paragraph |
| `.TP <num>` | Indent paragraph <num> spaces except first line |

```
.SH BUGS
.B mycommand
is always error free!

.SH SEE ALSO
myprogram(1), myshell(1)

.SH AUTHOR
.B Me.
Who did you think it was!
```

Remember to run the `catman -w` command periodically to keep the `apropos` and `whatis` data up to date. You might want to add it to roots `crontab`.

## 2.6 Feedback

The IBM Austin Information Design and Development group would like your feedback and comments concerning AIX documentation and the InfoExplorer help system and other AIX publications. An *InfoExplorer Readers Comment Form* is included as part of the system and is accessible from the *Topic & Task Index*. Follow the instructions on the form and return it to the address indicated. You can also e-mail comments to them at the following Internet address:

**aix6kpub@austin.ibm.com**

## 2.7 QwikInfo

*InfoExplorer:*

| | |
|---|---|
| `/usr/lpp/info` | InfoExplorer product directory |
| `/usr/lpp/man/$LANG` | Hypertext database directory (disk, CD-ROM, NFS) |
| `mount -v cdrfs -r /dev/cd0 /usr/lpp/info/$LANG` | Mount info CD-ROM |
| `info` | Motif interface |
| `info -a` | TTY interface |

*man Pages:*
AIX man page location and search order:

| | |
|---|---|
| 1. `/usr/man/cat?` | Formatted text |
| 2. `/usr/man/man?` | nroff format |
| 3. `/usr/lpp/info/$LANG` | Hypertext |

| | |
|---|---|
| `catman -w` | Update whatis database for apropos command |
| `/usr/lpp/bos/bsdadm` | Contains sample script to convert InfoExplorer hypertext to man text |

Chapter

# 3

# System Management Interface Tool—SMIT

UNIX has a bad reputation when it comes to system management. Most of the traditional UNIX management tools are the products of necessity, built by frustrated system programmers. Historically, UNIX development efforts have focused on designing the building blocks that support this "roll-your-own" methodology—`Perl` being a case in point.

In production enterprises, UNIX must conform to the management policies and practices that are the hallmarks of big iron operating systems. Ad hoc tool development is not acceptable in many of these environments. A new breed of UNIX management tools is required that will provide centralized control over distributed heterogeneous resources. The tools should also interoperate with the existing legacy tool sets. The Open Software Foundation is ready to license its *Distributed Management Environment* (DME), however, real shrink-wrapped DME tools remain products of the future.

Rather than wait, many vendors have begun testing the waters with their own UNIX management tools. In general, most of these tools integrate graphical interfaces with traditional UNIX commands to streamline system installation, configuration, and management tasks.

## 3.1 SMIT Overview

AIX provides a central administration and management tool called the *system management interface tool* (SMIT). SMIT is a complete administrator's toolbox that may be used to perform system management activities such as software installation and maintenance, device configuration, administration of user accounts, system backups, and diagnosis of problems. SMIT uses a menu-driven interface that streamlines and simplifies the complexity of many system management activities. SMIT does not inhibit or replace command line access to system management; rather, it uses these same commands under the cover of the menu-driven interface. Not all possible command and argument combinations are available under SMIT. Command and parameter selection is based on the most common use to complete a given management task.

For novice administrators, SMIT simplifies system management through the use of task-oriented dialogs. New users can zero in on a particular task by stepping through SMIT's submenu hierarchy. Menu options for a specific task are identified with descriptive field titles and contextual help. Error-checking routines validate argument type and range.

The advanced administrator may find that SMIT provides a faster interface to many management tasks. The SMIT script facility may be used to assist in creating complex administration scripts.

The choice is yours whether or not you elect to use SMIT to manage AIX. As you gain experience with SMIT and the AIX environment, you may find that you prefer to use SMIT for some management activities and the command line for others. Whether you love it or hate it, SMIT is here to stay. As they say, *SMIT happens!*

## 3.2 Using SMIT

SMIT is started by executing the `smit` command from the command line. By default, SMIT will enter the top-level system management menu (see Fig. 3.1). To enter SMIT at a particular task submenu, supply the SMIT fast-path name as an argument.

```
# smit            Start SMIT at top-level menu
# smit user       Start SMIT at the user admin submenu
```

SMIT allows you to take a test drive utilizing all of its features without making changes to the operating system. Invoke SMIT with the `-X` to kick the tires and get a feel for how it operates. SMIT will log the commands it would have executed in the `$HOME/smit.script` file.

```
# smit -X
```

You can also use the F6 key within SMIT to display the AIX command and arguments it will invoke before committing the update.

### 3.2.1 SMIT display

SMIT provides both an ASCII and a Motif based user interface. The Motif interface is invoked by default on an X11 managed display and employs a point-and-click feel. The Motif display (Fig. 3.2) enhances the operating environment through the use of buttons, slider bars, and submenu panels. The SMIT ASCII interface (Fig. 3.3) is invoked using the `smitty` or `smit -C` commands.

```
# smit user       SMIT X11 interface
# smitty user     SMIT ASCII interface
# smit -C user    SMIT ASCII interface
```

```
System Management

Move cursor to desired item and press Enter.

Installation and Maintenance

Devices

Physical & Logical Storage

Security & Users

Diskless Workstation Management

Communications Applications and Services

Spooler (Print Jobs)

Problem Determination

Performance & Resource Scheduling

System Environments

Processes & Subsystems

Applications

Using SMIT (information only)

F1 = Help          F2 = Refresh        F3 = Cancel        F8 = Image
F9 = Shell         F10 = Exit          Enter = Do
```

**Figure 3.1** System Management Interface Tool.

Each SMIT panel is divided into three parts. At the top of the panel the task *title* and *instructions* appear. The middle of the screen contains menu selections or input fields. Location in the set of fields is indicated by `[TOP]`, `[MORE...#]`, and `[BOTTOM]`. At the bottom of each panel, the set of valid function keys is listed in four columns. SMIT flags input field types and selection lists through the use of field mark characters (see Table 3.1) and buttons displayed to the far left and right of the input fields.

### 3.2.2 SMIT keys

To navigate between fields and options in a SMIT panel, use the `TAB` and `Arrow` keys, or the `mouse`. Input field values may be typed from the keyboard or, in some cases, selected from a list. The `Enter` key invokes and commits the selection or task. SMIT also provides a set of *function keys* to display additional information, access the shell, or exit (see Table 3.2).

### 3.2.3 SMIT help and messages

SMIT help can be invoked from any menu by pressing the `F1` key. The help and message text is located in `/usr/lpp/msg/$LANG/smit.cat` catalog. Note that the message catalog is a National Language (NLS)

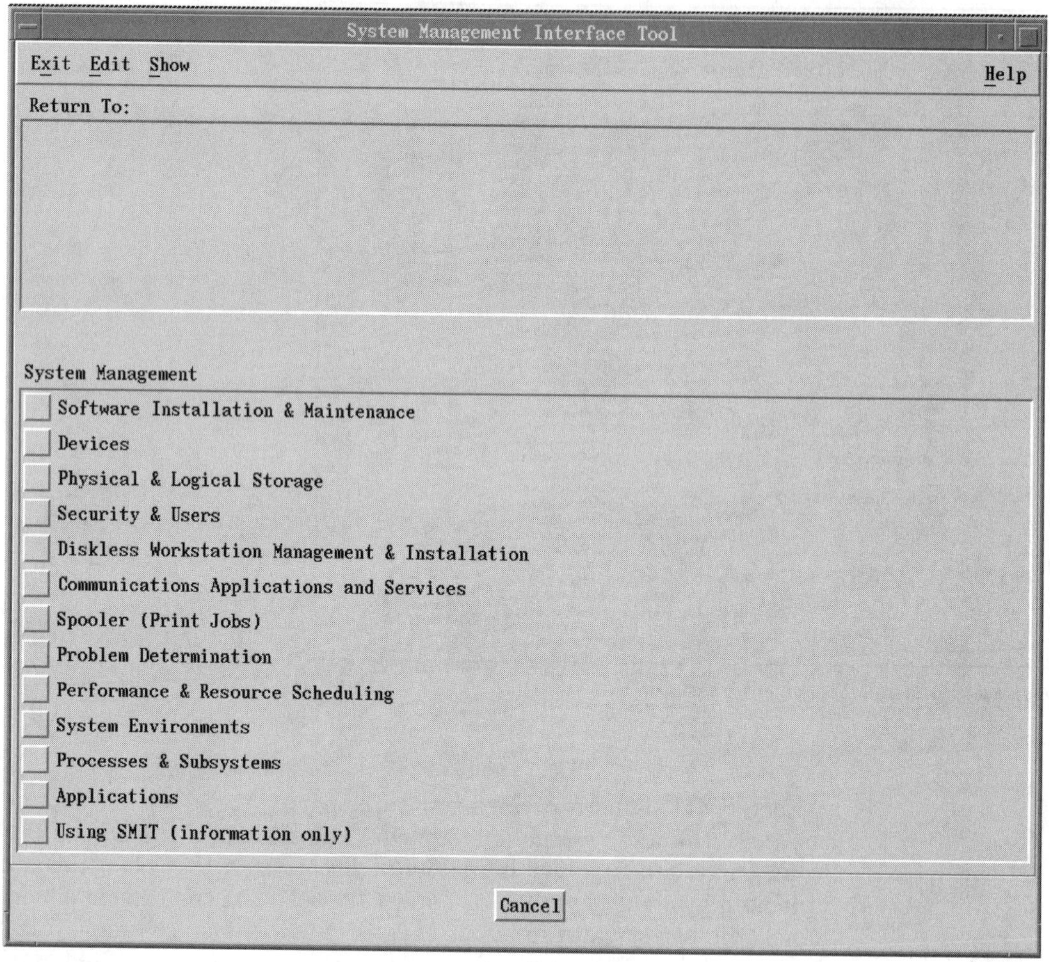

```
System Management Interface Tool
Exit  Edit  Show                                      Help
Return To:

System Management
  Software Installation & Maintenance
  Devices
  Physical & Logical Storage
  Security & Users
  Diskless Workstation Management & Installation
  Communications Applications and Services
  Spooler (Print Jobs)
  Problem Determination
  Performance & Resource Scheduling
  System Environments
  Processes & Subsystems
  Applications
  Using SMIT (information only)

                         Cancel
```

**Figure 3.2** SMIT X11 display.

catalog, and is thus dependent on the setting of the `$LANG` environment variable. An invalid or missing `$LANG` specification will result in missing or garbled help and message information.

```
1800-040 Cannot open SoftCopy help information
database. Help is not available for this
SMIT session. You may continue from here or
you can check the $LANG environment variable
setting or use local problem reporting
procedures. For the current setting of
"/usr/lpp/info/C/aix/aix.key",
"/usr/lpp/info/C/aix/aix.rom",
"/usr/lpp/info/C/sys.sys".
("/usr/lpp/info/C/aixmin/aixmin.key")
("/usr/lpp/info/C/aixmin/aixmin.rom")
("/usr/lpp/info/C/sys.sys")
```

```
Create User
Type or select values in entry fields.

Press Enter AFTER making all desired changes.

[TOP]                                      [Entry Fields]

* User NAME                                []
ADMINISTRATIVE User?                       false         +
User ID                                    []            #
LOGIN user?                                true          +
PRIMARY group                              []            +
Group SET                                  []            +
ADMINISTRATIVE groups                      []            +
SU groups                                  []            +
HOME directory                             []
Initial PROGRAM                            []
User INFORMATION                           []
Another user can SU to user?               true          +
User can RLOGIN?                           true          +
TRUSTED PATH?                              nosak         +

[MORE...12]

F1 = Help         F2 = Refresh       F3 = Cancel       F4 = List
F5 = Undo         F6 = Command       F7 = Edit         F8 = Image
F9 = Shell        F10 = Exit         Enter = Do
```

**Figure 3.3** SMIT ASCII interface.

**TABLE 3.1 SMIT Dialog Symbols**

| Symbol | Type | |
|---|---|---|
| * | Entry is required | |
| # | Numeric field | |
| X | Hexadecimal field | |
| / | File name field | |
| + | List available | (ASCII display only) |
| [] | Field delimiters | (ASCII display only) |
| Arrow button | Fixed set of options | (Motif display only) |
| List button | List of choices | (Motif display only) |

**TABLE 3.2 SMIT Function Keys**

| Key | Action |
|---|---|
| F1 | Help |
| F2 | Refresh screen |
| F3 | Cancel |
| F4 | Display selection list |
| F5 | Undo entry—reset to default |
| F6 | Display command and args |
| F7 | Edit or select |
| F8 | Display fast-path name |
| F9 | Shell escape |
| F10 | Exit SMIT |
| Enter | Execute |
| Tab/SHFT-Tab | Move between options |

### 3.2.4 SMIT log file

SMIT creates an audit log of each SMIT session in the user's `$HOME` directory named `smit.log`. The log file indicates the SMIT submenu path traversed during the session by object class ID, panel sequence number, title, and the fast-path name. Each new SMIT session is appended to the existing log file. Care must be taken to monitor the size of the log file over time. The location of the log file may be set using the `smit -l <PathName>` option. The level of logging verbosity may be increased using `smit -vt`.

```
# smit -l /tmp/smit.log -vt       Use /tmp to hold log file
```

*SMIT Log Example—Adding a 9-Track Tape Drive*

```
[Sep 07 1993, 13:29:36]
Starting SMIT
(Menu screen selected as FastPath,
id = "__ROOT__",
id_seq_num = "0",
next_id = "top_menu",
title = "System Management".)
(Menu screen selected,
FastPath = "top_menu",
id_seq_num = "0",
next_id = "top_menu",
title = "System Management".)
(Menu screen selected,
FastPath = "dev",
id_seq_num = "020",
next_id = "dev",
title = "Devices".)
(Menu screen selected,
FastPath = "tape",
id_seq_num = "080",
next_id = "tape",
title = "Tape Drive".)
(Selector screen selected,
FastPath = "maktpe",
id = "maktpe",
next_id = "maktpe_",
title = "Add a Tape Drive".)
(Selector screen selected,
FastPath = "maktpe",
id = "maktpe_9trk_scsi",
next_id = "maktpe_9trk_scsi_hdr",
title = "Add a Tape Drive".)
(Dialogue screen selected,
FastPath = "maktpe",
id = "maktpe_9trk_scsi_hdr",
title = "Add a Tape Drive".)
[Sep 07 1993, 13:29:50]
Command_to_Execute follows below:
>>mkdev -c tape -t '9trk' -s 'scsi' -p 'scsi1' -w '10'
[Sep 07 1993, 13:29:52]
Exiting SMIT
```

### 3.2.5 SMIT script file

Along with the log file, SMIT appends the AIX commands invoked during the session to a local `$HOME/smit.script` file. The script file information can be used to create complex management scripts or review the commands invoked during a previous session. For example, you might use SMIT to configure the first of a set of 64 TTY devices. Then edit the `$HOME/smit.script` file and duplicate the `mkdev` command 62 times for the remaining devices, changing each device name and attributes as required. The script file can be executed from the command line to complete the definition of the remaining devices. Use the `smit -s <PathName>` option to create a script file in a location other than your home directory.

```
# smit -s /tmp/smit.script       Create a script file in /tmp
```

*SMIT Script Example—Adding a 9-track Tape Drive*

```
#
# [Sep 07 1993, 13:29:50]
#
mkdev -c tape -t '9trk' -s 'scsi' -p 'scsi1' -w '10'
```

### 3.2.6 SMIT fast paths

SMIT allows you to bypass menu levels and enter a task directly through the use of a fast-path name. A fast-path name is an identifier for a particular SMIT panel (see Table 3.3). Fast-path names are recorded as part of the `$HOME/smit.log` information. The fast-path name is included as an argument to the `smit` command to enter a task panel directly.

```
# smit nfs       Access SMIT NFS management
```

Remembering all the fast-path names and management commands can be a real bear. Fortunately, the AIX developers implemented an easy-to-remember rule for remembering the fast-path and command names. A set of four prefixes, `ls`, `mk`, `ch`, and `rm` are appended to a root task name to `list`, `make`, `change`, and `remove` operating system objects. For example, to `make` a CD-ROM device, the fast-path or command name is `mkcdrom`. This doesn't work all the time, but it's better than nothing!

**TABLE 3.3 Common SMIT Fast-Path Names**

| | |
|---|---|
| `dev` | Devices management |
| `diag` | Diagnostics |
| `jfs` | Journaled file system management |
| `lvm` | Logical volume manager management |
| `nfs` | NFS management |
| `sinstallp` | Software installs and maintenance |
| `spooler` | Print queue management |
| `system` | System management |
| `tcpip` | TCP/IP management |
| `user` | User administration |

#### 3.2.6.1 Fast path and command algorithm

| | |
|---|---|
| operation | mk, ls, ch, rm |
| objects | dev, user, fs, vg, pv, tty, cdrom, diskette, tape, etc. |

## 3.3 Customizing SMIT

SMIT consists of a hierarchical set of menu panels, an NLS message catalog, command interface, and a logging and scripting facility. These components are integrated to provide a seamless interface for managing the operating system and system resources.

Three types of SMIT display panels are used to manage the dialog between the user and management tasks: *menu, selector,* and *Dialog.* Menu panels display management task selections. Selector panels present a range of values of which one or more is to be selected before proceeding with the management task. Dialog panels provide input fields for specifying command arguments and values. (See Table 3.4.)

SMIT panels, command link descriptions, option defaults, and attributes are stored as objects in the ODM database. SMIT object classes (see Table 3.5) reside in the `/usr/lib/objrepos` directory. Symbolic links are used to provide access from the default ODM database path, `/etc/objrepos`.

SMIT object classes may be manipulated using ODM commands just like any ODM object (see Chap. 6). After becoming experienced with the ODM and SMIT architectures, you may use ODM commands to customize SMIT. SMIT object class names and object identifiers are listed in the SMIT log file when SMIT is invoked with the verbose trace, **-vt** option.

```
# smit -vt        SMIT verbose tracing
```

To display an object class description associated with a SMIT object, identify the object class, identifier, and number from the log. Then use the `odmshow` or `odmget` commands to list the object description.

```
# odmshow sm_menu_opt        Display SMIT menu object class
```

**TABLE 3.4 SMIT Panel Types**

| | |
|---|---|
| Menu | List of task options |
| Selector | Request additional input before proceeding |
| Dialog | Request values for command arguments and options |

**TABLE 3.5 SMIT Object Classes**

| | |
|---|---|
| `sm_menu_opt` | Menu titles and options |
| `sm_name_hdr` | Selector titles, attributes, and links to other screens |
| `sm_cmd_hdr` | Dialog titles, base command, links |
| `sm_cmd_opt` | Defaults, input types, selector/dialog attributes |

`odmget` can be used to retrieve an existing entry for modification or as a template for a new object. After updating the definition, delete the old entry with `odmdelete` and add the new object using `odmadd`. This is not something I would recommend unless you are very familiar with the ODM and SMIT. Always back up the existing object class information before making any modifications.

## 3.4 Distributed Management Environment

The Open Software Foundation has defined a management standard for distributed systems called the *Distributed Management Environment* (DME). DME supplies a uniform and consistent set of tools and services which may be used to manage both stand-alone and distributed heterogeneous systems, applications, and networks.

DME combines a select set of vendor management technologies into a consistent framework based on a three-tier model. The lowest tier supports single-host management activities. The second level provides cell naming and security management in distributed environments. The top level encompasses enterprisewide management via Motif based GUI interfaces. DME routines communicate with managed objects using DCE, SNMP, and OSI CMIP.

*DME Technology Selections*

| | |
|---|---|
| IBM | Data Engine, System Resource Controller |
| MIT Project Athena | Palladium Print Services |
| Tivoli | WIzDOM Object Oriented Framework |
| Banyan | Network Logger |
| HP | Open View Network Management Server |
| | Software Distribution/Installation Utils |
| | Network License Manager |
| Groupe Bull | Consolidated Management API |
| Gradient | PC Ally and Client Lib for Net License Server |
| | PC Agent and Event Components |

The DME *Request For Technology* (RFT) was first issued in July 1990. After evaluation by OSF's Munich Development Office, a selection was made in September 1991. The selected technologies have gone through a period of integration and testing, during which time code snapshots have been made available to interested parties. DME Network Management Option version 1.0 is generally available from the OSF to all interested parties.

## 3.5 InfoExplorer Keywords

| | |
|---|---|
| smit | `LANG` |
| `smitty` | `ODM` |

| | |
|---|---|
| smit.log | odmshow |
| smit.script | odmget |
| NLS | odmadd |
| | odmdelete |

## 3.6 QwikInfo

| | |
|---|---|
| - SMIT | |
| smit | Motif Interface |
| smit -C, smitty | TTY Interface |
| smit -X | Inhibit updates, test-drive SMIT |
| F6 key | Display command to be executed by SMIT |
| smit <fast-path-name> | Display SMIT submenu |
| $HOME/smit.log | SMIT transaction log |
| $HOME/smit.script | SMIT command log |
| /etc/objrepos/sm_xxxxxx | SMIT ODM panel database |
| /usr/lib/objrepos/sm_xxxxxx | SMIT ODM panel database |

Part

# 2

# System Installation and Operation

Chapter

# 4

# AIX Installation and Maintenance

## 4.1 Installing AIX

One thing that IBM is well known for is documentation. It's a close bet whether the installation and maintenance documentation you receive with each RISC System/6000 weighs more than the hardware. Although I have mixed feelings about the information provided in some of the IBM documentation, the *IBM AIX Version 3.2 for RISC System/6000 Installation Guide* is a first-rate document. It's easy to follow, helps get the job done, and exercises your upper body each time you pick it up.

Another thing IBM is known for is changing the maintenance procedures with each new release. Each time you install AIX, I recommend that you follow the installation guide *carefully* (even when you feel like you can do it in your sleep). I can tell you from experience that cutting corners can have catastrophic results. Follow the install path that fits your environment and you'll keep surprises at a minimum. Rather than duplicate the information in the install document, I'll concentrate on condensing the install process down to the general tasks. I'll also make a few suggestions to help keep your existing environment isolated from the install and maintenance process.

While writing this text, the AIX maintenance procedures have changed three times. I recommend staying as close to the current release as is comfortable. I will concentrate on installation and maintenance function at the AIX 3.2.5 level, since it is the last one I have personally used. Most of the SMIT panels are similar to those used in earlier releases. The fast-path names have changed in 3.2.5. If you are running an older release of AIX, read this text while looking through a glass of water. If you're still uneasy, start at the top and proceed through the SMIT software maintenance submenus until you find what you're looking for.

### 4.1.1 Installation and maintenance planning

Installing a brand new operating system or application is like painting on clean canvas. You're not encumbered with preserving or working within any existing paradigm. You have the freedom to plan your environment from scratch. Planning is the key word here. Operating system and product file system configuration should not waste disk space. Implement a configuration that facilitates future product upgrades and maintenance tasks. Reserve disk space for non-`rootvg` volume groups to hold your user and local product file systems. If you are installing multiple machines, consider installing one system as a reference system, which can then be cloned from a *network install server*. Eliminate duplicate file system requirements for diskless client *shared product object trees* (SPOT). Make use of the worksheets provided in the planning section of the installation guide. The planning sheets make a good reference set when you need to review your installation plan at some time in the future.

#### 4.1.1.1 Installation considerations

- Installation media
- Additional maintenance
- BOS disk space
- Product disk space
- Paging space
- `/tmp space`
- Separate volume group for local user and product file systems
- Reference system and install server
- Network parameters
- SPOT support for diskless clients
- Preservation of configuration and data on existing systems

Before jumping in with both feet, read any product-related readme files. Contact IBM support representatives concerning the latest maintenance level and *preventative service planning* (PSP) information for the release level being installed. Before you contact an IBM service representative or IBM software manufacturing, make sure you have your AIX version and release numbers, your service modification level, machine serial number, model number, and your customer number. To identify the version and release numbers for an existing system use the `uname` command. AIX 3.2.4 provided a new command for identifying the operating system level: `oslevel`. The "<>" characters indicate whether you are "<" at a lower level, ">" at a higher level, or "<>" equal to the displayed level.

| | |
|---|---|
| `# uname -v -r`<br>`2 3` | Note that uname will give the release level first, regardless of the argument order. Thus, "2 3" indicates V3 R2. |
| `# uname -m` | Display machine id |
| `xxyyyyyymmss` | |
| `xx` | 00 for RS/6000 |
| `yyyyyy` | CPU ID |
| `mm` | Model identifier |
| `ss` | Submodel identifier |
| `# oslevel` | AIX 3.2.5 product level |
| `<>3250` | |

Your system maintenance level can be inferred from `bos.obj` history. Use the `lslpp -h` command to display the maintenance history and state.

`# lslpp -h bos.obj` Short listing

```
Name
Fix Id      Release         Status    Action    Date      Time      User Name
Path: /usr/lib/objrepos
bos.obj
        03.02.0000.0000 COMPLETE  COMMIT  12/31/69  16:00:00    root
Path: /etc/objrepos
bos.obj
        03.02.0000.0000 COMPLETE  COMMIT  12/31/69  16:00:00    root
```

`# lslpp -a -h bos.obj` Verbose listing

```
Name
Fix Id      Release         Status    Action    Date      Time      User Name
Path: /usr/lib/objrepos
bos.obj
        03.02.0000.0000 COMPLETE  COMMIT  12/31/69  16:00:00    root
U401864 03.02.0000.0000 COMPLETE  COMMIT  09/04/92  13:00:00    root
        03.02.0000.0000 COMPLETE  APPLY   09/04/92  12:50:00    root
U401962 03.02.0000.0000 COMPLETE  COMMIT  11/24/92  10:31:46    root
        03.02.0000.0000 COMPLETE  APPLY   11/24/92  09:49:40    root
U401963 03.02.0000.0000 COMPLETE  COMMIT  11/24/92  10:31:47    root
        03.02.0000.0000 COMPLETE  APPLY   11/24/92  09:49:55    root
U401968 03.02.0000.0000 COMPLETE  COMMIT  09/04/92  17:55:46    root
        03.02.0000.0000 COMPLETE  APPLY   09/04/92  15:07:20    root
U401969 03.02.0000.0000 COMPLETE  COMMIT  09/04/92  17:55:46    root
        03.02.0000.0000 COMPLETE  APPLY   09/04/92  15:06:42    root
U401970 03.02.0000.0000 COMPLETE  COMMIT  09/04/92  17:55:47    root
        03.02.0000.0000 COMPLETE  APPLY   09/04/92  15:10:20    root
U401972 03.02.0000.0000 COMPLETE  COMMIT  11/24/92  10:31:47    root
        03.02.0000.0000 COMPLETE  APPLY   11/24/92  09:50:10    root
U401977 03.02.0000.0000 COMPLETE  COMMIT  09/04/92  13:26:34    root
        03.02.0000.0000 COMPLETE  APPLY   09/04/92  13:25:06    root
U401979 03.02.0000.0000 COMPLETE  COMMIT  09/04/92  17:55:46    root
        03.02.0000.0000 COMPLETE  APPLY   09/04/92  15:07:57    root
U401980 03.02.0000.0000 COMPLETE  COMMIT  09/04/92  12:59:59    root
        03.02.0000.0000 COMPLETE  APPLY   09/04/92  12:43:57    root
U401986 03.02.0000.0000 COMPLETE  COMMIT  09/04/92  13:00:00    root
        03.02.0000.0000 COMPLETE  APPLY   09/04/92  12:45:17    root
U402027 03.02.0000.0000 COMPLETE  COMMIT  09/04/92  13:00:00    root
        03.02.0000.0000 COMPLETE  APPLY   09/04/92  12:49:18    root
```

```
U402043 03.02.0000.0000 COMPLETE COMMIT  11/24/92  10:31:43     root
        03.02.0000.0000 COMPLETE APPLY   11/24/92  09:46:37     root
U402044 03.02.0000.0000 COMPLETE COMMIT  09/04/92  13:00:01     root
        03.02.0000.0000 COMPLETE APPLY   09/04/92  12:52:06     root
U402093 03.02.0000.0000 COMPLETE COMMIT  09/04/92  17:55:59     root
        03.02.0000.0000 COMPLETE APPLY   09/04/92  15:55:50     root
U402098 03.02.0000.0000 COMPLETE COMMIT  09/04/92  17:55:48     root
        03.02.0000.0000 COMPLETE APPLY   09/04/92  15:11:46     root
U402099 03.02.0000.0000 COMPLETE COMMIT  09/04/92  17:56:18     root
        03.02.0000.0000 COMPLETE APPLY   09/04/92  17:09:50     root
U402101 03.02.0000.0000 COMPLETE COMMIT  09/04/92  17:56:54     root
        03.02.0000.0000 COMPLETE APPLY   09/04/92  16:42:26     root
```

A quick snapshot of maintenance history can be obtained using the -L option to `lslpp`.

```
# lslpp -L bos.obj
Processing.....Please Wait.
Description                                    State      Fix Id

bos.obj 3.2.0.0
  3250 bos Maintenance Level                     C        U491123
    Vital User Information                       C        U423515
    Device Drivers                               C        U423535
    Character Stream Editing Utilities           C        U423643
    Device Diagnostics                           C        U423761
```

Look for the following fix numbers in the output stream. It will give you an indication of the modification level of your system.

| PTF | Level |
|---|---|
| U493250 | 3.2.5 |
| U420316 | 3.2.4 |
| U411711 | 3.2.3 Extended |
| U409490 | 3.2.3 |
| U403173 | 3.2.2 |
| U401864 only | 3.2.0 else 3.2.1 |

In the United States, you can order software updates from IBM Software Manufacturing:

IBM Software Manufacturing
1-800-879-2755

For specific problem fixes, contact IBM Support:

IBM Support
1-800-237-5511

IBM AIX/6000 support offers a number of options for specialist assistance for installation, problem solving, and tuning. For general information contact AIX support at:

AIX/6000 Support Family
40-B2-05
IBM Corporation
P.O. Box 9000
Roanoke TX 76262-9989

1-800-CALLAIX
FAX: (817) 962-6723
call-aix@vnet.ibm.com

You can review the problem and service database yourself if you have access to *IBMLink.* If you don't have access to IBMLink, IBM provides periodic snapshots of the IBMLink question and service databases on CD-ROM; order *AIX Technical Library/6000 CDROM.* IBMLink may be accessed via the Internet:

```
telnet IBMLink.advantis.com
```

If you have access to the Internet or Usenet news, reference the `comp.unix.aix` discussion and archives. The best information comes from peers who are using AIX in various production environments. IBM support personnel and developers also watch these groups and may lend assistance.

### 4.1.2 Apply and commit

*To commit or not to commit—that is the question.*

Before installing new software or maintenance on an existing system, you need to have a backout strategy in the event that problems occur during or after the installation. The AIX default is used to add new software and maintenance to the system using the APPLY option. This option keeps a history file and a backup copy of each object replaced by the software update. If you are not happy with the update, you can REJECT it and restore the previous version. When using SMIT to install software updates, use the default `COMMIT software? no` option.

```
# installp -qa -d /inst.images -X all      APPLY updates
# installp -rB -X all                      REJECT updates
```

Once satisfied with the update, you can COMMIT the update to remove the backup copy of the previous version:

```
# installp -c -g -X all      COMMIT updates
```

The caveat of installing using the APPLY option is that additional disk space is required in `/usr/lpp` to hold the old version. This additional space is also difficult to reclaim once the new software is committed. If you don't have the disk space to spare, you may elect to install the update with COMMIT. This option will save on disk space, but does not provide a simple backout mechanism. Make a full dump of your root file systems prior to installing with COMMIT. In the event of a problem, you can restore the backup.

```
# installp -qa -d /inst.images -c -N all      Install with COMMIT
```

In the event that you must back out a committed lpp, there is a script originally provided by IBM Support that can be used to remove the update and associated links.

### 4.1.3 File system expansion

To ensure that sufficient file system space is available, you can elect to have file system size automatically increased during the installation. Unfortunately, this process tends to overallocate file system space, the result being wasted disk space at the end of the installation. Automatic file system expansion can also cause the installation to abort if the requested increment in logical partitions is not available. In most cases, you will be better off calculating the space required for the update and allocating the space manually. Remember, you cannot easily shrink a file system once it is overallocated.

```
# installp -qa -d /inst.images -X all      Autoexpansion
# installp -qa -d /inst.images all         No autoexpansion
```

### 4.1.4 System state

When installing a new product release or maintenance, limit the activity on your system. For some products, this may only involve restricting access to the application being updated and stopping any related subsystems and subservers. Use the `stopsrc` command to shut down subsystems and subservers.

```
# stopsrc -g tcpip      Stop tcpip subsystem
```

For operating system updates or when updating a group of products, it is easier to reduce system activity by shutting down to maintenance mode. This will stop all subsystems and restrict access to the system other than from the system console.

```
# telinit M      Shut down to maintenance mode
```

You can temporarily inhibit login access by creating a `/etc/nologin` file. The `tsmlogin` command will display the contents of the `/etc/nologin` file at each login attempt and then exit.

*Example* /etc/nologin

```
Login access is temporarily inhibited due to system maintenance
activities. Please try again later.
```

### 4.1.5 Installing preloaded systems

If you are installing a brand new RISC System/6000, parts of the basic operating system (BOS) and product run-time environments are preinstalled on the system. Note that the preinstalled system does not represent the full product or maintenance set. You must complete the installation of the remaining products and maintenance before configuring the system for use. Preloaded software is located in the /usr/sys/inst.images directory.

#### 4.1.5.1 Preloaded install steps

0. Complete installation planning.
1. Power up the system with the key switch in the NORMAL position.
2. Log in as root and set the TERM environment variable for your terminal type.

| | |
|---|---|
| `# echo TERM` | Display current setting |
| `# export TERM = <type>` | Set new terminal type |

3. Check and set NLS language LANG environment variable.

| | |
|---|---|
| `# echo LANG` | Query language setting |
| `# export LANG = <NLSlang>` | Set new NLS language |

4. Review the BOS readme file.

```
# more /usr/lpp/bos/README
```

5. Install preloaded software and maintenance. Use SMIT fast path sinstallp or the installp command. It's a good idea to copy any additional maintenance into the preloaded software directory /usr/sys/inst.images and install software and updates as a unit.
6. Complete postinstallation tasks described in Sec. 4.4

### 4.1.6 Upgrading existing AIX systems

Installing an upgrade or maintenance to an existing AIX system is much easier if you have kept your user file systems and local product data on non-rootvg volume groups. Before installing the upgrade or maintenance, these volume groups may be exported, protecting them from update problems. Once the update is complete, they can be imported.

```
# exportvg <VGname>
```

Install upgrade

```
# importvg <VGname>
```

You may wish to save some configuration files—for example, password files, auditing configuration, printing `qconfig`, network tables, etc. If you know the installation date of your last upgrade, you can use the `find` command to walk the `rootvg` file systems and log file names modified since the last upgrade date. Edit the log file and remove any unnecessary file names. The log file can be easily converted to a script to copy the desired configuration files to a safe location or backup medium.

```
# find /etc -mitime <Ndays> -print > save-config
# find /usr/lib -mitime <Ndays> -print >> save-config
```

AIX installation procedures provide a *preservation install* option which does not destroy all of the `rootvg` file systems. Only the `/usr`, `/tmp`, `/var`, and / file systems are overwritten. There is a set of upgrade utilities for AIX V3.1 sites which preserve some configuration files for later restoration on the AIX V3.2 system. Beware that there is a problem with preservation installs if you change the logical device names of the default paging volumes.

Before initiating a preservation install, record location, layout, and space on each of the physical volumes to be used by the install process. Begin by displaying the physical volume names.

```
# ipl_varyon -i
```

| PVNAME | BOOT DEVICE | PVID | VOLUME GROUP ID |
|---|---|---|---|
| hdisk0 | YES | 000004065a4ad7ce | 0000406042e9db9f |
| hdisk1 | NO | 000004065a4b372d | 0000406042e9db9f |
| hdisk2 | NO | 00000444d7afade3 | 00004060db76b544 |

For each physical volume display the location information.

```
# lsdev -C -l hdisk0
hdisk0 Available 00-08-00-00 670 MB SCSI Disk Drive
```

Use `df` and `lsvg` to total the used and free space making up the root file systems and the root volume group.

```
# df -v / /usr /tmp /var
```

```
Filesystem   Total KB    used    free $used   iused  ifree  %iused Mounted
/dev/hd4       32768    29796   2972   90$    1864   6328     22%    /
/dev/hd2      499712   456704  43008   91$   17438 107490     13%    /usr
/dev/hd3      323584    21068 302516   6$     103   81817     0%     /tmp
/dev/hd9var  1048576   227520 821056  21$    1635  260509     0%     /var

# lsvg rootvg

VOLUME GROUP:    rootvg             VG IDENTIFIER:    00001508fce80427
VG STATE:        active/complete    PP SIZE:          4 megabyte(s)
VG PERMISSION:   read/write         TOTAL PPs:        574 (2296 megabytes)
MAX LVs:         256                FREE PPs:         60 (240 megabytes)
LVs:             10                 USED PPs:         514 (2056 megabytes)
OPEN LVs:        9                  QUORUM:           2
TOTAL PVs:       2                  VG DESCRIPTORS:   3
STALE PVs:       0                  STALE PPs         0
ACTIVE PVs:      2                  AUTO ON:          yes
```

### 4.1.7 Installing from distribution media

Three types of BOS installation procedures are available for *diskfull* workstations: *new installation, preservation installation,* and *complete overwrite installation.* A new installation assumes you are installing to clean disks. The latter two options assume an existing system and allow you to retain nonroot file systems (preservation) or wipe clean the existing installation (overwrite).

#### 4.1.7.1 Media install steps

0. Complete installation planning.
1. Power up the system from the bootable media with the key switch in the SERVICE position. If you are booting from diskettes, the LED display will prompt `c07` for each boot and display diskette. A status of `c03` indicates the wrong diskette was inserted, and a status of `c05` indicates a diskette error.
2. Select the device to be used as the console. The LED display reads `c31` and a message is displayed on each attached tty or hft device prompting for selection of the system console. If you are booting from diskettes, you are prompted to insert the *install/maint diskette.*

   ```
   Insert BOS Install/Maint Diskette and Press Enter
   ```

3. Select *Install AIX from the Installation and Maintenance menu*

   AIX 3.2 INSTALLATION AND MAINTENANCE

   >>> 1 Install AIX

   2 Install a system that was created...

   3 Install this system for use with a `/usr`...

   4 Start a limited function maintenance ...

4. At this point, you must commit to proceeding with either the preservation install or the overwrite install. The same menu options will be presented in either case, with the exception that menus for the preservation install assume existing volume groups will be used.

   METHOD OF INSTALL

   1 Preservation install

   2 Complete overwrite install

5. Verify that the correct disks or volume group will be used for the install. In the case of a preservation install, use the volume group identifier that you recorded on the planning worksheet to select the volume group to be used for installation.

| PRESERVATION INSTALL | COMPLETE OVERWRITE INSTALL |
|---|---|
| 1 LOCALE (language) | 1 LOCAL (language) |
| 2 INPUT Installation Device | 2 INPUT Installation Device |
| >>> 3 DESTINATION root VG | >>>3 DESTINATION Disks |
| | >>>4 STARTUP (boot) Device |

6. Select the *LOCAL language* and INPUT installation device. Installation media include diskette, tape, CD-ROM, and network device types.
7. Install BOS.

   FINAL WARNING

   Base operating system installation ...

   99 Return to previous menu

   >>> 0 Continue with install

8. Once installation is complete, remove the install media, switch the key to NORMAL, and reboot the system.

   AIX base operating system installation is complete

   1 Make sure your installation media () has been removed from the input device

   2 Turn the system key to the NORMAL position

   3 Press the ENTER key to restart (reboot) the system

9. Log in as root and review BOS readme file.

```
# more /usr/lpp/bos/README
```

10. Install remaining software and maintenance. Use SMIT fast path `sinstallp` or the `installp` command. It's a good idea to copy any additional maintenance into the preloaded software directory `/usr/sys/inst.images` and install software and updates as a unit.
11. Complete post installation tasks described in Sec. 4.4.

## 4.2 Installing Applications

Installing program products in backup format can be managed using the SMIT `install` fast path or by using the `installp` command.

```
# installp -qa -d /inst.images -X all       APPLY updates
```

Products and maintenance will usually be installed into the *licensed program product* (LPP) directory, `/usr/lpp.` A separate subdirectory is created for each product.

```
# ls -aF /usr/lpp
./              bseiEn_US/      inu_LOCK*           xdt3/
../             bsl/            jls/                xlc/
DPS/            bsmEn_US/       msg@                xlccmp/
X11/            bspiEn_US/      ncs/                xlf/
X11_3d/         bssiEn_US/      nfs/                xlfcmp/
X11dev/         cobolcmp/       pci/                xlfcmpiEn_US/
X11deviEn_US/   cobolrte/       pcsim/              xlfcmpmEn_US/
X11fnt/         colormaps/      pcsimmEn_US/        xlfrte/
X11mEn_US/      cpp/            rlm/                xlfrtemEn_US/
X11rte/         diagnostics/    tcpip/              xlfrtemsg/
bos/            fonts/          tty/                xlp/
bosadt/         gai/            txtfmt/             xlpcmp/
bosext1/        hanfs/          vdi/                xlpcmpiEn_US/
bosext2/        hft/            x3270/              xlpcmpmEn_US/
bosinst/        ibmgl@          x3270.sav/          xlprte/
bosnet/         info/           x_st_mgr/           xlprtemEn_US/
bosperf/        infoxl/         x_st_mgrmEn_US/     xlprtemsg/
```

The contents of the installation media may be reviewed by selecting `List All Software on Installation Media` from the SMIT `install` menu or executing `installp` with the `-l` option.

```
# installp -q -d /inst.images -l
```

| Option name | Level | I/U | Q content |
|---|---|---|---|
| xlfrtemEn_US.msg | 02.03.0000.0000 | I | N usr |
| # AIX XL FORTRAN Run Time Environment/6000 Messages - | | | |
| xlfcmpmEn_US.msg | 02.03.0000.0000 | I | N usr |
| # AIX XL FORTRAN Compiler/6000 Messages - U.S. English | | | |
| xlfcmp.obj | 02.03.0000.0000 | I | N usr,root |
| # AIX XL FORTRAN Compiler/6000 | | | |
| xlfrte.obj | 02.03.0000.0000 | I | N usr |
| # AIX XL FORTRAN Run Time Environment/6000 | | | |

In the event that one or more of the applications will be installed on multiple machines, you might want to copy the contents of the install media to disk for use with an install server. Select `Copy Software to Hard Disk for Future Installation` from the SMIT `install_update` menu (see Fig. 4.1), and refer to Sec. 4.5.3 for details on configuring and using an install server. You may also use the `bffcreate` command to copy the software update to disk.

```
# bffcreate -qv -d'/dev/rmt0' -t'/inst.images' '-X' all
# smit install_update
```

To install ALL software and maintenance on the media, invoke SMIT with the `install_all` fast-path name. You will be prompted for the media type and installation will proceed using default options. If you want to select other update options or install a subset of the updates on the media, start SMIT using the `install_latest` fast path. Use the F4 key to list the products available on the media. Individual entries may be tagged using F7. (Refer to Fig. 4.2.)

```
# smit install_latest
```

In the previous section on installation planning, the pros and cons of installing with COMMIT and automatically extending the file system were discussed. The same arguments relate to product and maintenance updates. If you have extra disk space to play with, electing not to COMMIT and allowing file system extension will make the install smoother.

During the installation and update process, progress information is displayed by SMIT and `installp.` SMIT will log this information to the `smit.log` file. You may wish to redirect output from the `installp` to a file if it was invoked from the command line. Once the install has completed, verify the status of the update (see Sec. 4.4 for details on product and maintenance installation status).

```
                   Install/Update Software

Move cursor to desired item and press Enter.

Install/Update Selectable Software (Custom Install)
Install ALL Software Updates on Installation Media
Copy Software to Hard Disk for Future Installation
Clean Up After a Failed Installation
List All Software on Installation Media
List All Problems Fixed by Software on Installation Media

F1 = Help         F2 = Refresh        F3 = Cancel         F8 = Image
F9 = Shell        F10 = Exit          Enter = Do
```

**Figure 4.1** SMIT install update panel.

```
          Install Software Products at Latest Available Level

Type or select values in entry fields.
Press Enter AFTER making all desired changes.

                                                     [Entry Fields]
* INPUT device / directory for software            /inst.images
* SOFTWARE to install                              []                +
  Automatically install PREREQUISITE software?     yes               +
  COMMIT software?                                 yes               +
  SAVE replaced files?                             no                +
  VERIFY Software?                                 no                +
  EXTEND file systems if space needed?             yes               +
  REMOVE input file after installation?            no                +
  OVERWRITE existing version?                      no                +
  ALTERNATE save directory                         []

F1 = Help        F2 = Refresh     F3 = Cancel     F4 = List
F5 = Reset       F6 = Command     F7 = Edit       F8 = Image
F9 = Shell       F10 = Exit       Enter = Do
```

**Figure 4.2** SMIT selective install panel.

### 4.2.1 Non-LPP products

It's a good idea to keep local, public domain, and vendor products separate from BOS directories. This will ensure that they will not be clobbered by BOS upgrades and installations. A common practice is to create a local product file system called `/usr/local`. Within `/usr/local`, create subdirectories `bin`, `lib`, `etc`, and `src`. You can add these directories to the default command PATH and create symbolic links from BOS directories if required.

## 4.3 Applying Maintenance

The first and foremost rule of system maintenance is: *If it isn't broken, don't fix it!* If only it was that easy! The AIX operating system and product set is made up of a large number of subsystems. Each subsystem contains hundreds or thousands of components. In this not-so-perfect world, problems *will* crop up in many of these objects. You have to decide which bugs will be tolerated and which ones must be fixed. Each new fix set that is applied to the system or subsystem will include a new set of gremlins. The trick is to find a maintenance level that provides stability for your environment and is within current maintenance levels supported by the vendor.

All the operating system and applications vendors are doing their best to drive product error rates down. This is a very difficult task, which is complicated in shared library environments. Think of the number of commands and subsystems that depend on `libc.a`! IBM has addressed the problems encountered with the old *selective fix* strategy in AIX 3.2.4+ by packaging fixes by subsystem. In the selective fix environment it was difficult to collect all the *prerequisite* (prereq) and *corequisite* (coreq) fixes that represented a particular system snapshot. A prereq or coreq often involves a component not related to the problem being addressed. The unrelated component often requires other fixes. Components were duplicated many times in the fix set. You ended up with a 50-megabyte fix tape to fix a small problem in csh.

AIX 3.2.4+ comes with a new maintenance strategy that packages prereq and coreq fixes by subsystem. A subsystem is a set of functionally related software components. The new strategy is called the *preventative maintenance package* (PMP). Each PMP represents a tested subsystem snapshot that includes all maintenance since the previous PMP. PMPs will be provided at a frequency of three or four times a year.

*Preventative Maintenance Packages*

| | |
|---|---|
| Subsystem selective fix | Correct specific subsystem problem |
| Selective enhancement | Provides new subsystem function |
| Maintenance level | Contains all fixes since last release |

AIX 3.2.4+ also provides a new installp option, -t <PathName>, that allows you to save files replaced by maintenance into the directory path of your choice. This feature saves on disk space requirements in /usr.

The rules for installing maintenance are the same as described in the previous section on installing program products. For distributed environments, you may wish to copy the maintenance set to disk for access from an install server. You might also choose to build a reference system image accessible from an install server (see Sec. 4.5.3 for details).

In many cases, maintenance updates involve the installation of a new installp command set before proceeding with the installation. Read the maintenance documentation carefully before beginning the update. A short description of each fix on the media may be displayed by selecting "List All Problems Fixed by Software on Installation Media" from the SMIT sinstallp menu or using the installp -A option.

```
# installp -qA -d /dev/rmt0 all        Display fix information

Fix information

files restored: 1
   usr/share fix information for
   x_st_mgr.obj 1.4.0.0.U412032
IX31874 x_st_mgr Create supersede PTF so KR and TW locales can install.

files restored: 1
   usr/share fix information for
   x_st_mgr.obj 1.3.0.0.U406206
```

```
IX28806 X Station Manager changes to support ko_KR and zh_TW locales.

    X Station Manager changes to support ko_KR and zh_TW locales.
```

Follow the procedure outlined in Sec. 4.3 when installing system maintenance.

## 4.4 Postinstallation and Maintenance Tasks

With the installation or maintenance process complete, there is still a bit of tidying up to be done before making the system available for use. A new installation requires that you set default system and environment variables. If you installed over an existing system, you will need to restore the previous environment. Product updates or maintenance will require testing before committing or rejecting the update. Finally, create new stand-alone media and take a fresh backup of the new system. A clean snapshot can be used as a reference point for installing additional machines or as a fallback should problems arise in the future.

### 4.4.1 Review install/update status

Review the status of software product and maintenance updates using `List All Applied but Not Committed Software` from the SMIT `sinstallp` menu or by invoking `lslpp` from the command line.

```
# lslpp -h bos.obj       Display lpp history

Name
Fix Id       Release         Status    Action     Date      Time      User Name
Path: /usr/lib/objrepos
bos.obj
       03.02.0000.0000  COMPLETE  COMMIT  12/31/69  16:00:00     root

Path: /etc/objrepos
bos.obj
       03.02.0000.0000  COMPLETE  COMMIT  12/31/69  16:00:00     root

# lslpp -pB U411227      Display fix status

Name        Fix Id      State         Prerequisites
Path:       /usr        /lib          /objrepos
bos.obj     U411227     COMMITTED     *ifreq bosadt.lib.obj p = U411212
                                      *prereq bos.obj v = 03 r = 02 m = 0000
Path: /etc/objrepos
bos.obj     U411227     COMMITTED     *ifreq bosadt.lib.obj p = U411212
                                      *prereq bos.obj v = 03 r = 02 m = 0000
```

LPP software can be in one of the following states:

APPLIED — Software was applied successfully but has not been committed.

COMMITTED — Software has been applied and committed.

| | |
|---|---|
| AVAILABLE | Software has not been installed but is available on installation media. |
| BROKEN | Software installation was not successful. Reinstall the product. |
| APPLYING | Software has not been successfully applied. Run CLEANUP and reinstall. |
| COMMITTING | COMMIT did not complete successfully. |
| REJECTING | REJECT failed for the software product. |

In the event of problems with the update, invoke CLEANUP and reinstall. LPP cleanup can be executed from the `Clean Up After Failed Installation` option on the SMIT `sinstallp` menu or via the `installp -C` option. Installations using SMIT or the `installp` command will normally perform any clean up automatically in the event of a failure.

```
# installp -C <ProductName>        Clean up failed install
```

### 4.4.2 Restoring your environment

Setting default *system environments* is a final step for the installation paths described thus far (see Fig. 4.3). This involves setting or validating the default language, time zone, console type, number of licensed users, and number of virtual terminals. IBM has kindly provided a SMIT fast path that addresses each of these variables. With `root` permissions invoke SMIT `startup`:

```
# smit startup
```

In a networked environment, you will need to set your network interface address and characteristics (see Part 4, "Network Configuration and Customization").

Set the `root` account password. The default installation does not provide a password for root. Need I say more?

```
                    System Environments

Move cursor to desired item and press Enter.

Assign the Console
Change Number of Virtual Terminals at Next System Restart
Change / Show Date, Time, and Time Zone
Change / Show Characteristics of Operating System
Manage Language Environment
Change Number of Licensed Users

F1 = Help        F2 = Refresh     F3 = Cancel      F8 = Image
F9 = Shell       F10 = Exit       Enter = Do
```

**Figure 4.3** SMIT system configuration panel.

Restore any configuration tables from the previous system, and reimport any volume groups exported as part of the preliminary installation planning.

```
# importvg <VGname>
```

### 4.4.3 Create new bootable media and backups

Next make sure you have multiple copies of stand-alone bootable media that reflect the new systems install and maintenance level. Notice I said *multiple copies.*. I must admit that I have been bitten more than once by having only a single copy of some crucial bit of data. Let's start with the *BOSboot diskettes.* If you carefully read the *AIX Installation Guide,* there is a chapter on creating stand-alone boot diskettes. This procedure is version-dependent, so make sure you have the right documentation in hand. Following the procedures in the install guide, you will create a set of diskettes that contain a small bootable kernel, device drivers for your console display type, and the AIX installation/maintenance shell.

| | |
|---|---|
| `# format` | Format a diskette |
| `# bosboot -a -d fd0` | Boot diskette |
| `# mkdispdskt` | Display diskette |
| `# mkextdskt` | Display extension diskette |
| `# mkinstdskt` | BOS install/maint diskette |

Unless you're the gambling type, test the diskettes you have created. It will bring you peace of mind and familiarize you with the stand-alone boot procedure.

#### 4.4.3.1 Stand-alone boot procedure

1. Insert the boot diskette/tape and power on/reset.
2. At LED `c07` insert the display diskette.
3. When prompted, select the console display.
4. Insert the BOS install/maint diskette and press ENTER.
5. Select `Start a limited function maintenance shell` from the menu.
6. Access and mount the root volume group: `getrootfs hdisk0`.

Now is a good opportunity to move the `/usr/sys/inst.images` directory into a separate file system, for example, `/inst.images`. The `/usr` file system is not a good target for present or future installation and maintenance activities. The `inst.images` subdirectory requires constant resizing to accommodate new install and maintenance images. Create a new JFS file system called `/inst.images`, and move the current contents of `/usr/sys/inst.images` into the new directory. If you want to continue using the `/usr/sys/inst.images` path, use it as the mount point for the new installation and maintenance file system.

Create a *vanilla* bootable image of the new `rootvg` on tape using the `mksysb` command. The tape can be used to recover from a disk failure or it can be used to install additional machines. Begin by using the `mkszfile` command to create a `/.fs.size` file. This file contains descriptive information about the file systems in the `rootvg`. Edit this file so that it contains only those file systems you wish to include in your reference set. Execute `mksysb` to create the bootable image. When booting from the stand-alone tape, the AIX install/maint shell is executed which will guide you through the restoration process.

```
# mkszfile              Create rootvg description
# mksysb /dev/rmt0      Boot tape and rootvg image
```

Once you are satisfied with the new configuration, backup everything. The extra time is worth the peace of mind. I suggest making both `mksysb` and `backup` full dumps of the new system state.

## 4.5 Distributed Systems

If installing or updating a single system isn't problem enough, think about repeating the process over and over again in a multisystem environment! In many cases, these systems represent both diskfull and diskless configurations.

### 4.5.1 NFS installation support

In networked environments, copy product and maintenance images to a file system, `/inst.images`. NFS exports this file system to each of the remote sites. This method requires repeating the installation process on each machine. It provides the capability of individually tailoring the update on each system.

### 4.5.2 Creating a reference system

To minimize the amount of time and work required to update multiple diskfull systems, create a single *reference system* image that can be cloned on each machine.

1. Update and tailor one system that represents your base configuration.
2. Invoke `mkszfile` to create a `/.fs.size` table.

3. Edit the `/.file.size` table such that it contains only those file systems you want to include in your reference system image.
4. Invoke `mksysb` to create a bootable reference image. In nonnetworked environments, direct `mksysb` output to portable media. If network access is available, direct the output image to a file system, `/inst.images`.
5. Create a *network install server* in networked environments with NFS and TCP/IP support.

### 4.5.3 Network install server

A *network install server* can be used to serve BOS, maintenance, and `mksysb` backup images to remote sites on TCP-based networks. Each remote machine connects to the install server from the stand-alone install/maintenance system. To create a network install server, complete the following steps:

1. Create an AIX account named `netinst`.

```
# smit mkuser
```

2. Copy `inst` server code to `$HOME/netinst` from `/usr/lpp /bosinst`.

```
# cd /usr/lpp/bosinst
$ find bin db scripts -print | cpio -dumpv /home/netinst
$ chmod -R 500 *
$ chown -R netinst.staff *
```

3. Create a file system to hold product, maintenance, and `mksysb` backup images with mount point `/inst.images`.

```
# smit crjfs
```

4. Install the product, maintenance, and `mksysb` backup images in `/inst.images`.
5. Set access permissions for objects in `/inst.images`.

```
# find . -type d -print | xargs chmod 755
$ find . -type f -print | xargs chmod 444
```

6. Create and maintain a `choices` file that lists the image names available from the server.

```
# cd /home/netinst/db
$ echo `/inst.images/<path>/*' >> choices
```

7. Add the install server port to `/etc/services`.

```
instsrv 1234/tcp
```

8. Add the install server to `/etc/inetd.conf`.

```
instsrv stream tcp nowait netinst /u/netinst/bin/instsrv
```

9. NFS export `/inst.images` to each remote site.

```
# smit mknfsexp
```

### 4.5.4 Accessing the network install server

To install images from the network install server, shut down the remote machine and reboot from the stand-alone boot media.

#### 4.5.4.1 Stand-alone boot procedure

1. Insert the boot diskette/tape and power on/reset.
2. At LED `c07` insert the display diskette.
3. When prompted, select the console display.
4. Insert the BOS install/maint diskette and press ENTER.
5. Select `Install a system that was created with the SMIT "Backup the System" function or the "mksysb" command` from the menu.
6. Select the network interface type and IP numbers of the local machine and the install server.
7. After the `choices` information is displayed, select the image to be installed and start the installation.

Installation will proceed by creating the `rootvg` file systems; then `tar` the image contents to the local file systems. The network BOS install process takes about 20 minutes over Ethernet.

## 4.6 Diskless Installation

Diskless workstations are systems configured with local cpu, memory, and external peripherals, but, as the name implies, no local disk. Disk support for kernel images, paging space, and file systems is provided by a network server. The network server must be configured with the *Diskless Workstation Management* software. This software is standard on AIX 3.2, or it may be installed on non-AIX servers. The network server provides a boot image and tailored copies of the `/usr` file system called shared product object trees (SPOTs) for each diskless client. SPOTs, identified by a client group name, reside in the `/export/root` directory and are created using the `mkspot` command.

```
            Diskless Workstation Management

Move cursor to desired item and press Enter.

Start Daemons on Server
Manage Shared Product Object Trees (SPOTs)
Install/Maintain Software
Manage Software Inventory
Manage Clients

F1 = Help        F2 = Refresh       F3 = Cancel       F8 = Image
F9 = Shell       F10 = Exit         Enter = Do
```

**Figure 4.4** SMIT diskless workstation panel.

To access a boot image and associated SPOT, a diskless workstation sends a `bootp` request to the network SPOT server (see Fig. 4.4). Once the server receives the `bootp` packet and the client address is established, the server downloads a copy of the boot image to the client using `tftp`. The diskless client boots the copied image and mounts the SPOT file system from the server, using `NFS`.

AIX supports three types of diskless clients:

| | |
|---|---|
| diskless | Remote file systems, paging, and dump. Bootstrap ROM for network boot. |
| dataless | Remote file systems. Local paging and dump. Bootstrap ROM for network boot. Better performance than `diskless` configuration. |
| remote /usr | Remote `/usr` file system. |

To tailor a SPOT server and manage diskless clients, invoke the SMIT `diskless` fast path.

```
# smit diskless
```

### 4.6.1 Configuring an install server

To create a server for diskless clients complete the following steps:

1. For non-AIX servers, install the *diskless workstation code* from the `bos.obj` installation image. The following example assumes that the `bos.obj` image has been copied from the installation media to the `/inst.images` directory.

```
# tar -xvf /inst.images/bos.obj ./usr/lib/dwm
```

   Tailor the `/usr/lib/dwm/dwm_platform` file to match the architecture parameters associated with the non-AIX server. See `/usr/lpp/bos/README.diskless` for more information. Non-AIX servers require that one diskless client be identified as a *superclient.* The superclient will be used to install optional software products.

2. Verify that `bootpd` and `tftpd` services are defined in `/etc/inetd.conf` and `/etc/services`.

```
/etc/inetd.conf:

bootps    dgram    udp    wait    root      /etc/bootpd bootpd
tftp      dgram    udp    wait    nobody    /etc/tftpd tftpd -n

/etc/services:

bootps    67/udp    # bootp server port
bootpc    68/udp    # bootp client port
tftp      69/udp
```

3. Verify the existence of the `/etc/bootptab` file. This file is used to locate boot images for `bootp` requests.
4. Create non-`rootvg` file systems for the diskless clients using the following mount points. You can save some disk space by using the servers `/usr` for the client SPOT. Planning worksheets for file system size calculations are provided in *AIX for RISC System/6000—Installation Guide.*

| | |
|---|---|
| `/export/root` | Size + (4 × 2048 × num clients) |
| `/export/home` | MB/user × num users on all clients |
| `/export/dump` | |
| `/export/swap` | Total client RAM × 2 × 2048 |
| `/export/exec` | |
| `/export/share` | |
| `/tftpboot` | |

   Mount and verify the file system sizes after they have been created.

5. Create a SPOT from either the server's `/usr` file system or from the AIX 3.2 distribution media. Use the `mkspot` command or the `Add a SPOT` option from the SMIT `diskless` menus.

```
# mkspot -A /usr -v <SPOTName>          User servers /usr
# mkspot -f /dev/rmt0.5 <SPOTName>      AIX 3.2 install media
```

   You can list the SPOT configuration after it is created by invoking the `lsspot` command.

```
# lsspot -L <SPOTName>
```

6. Customize common configuration files in the SPOT that will be used by the diskless clients.

   Examples:

```
/export/exec/<SPOTName>/usr/lpp/bos/inst_root/resolv.conf
/export/exec/<SPOTName>/usr/lpp/bos/inst_root/syslog.conf
```

```
/export/exec/<SPOTName>/usr/lpp/bos/inst_root/rc.local
/export/exec/<SPOTName>/usr/lpp/bos/inst_root/.profile
```

7. Initialize NFS services on the server if not already running.

```
# startsrc -g nfs
```

8. Add diskless clients.

### 4.6.2 Adding diskless clients

Each diskless client must be identified to the server. To add a diskless client, use the SMIT `mkdclient` fast path or the `mkdclient` command (see Fig. 4.5).

```
# mkdclient -a -E<SPOTName> - A<HardwareAddress> -v <ClientName>
# smit mkdclient
```

A list of configuration parameters and resources for each diskless client can be displayed using the `lsdclient` command.

```
# lsdclient -L <ClientName>
```

```
                         Add a Diskless Client

Type or select values in entry fields.
Press Enter AFTER making all desired changes.

                                                   [Entry Fields]
*CLIENT name                                    [lisa.dom.org]
  SPOT name                                     SPOT1

  NETWORK HARDWARE type                         [1]                    +#
*HARDWARE address of client machine             [10005a215c3a]
  GATEWAY INTERNET (IP) address                 []
  NETWORK SUBNETMASK                            []
  ROOT parent directory                         [/export/root]
  HOME parent directory                         [/export/home]
  DUMP parent directory                         [/export/dump]
  PAGING parent directory                       [/export/swap]
  PAGING size in blocks                         [65536]                 #
  MICROCODE directory                           [/export/exec/SPOT1/usr>
  TIME zone                                     CST                     +
  LANGUAGE                                      [1]                    +#
  KEYBOARD                                      [1]                    +#
  SUPERCLIENT?                                  No                      +
  INSTALLATION files directory                  [/export/exec/SPOT1/usr>
  DETAILED messages during client creation?     Yes                     +

F1 = Help        F2 = Refresh      F3 = Cancel      F4 = List
F5 = Undo        F6 = Command      F7 = Edit        F8 = Image
F9 = Shell       F10 = Exit        Enter = Do
```

**Figure 4.5** SMIT diskless client panel.

If maintenance or software updates are applied to the root server, synchronize the updates with the diskless clients using the SMIT `diskless_instupdt` fast path.

```
# smit diskless_instupdt
```

## 4.7 InfoExplorer Keywords

| | | |
|---|---|---|
| uname | importvg | mkszfile |
| oslevel | find | SPOT |
| lpp | rootvg | mkspot |
| bos.obj | lsvg | bootp |
| lslpp | df | tftp |
| installp | bosboot | diskless |
| bffcreate | mkdispdskt | lsspot |
| stopsrc | mkextdskt | mkdclient |
| startsrc | mkinstdskt | lsdclient |
| telinit | mksysb | |
| tsmlogin | | |
| exportvg | | |

## 4.8 QwikInfo

*Software install/maintenance information and support:*

| | |
|---|---|
| 1-800-CALLAIX | |
| 1-800-879-2755 | Software support |
| 1-800-237-5511 | Problem support |
| aixserv | E-mail problem support |
| | Requires script contact: |
| | services@austin.ibm.com |
| IBMlink.advantis.com | Internet telnet IBMLink |

Maintenance level and history:

| | |
|---|---|
| `oslevel` | AIX 3.2.4 1 version and release level |
| `uname -v -r` | Display version and release level |
| `lslpp -a -h <product>` | List maint history |

*Backup* `rootvg`:

| | |
|---|---|
| `mkszfile` | Create .fs.size file for mksysb |
| `mksysb /dev/rmt0` | Backup rootvg to tape |

*Maintenance installation:*

| | |
|---|---|
| `smit install_update` | Base install panel |
| `smit install_latest` | Selective install panel |
| `smit install_all` | Install ALL products |
| `bffcreate -qv -d <media> -f <disk-path>` | Copy maint to disk |
| `installp -qa -d <media-path> -X all` | APPLY updates |
| `installp -rB -d -X all` | REJECT updates |
| `installp -c -g -X all` | COMMIT updates |
| `installp -C <product>` | CLEANUP failed install |

*Diskless workstations system product object tree* (SPOT):

| | |
|---|---|
| `mkspot/lsspot` | Manage SPOT |

Chapter

# 5

# System Boot and Shutdown

## 5.1 AIX Boot Process

Each time you power up an RS/6000, a complex series of system checkout and initialization tasks are executed. The only outward sign of this activity is the play of numbers across the three-digit LED display on the front panel. This system start-up process is what you might be familiar with on other UNIX systems as *bootstrapping*. Bootstrapping the system involves a hardware initialization phase, followed by AIX kernel initialization. IBM refers to the hardware phase as *read only storage initial program load* (ROS IPL). Sometimes it is referred to as *ROS init.*

You may find that the terms "IPL" and "boot" are often used interchangeably in many of the IBM documents. Since IPL conjures images of 370/390 MVS or VM architectures and boot is more common in UNIX circles, I'll tend to use boot in the remainder of the chapter. Old habits are hard to break!

Whatever you call it, it's important that the system administrator be familiar with the sequence of events that is taking place under the system unit cover at boot time. Understanding the system start-up flow of control will assist in diagnosing hardware and configuration problems when they occur. (Notice that I said "*when* they occur"!)

## 5.2 Booting the System

AIX on the RS/6000 may be started in one of three ways.

*Normal boot.* Boot from a local disk. System initialized with runtime kernel. Key mode switch in NORMAL position. Normal mode of operation.

*Stand-alone boot.* Similar to normal boot, but the system is brought up with a single-user maintenance/install or diagnostic mode kernel. The system is booted from local disk, tape, or diskettes. Key mode switch in SERVICE position. Used when installing software or performing maintenance or diagnostics. (See Sec. 5.2.1.)

*Network boot.* Boot information and kernel provided by network-based file server. ROS broadcasts a boot REQUEST packet to locate a `bootp` server. The REPLY packet from the server indicates how to load the boot image from the server. The boot kernel and file system are copied from the server via TFTP. (See Sec. 4.6.)

Once the boot kernel and file system are loaded, generally the same steps are followed in all three modes to initialize a run-time AIX kernel.

Assuming that the system is configured correctly, normal and network boot proceed with bringing AIX up to *multiuser mode* after power-on without additional intervention. The boot sequence of events is outlined in Sec. 5.4 and in detail later in the chapter.

### 5.2.1 Stand-alone boot

In the event of a system problem or when required for AIX installation or maintenance, you may need to start the system in *stand-alone mode.* In stand-alone mode, the system is running the boot kernel and provides minimal access to the volume groups and file systems on disk. Booting the system in stand-alone mode will assist you in recovering corrupted system configuration files and file systems.

#### 5.2.1.1 Stand-alone boot procedure

1. Insert a diskette/tape containing a boot image and power on the system.
2. At LED `c07`, insert the display diskette.
3. When prompted, select the console display.
4. Insert the BOS install/maint diskette and press ENTER.
5. Select `Maintenance` option from the menu.
6. Select `Standalone Maintenance Shell` option from the menu.
7. Access the root volume group: `getrootfs hdisk0`.

## 5.3 Creating Bootable Media

In order to boot AIX, a *boot image* or *bootstrap kernel* must be available on one or more *boot devices* specified by *boot lists* stored in nonvolatile system RAM. ROS boot code will attempt to access each device in the list until a valid boot device is found from which to load the boot image.

The boot device characteristics and the location and size of the boot image on the device are described by a *boot record.* The boot record may be added to the beginning of the boot image, or, in the case of a disk device, the boot record is written to the first sector of the disk. The boot image and file system may or may not be compressed to save space and access speed.

### 5.3.1 Configuring the boot list

At system start-up, the ROS boot code will attempt to access boot devices from a list of boot devices stored in nonvolatile RAM (NVRAM). The boot list can be tailored or recovered by invoking the `bootlist` command or from the RS/6000 diagnostic diskettes.

Examples:

```
# bootlist -m normal hdisk0 fd0 rmt0
# bootlist -m ent0 gateway = 128.95.135.100 \
bserver = 128.95.132.1 \
client = 128.95.135.10 fd0
```

Separate lists are maintained for *normal boot, service boot,* and *previous boot.* Valid boot device types are listed in Table 5.1.

Device drivers for each of these device types are available in NVRAM. New device drivers may be loaded using the `nvload` command for custom boot configurations.

### 5.3.2 Installing a boot image

A boot image consists of a stripped kernel and skeleton root file system tailored for the boot device and boot type (normal, service, or both). The kernel is stripped of symbols to reduce its resident size. The boot file system contains the device configuration tables, driver routines, and commands that will be required to gain access to the systems devices and file systems. To create a boot image for a particular boot device, use the `bosboot` command. The boot image type is specified by the [-M normal,serv,both] flag.

*Examples:*

| | |
|---|---|
| `# bosboot -a -d -M both /dev/hdisk0` | Disk image |
| `# bosboot -s -z -M both -d /dev/network` | Compressed network |

Just in case bosboot fails when creating a new boot image on the default boot device `hdisk0`, DON'T attempt to reboot the system. It's quite likely that the old boot image is corrupted, and it's no fun

**TABLE 5.1 Boot Device Types**

| | |
|---|---|
| `fdXX` | Diskette |
| `hdiskXX` | Disk |
| `cdXX` | CD-ROM |
| `rmtXX` | Tape |
| `entXX` | Ethernet |
| `tokXX` | Token ring |

rebuilding a system from scratch. Attempt to determine the reason for the failure. Get it corrected and try again.

### 5.3.3 Creating stand-alone boot diskettes

It should go without saying that a local boot device be configured as part of your standard boot list for maintenance purposes. This device will be used to boot the stand-alone media created in Sec. 4.4.3. Remember to keep multiple copies of the stand-alone boot media that reflect your AIX maintenance level. See Sec. 5.8, "Troubleshooting," for the stand-alone boot procedure.

## 5.4 Boot Sequence of Events

In a nutshell, when the power switch is toggled to the ON (1) position, the system start-up begins by self-checking and initializing hardware. Once hardware has been reset, a boot device is located and a boot kernel and file system is loaded into memory. Peripheral devices and adapters are identified and enabled. Virtual memory support and the process scheduler are initialized. The root volume group is varied online and the root file systems checked and mounted. Run-time init is dispatched to complete system configuration, check and mount remaining file systems, and start the service daemons. Login processing is enabled and the system is up and ready for use. Sounds simple!

In the following sections we will dissect each of the boot stages and explore them in more detail. (See Fig. 5.1.) I'll list the steps performed at each stage in the boot process and the three-digit LED code that is associated with each major step being performed. You can use the LED indicators as road signs to assist you in following the boot process in real time. Being able to identify boot stages from the LED information will give you a better feel for when to start getting worried during system power-up!

The orchestration of steps conducted at boot time depends on the hardware state, key mode switch setting, available boot devices, and the system reset count retained in memory from the previous run.

### 5.4.1 Key mode switch position

There are three selectable options for the front panel key mode switch: NORMAL, SECURE, and SERVICE.

- NORMAL position is used for standard AIX operation. The system will boot to multiuser mode and support user login. The RESET button is operational.
- SECURE position is used to inhibit rebooting a running system or starting a system that has been shut down. The RESET button is

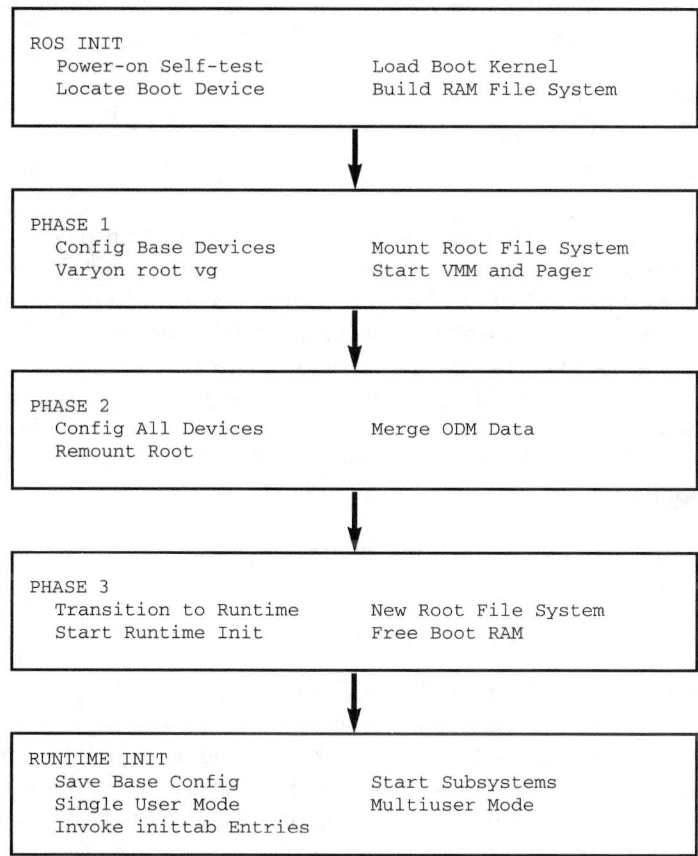


**Figure 5.1** Boot block diagram.

not operational. This position secures changes in the run state of the system.

- SERVICE position is used when you want to run system diagnostics or bring the system up in stand-alone mode. See Sec. 5.8 for more information on running system diagnostics.

As a precaution, keep one of the two keys supplied with the system unit and the other tucked away where you won't easily forget it. You can always get a replacement key from IBM; however, turnaround time may be a problem for your users.

## 5.5 ROS Initialization

A ROS IPL is invoked when hardware events trigger a system reset. Normally this occurs when you turn the system on or press the RESET button. Resets also occur in the event of a hardware failure or machine check. One of two types of IPL is performed, depending on the value of the system reset count—*cold IPL* or *warm IPL*.

```
Cold IPL Reset Count = 0 OCS BIST Checkout, OK LED = 100.
Warm IPL Reset Count = 1 BIST Bypassed. ROS IPL.
```

### 5.5.1 Built-in self-test (BIST)

A cold IPL is started each time the computer is turned on (see Fig. 5.2). If the model is equipped with an *on-card sequencer* (OCS), the OCS performs a *built-in self-test* (BIST) of the processor complex. The OCS is an 8-bit 8051 processor with 4 KB of ROM. The OCS fetches 31-bit seed and signature patterns from ROM to test and validate each processor component. The seed pattern is sent to a *common on-chip processor* (COP) resident on each of the processor chips. Test results are compared with the signature data. BIST performs the following functions:

1. Initialize and test COPs and embedded chip memory
2. Test ac/dc logic
3. Initialize and reset hardware for ROS IPL

A warm IPL occurs when the RESET button is pressed on a running system or initiated via software control. For example, a warm IPL results when the `reboot` command is executed at run time. The BIST phase is bypassed during a warm IPL. Processor memory, cache, and registers are reset and the system branches to the warm IPL entry point in ROS.

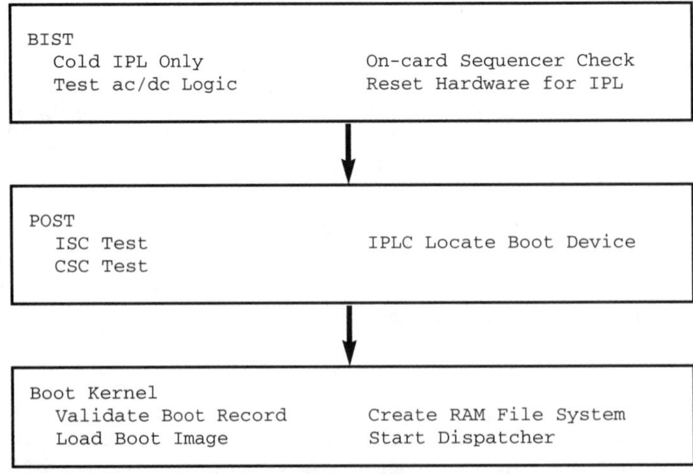


**Figure 5.2** ROS initialization block diagram.

### 5.5.2 Power-on self-test (POST)

At this point, the power-on self-test (POST) code is executed. POST processing further verifies system components. There are three phases to POST processing: *initial sequence controller* (ISC) tests, *core sequence controller* (CSC) tests, and *IPL controller* (IPLC) boot device interrogation and kernel load.

### 5.5.3 Initial sequence controller test

ISC begins by performing a CRC check on system ROM. If an error is found, you may be able to refresh ROM by switching the key mode switch to the SERVICE position and rebooting. If the CRC still fails, it's time to place a call to IBM Service.

Next, ISC inspects the *system check stop count* stored in NVRAM. Under normal circumstances, the value is 0. A nonzero value indicates that some type of noncorrectable machine check has occurred. The system is halted and the error code associated with the machine check is displayed on the front panel LED display.

Physical memory is interrogated and a bit map is built representing each 16-KB block of available memory in the system. This bit map is stored in the IPL control block for later use (see `/usr/include/sys/iplcb.h`). The ISC verifies that 1 MB of contiguous memory is available for loading the boot image from a boot device.

1. Perform CRC on system ROM. Error LED = 211.
2. Inspect system check stop value in NVRAM.
   If nonzero, halt; LED = error code.
3. RAM POST—check physical memory.
4. Build and store memory bit map in IPL control block.
5. Reserve 1-MB boot image area.

### 5.5.4 Core sequence controller test

ISC passes control to CSC, which completes POST testing. Routines stored in ROS are used by CSC to test and validate the operational presence of all devices required for successful booting of the system. CSC records the IDs of all devices and adapters discovered in the IPL control block.

1. Locate and validate boot devices.
2. Complete DMA, I/O, interrupt, SCSI POSTs.
3. Recorded device information in IPL control block.

### 5.5.5 IPL controller load boot image

IPLC takes control and begins looking for a boot device and path from which to load an IPL record and boot image. The boot device list is read from NVRAM corresponding to the boot type, and each device in the list is polled in turn until a valid boot record is found. If the selection process fails, IPLC will enter a boot list rebuild/retry loop in an attempt to locate a valid boot device. The front panel LED alternates between 229 and 223 for each iteration of the retry loop. If the NVRAM boot list is invalid, then the system default boot list is used.

Once the boot device is located, the system validates the IPL record. The IPL record describes the media characteristics and the location, length, and entry points of the boot kernel code and file system (see `/usr/include/sys/bootrecord.h`). IPLC loads the boot record into memory and makes it part of the IPL control block. From the information contained in the boot record, IPLC begins loading the boot kernel into the 1-MB memory area reserved by the ISC.

If the reserved memory space is exhausted during kernel loading, noncontiguous memory may be used if the fragmentation flag is set in the boot record. If fragmentation is disallowed, then IPLC aborts and tries the next device in the bootlist. Upon load completion, interrupts are disabled and control is passed to the boot kernel along with a pointer to the IPL control block. ROS initialization is complete.

1. Retrieve boot device list from NVRAM.
2. Locate boot device from list.
3. Load and validate boot record.
4. Load boot image into reserved 1-MB RAM.
5. Pass control to boot kernel.

## 5.6 Boot Kernel Configuration

We're still a long way from user and process scheduling at this point. The *object data manager* (ODM) has yet to be configured, there is no *logical volume manager* (LVM) support, and the scheduler and pager services are not available.

The newly loaded boot kernel determines the type of RS/6000 it is running on and saves base custom *vital product data* (VPD) for subsequent ODM configuration. A free list of memory is built based on the bit map created earlier by the ISC. The kernel uses a section of this memory space to create a RAM disk, `/dev/ram0`, which will be used to support the RAM file system data read from the boot device. The RAM file system contains the programs and file system structures required to support the remainder of kernel initialization. A prototype template defines which files will make up the RAM file system based on the boot device type. These templates are used by the `mkfs` command when creating the boot file system.

| | |
|---|---|
| `disk.proto` | Disk template |
| `diskette.proto` | Diskette template |
| `tape.proto` | Tape template |
| `net.proto` | Network template |
| `cdrom.proto` | CD-ROM template |

*Virtual memory manager* (VMM) services are next on the list. Structures for page device, page frame, repage, and hash tables are created. These tables will be used by the VMM to track and allocate virtual memory for each process in the running system. *Translation look-aside buffers* (TLB) and kernel stack areas are allocated.

Address translation is enabled. The RS/6000 uses 32-bit effective addresses in conjunction with a segment address to designate virtual memory locations. The most significant 4 bits of the effective address are used to index into one of sixteen memory segment registers. The indexed 24-bit segment address is then concatenated with the remaining 28 bits of the effective address to create a 52-bit virtual address. Each segment represents 256 MB of virtual memory. The RS/6000 hardware supports 2**24 segments per register.

The I/O subsystem is started after VMM initialization is completed. First-level interrupts are enabled for attached devices and adapters. *Input/output channel controller* (IOCC) support and the planar I/O address space is initialized. The IOCC provides the I/O pipe between the *Micro Channel bus* and the planar CPU complex.

The process table is allocated and the remaining kernel structures and services defined in `init_tbl` are set up. The *system dispatcher* is invoked as pid(0) and process table entries for `init` and `wait` are defined. Default exception handlers are set. The dispatcher is now ready to begin process scheduling. From here on, the dispatcher is referred to as the *scheduler.*

The scheduler maintains fair-share allocation of CPU resources by periodically scanning the process table and recomputing process CPU priorities and time slices. The scheduler also maintains *repage* history in order to manage *thrashing* conditions. Thrashing and repaging occur when memory has been overallocated, forcing processes to refetch pages required for execution each time they are dispatched. Thus, the term "thrashing" is used to describe this rapid page-in/page-out process. When the system repage rate exceeds 30 pages/sec, the scheduler temporarily suspends processes to reduce thrashing.

1. Save base VPD.
2. Create `/dev/ram0` and RAM file system.
3. Initialize VMM.
4. Initialize I/O subsystem.
5. Set up kernel tables and structures.
6. Start the dispatcher/scheduler.

### 5.6.1 Phase 1

The `boot init` image is loaded by the scheduler as pid(1) from `/usr/lib/boot/ssh` in the RAM file system. This heralds the beginning of *Phase 1* (See Fig. 5.3). Phase 1 is also referred to as *base device configuration phase.* `boot init` starts by forking a shell and invoking the `/etc/rc.boot` script with an argument value of 1. Base device customization information is restored by invoking `restbase` to build the object data manager (ODM) `/etc/objrepos` database. `cfgmgr` is executed and the `Config_Rules` object class is queried for all configuration rules with a phase value of 1. The `bootmask` for each rule is checked to see if the rule is to be included for this boot type. Custom configuration rule sequences can be defined by manipulating the bootmask for each rule or method. See `/usr/include/sys/cfgdb.h` for more information.

| `# cfgmgr -m <mask>` | Run rules with specified mask |
|---|---|

| Boot mask | Bits |
|---|---|
| DISK_BOOT | 0x0001 |
| TAPE_BOOT | 0x0002 |
| DISKETTE_BOOT | 0x0004 |
| CDROM_BOOT | 0x0008 |
| NETWORK_BOOT | 0x0010 |
| PHASE0_BOOT | 0x0020 |

*Note:* bootmask 0 always run.

A list of Phase 1 rules is established and sorted by sequence number. `cfgmgr` invokes each method using `odm_run_method()` to

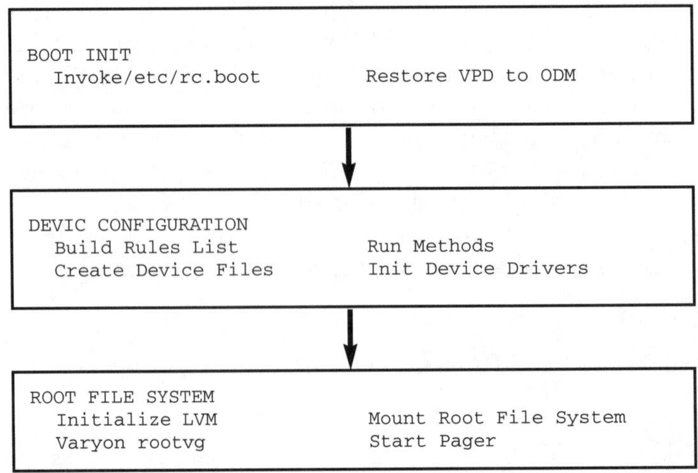


**Figure 5.3** Phase 1 block diagram.

establish device state information in the ODM. Predefined methods are located in `/usr/lib/methods`.

| Device states | Status |
|---|---|
| DEFINED | Device listed in the custom DB. Not configured or available. |
| UNDEFINED | Not represented in the custom DB. |
| AVAILABLE | Configured and available for use. |
| STOPPED | Configured but not available for use. |

The `defsys` method establishes the top-level system object `sys0`. `cfgmgr` forks a child process for each dependent method until all devices are configured. ODM *custom device* (CuDv) and *custom attribute* (CuAt) status entries are updated and the associated methods run. These methods define device special files and install device drivers. Each device is initialized by `sysconfig()` and the device switch table updated by a call to `devswadd()`. Microcode is downloaded to the device if required and VPD information is updated.

It's worth noting that you may experience problems with third-party SCSI disks when the `cfgscsi` method is run. `cfgscsi` attempts to start `SCIOSTART` and query `SCIOINQU` each device identified at each *SCSI ID/logical unit number* (LUN) location. Devices identify themselves via a 5-byte header and optional vendor data. Disk device methods attempt to spin up each disk and query the *physical volume ID* (PVID) associated with the disk. This can cause problems for external disk devices that may have already spun up, and it results in a ghost device defined with no PVID at the same SCSI-ID and LUN. The old PVID definition is left in the DEFINED state. Each PVID in a logical volume group must be set to the AVAILABLE state before the volume group can be varied on-line. You can usually fix this problem by removing the ghost PVID entry and rebooting the system after powering the disks off and on.

Phase 1 completes by initializing the logical volume manager (LVM). The LVM is defined as a pseudodevice in the ODM. The LVM device driver, `lvdd`, interfaces to the SCSI device driver, `hscsidd`, to provide logical disk volumes.

Method list:

| | | |
|---|---|---|
| | Start method invocation | LED 538 |
| `cfgsys` | System/memory/IO planar | LED 813 |
| `cfgbus` | Micro Channel bus | LED 520 |
| `cfgscsi` | SCSI adapters/devices | LED 869 |
| `deflvm` | Logical volume manger | LED 591 |
| | Complete methods | LED 539 |
| | Phase 1 complete | LED 512 |

Phase 1 completes by varying the root volume group (`rootvg`) online. The root file systems are checked and mounted. At this point, root, "/", is mounted over `/mnt`. The *pager* is started via `swapon`.

*Phase 1:*

1. `boot init` invoked as pid(1).
2. Invoke `/etc/rc.boot 1`.
3. Invoke `restbase` to restore VPD to ODM.
4. Build Phase 1 config rules list.
5. Run Phase 1 methods, planar, MCA, SCSI, etc.
6. Create device special files, device drivers, etc.
7. Initialize LVM.
8. Varyon `rootvg`.
9. Check and mount root file systems.
10. Start pager.
11. Phase 1 complete.

### 5.6.2 Phase 2

Control is returned to `boot init`, which restarts the `/etc/rc.boot` script with an argument value of 2 to begin *Phase 2* (see Fig. 5.4). The volume group map, device special files, and ODM object classes created during Phase 1 are merged into the real root file system. Hardware VPD information is deleted from the user customized ODM entries. Devices not configured in Phase 1 are configured. After all device configuration information has been updated in the root file system, the

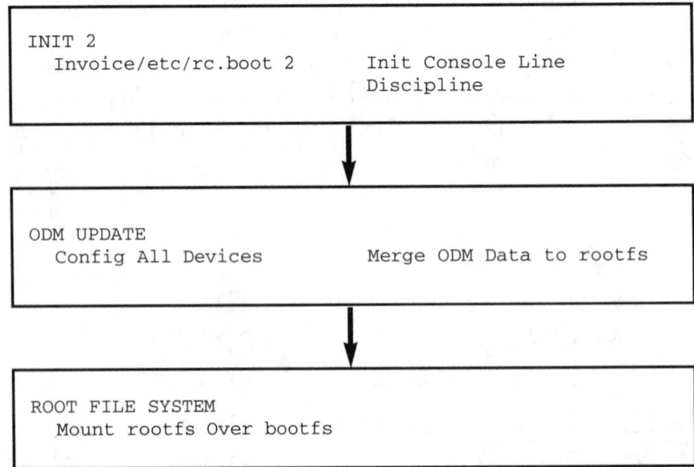


**Figure 5.4** Phase 2 block diagram.

root file system is remounted as "/" over the boot file system and `newroot` is invoked.

*Phase 2:*

1. `init` invokes `/etc/rc.boot 2` LED = 551.
2. Console line discipline initialized.
3. Merge RAM ODM and device files into `rootfs`.
4. Configure any devices not configured by Phase 1.
5. Remount `rootfs` over `bootfs`; LED = 517.
6. Phase 2 complete; LED = 553.

### 5.6.3 Phase 3

*Phase 3* marks the transition from `boot init` to `runtime init` or *Phase 2 service mode* (see Fig. 5.5). Service mode is entered when the key switch is set in the SERVICE position. All running processes except the scheduler and `boot init` are killed. After all of its children exit, `boot init` exits and becomes a ZOMBIE process. The scheduler discovers that pid(1) has exited and invokes `newroot`. `newroot` releases the RAM file system, remounts the virtual root file system and invokes `proc1restart()`, which starts `/etc/init` as pid(1). `boot init` has now been replaced by `runtime init`.

*Phase 3:*

1. Kill all running processes.
2. `boot init` exits.
3. Scheduler invokes `newroot`.
4. Old RAM file system freed.
5. VFS points at real `rootfs`.
6. `proc1restart` invokes `runtime init`.

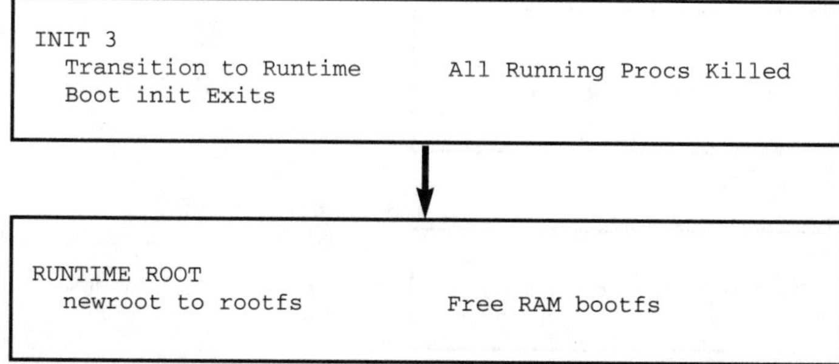


**Figure 5.5** Phase 3 Block diagram.

### 5.6.4 Runtime

runtime init begins by setting the init state to *single-user mode* (see Fig. 5.6). It examines entries in /etc/inittab and invokes /etc/rc.boot with argument of 3. The /tmp file system is checked and mounted. cfgmgr is invoked based on the key mode switch setting. If the key position is NORMAL, cfgmgr runs Phase 3 rules. If the key position is SERVICE, cfgmgr runs Phase 2 rules. Phase 1 methods are rerun. The console pseudodevice is configured and assigned. savebase is executed to save custom ODM entries to NVRAM for subsequent system boots. If the key mode switch is in the service position, then system diagnostic pretest is run. If the key is in the NORMAL position, the remaining single-user mode /etc/inittab entries are run. srcmstr is started, which, in turn, invokes subsystems defined in /etc/inittab. The init state is set to 2 and the system transitions to *MULTIUSER MODE*. Login processing is now available to your user base. The system's up! Start hacking!

*Runtime:*

1. init state to 1 SINGLE USER.
2. /etc/inittab entries invoked.
3. /etc/rc.boot 3 started.
4. fsck and mount /tmp.
5. cfgmgr Phase 2 if key = normal, Phase 3 if key = service.
6. Phase 1 rules rerun.
7. Config and Assign console pseudodevice.

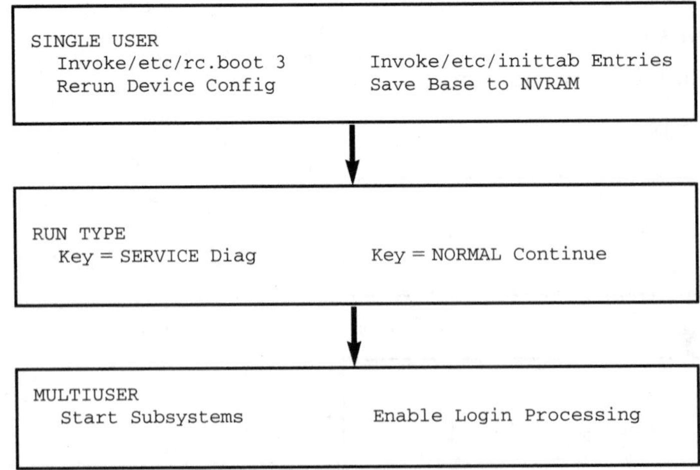


**Figure 5.6** Runtime init block diagram.

```
/dev/hft0 LED = c32
/dev/tty0 LED = c33
```

8. Invoke `savebase` to save custom settings to NVRAM.
9. If key = service then invoke diagnostics, key = normal complete `/etc/inittab` entries.
10. Set `init state` to MULTI USER.
11. Start `srcmstr` and `subsystems`.
12. Enable login processing.

## 5.7 Stopping the System

Like all things in life, runtime must occasionally come to an end. In this event, you can use the `shutdown` or `reboot` to gracefully bring services and the system off-line.

The `shutdown` command supports a number of flags to control how the system is to be brought down. By default, it will warn users to wait one minute, terminate active processes, sync the file systems, and halt the CPU. You may indicate that the system is to be immediately restarted after shutdown by using the `-r` flag, or by invoking the `reboot` command.

| | |
|---|---|
| `# shutdown -m +5` | System down to single user in 5 min |
| `# shutdown -r` | Shut down and reboot |
| `# shutdown now` | Shut down immediately |
| `# shutdown -k` | Abort shutdown procedures |

## 5.8 Troubleshooting

The RS/6000 is very good about checking its hardware during the built-in self-test (BIST) at power-up time. Keeping track of the LED information during system power-up will assist you in debugging hardware problems. If you suspect hardware problems or the system won't boot, use the *RS/6000 Diagnostic Programs* to assist in determining the failure. The diagnostic programs may be run in stand-alone mode from diskettes, or in concurrent mode with AIX on-line, using the `diag` command. For concurrent mode operation, as superuser, enter the `diag` command and follow the menu instructions. Stand-alone mode is similar to booting from diskette as described previously. There are two different boot diskettes depending on whether you have 8 M of memory or greater than 16 MB. There is a console display definition diskette and several diagnostic diskettes for testing and configuring adapters.

*Booting from diagnostics diskettes:*

1. With the system powered down, turn the key to service.

2. Insert either the 8-M or 16-MB boot diskette per your config.
3. Turn the power switch on.
4. At each `c07` LED prompt, insert the next diskette #.
5. At the `c31` LED prompt, select the console.
6. Follow the diagnostic instructions displayed on the console.

While loading the diagnostics diskettes, if a `c02` or `c03` LED status is displayed, you have either loaded the diskettes out of sequence or inserted the wrong diskette, respectively.

## 5.9 InfoExplorer Keywords

| | |
|---|---|
| bootlist | nvram |
| bosboot | getrootfs |
| mkboot | mkboot |
| restbase | mkdispdskt |
| savebase | mkextdskt |
| reboot | mkinstdskt |
| shutdown | diag |

## 5.10 QwikInfo

*System boot:*

| | |
|---|---|
| bootlist | Set boot device list |
| bosboot | Create new boot image |

*Stand-alone boot procedure:*

1. Insert a diskette/tape containing a boot image and power-on the system.
2. At LED `c07,` insert the display diskette.
3. When prompted, select the console display.
4. Insert the BOS install/maint diskette and press ENTER.
5. Select the `Maintenance` option from the menu.
6. Select the `Standalone Maintenance Shell` option from the menu.
7. Access the root volume group: `getrootfs hdisk0.`

*Start-up files:*

| | |
|---|---|
| /etc/rc.boot | Boot phases |
| /etc/inittab | Subsystem start-up |

*System shutdown:*

| | |
|---|---|
| `shutdown now` | Shut down immediately |
| `shutdown -m` | Shut down to single user |
| `shutdown -k` | Abort shutdown |
| `reboot` | Shut down and restart |
| `telinit` | Set system run level |

Part

# 3

# System Configuration and Customization

Chapter

# 6

# Devices Configuration and the Object Data Manager

## 6.1 AIX Dynamic Device Configuration

Unlike many traditional UNIX systems, AIX supports dynamic device configuration and management. In many cases, you can connect external devices to a running system, configure the device attributes, and begin using the new device. No kernel rebuild! No system reboot! How this works is that AIX allows dynamic kernel extensions and device driver installation to a running kernel, and dynamic device configuration through the *object data manager* (ODM). If you spend much time with AIX, it's essential that you develop a good understanding of ODM structure and operation. Since device management and the ODM are so tightly coupled, it makes sense to begin the discussion on devices by outlining the functional characteristics of the ODM.

## 6.2 ODM Overview

In the beginning, there were UNIX system configuration tables. They were sent forth to the BSD and SYSV masses, bringing all into a common fold of administration. But lo, workstations multiplied and prospered. Configuration tables became large and unwieldy. Out of this mire of table parsing, a new doctrine was prophesied which would reduce the wailing and gnashing of teeth during login processing and password updates. It was called `dbm` and it was good. `dbm` routines reduced large configuration tables into a database of *key-content* pairs. Items in a database are retrieved in one or two file I/Os. `dbm` databases are represented as an index file, `*.dir` and a data file, `*.pag`. A common example of a `dbm` database is the password `passwd.dir` and `passwd.pag` file.

IBM decided to take the dbm doctrine one step further by introducing a hierarchical object-oriented database for configuration data called the object data manager (ODM). The ODM centralizes a number of the standard configuration tables into a single management structure with update validation. AIX commands and kernel routines access ODM objects using SQL-like semantics.

## 6.3 ODM Components

The ODM consists of a database of object classes based on a simple UNIX file access method. The database is managed using a library of routines and commands. Information is stored as objects within an object class. Each object is associated with a set of attributes associated with the object class definition.

### 6.3.1 ODM database

Object classes are implemented as standard UNIX files in a directory which represents the ODM database. The ODMDIR environment variable defines the directory path used as the ODM database. The default ODMDIR path is set to /etc/objrepos in the /etc/environment file. ODMDIR may be manipulated to designate custom application databases.

```
/etc/objrepos          Default object class directory

./                  FRUB              SRCodmlock        lvm_lock
../                 FRUs              SRCsubsvr         product
CDiagDev            InetServ          SRCsubsys         product.vc
Config_Rules        MenuGoal          TMInput           sm_cmd_hdr@
CuAt                PDiagAtt@         boot/             sm_cmd_hdr.vc@
CuDep               PDiagAtt.vc@      config_lock       sm_cmd_opt@
CuDv                PDiagDev@         errnotify         sm_cmd_opt.vc@
CuDvDr              PDiagDev.vc@      history           sm_menu_opt@
CuVPD               PdAt@             history.vc        sm_menu_opt.vc@
DAVars              PdCn@             inventory         sm_name_hdr@
DSMOptions@         PdDv@             inventory.vc      sm_name_hdr.vc@
DSMOptions.vc@      SNMPD             lpp
DSMenu@             SRCnotify         lpp.vc

/usr/lib/objrepos      Additional AIX 3.2 directory

./                  PDiagAtt.vc       inventory         sm_cmd_opt.vc
../                 PDiagDev          inventory.vc      sm_menu_opt
Config_Rules@       PDiagDev.vc       lpp               sm_menu_opt.vc
DSMOptions          PdAt              lpp.vc            sm_name_hdr
DSMOptions.vc       PdCn              product           sm_name_hdr.vc
DSMenu              PdDv              product.vc        swconfig_info
GAI                 boot/             sm_cmd_hdr        swconfig_info.vc
GAI.vc              history           sm_cmd_hdr.vc
PDiagAtt            history.vc        sm_cmd_opt
```

### 6.3.2 Objects and object classes

ODM *objects* are the data items which make up *object classes*. Object attributes are mapped to a C language structure which represents the object class definition. The object class definition describes the *descriptor = value* pairs which make up an object. Object classes may be relationally joined to other object classes using a special *link* descriptor.

Initially the object class definition is constructed as an ASCII text file identified by a `.cre` extension. This description file is read by the `odmcreate` command to create the object class. The result is an empty object class and a `.h` header file which may be used by application programs to populate and manipulate members in the object class. As an example, consider the generic attributes of an inventory object class for a music store.

`inventory.cre` *object class definition*

```
class Inventory {
   char item[20];
   char description[80];
   char color[20];
   short unit_number;
   char manufacturer[20];
   long quantity;
   long unit_price;
   method order_more;
}

# odmcreate inventory.cre        Create an object class called inventory
```

*Inventory object member*

```
Inventory:
   item         = "Drum Sticks"
   description  = "Rudimental drum sticks, plastic tip"
   color        = "black"
   unit_number  = 293
   manufacturer = "Prehistoric Logs"
   quantity     = 20
   unit_price   = 2050
   order_more   = /usr/local/bin/check_inventory
```

The object class definition may specify a *method* descriptor (see Table 6.1). The method defines a program that is to be invoked by the

**TABLE 6.1 ODM Descriptors**

| | |
|---|---|
| short | 2-byte short integer |
| long | 4-byte long integer |
| char | Fixed-length null-terminated string |
| vchar | Variable-length null-terminated string |
| binary | Arbitrary bit string |
| link | Link to another object class |
| method | Fork and exec child command or program |

odm_run_method routine. The method updates the state of the object. In the example, the method would check the inventory and change state when the inventory was exhausted. Each object in the object class may specify a unique method program. Methods are represented as null-terminated 255-character strings. The special character "&" may be appended to the method for asynchronous execution.

### 6.3.3 Command and library interface

Users and applications manipulate ODM data via commands, library routines, and the odme ODM editor. The list of commands and library routines in Table 6.2 will give you a feeling for types of operations permitted on ODM data.

## 6.4 ODM Editor

The odme editor is an excellent tool for browsing through configuration information. In a *real* bind, it can be used to update problem data. DO NOT TRY THIS UNLESS YOU ARE VERY FAMILIAR

**TABLE 6.2 ODM Commands and Library Routines**

| Library routine | Command | |
|---|---|---|
| odm_set_path | ODMDIR | Set odm database location. ODMDIR represents a shell environment variable. |
| | odme | Object class editor. |
| | restbase | Retrieve customized objects from boot image and store in ODM. |
| | savebase | Store ODM customized objects in boot image. |
| | odmdrop | Remove an object class. |
| | odmshow | Display object class definition. |
| odm_create_class | odmcreate | Create empty object class with associated C headers for applications. |
| odm_add_obj | odmadd | Add an object to an object class. |
| odm_change_obj | odmchange | Modify object attributes. |
| odm_rm_obj | odmdelete | Delete object from an object class. |
| odm_get_obj | odmget | Retrieve an object in odmadd format. |
| odm_get_by_id | | Retrieve an object by its ID. |
| odm_rm_by_id | | Remove an object by its ID. |
| odm_get_first | | Retrieve first object that matches criteria. |
| odm_get_next | | Retrieve next object that matches criteria. |
| odm_get_list | | Retrieve a list of objects that match criteria. |
| odm_free_list | | Free memory allocated for odm_get_list. |
| odm_run_method | | Execute method associated with an object. |
| odm_close_class | | Close object class. |
| odm_err_msg | | Retrieve error message string. |
| odm_lock | | Lock object for update. |
| odm_unlock | | Unlock object. |
| odm_initialize | | Initialize ODM session. |
| odm_terminate | | Terminate an ODM session. |

WITH THE OBJECT CLASS RELATIONSHIPS! Use odme from an account without write permissions for the object classes you would like to browse to ensure integrity. Begin by selecting the object class name of interest. You may then display and manipulate information in the selected class.

As an exercise, set the ODMDIR environment variable to point to a subdirectory in your $HOME directory. Use an editor to create a sample object class and invoke odmcreate to build the new object class. Use odme and the commands listed in the previous section to manipulate data in the test object class. (See Figs. 6.1 and 6.2.)

```
# odme
```

Set the default object class type and then select Retrieve/Edit objects.

## 6.5 Configuration Tables and the ODM

To support traditional UNIX administration techniques, some ODM information is mirrored in traditional UNIX configuration tables. Care must be taken to make certain that ODM information is kept synchronized with configuration table contents. ODM and table synchronization is performed automatically if updates are introduced using SMIT. In some cases you can edit the standard configuration file and invoke synchronization commands to incorporate the updates into the ODM. For example, the TCP/IP /etc/services and /etc/inetd.conf tables may be built from ODM data using the inetexp command, updated with an editor, then incorporated back into the ODM using the inetimp command.

```
# inetexp     Build /etc/services and /etc/inetd.conf from ODM information
# inetimp     Import /etc/services and /etc/inetd.conf data into the ODM
```

```
                    Object Data Manager Editor

                 Set default object class
                 Display relational graphs
                 Create an object class
                 Selective search
                 Retrieve/Edit objects
                 Object class management
                 Delete an object class

         <Esc>1 = Help                <Esc>3 = QUIT
```

**Figure 6.1** Object data manager editor.

Object Display

Object Class : CuDv Object: 1 Descriptor: 1 of 8

| name ODM_CHAR | status ODM_SHORT | chgstatus ODM_SHORT | ddins ODM_CHAR | location ODM_CHAR |
|---|---|---|---|---|
| sys0 | 1 | 1 | | 00-00 |
| sysplanar0 | 1 | 1 | | 00-00 |
| ioplanar0 | 1 | 1 | | 00-00 |
| bus0 | 1 | 1 | | 00-00 |
| sio0 | 1 | 2 | | 00-00 |
| scsi0 | 1 | 2 | hscsidd | 00-08 |
| ent0 | 1 | 2 | entdd | 00-06 |
| sysunit0 | 1 | 1 | | 00-00 |
| fpa0 | 1 | 1 | | 00-00 |
| mem0 | 1 | 2 | | 00-0B |
| mem1 | 1 | 2 | | 00-0D |
| mem2 | 1 | 2 | | 00-0F |
| mem3 | 1 | 2 | | 00-0H |
| fda0 | 1 | 2 | | 00-00-0D |
| siokb0 | 1 | 2 | kts_load | 00-00-0K |
| siotb0 | 1 | 2 | kts_load | 00-00-0T |

<Esc>1 = Help <Esc>2 = Search <Esc>3 = EXIT <Esc>4 = Add <Esc>5 = Delete
<Esc>6 = Copy <Esc>7 = PgUp <Esc>8 = PgDown <Esc>9 = Left <Esc>0 = Right

**Figure 6.2** Sample odme panel.

## 6.6 Device Configuration

Device interface definitions and configuration attributes are stored as objects in the ODM database. Each time the system is booted, the `cfgmgr` walks the I/O bus and Micro Channel and identifies all devices present on the system. Device location and type information is stored in the ODM and the associated configuration rules and initialization methods are run to make the devices available for use (see Chap. 5).

`cfgmgr` can also be invoked on a running system from the SMIT `devices` menus (see Fig. 6.3) or by executing `cfgmgr`, `mkdev`, `chdev`, or `rmdev` from the command line. The same dynamic device configuration activities performed at boot time are invoked while the system is up and available for use. This feature allows you to make new devices available without requiring a system reboot.

```
# smit devices
```

| | |
|---|---|
| `# mkdev -l tty0` | Add a tty device |
| `# lsdev -C -s scsi -H` | List existing SCSI devices |
| `# chdev -l rmt0 -a block_size = 0` | Change tape block size |
| `# lsattr -D -l rmt0` | List tape attributes |
| `# rmdev -l rmt0 -d` | Remove a tape device |
| `# cfgmgr` | Update ODM and kernel |

```
Devices
Move cursor to desired item and press Enter.
    Configure Devices Added After IPL
    Printer/Plotter
    TTY
    Asynchronous Adapters
    PTY
    Console
    Fixed Disk
    CD-ROM Drive
    Diskette Drive
    Tape Drive
    Communications
    High Function Terminal (HFT)
    SCSI Initiator Device
    SCSI Adapter
    Asynchronous I/O
    Multimedia
    List Devices
F1 = Help      F2 = Refresh     F3 = Cancel     F8 = Image
F9 = Shell     F10 = Exit       Enter = Do
```

**Figure 6.3** SMIT devices panel.

**TABLE 6.3 Sampling of AIX Object Classes**

| | |
|---|---|
| `PdDv` | Predefined devices supported by AIX |
| `PdAt` | Predefined device attributes |
| `PdCn` | Predefined device subclass connections |
| `CuDv` | Customized devices attached to the system |
| `CuDvDr` | Customized device drivers |
| `CuAt` | Customized device attributes |
| `CuDep` | Custom device dependencies |
| `CuVPD` | Customized vital product data |
| `Config_Rules` | Configuration rule sets |

## 6.7 Predefined and Customized Devices

Device configuration information is separated into `predefined` and `customized` object classes (see Table 6.3). Predefined object class information represents default configuration information for all devices supported by AIX. Customized object classes represent the devices actually present on the system.

| | |
|---|---|
| `/etc/objrepos/Pdxxx` | ODM predefined devices/attributes |
| `PdAt PdCn PdDv` | |
| `/etc/objrepos/Cuxxx` | ODM customized devices/attributes |
| `CuAt CuDep CuDv CuDvDr CuVPD` | |

Device object classes are linked hierarchically into subclasses. For example, `7207` and `3490E` tape devices represent subclasses under the tape object class. The tape object class in turn is a subclass of the scsi object class. This hierarchy enforces configuration relationships.

Parent object class information must be configured before child subclass configuration.

Parent object class information may not be modified if child subclasses exist.

Parent object classes may not be removed if child subclasses exist.

A special object class, *predefined connections* (PdCn), defines the hierarchy of device classes and subclasses. Device attributes are maintained as separate attribute object classes.

You can display object class definitions using the odmshow command.

```
# odmshow <ObjectClassName>
```

Tables 6.4 through 6.7, representing the predefined and customized device and attribute descriptors, will give you some idea how device information is represented and linked.

## 6.8 Device States

The cfgmgr routine is responsible for updating custom device information using the configuration rule sets. cfgmgr invokes the method

**TABLE 6.4 PdDv Descriptors**

| | |
|---|---|
| type | Device type |
| class | Device class |
| subclass | Device subclass |
| prefix | Prefix name |
| devid | Device ID |
| base | Base device flag |
| has_vpd | VPD flag |
| detectable | Device detectable flag |
| chgstatus | Change status flag |
| bus_ext | Bus extender |
| fru | FRU flag |
| led | LED value |
| setno | Set number |
| msgno | Message number |
| catalog | Catalog number |
| DvDr | Device driver name |
| Define | Define method |
| Configure | Configure method |
| Change | Change method |
| Unconfigure | Unconfigure method |
| Undefine | Undefine method |
| Start | Start method |
| Stop | Stop method |
| inventory_only | Inventory only flag |
| uniquetype | Unique type |

**TABLE 6.5 PdAt Descriptors**

| | |
|---|---|
| uniquetype | Unique type |
| attribute | Attribute name |
| deflt | Default value |
| values | Attribute values |
| width | Width |
| type | Type flags |
| generic | Generic flags |
| rep | Representative flags |
| nls_index | NLS index |

**TABLE 6.6 CuDv Descriptors**

| | |
|---|---|
| name | Device name |
| status | Device status flag |
| chgstatus | Change status flag |
| ddins | Device driver instance |
| location | Location code |
| parent | Parent device |
| connwhere | Where connected |
| PdDvLn | Link to predefined device |

**TABLE 6.7 CuAt Descriptors**

| | |
|---|---|
| name | Device name |
| attribute | Attribute name |
| value | Attribute value |
| type | Attribute type |
| generic | Generic flags |
| rep | Representative flags |
| nls_index | NLS index |

specified for each attached device and updates the devices state. After the device method is complete, the device is set to one of three states, DEFINED, STOPPED, or AVAILABLE.

*Device states*

| | |
|---|---|
| DEFINED | Device defined but not available for use |
| STOPPED | Device configured but not available |
| AVAILABLE | Device configured and available |

## 6.9 Boot Devices

A small ODM database representing device configuration information is maintained as part of the AIX boot images. This information can be updated from the master ODM database using the savebase command. Likewise, ODM information from the boot image can be restored to the master ODM database by invoking the restbase command (see Chap. 5).

| | |
|---|---|
| `# savebase` | Save master ODM custom device data to the boot image |
| `# restbase` | Restore custom ODM data from the boot image to the master ODM database |

## 6.10 Small Computer System Interface

The most common device interface for the RISC System/6000 is the *small computer system interface* (SCSI). The SCSI standard defines a generic interface and command protocol that will support most device types. Devices are attached in a daisy chain fashion to the host adapter. The total chain length cannot exceed the distance maximum for the adapter type.

### 6.10.1 SCSI-1 and SCSI-2

The RISC System/6000 supports both SCSI-1 and SCSI-2 adapters and devices. Both SCSI-1 and SCSI-2 devices may be mixed on either adapter type; however, throughput to the device will be limited to SCSI-1 speeds. The `cfgmgr` queries the device type during SCSI device configuration and records the SCSI type. This eliminates the need for device drivers to continually query the SCSI type to determine if extended SCSI-2 commands are supported. SCSI-1 support provides transfer rates up to 4 MB/s. SCSI-2 *Fast SCSI* mode extends synchronous transfer rates to 10 MB/s. SCSI-2 signal control is also two to three times faster than SCSI-1.

### 6.10.2 Cables and adapters

The SCSI-2 cable uses the same pin assignments as the SCSI-1 adapter. The only difference is that on the adapter end, the SCSI-2 adapter only has 50 pins like the integrated SCSI cable.

If you are sharing a SCSI string between two machines, use IBM *Pass Through Terminator* (PTT) cables between the first device and the adapter on each end of the shared string. Device-to-device connections can use standard SCSI cables.

### 6.10.3 Single-ended and differential SCSI

Single-ended SCSI connections have a combined distance limitation of 6 meters. Logic level of each wire is based on the voltage difference with a common ground. Differential SCSI connections can run up to 25 meters. Logic levels on differential connections are based on the potential difference between two signal wires.

Single-ended connections can be a real problem with some RS/6000-9XX systems. The SCSI cable management arm in early 9XX racks eats up approximately 4.75 meters of the total 6-meter cable length. A single-ended SCSI to differential SCSI adapter can be used to get around the problem.

### 6.10.4 SCSI addressing

Each SCSI string supports eight addresses (0–7)that must be divided up between the devices and the adapter. Some device controllers support multiple devices from a single SCSI ID using *logical unit numbers* (LUN). In most cases, you are only going to have seven addresses that may be assigned to seven devices on the chain. The SCSI adapter requires one of the addresses, normally SCSI ID 7. Arbitration on a SCSI chain begins with the high address numbers, so better response is provided to devices with larger SCSI IDs. Device SCSI IDs are commonly selectable via jumpers or from a selector wheel on the device frame or housing.

*SCSI address format*

| | |
|---|---|
| `AB` | Two-digit SCSI address where:<br>`A` represents the SCSI ID<br>`B` represents the logical unit number |

Devices are identified by a location code. Verify that the location code matches the actual hardware slot and interface using the `lsdev` command.

*Device location codes*

```
AA-BB-CC-DD
```

| | |
|---|---|
| `AA` | Drawer location or planar |
| `BB` | I/O bus and slot |
| `CC` | Adapter connector number |
| `DD` | SCSI ID or port number |

## 6.11 Updating the Product Topology Diskette

It's a good idea to update the topology diskette supplied with your system each time you add a new device. These diskettes are used by IBM service and support representatives to keep a record of your system configuration. These are especially helpful for sites that have a number of machines. After updating the diskette, send a copy to IBM Hardware Support using the mailer and address label supplied with the update diskette.

*Topology update procedure*

1. Shut down the system.
2. Set the key switch to the SERVICE position.
3. Boot the system.
4. At the `DIAGNOSTICS OPERATING INSTRUCTIONS` display press enter.

5. At the `FUNCTION SELECTION` menu, select the `Service Aid` option.
6. At the `SERVICE AIDS SELECTION` menu, select the `Product Topology` options.
7. Follow the instructions displayed. When prompted "Do you have any update diskettes that have not been loaded?" answer "yes" and insert the *Product Topology Update* diskette. Follow the instructions to update the *Product Topology System* diskette. If the `EC AND MES UPDATES` screen is displayed, select the PF key to commit updates.
8. Repeatedly press PF3 to exit all `DIAGNOSTICS` menus.
9. Reset the key switch to the NORMAL position.
10. Reboot the system.

## 6.12 InfoExplorer Keywords

| | |
|---|---|
| dbm | inetimp |
| ODM | cfgmgr |
| ODMDIR | mkdev |
| odmcreate | chdev |
| method | rmdev |
| odme | savebase |
| inetexp | restbase |

## 6.13 QwikInfo

*Object data manager*

| | |
|---|---|
| /etc/objrepos | ODM database directory |
| /usr/lib/objrepos | ODM database directory |
| export ODMDIR = <path> | Set ODM database path |
| odme | ODM editor |
| inetimp/inetexp | Import/export TCP config files data from/to ODM |

*Devices*

| | |
|---|---|
| cfgmgr | Add devices after IPL |
| lsdev, mkdev, chgdev, rmdev | Manage devices |

# Chapter 7

# Tapes

Magnetic tape, due to its large storage capacity, low cost, and long storage life (usually more than 2 years), has been the secondary storage medium of choice for many years. The RISC System/6000 supports QIC $\frac{1}{4}$-in, 4-mm, 8-mm, 9-track, and 18-track drives.

## 7.1 Tape Characteristics

Before we look at the attributes of the individual device types and tape formats, it will be helpful to do a level set concerning general tape characteristics. An understanding of how data is represented on the media will assist you in making better use of the resource.

### 7.1.1 Physical characteristics

The earliest use of magnetic tape was German *Magnetophons.* These devices used a plastic tape doped with iron oxide. Later on, the United States experimented with paper tape coated with iron oxide. This was followed by acetate and, finally, polymer-based tape. The thickness of the oxide coating, particle density, and particle distribution on the tape surface determines the signal strength which may be encoded. A thicker and denser oxide layer improves the signal strength, but reduces high-frequency response for audiotape. If the layer is too thin, *print through* may occur. Print through is the transfer of recorded magnetic signal between tape layers on the reel. Tape thickness and base substrate also determine transport friction, media durability, and shelf life. Data-grade tape employs a thicker and denser oxide coating than standard audiotape and is usually more expensive. This is changing somewhat with *digital audio tape* (DAT). The same is true for data and video 8-mm tape. Good quality videotape will work in your RISC System/6000 tape drive, but I wouldn't recommend it. I learned the hard way!

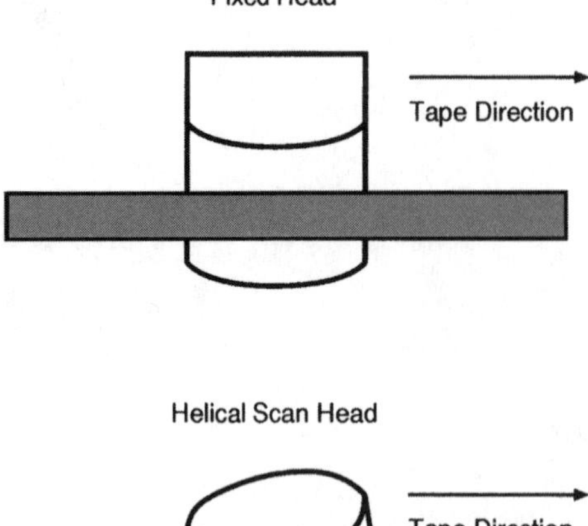


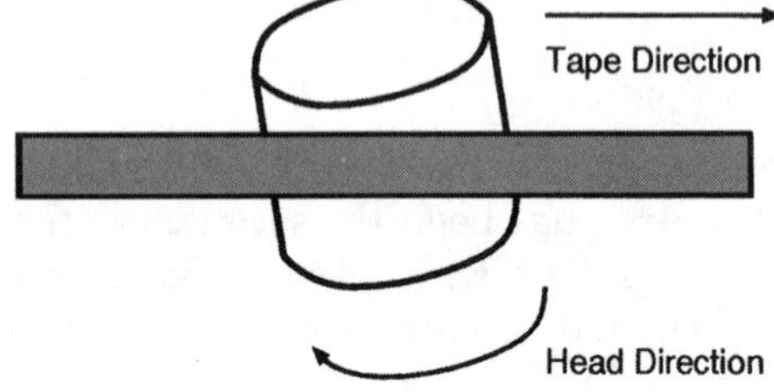


**Figure 7.1** Fixed head and helical-scan head.

Over the last few years we have also seen improvements in mechanical transport and head technologies. *Helical-scan* heads are replacing fixed head configurations for digital recording (see Fig. 7.1). Helical-scan heads spin as the tape moves across the head surface. This reduces the transport speed requirements for the tape moving from spindle to spindle. Data is written diagonally across the tape surface. This will be an important point to remember when we talk about block sizes later in the next section.

### 7.1.2 Data format

Data is recorded on tape in *blocks.* Each block of data is separated from the next by an interrecord gap. (See Fig. 7.2.) Files on a tape are delimited by *tape marks* or *file marks.* A tape mark indicates the *beginning of tape* (BOT). Two tape marks in succession indicate *end of tape* (EOT). BOT may also be followed by a special file called a *tape label.* The label indicates the volume name, size, and sequence number in a multivolume set.

Blocks are either fixed or variable in length. Fixed block format means that data is read and written in chunks which are all the same size. The amount of data read and written to the media must be done in multiples of the block size. Variable block format leaves it up to the application to determine the length of each block of data. A request to read more data than is available in the next tape block will result in a

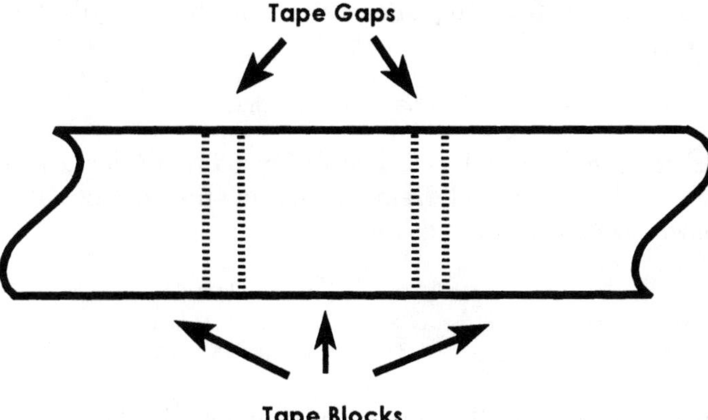


**Figure 7.2** Tape block and gap format.

*short read* when using variable format. This feature is useful for commands like `dd` that will support short reads, but is detrimental to less forgiving commands like `tar`, `cpio`, `backup`, and `restore`. The good news is that when using variable block size, the `dd` command can be employed with an excessive block size to buffer input to `tar`, `cpio`, `backup`, and `restore`.

```
# dd if = /dev/rmt0.1 ibs = 64k obs = 512 | restore -xvB
# dd if = /dev/rmt0.1 ibs = 64k obs = 5120 | tar -xvBf -
# dd if = /dev/rmt0.1 ibs = 64k obs = 5120 | cpio -ivB
```

### 7.1.3 Block size

Block size is an important consideration and will effect the total media capacity and the time required to read or write data on the device. Larger block sizes reduce the number of interrecord gaps and make better use of the tape. The block size should also reflect the physical block size written by the device. For example, an 8-mm tape drive writes 1024 bytes per block diagonally across the width of the tape. If the block size defined to AIX for the device is fixed 512-byte blocks, then the device will write out 512 bytes of data and pad the remaining 512 bytes in the physical 1024-byte block. This effectively reduces the media capacity by half. When variable length blocks are defined in AIX for the example 8-mm device, block sizes larger than 1024 will fill each physical block on the tape. If the block size used by the application is not a multiple of 1024, then the last physical block written will be padded.

Block size is application-dependent. Selecting the wrong block size can inhibit the ability to read AIX distribution and backup media, and cause portability problems. IBM uses a default block size of 512 bytes for product distribution media. You must also use a block size of 512 bytes for backups of the root volume group. If you do not use a block size of 512, the installation and restore programs will abort with the error message:

```
/dev/rmt0: archive not in backup format
```

You can change the default block size defined to AIX for a tape device using the chdev command. Remember that this does not alter the physical block size used by the device.

| | |
|---|---|
| `# chgdev -l rmt0 -a "block_size = 0"` | Variable block size |
| `# chgdev -l rmt0 -a "block_size = 512"` | Fixed 512-byte block size |
| `# chgdev -l rmt0 -a "block_size = 1024"` | Fixed 1024-byte block size |

If portability is an issue, you will want to define a default block size of 0, which indicates a variable block size. Byte ordering and ASCII/EBCDIC conversion can be handled by the conv option to the dd command.

| | |
|---|---|
| `# dd if = /dev/rmt0 conv = swab` | Swap byte pairs |
| `# dd if = /dev/rmt0 conv = ascii` | Convert EBCDIC to ASCII |
| `# dd if = /dev/rmt0 ibs = 512 obs = 1024 conv = sync` | Pad blocks |

Table 7.1 provides a few hints when using tar to move data from an RS/6000 to one of the listed vendor types.

### 7.1.4 Device names

Along with the block size, you must also be aware of the implicit tape ioctl operations associated with the device special file names. Device special file names are associated with a unique major number that identifies the tape device driver location in the device switch table. A per-device unique minor number identifies entry points in the tape device driver that correspond to various density and tape control operations. If you are familiar with other UNIX tape systems, you know that nearly everyone uses their own scheme for naming device special files. Table 7.2 represents the AIX V3 default device names and the corresponding control operations and density.

**TABLE 7.1 RS/6000 Tape Conversions Using tar**

| | |
|---|---|
| DEC | Ok. Check for compatible tape type/density. |
| Sun | Sun uses 512-byte blocks by default. On RS/6000, set block size to 512 or use dd conv = sync to pad blocks when reading Sun tapes. |
| HP | Ok. Check for compatible tape type/density. |
| SGI | Swap byte pairs using dd conv = swab. |

**TABLE 7.2 Tape Device Name Implicit Options**

| File name | Rewind on close | Retension on open | Density |
|---|---|---|---|
| /dev/rmt* | Yes | No | HIGH |
| /dev/rmt*.1 | No | No | HIGH |
| /dev/rmt*.2 | Yes | Yes | HIGH |
| /dev/rmt*.3 | No | Yes | HIGH |
| /dev/rmt*.4 | Yes | No | LOW |
| /dev/rmt*.5 | No | No | LOW |
| /dev/rmt*.6 | Yes | Yes | LOW |
| /dev/rmt*.7 | No | Yes | LOW |

**TABLE 7.3 IBM Density Modes**

| Mode # | Description |
|---|---|
| 140 | 8-mm 5-GB compression mode |
| 20 | 8-mm 2.3-GB mode |
| 0 | 8-mm 5-GB compression mode |
| 15 | 7207-12 QIC-120 |
| 16 | 7207-12 QIC-150 |
| 17 | 7207-12 QIC-525 |
| 21 | 7207-12 QIC-1000 |
| 0 | 7207-12 QIC-1000 |
| 15 | 7207-11 QIC-120 |
| 16 | 7207-11 QIC-150 |
| 17 | 7207-11 QIC-525 |
| 0 | 7207-11 QIC-525 |
| 15 | 7207-01 QIC-120 |
| 16 | 7207-01 QIC-150 |
| 0 | 7207-01 QIC-150 |
| 3 | 9-track 6250 bpi |
| 2 | 9-track 1600 bpi |
| 0 | Sensed tape density |

The high and low density values are dependent upon the device. Consult the vendor documentation concerning the device characteristics. The mode numbers in Table 7.3 identify the density for the particular IBM device.

Make sure you take a close look at the `rmt` man page information on how BOT, EOF, and EOT are handled for both reading and writing. You may be in for a surprise if you do not select the correct device name for your applications requirements. This can be especially true for EOT handling on 9-track tape drives. UNIX generally does not sense EOT before reaching it. Improper tape positioning at EOT can cause the application to run the tape off the end of the reel. You will make few friends in the operations staff if you do this very often.

### 7.1.5 Tape positioning

The tape device driver supports a somewhat standard set of ioctl operations used to control tape positioning. These operations can be invoked from the local command line, remotely, or within a program.

Local and remote positioning is handled by the `tctl` and `rmt` commands, respectively. If you are familiar with the `mt` command on other UNIX platforms, you can link `mt` to `tctl`, since their operation is similar. `rmt` is used in conjunction with `rcmd` or `rexec`.

```
# tctl -f /dev/rmt0 rewind
```

For remote operation, be aware that AIX ioctl call numbers don't necessarily map one-for-one with those on the remote system. You can fix the mapping problem by creating a wrapper for `rmt` to remap the command line parameters to those in use by the remote system. (See Table 7.4.)

Be aware of where you are during tape operations. After each program read() or write() operation, the tape head is positioned at the beginning of the next block or the beginning of blank space. Tape marks are treated exactly like a file, so they must be accounted for when skipping from file to file on a tape.

### 7.1.6 Permissions

Restricting access to tape devices tends to be a problem on many UNIX systems. The device special files are commonly set "rw" by the world. In the absence of additional tape allocation software, you can easily create your own drive reservation application using the following algorithm:

1. Check for a free device (absence of device lock files).

   All devices in use then exit

   Else continue

2. Fork and spawn a new shell.

**TABLE 7.4 AIX to UNIX ioctl Mapping**

| AIX | ioctl # | Remote | ioctl # | Comment |
|---|---|---|---|---|
| STOFFL | 5 | MTOFFL | 6 | Rewind unload tape |
| STREW | 6 | MTREW | 5 | Rewind tape |
| STERASE | 7 | MTERASE | 9 | Erase tape |
| STRETEN | 8 | MTRETEN | 8 | Retension tape |
| STWEOF | 10 | MTWEOF | 0 | Write end-of-file marker |
| STFSF | 11 | MTFSF | 1 | Forward-space file |
| STRSF | 12 | MTBSF | 2 | Backspace file |
| STFSR | 13 | MTFSR | 3 | Forward-space record |
| STRSR | 14 | MTBSR | 4 | Backspace record |
| N/A | N/A | MTNOP | 7 | NO-OP |
| N/A | N/A | MTEOM | 10 | End-of-media |
| N/A | N/A | MTNBSF | 11 | Backspace to BOF |

Wait until process exit to release device

3. Create lock file for selected device.
4. Set permissions and ownership to requester.

*Default device permissions*

```
# ls -al /dev/rmt*
crw-rw-rw-   1 root   system   22,   0 Aug 23 12:54   /dev/rmt0
crw-rw-rw-   1 root   system   22,   1 Aug 23 12:54   /dev/rmt0.1
crw-rw-rw-   1 root   system   22,   2 Aug 23 12:54   /dev/rmt0.2
crw-rw-rw-   1 root   system   22,   3 Aug 23 12:54   /dev/rmt0.3
crw-rw-rw-   1 root   system   22,   4 Aug 23 12:54   /dev/rmt0.4
crw-rw-rw-   1 root   system   22,   5 Aug 23 12:54   /dev/rmt0.5
crw-rw-rw-   1 root   system   22,   6 Aug 23 12:54   /dev/rmt0.6
crw-rw-rw-   1 root   system   22,   7 Aug 23 12:54   /dev/rmt0.7
```

## 7.2 Tape Tools

AIX provides a limited set of tape utilities. The following set of commands support tape manipulation:

| | |
|---|---|
| `dd` | Read/write variable block sizes and perform data conversion |
| `tcopy` | Display tape directory or copy tape to tape |
| `tapechk` | Verify QIC tapes for errors |
| `tar,cpio,backup/restore` | Archive tools that may use tape as a medium |

## 7.3 Public Domain Tape Tools

Due to the absence of tape allocation mechanisms, label support, and tape librarians in UNIX, a number of vendor and public domain tape handling applications have been developed. Vendor packages change faster than the publication life of this book, so I encourage you to refer to advertisements and reviews in publications like *RS/Magazine.* I found the following set of public domain tools after spending a few minutes with `archie`, searching on "tape." No warranty or guarantees implied! Use `archie` to locate the archive site nearest you.

| | |
|---|---|
| `ansitape:` | Read and write ANSI and IBM standard labels in ASCII and EBCDIC. Read multivolume tapes. Requires ioctl command changes ala `rmt` on AIX. |
| | comp.unix.sources archive v08i099. |
| `cmstape` | Process IBM VM/CMS TAPE DUMP format. |
| | comp.unix.sources archive v07i008. |
| `copytape` | Tape-to-tape copy program. |
| | comp.unix.sources archive v10i099. |
| `dectp` | Map and read a DEC ANSI labeled tape. |
| `exatoc` | Manipulate a table of contents on the beginning of an 8-mm tape. |
| `ibmtape` | Read IBM standard labeled tape. |

| | |
|---|---|
| magtapetools | Package of tape tools supporting: interrogating tape contents, tape copy, read random blocks, and read/write ANSI labels. |
| rmtlib2 | Library and generic rmt.h file supporting remote tape operations from a program similar to rmt. |
| | comp.unix.sources archive v18i109. |
| tapemap | Map a tape. Reports minimum/maximum block size and block count for each file on the tape. |
| tprobe | Copy tape package. |
| | comp.sources.3b1 archive volume02. |
| with | Tape device reservation with operator messages. |

## 7.4 IBM Tape Devices and Characteristics

For third-party devices, see documents in pub/oemhw available via anonymous FTP from ibminet.awdpa.ibm.com.

Figuring out QIC tape portability characteristics is an art unto itself. The following table for IBM 7207 models (Table 7.6) is based on data put together by Brian Murphy from IBM Development. Brian's original information is available from comp.unix.aix archives May 93.

Column numbers represent 7207 model. DC300XLP and DC600A tapes are not recommended and may cause head damage. DC9135, DC9164, DC9200, and DC9210 tapes are not supported.

## 7.5 InfoExplorer Keywords

| | |
|---|---|
| dd | ioctl |
| tar | tctl |
| cpio | mt |
| backup | rcmd |
| restore | rexec |
| rmt | |

**TABLE 7.5 IBM Tape Device Characteristics**

| Model | Format | Max. capacity | Max. transfer rate | Interface |
|---|---|---|---|---|
| 7207-01 | QIC | 150-MB | 90-KB/s | SE SCSI |
| 7207-11 | QIC | 525-MB | 200-KB/s | SE SCSI |
| 7207-12 | QIC | 1.2-GB | 300-KB/s | SE SCSI |
| 7206 | 4-mm | 4.0-GB | 732-KB/s | SE SCSI |
| 7208-1 | 8-mm | 2.3-GB | 245-KB/s | SE SCSI |
| 7208-2* | 8-mm | 2.3-GB | 245-KB/s | DF SCSI |
| 7208-11 | 8-mm | 10.0-GB | 500-KB/s | SE SCSI |
| 7208-12* | 8-mm | 10.0-GB | 500-KB/s | DF SCSI |
| ½ Inch | 9-trk | 180-MB | 768-KB/s | SE SCSI |
| 3480/3490 | 18-trk | 2.4-GB | 3-MB/s | 370 Channel |
| 3490E | 18-trk | 2.4-GB | 3-MB/s | DF SCSI |

*AS/400 compatible.

**TABLE 7.6 IBM 7207 QIC Tape Compatibility**

| Read Compatibility | | | | | |
|---|---|---|---|---|---|
| | QIC-24 | QIC-120 | QIC-150 | QIC-525 | QIC-1000 |
| DC300XLP | 01,11,12 | | | | |
| DC600A | 01,11,12 | 01,11,12 | | | |
| DC6150 | 01,11,12 | 01,11,12 | 01,11,12 | | |
| DC6250 | 01,11,12 | 01,11,12 | 01,11,12 | | |
| DC6037 | 01,11,12 | 01,11,12 | 01,11,12 | | |
| DC6320 | 01,11,12 | 01,11,12 | 01,11,12 | 11,12 | |
| DC6525 | 01,11,12 | 01,11,12 | 01,11,12 | 11,12 | |
| DC6080 | 01,11,12 | 01,11,12 | 01,11,12 | 11,12 | |
| DC9100 | | | | | 12 |
| DC9120 | | | | | 12 |
| **Write Compatibility** | | | | | |
| | QIC-24 | QIC-120 | QIC-150 | QIC-525 | QIC-1000 |
| DC300XLP | | | | | |
| DC600A | | 01 | | | |
| DC6150 | | 01,11,12 | 01,11,12 | | |
| DC6250 | | 01,11,12 | 01,11,12 | | |
| DC6037 | | 01,11,12 | 01,11,12 | | |
| DC6320 | | 01,11,12 | 01,11,12 | 11,12 | |
| DC6525 | | 01,11,12 | 01,11,12 | 11,12 | |
| DC6080 | | 01,11,12 | 01,11,12 | 11,12 | |
| DC9100 | | | | | 12 |
| DC9120 | | | | | 12 |

## 7.6 QwikInfo

*Tapes*

| | |
|---|---|
| `chgdev -l <device> -a block_size = NNN` | Set block size |

| | | |
|---|---|---|
| where NNN = | 0 | Variable block size for compatibility |
| | 512 | Backup/install block size |
| | 1024 | Efficient block size for 8-mm devices |

| | |
|---|---|
| `tar, cpio, backup` | Archive commands |
| `dd` | Data dump tool, conversion, reblocking |
| `tcopy` | Copy tape to tape |
| `tctl` | Control tape device |

Chapter

# 8

# Disks and File Systems

## 8.1 Disk Evolution

Are your file systems half full or are they half empty? It doesn't matter how much disk space you throw into a system, they are *always half full and growing fast!* With multimedia tools becoming commonplace, it's not unusual to see large numbers of audio and video files where minimum sizes are well over a megabyte. It won't be long before multimedia electronic mail will be shipping these multi-megabyte files all over the network. If you aren't already thinking in terms of multi-gigabyte personal computer and workstation storage, then you are not going to be ready for the storm. A full-blown AIX BOS installation requires one-third of a gigabyte just for the operating system. The InfoExplorer information bases can eat up another third of a gigabyte. Remember when 10-MB hard files on an IBM PC/XT seemed like more storage than you could ever use? What all this means is that you better get comfortable installing new disks and managing file systems.

## 8.2 Disk Hardware

Workstation and personal computer disk drives have primarily been either an *integrated drive electronics* (IDE) drives or *small computer system interface* (SCSI) drives. IDE drives integrate all the controller functions into the disk housing. SCSI drives also integrate controller function in the disk assembly, but require a more complex adapter card on the I/O bus. The RISC System/6000 supports internal SCSI disks and Micro Channel adapters for external single-ended SCSI/SCSI-2 and differential SCSI-2 devices.

The disks themselves are multiple platters stacked like records on a hub (see Fig. 8.1). Each platter is coated with a magnetic substrate. One or more electromagnetic heads may be moved back and forth across a platter from outer edge to inner edge. The heads react to the

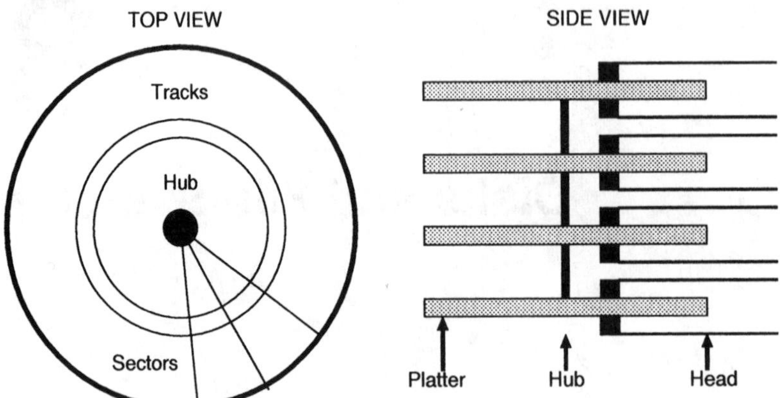


**Figure 8.1** Fixed-disk architecture.

polarization of the magnetic particles formatted in circular tracks around the surface of the platter. The heads are positioned on the platters by a disk controller circuit, which receives its instructions from the operating system.

Most disks come preformatted with a bad-sector map allocated. If you have to format a disk, invoke the `diag` command or reboot the system from the diagnostic diskettes. From the function menu, select `Service Aid`, followed by `Disk Media` and `Format Disk and Certify.`

```
# diag
Function Menu
    Service Aid
        Disk Media
            Format and Certify
```

Formatted space on the disk is made up of sectors or blocks. The sector size will vary with make and model and may be either fixed or variable. Tracks are made up of sectors aligned in circles on each platter. Stacked tracks on the platters make up a cylinder.

## 8.3 Disk Installation

To add a new SCSI disk to the system, plug the disk onto one of the SCSI adapters on the back of the system unit. This is best done with the system powered down, but can be done on-line if you are *very careful.* Multiple SCSI devices may be daisy chained off of a single SCSI adapter. Each disk must represent a unique SCSI ID and logical unit number (LUN) in the chain. The SCSI ID is jumper- or switch-selectable on the drive assembly or casing. SCSI IDs range from 0 through 7, with 7 usually assigned to the adapter. When the system is booted, the new disk is automatically identified and recorded in ROS and the ODM database. You can update device information on-line by invoking `cfgmgr` or using the `mkdev` command. The new disk is assigned the next available `hdisk<nn>` label.

```
# mkdev -c disk -s scsi -t osdisk -p scsi2 -a pv=yes
# SMIT cfgmgr
```

Use the `diag` command to verify that the system can access the new device.

```
# diag
```

## 8.4 Logical Volume Manager

The physical disk is now available for partitioning. A partition is a section of disk space which can be used for file systems or paging space. Legacy UNIX systems restrict partitions to contiguous space on a single disk. AIX uses the concept of *logical volumes* as indirection to physical space. A logical volume is represented by a mapping of contiguous logical partitions to discontiguous physical partitions residing on one or more physical disks. Each physical disk may contain up to 65,535 physical partitions ranging in size from 1 to 256 MB in powers of 2. The default physical partition size is 4 MB. One to three physical partitions may be mapped to a logical partition. Logical volumes are allocated from logical partitions within a *logical volume group* (LVG). Each LVG is made up of 1 to 32 physical disks. Partition mapping, volume management, and interfaces are implemented through a pseudodevice driver and manager called the *logical volume manager* (LVM). (Refer to Figs. 8.2 and 8.3.)

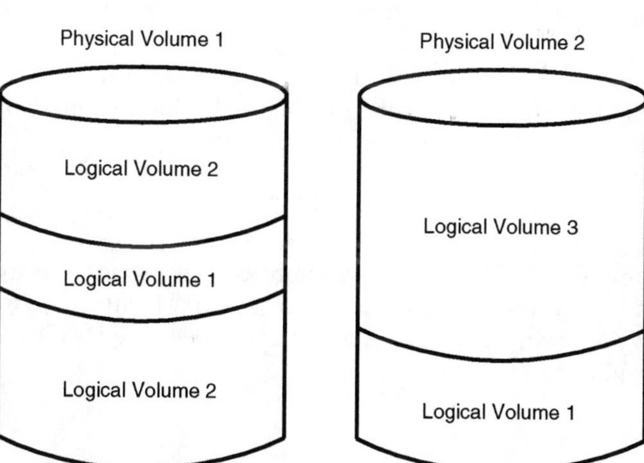


**Figure 8.2** PV to VG to LV mapping.

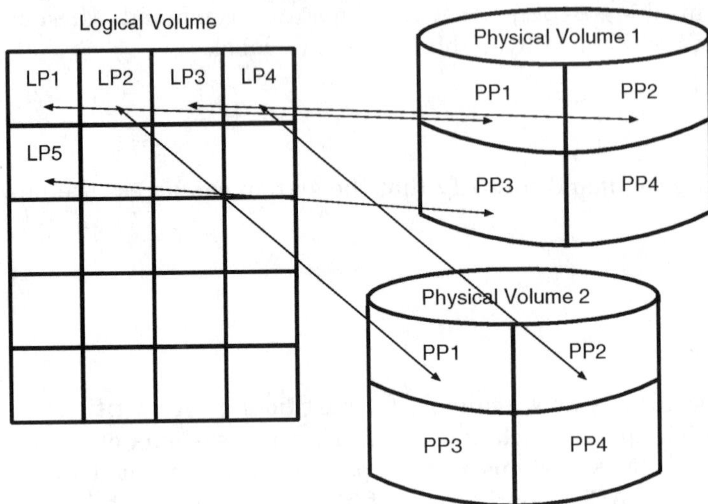


**Figure 8.3** LV to LP to PP mapping.

Using the abstraction of logical to physical partition mapping, AIX is able to dynamically increase the size of volume groups, logical volumes, and, ultimately, file systems without service interruption. Prior to LVM support, you had to back up a file system to disk or tape, destroy it, rebuild it with the new allocation sizes, and restore the backup. LVM allows you to dynamically manage disk space on-line rather than requiring hours of file system down time.

Tailoring the logical partition mapping allows you to optimize file system placement. Busy file systems should be located in the center of the physical disk and spread across multiple physical disks. The LVM also supports *mirroring,* making duplicate copies of a logical volume available for concurrent read access. Mirroring also improves data availability.

Logical volume services are also a part of the Open Software Foundation's OSF/1 operating system. Although the implementation is different, the conceptual services are very similar.

## 8.5 Configuring Volume Groups

In order for a new disk to be made available to the logical volume manager (LVM), it must be designated a physical volume and assigned a *physical volume identifier* (PVID) and *label.* The PVID is a sixteen-digit hexadecimal number.

```
# chdev -l hdisk<n> -a -pv=yes
```

You can list physical disks on your system using `lsdev`.

```
# lsdev -C -c disk
```

`hdisk0` Available 00-00-0S-00 1.2-GB SCSI disk drive (in 2.4-GB Disk Unit)

`hdisk1` Available 00-00-0S-10 1.2-GB SCSI disk drive (in 2.4-GB Disk Unit)

`hdisk2` Available 00-04-00-30 Other SCSI disk drive

`hdisk3` Available 00-04-00-40 Other SCSI disk drive

`hdisk4` Available 00-04-00-50 Other SCSI disk drive

`hdisk5` Available 00-04-00-00 Other SCSI disk drive

`hdisk6` Available 00-04-00-10 Other SCSI disk drive

`hdisk7` Available 00-04-00-20 Other SCSI disk drive

To list the PVIDs associated with these disks, use the `lspv` command.

```
# lspv
hdisk0      000008870001c7e1     rootvg
hdisk1      00001508fce5bbea     rootvg
hdisk2      00004060c388efc4     vg00
hdisk3      000015082c6e92df     vg00
hdisk4      0000150837cc1a85     vg01
hdisk5      000015082c28f5c7     vg01
hdisk6      000015082c2931f5     vg01
hdisk7      000015082c296d8f     vg01
```

To add the new disk to a new or existing volume group use SMIT or the `mkvg` and `extendvg` commands. (Refer to Fig. 8.4.)

| | |
|---|---|
| `# mkvg -f -y vg10 hdisk10 hdisk11` | Create a volume group vg10 using physical disks 10 and 11 |

```
                        Add a Volume Group

Type or select values in entry fields.
Press Enter AFTER making all desired changes.

                                                        [Entry Fields]
  VOLUME GROUP name                                        []
  Physical partition SIZE in megabytes                     4        +
  * PHYSICAL VOLUME names                                  []       +
  Activate volume group AUTOMATICALLY at system restart?   yes      +
  * ACTIVATE volume group after it is created?             yes      +
  Volume group MAJOR NUMBER                                []       +#

F1 = Help      F2 = Refresh      F3 = Cancel      F4 = List
F5 = Undo      F6 = Command      F7 = Edit        F8 = Image
F9 = Shell     F10 = Exit        Enter = Do
```

**Figure 8.4** SMIT add volume group panel.

```
# extendvg -f rootvg hdisk8      Add disk 8 to the rootvg volume group
# smit mkvg
```

A *volume group identifier* (VGID) is assigned to each volume group. The VGID is a sixteen-digit hexadecimal number. Each VGID in the system is represented by an entry in the /etc/vg directory.

```
# ls /etc/vg
./                    vg0000150837CC1FBA    vg00001508CECC7A4C
../                   vg000015084549417D    vg00001508EA5D85C7
lvdd_kmid             vg000015084549F2C6    vg00001508EA5DEB29
vg0000150837CAEE45    vg00001508AC04C232    vg00001508EA5F84DA
vg0000150837CB78DD    vg00001508CA7846C0    vg00001508FCE80427
```

To display the configuration of the existing volume groups on your system use the lsvg command.

```
# lsvg      List volume groups
rootvg
vg01
vg02
vg03
# lsvg -p rootvg      List physical volumes in the root volume group


rootvg:
PV_NAME     PV STATE     TOTAL PPs     FREE PPs     FREE DISTRIBUTION
hdisk0      active       287           17           00..12..04..01..00
hdisk1      active       287           43           00..17..00..00..26
```

### 8.5.1 Quorum

Each physical volume in the volume group is marked with a *volume group descriptor area* (VGDA) and a *volume group status area* (VGSA). The VGDA contains identifiers for all logical and physical volumes and partitions that make up the volume group. The VGSA is a bit map used to indicate which physical partitions on the disk are stale and require synced update.

When a volume group is activated using the varyonvg command or using SMIT, the LVM verifies that it has access to at least 51 percent of the VGDA and VGSA copies before going on-line. This majority is called a *quorum* and is required by the LVM to ensure data integrity. Any physical volume not available is reported. The system administrator must decide whether to continue if a device is not accessible. If a majority quorum is not established for the volume group, it is not activated.

```
# varyonvg <VGname>
```

You can take a volume group off-line using the `varyoffvg` command or via SMIT. Note that all access to logical volumes in the volume group must be terminated. Any file systems located in the volume group must be unmounted and any paging space must not be active.

```
# varyoffvg <VGname>
# smit varyoffvg
```

To remove or replace physical volumes in a volume group for maintenance purposes, use SMIT or the `chpv` command.

```
# chpv -vr <PVname>       Remove disk from VG
# chpv -va <PVname>       Replace disk in VG
```

An entire volume group may be moved as a unit from one system to another. Use SMIT or the `exportvg` and `importvg` commands to export a volume group from the old system and import it onto the new system. The volume group must first be deactivated before attempting to export it from the system. When the volume group is exported, all references to it are removed from the system tables. When the volume group is imported on the new system, all device table, special file, and `/etc/filesystem` entries are added automatically. You can export and import a volume group on the same system to resynchronize the VGDA and ODM information.

```
# exportvg <VGname>
# importvg <VGname> <PVname>
```

### 8.5.2 Root volume group—`rootvg`

A special VG called `rootvg` is used by AIX for the operating system's root file systems and the default paging areas. It's a good idea to use separate volume groups for user and local application file systems. This way you can export and import these volume groups before and after operating system upgrades. Each AIX BOS installation destroys all or part of `rootvg`.

## 8.6 Configuring Logical Volumes

To make use of the disk space available in a volume group you will need to create a *logical volume.* Logical volumes are analogous to *partitions* on other UNIX systems, but they provide some significant enhancements. The structure and features provided by logical volumes should be well understood before proceeding with allocating space for file systems or paging areas.

Logical volume type
Size in logical partitions
Interdisk partition layout
Write scheduling policy
Intradisk partition layout
Will it be mirrored

### 8.6.1 Logical volume types

The LVM basically manages all logical volume types the same way. A logical volume may warrant special consideration when defining some of the other attributes. For example you may wish to locate paging logical volumes in the center of the disks to reduce head movement. There are five logical volume types used by AIX:

| | |
|---|---|
| File system | Holds file system data and metadata |
| Log | Holds JFS metadata update log |
| Paging | Paging areas |
| Boot logical volume | Boot block and RAM file system code |
| Dump area | Holds panic dumps |

### 8.6.2 Logical volume size

When you create a new logical volume or add space to an existing logical volume, you will be working in logical partition units. If you accepted the default 4-MB partition size, then a 512-MB logical volume will require 128 logical partitions. Define a maximum number of logical partitions that will be used for the logical volume. This value limits the size a file system may grow within the logical volume. If additional file system space is required at a later date, the maximum limit may be increased.

You may notice that, when you add up the number of partitions represented by the physical volumes in a volume group, you have lost somewhere between 7 to 10 percent of the total formatted space. This is due to space overhead required by the LVM to manage the volume group. Remember the VGDA and VGSA structures described in the previous sections?

### 8.6.3 Interdisk policy

The *interdisk* layout policy determines the range of physical disks that may be used to allocate partitions for the logical volume. The interdisk policy may be either `MINIMUM` or `MAXIMUM`, along with a `RANGE` limit governing the number of physical disks that may be used.

`MINIMUM` Provides highest availability. All partitions are allocated on a single physical volume. For mirrored logical volumes, the first copy will be allocated on a single physical disk. The second copy can be allocated across multiple physical volumes up to the RANGE limit unless the strict option is selected.

`MAXIMUM` Provides the best performance. Each logical partition in the logical volume will be allocated sequentially across up to RANGE physical volumes. If one of the physical disks fails, then the entire logical volume is unavailable.

### 8.6.4 Intradisk policy

The *intradisk* layout policy (Fig. 8.5) defines where partitions will be allocated within a physical disk. One of five regions may be selected: *inner edge, inner middle, center, middle,* and *outer edge.* Inner edge and outer edge have the slowest seek times. Average seek times decrease toward the center of the disk. Use the `lsvg` command to display the layout of existing logical volumes and the number of free partitions.

```
# lsvg rootvg
```

| | | | |
|---|---|---|---|
| VOLUME GROUP: | `rootvg` | VG IDENTIFIER: | 00001508fce80427 |
| VG STATE: | active/complete | PP SIZE: | 4 MB |
| VG PERMISSION: | read/write | TOTAL PPs: | 574 (2296 MB) |
| MAX LVs: | 256 | FREE PPs: | 60 (240 MB) |

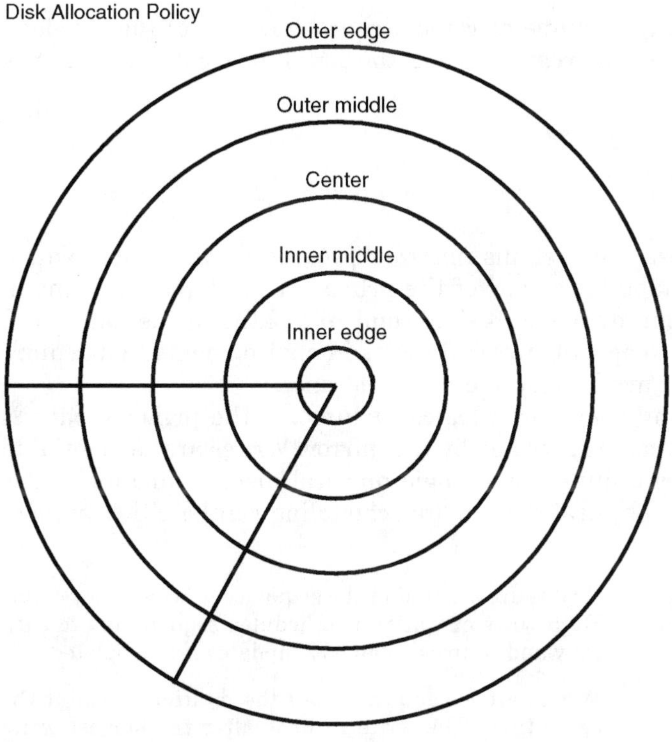

**Figure 8.5** Intradisk policies.

| | | | |
|---|---|---|---|
| LVs: | 10 | USED PPs: | 514 (2056 MB) |
| OPEN LVs: | 9 | QUORUM: | 2 |
| TOTAL PVs: | 2 | VG DESCRIPTORS: | 3 |
| STALE PVs: | 0 | STALE PPs: | 0 |
| ACTIVE PVs: | 2 | AUTO ON: | yes |

```
# lsvg -l rootvg
```

```
rootvg:
```

| LV name | Type | LPs | PPs | PVs | LV state | Mount point |
|---|---|---|---|---|---|---|
| hd5 | boot | 2 | 2 | 1 | closed/syncd | /blv |
| hd6 | paging | 6 | 6 | 1 | open/syncd | N/A |
| hd61 | paging | 6 | 6 | 1 | open/syncd | N/A |
| hd8 | jfslog | 1 | 1 | 1 | open/syncd | N/A |
| hd4 | jfs | 8 | 8 | 2 | open/syncd | / |
| hd2 | jfs | 122 | 122 | 1 | open/syncd | /usr |
| hd3 | jfs | 79 | 79 | 2 | open/syncd | /tmp |
| hd1 | jfs | 33 | 33 | 1 | open/syncd | /home |
| hd9var | jfs | 256 | 256 | 2 | open/syncd | /var |
| hd7 | sysdump | 1 | 1 | 1 | open/syncd | /mnt |

### 8.6.5 Adding a logical volume

After selecting the volume placement characteristics for the new logical volume, you can create it using the SMIT fast path, `mklv`. (See Fig. 8.6.)

```
# smit mklv
```

### 8.6.6 Mirrors

For high-access file systems, *mirrors* provide a mechanism which improves availability (a copy of the primary logical volume is maintained), and improves access time (multiple paths to the data). You may choose to keep two mirrored copies in environments that require higher levels of availability and fault tolerance.

When reading a mirrored logical volume, if the primary path is busy, the read can be satisfied by the mirror. Writes are sequential to logical volumes confined to a single physical disk. If mirrors occupy more than one physical disk, write scheduling can be either *sequential* or *parallel.*

Sequential writes — Writes are ordered in the sequence in which they occur. Each write operation is scheduled sequentially to each copy and returns when both updates are completed.

Parallel writes — Writes are scheduled across the multiple disks at the same time. The write returns after the longest write completes.

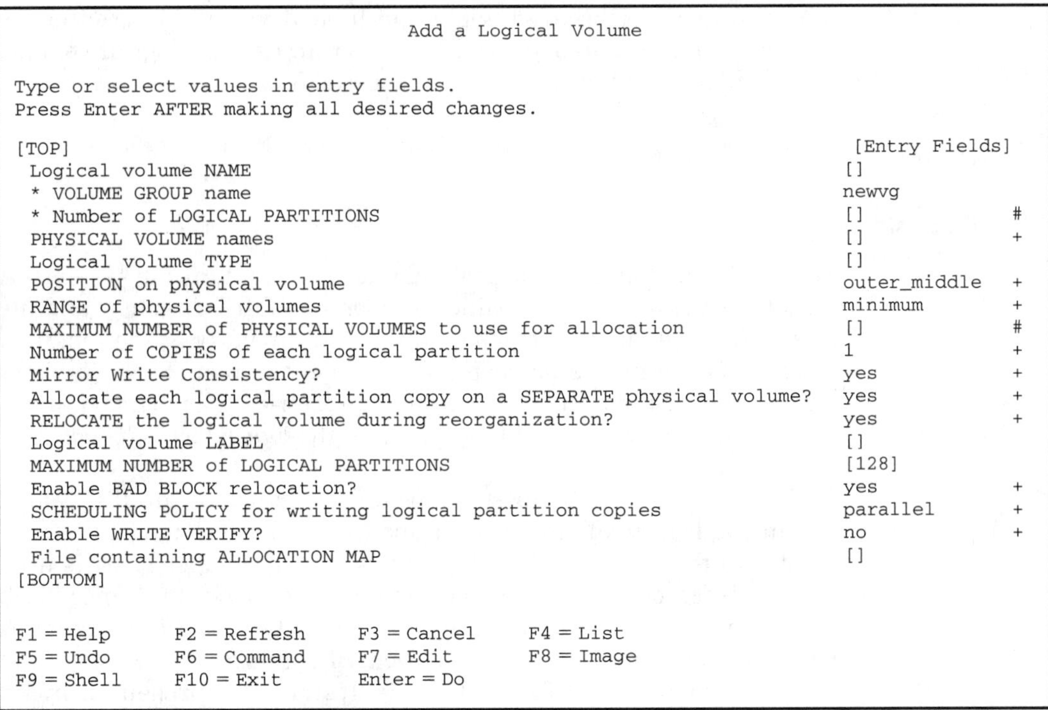

```
                              Add a Logical Volume

Type or select values in entry fields.
Press Enter AFTER making all desired changes.

[TOP]                                                              [Entry Fields]
  Logical volume NAME                                             []
  * VOLUME GROUP name                                             newvg
  * Number of LOGICAL PARTITIONS                                  []              #
  PHYSICAL VOLUME names                                           []              +
  Logical volume TYPE                                             []
  POSITION on physical volume                                     outer_middle    +
  RANGE of physical volumes                                       minimum         +
  MAXIMUM NUMBER of PHYSICAL VOLUMES to use for allocation        []              #
  Number of COPIES of each logical partition                      1               +
  Mirror Write Consistency?                                       yes             +
  Allocate each logical partition copy on a SEPARATE physical volume? yes         +
  RELOCATE the logical volume during reorganization?              yes             +
  Logical volume LABEL                                            []
  MAXIMUM NUMBER of LOGICAL PARTITIONS                            [128]
  Enable BAD BLOCK relocation?                                    yes             +
  SCHEDULING POLICY for writing logical partition copies          parallel        +
  Enable WRITE VERIFY?                                            no              +
  File containing ALLOCATION MAP                                  []
[BOTTOM]

F1 = Help       F2 = Refresh      F3 = Cancel      F4 = List
F5 = Undo       F6 = Command      F7 = Edit        F8 = Image
F9 = Shell      F10 = Exit        Enter = Do
```

**Figure 8.6** SMIT add logical volume panel.

```
                         Add Copies to a Logical Volume

Type or select values in entry fields.
Press Enter AFTER making all desired changes.


                                                                   [Entry Fields]
  * LOGICAL VOLUME name                                           lv01
  * NEW TOTAL number of logical partition copies                  1               +
  PHYSICAL VOLUME names                                           []              +
  POSITION on physical volume                                     outer_middle    +
  RANGE of physical volumes                                       minimum         +
  MAXIMUM NUMBER of PHYSICAL VOLUMES to use for allocation        [32]            #
  Allocate each logical partition copy on a SEPARATE physical volume? yes         +
  File containing ALLOCATION MAP                                  []
  SYNCHRONIZE the data in the new logical partition copies?       no              +

F1 = Help       F2 = Refresh      F3 = Cancel      F4 = List
F5 = Undo       F6 = Command      F7 = Edit        F8 = Image
F9 = Shell      F10 = Exit        Enter = Do
```

**Figure 8.7** SMIT mirror logical volume panel.

Mirrors can be created when the logical volume is created by requesting more than one copy. To mirror an existing logical volume, use the SMIT fast path, `mklvcopy` (see Fig. 8.7).

```
# smit mklvcopy lv01        Start SMIT and select logical volume to be mirrored
```

## 8.7 File Systems

The most common use of logical volumes is to contain file systems. A *file system* is the structure which supports a UNIX directory and file tree. A file system tree begins with the root directory at the top, with subdirectory branches preceding down from the root. Each directory level in the tree may contain files and directories. The primary structures which make up the file system are the *super block, inodes,* and *data blocks.*

The super block describes the overall structure of the file system within the logical volume. It contains the file system name, the size, pointer to the inode and free block lists, etc. The super block is used to keep track of the file system state during operation. Super block information is also used to verify the integrity of the file system as part of the boot process and in the event of a failure.

Each directory and file in the file system is represented by an inode. The inode can be thought of as an index entry. Each inode is sequentially numbered from 1 up to the maximum number of inodes defined for the file system. The inode identifies the attributes of the file or directory it represents.

File mode

File type

Owning UID and GID

Date and time stamps

Number of links

Pointer to data blocks

Size in bytes

Size in blocks

The number of inodes created for file systems is based on the size of the file system. The native AIX JFS file system doesn't permit granular control over the number of inodes allocated. This means more wasted space for file systems that will contain a small number of very large files—for example, databases. Each JFS inode is mapped to a 4-KB block. You can list the inode numbers associated with files and directories using the `-i` flag to the `ls` command.

```
# ls -ailF
total 1088
18   drwx------     13   deroest   system   1024   Aug 23 15:03   ./
 2   drwxr-xr-x     10   bin       bin       512   May 07 13:19   ../
25   -rwx------      1   deroest   system     27   Jan 11 1993    .forward*
21   -rwxr-x--       1   deroest   system   1499   Dec 23 1992    .kshrc*
24   -rwxr-x--       1   deroest   system    315   Nov 20 1992    .login*
```

Information for a particular inode can be displayed using the `istat` command.

```
# istat 25 /dev/hd1
Inode 25 on device 10/8 File
Protection: rwx------
Owner: 4084(deroest) Group: 0(system)
Link count: 1 Length 27 bytes
Last updated:    Tue Apr 20 08:15:50 1993
Last modified:   Mon Jan 11 14:01:24 1993
Last accessed:   Fri Aug 20 00:00:39 1993
Block pointers:
25    0    0    0    0    0    0    0
```

To find the file name associated with the inode number use the `-inum` flag with the `find` command.

```
# find /home -xdev -inum 25 -print
/home/deroest/.forward
```

Data blocks are used to store the actual file data in the file system. Each inode contains 13 data block address slots. The first 8 address slots point at the first 8 file data blocks of the file. The 9th address points to an *incore inode structure.* The disk inode information is copied to this structure when the file is opened. The 10th through 13th addresses point to *indirect data blocks* which are used to address data blocks for large files. Each indirect block supports 1024 addresses. Because file addressing is restricted to 32 bits, third-level indirection is not used.

### 8.7.1 Virtual file system

AIX V3 supplies a generic file system interface called the *virtual file system* (VFS) that permits it to support a number of file system types. VFS is an abstraction of the underlying physical file system mount structure, inodes, and operations.

The underlying physical file system is represented in VFS by a generic mount structure and an array of operations permitted on the physical file system called `vfsops`. VFS uses a paired abstraction of `vnodes` and `gnodes` to reference the underlying file system inode structures. One or more vnode structures reference a gnode which is linked to the real inode. VFS operates on the underlying inodes using vnode operations called `vnodeops`. VFS-supported file system types are defined in `/etc/vfs`.

**/etc/vfs**

```
# @(#)vfs @(#)77 1.20 com/cfg/etc/vfs, bos, bos320 6/7/91 07:47:30
#
# COMPONENT_NAME:  CFGETC
#
# FUNCTIONS:
#
# ORIGINS:  27
#
# (C) COPYRIGHT International Business Machines Corp. 1985, 1989
# All Rights Reserved
# Licensed Materials—Property of IBM
#
# US Government Users Restricted Rights—Use, duplication or
# disclosure restricted by GSA ADP Schedule Contract with IBM Corp.
#
# this file describes the known virtual file system implementations.
# format: (the name and vfs_number should match what is in
# <sys/vmount.h>)
#
# The standard helper directory is /etc/helpers
#
# name vfs_number mount_helper filsys_helper
#
# Uncomment the following line to specify the local or remote default
# vfs.
%defaultvfs jfs nfs
#
cdrfs  5  none                     none
jfs    3  none                     /sbin/helpers/v3fshelper
nfs    2  /sbin/helpers/nfsmnthelp  none                      remote
```

### 8.7.2 Journaled file system configuration

The native file system in AIX V3 is a log-based file system called the *journaled file system* (JFS). Log-based file systems like JFS improve recovery by maintaining a circular update log. In the event of a failure, the JFS log is replayed to recover the file system state. Log recovery of a file system is completed orders of magnitude faster than a full `fsck` walk of a file system. AIX provides the `fsck` to assist in disaster recovery; however, it is not invoked as part of the standard boot procedure.

When a JFS file system is created, a log logical volume is also created if it does not already exist. A log logical volume can support several file systems within a volume group.

Create or update a JFS file system using the SMIT fast path or the `crfs` and `chfs` commands. A new JFS file system may be created in an existing empty logical volume, or a new logical volume will be built to hold the new file system (see Fig. 8.8). Be careful when specifying the size of the file system! File system blocks are 512 bytes in size. The general rule of thumb is as follows:

| Block size | Action |
|---|---|
| 512 | Updating new or existing file system size |
| 1024 | AIX commands that report file system use |
| 4096* | Managing logical partitions for logical volumes |

*Default logical partition size.

```
                  Add a Journaled File System

Type or select values in entry fields.
Press Enter AFTER making all desired changes.

                                                    [Entry Fields]
Volume group name                                   rootvg
* SIZE of file system (in 512-byte blocks)          [500000]       #
* MOUNT POINT                                       [/myjfs]
Mount AUTOMATICALLY at system restart?              yes            +
PERMISSIONS                                         read/write     +
Mount OPTIONS                                       []             +
Start Disk Accounting?                              no             +

F1 = Help       F2 = Refresh      F3 = Cancel      F4 = List
F5 = Undo       F6 = Command      F7 = Edit        F8 = Image
F9 = Shell      F10 = Exit        Enter = Do
```

**Figure 8.8** SMIT add journaled file system panel.

If it was any clearer than this, it wouldn't be UNIX, and it sure wouldn't be AIX.

```
# crfs -v jfs -g uservg1 -m /u4 -a size = 1048576
SMIT crjfs
```

The file system attributes are recorded in the ODM custom databases and the `/etc/filesystem` file. You may want to edit the /etc/filesystems entry for the new file system to implement accounting or disk quotas (see Chaps. 21 and 23).

**/etc/filesystems**

```
*
* COMPONENT_NAME:  CFGETC
*
* FUNCTIONS:
*
* ORIGINS:  27
*
* (C) COPYRIGHT International Business Machines Corp. 1985, 1991
* All Rights Reserved
* Licensed Materials—Property of IBM
*
* US Government Users Restricted Rights—Use, duplication or
* disclosure restricted by GSA ADP Schedule Contract with IBM Corp.
*
*
*
* This version of /etc/filesystems assumes that only the root file
* system is created and ready. As new file systems are added, change the
* check, mount, free, log, vol and vfs entries for the appropriate
* stanza.
*

/:
    dev         = /dev/hd4
    vfs         = jfs
```

```
        log         = /dev/hd8
        mount       = automatic
        check       = false
        type        = bootfs
        vol         = root
        free        = true

/home:
        dev         = /dev/hd1
        vfs         = jfs
        log         = /dev/hd8
        mount       = true
        check       = true
        vol         = /home
        account     = true
        free        = false
        quota       = userquota

/usr:
        dev         = /dev/hd2
        vfs         = jfs
        log         = /dev/hd8
        mount       = automatic
        check       = false
        type        = bootfs
        vol         = /usr
        free        = false

/var:
        dev         = /dev/hd9var
        vfs         = jfs
        log         = /dev/hd8
        mount       = automatic
        check       = false
        type        = bootfs
        vol         = /var
        free        = false

/tmp:
        dev         = /dev/hd3
        vfs         = jfs
        log         = /dev/hd8
        mount       = automatic
        check       = false
        vol         = /tmp
        free        = false

/mnt:
        dev         = /dev/hd7
        vol         = "spare"
        mount       = false
        check       = false
        free        = false
        vfs         = jfs
        log         = /dev/hd8

/blv:
        dev         = /dev/hd5
        vol         = "spare"
        mount       = false
        check       = false
        free        = false
        vfs         = jfs
        log         = /dev/hd8
```

```
/usr/bin/blv.fs:
   dev       = /usr/bin/blv.fs
   vol       =  "/"

/usr/lpp/info/En_US:
   dev       =  /usr/lpp/info/En_US
   vfs       =  nfs
   nodename  =  fracio.geo.meca.com
   mount     =  true
   type      =  nfs
   options   =  ro,bg,hard,intr
   account   =  false
```

You may remove a file system using SMIT or the `rmfs` command.

```
# rmfs /n5        Remove file system /n5
# smit rmjfs
```

### 8.7.3 Mounting file systems

File system data is made accessible by mounting the file system on a *mount point.* The mount point is a directory in a previously mounted file system like the `root` file system. You might think that this is a "chicken and egg" problem; however, the boot procedure handles the special case of mounting the `root` file system (see Chap. 5). The mount point is usually an empty directory, but that is not a requirement. If you mount a file system over a populated directory, the previous subdirectory tree is not harmed, but it is no longer accessible until the file system has been unmounted.

File systems may be mounted or unmounted from SMIT or using the `mount` and `umount` commands. (See Fig. 8.9.)

```
                          Mount a File System

Type or select values in entry fields.
Press Enter AFTER making all desired changes.

                                                                [Entry Fields]
 FILE SYSTEM name                                                   []     +
 DIRECTORY over which to mount                                      []     +
 TYPE of file system                                                       +
 FORCE the mount?                                                   no     +
 REMOTE NODE containing the file system to mount                    []
 Mount as a REMOVABLE file system?                                  no     +
 Mount as a READ-ONLY system?                                       no     +
 Disallow DEVICE access via this mount?                             no     +
 Disallow execution of SUID and sgid programs in this file system   no     +

F1 = Help       F2 = Refresh     F3 = Cancel     F4 = List
F5 = Undo       F6 = Command     F7 = Edit       F8 = Image
F9 = Shell      F10 = Exit       Enter = Do
```

**Figure 8.9** SMIT mount file system panel.

```
# mount /dev/hd5 /n5        Mount /dev/hd5 on /n5
# umount /n6                Unmount file system /n6
# smit mountfs
```

You cannot unmount a file system that is busy. A file system is busy if any application has a file or directory open. This can be caused by an executing process or a user whose current directory path is within the file system. Use tools like `fuser` and the public domain `lsof` commands to identify which processes and users have files open.

```
# fuser -u /dev/hd1        AIX open file listing

/dev/hd1: 32605c(deroest) 43100c(deroest) 47029(root)


# lsof /dev/hd1        Public domain open file listing
```

| Command | PID | User | FD | Type | Device | | Size/off | | Inode/name |
|---|---|---|---|---|---|---|---|---|---|
| ksh | 32605 | deroest | cwd | VDIR | 10, | 8 | 1536 | 18 | /home (/dev/hd1) |
| aixterm | 43100 | deroest | cwd | VDIR | 10, | 8 | 1536 | 18 | /home (/dev/hd1) |
| ksh | 47029 | root | 63u | VREG | 10, | 8 | 2678 | 78 | /home (/dev/hd1) |

Specify which file systems are to be mounted automatically at boot time by adding the `mount = automatic` or `mount = true` parameters for each file system stanza in the `/etc/filesystems`.

File systems may also be identified as a group by adding a `type = <name>` parameter for the group in `/etc/filesystems`. The group name can then be used to mount or unmount all the file systems in the group from a single command.

```
# mount -t nfs        Mount all file systems in /etc/filesystems with type = nfs
```

To display the currently mounted file systems and their state use the `df` and `mount` commands.

```
# df -v
```

| File system | Total KB | Used | Free | % used | iused | ifree | % iused | Mounted on |
|---|---|---|---|---|---|---|---|---|
| /dev/hd4 | 32768 | 21876 | 10892 | 66% | 1239 | 6953 | 15% | / |
| /dev/hd2 | 499712 | 456776 | 42936 | 91% | 17440 | 107488 | 13% | /usr |
| /dev/hd9var | 1048576 | 235524 | 813052 | 22% | 1687 | 260457 | 0% | /var |
| /dev/hd3 | 323584 | 19260 | 304324 | 5% | 101 | 81819 | 0% | /tmp |
| /dev/hd1 | 135168 | 74824 | 60344 | 55% | 236 | 33556 | 0% | /home |
| /dev/lv02 | 909312 | 798232 | 111080 | 87% | 21 | 227307 | 0% | /inst.images |

```
# mount
```

```
node           mounted        mounted    date           options
                              over vfs
/dev/hd4       /              jfs        Aug 23 12:53   rw,log = /dev/hd8
/dev/hd2       /usr           jfs        Aug 23 12:53   rw,log = /dev/hd8
/dev/hd9var    /var           jfs        Aug 23 12:53   rw,log = /dev/hd8
/dev/hd3       /tmp           jfs        Aug 23 12:53   rw,log = /dev/hd8
/dev/hd1       /home          jfs        Aug 23 12:55   rw,log = /dev/hd8
/dev/lv02      /inst.images   jfs        Aug 23 12:55   rw,log = /dev/loglv
```

### 8.7.4 AIX root tree

The root file system tree was reorganized with version 3.2 of AIX. This was done to organize the data types in the root file system tree to facilitate mounting and maintenance. It also improves compatibility with root trees available on other UNIX platforms. For backward comparability sake, AIX 3.2 incorporates symbolic links emulating the old 3.1 root file system tree.

The AIX 3.2 root file system tree groups operating system files into the following structure:

| AIX 3.2 | AIX 3.1 Link | Description |
|---|---|---|
| / | | Root mount point and superuser shell files |
| /etc | | Machine-dependent configuration files |
| /usr | | Shared executables and files |
| /usr/bin | /bin | |
| /usr/lib | /lib | |
| /usr/sbin | | |
| /sbin | | Executables and files needed to boot and mount /usr |
| /dev | | Device special files |
| /tmp | | Temporary work files |
| /var | | Machine-dependent logs and spool files |
| /home | /u | User home directories |
| /export | | Server files exported to remote clients |

## 8.8 Paging Space

Paging (swap) space is used by AIX to support virtual memory services. When free memory becomes low or exhausted, AIX moves data pages from primary storage to the paging areas based on a least-recently-used algorithm. A threshold is maintained for virtual memory usage by the operating system. When the threshold is exceeded a `SIGDANGER` signal is sent to all processes. If a second threshold called the *kill level* is exceeded, then the operating system sends `SIGKILL` signals to the biggest memory offenders. This process continues until memory utilization falls below the threshold levels.

In order to keep this kind of trouble from occurring, you need to make sure that sufficient paging space is available. How much is going to depend on your system use profile. What are the average working set sizes required by your work load? Multiuser systems running a number of processes with large working sets may require two or more times the available real memory as paging space. A single-user workstation can get away with far less, depending on available real memory and disk. Paging space is allocated as paging logical volumes. You can split up paging space as separate logical volumes on separate physical disks to improve paging performance. Try to limit paging partitions to one per physical disk.

Paging logical volumes can be managed using SMIT or the `mkps`, `chps`, and `rmps` commands. Note that you must deactivate a paging logical volume and reboot the system before you can remove it. You may increase paging logical volumes while they are active (see Fig. 8.10).

```
# mkps          Add a new paging area
# chps          Increase the size of a paging area
# rmps          Remove a paging area
# smit mkps
```

New paging areas may be activated with the system up, using SMIT or the `swapon` command. Paging areas that are activated by a `swapon -a` are identified in the `/etc/swapspaces` file.

```
# swapon -a
/etc/swapspaces
* /etc/swapspaces
*
* This file lists all the paging spaces that are automatically put into
* service on each system restart (the 'swapon -a' command executed from
* /etc/rc swaps on every device listed here).
*
* WARNING: Only paging space devices should be listed here.
*
* This file is modified by the chps, mkps, and rmps commands and ref-
* erenced by the lsps and swapon commands.
```

```
                         Add Another Paging Space

Type or select values in entry fields.
Press Enter AFTER making all desired changes.

                                                            [Entry Fields]
 Volume group name                                            newvg
 SIZE of paging space (in logical partitions)                 []        #
 PHYSICAL VOLUME name                                                   +
 Start using this paging space NOW?                           no        +
 Use this paging space each time the system is RESTARTED      no        +

F1 = Help       F2 = Refresh     F3 = Cancel     F4 = List
F5 = Undo       F6 = Command     F7 = Edit       F8 = Image
F9 = Shell      F10 = Exit       Enter = Do
```

**Figure 8.10** SMIT add paging space panel.

```
hd6:
dev = /dev/hd6
hd61:
dev = /dev/hd61
paging00:
dev = /dev/paging00
```

To display the current allocated paging logical volumes use the `lsps` command.

```
# lsps -a
Page Space Physical Volume Volume Group Size  %Used Active Auto Type
paging00   hdisk2          fujivg       400MB 29    yes    yes  lv
hd61       hdisk1          rootvg       40MB  61    yes    yes  lv
hd6        hdisk0          rootvg       40MB  73    yes    yes  lv
```

Occasionally stale pages from processes are left on the paging logical volumes. To clean up paging space, use the `slibclean<n> command.`

```
# slibclean       Clean up paging space
```

## 8.9 Volume Maintenance

Other than the cases of reducing the size of existing file systems or paging areas, the AIX LVM and JFS systems make disk management a breeze. It's the "other than" cases that still require a bit of work.

### 8.9.1 Moving file systems

File systems may be moved within a machine, provided there is sufficient free disk space. If you are short on disk space, follow the procedure as described in Sec. 8.9.3 concerning resizing file systems. To migrate the file system logical volume to a new location, use the `migratepv` command or the SMIT `pv` fast path.

1. Use `lslv` to identify the current logical volume location and produce a physical disk map.
2. Use the `migratepv -l` to move the logical volume to its new location.

### 8.9.2 Moving volume groups

You can also move a volume group from one system to another using the `exportvg` and `importvg` commands or from using SMIT `vg` fast path.

1. Unmount all the file systems and deactivate any paging areas contained in the volume group to be moved.
2. Export the volume group using `exportvg`.

3. Move the physical disks containing the volume group to the new system.
4. Import the volume group on the new system using `importvg`. All table references will be updated automatically.
5. Mount the file systems and active paging space on the new system.

### 8.9.3 Resizing file systems

Increasing the size of a file system, logical volume, or volume group can be done on the fly with SMIT as described in the previous sections. To decrease the size of a file system requires doing things the old-fashioned way: back up the file system, recreate it, and restore the backup. It gets even trickier if you are resizing one of the operating system file systems, like `/usr`. Let's use `/usr` as an example since it's a worst-case scenario. The procedure is also a bit different on AIX 3.1.

Before you begin, if you will be using tape as a backup device, make sure that the block size is set to 512.

```
# chdev -l rmt0 -a block = 512 -T
```

*AIX 3.1*

1. Back up old `/usr`.

```
# find /usr -print | backup -ivf /dev/rmt0
```

2. Shutdown to maintenance mode.

```
# shutdown -Fm
# export LANG = C
```

3. Remove the old `/usr` file system.

```
# umount /usr
# rmfs /usr
```

4. Create new `/usr` file system. The new <size> is specified in logical partition units.

```
# mklv -yhd2 -a'e' rootvg <size>
# crfs -vjfs -dhd2 -m'/usr' -Ayes -p'rw'
# /etc/mount /usr
```

5. Restore the `/usr` backup.

```
# restore -xvf/dev/rmt0
```

*AIX 3.2*

1. Export any non-`rootvg` volume groups. This makes for peace of mind.

```
# exportvg <VGname>
```

2. Invoke `mkszfile` to create a `.fs.size` table of the current file system attributes.

```
# mkszfile
```

3. Edit the `.fs.size` and set the new size for `/usr`. Remove any non-`rootvg` file systems if any are present in the file.

   *Example:* `rootvg 4 hd2 /usr 10 40 jfs`

   The number 10 is the number of logical partitions and the number 40 is the size in megabytes. MAKE CERTAIN YOU LEAVE ENOUGH SPACE TO RESTORE THE `/usr` CONTENTS.
4. Create a `rootvg` backup using `mksysb`.

```
# mksysb /dev/rmt0
```

5. Reboot the system from the maintenance diskettes. After the `AIX 3.2 Installation and Maintenance` menu is displayed, select 2 "Install a system that was created with the SMIT `Backup the System`" function or the `mksysb` command. Follow the instructions for selecting the restore device.
6. Reboot the system after the restore is complete and import the non-`rootvg` file systems that were exported in step 1.

```
# importvg <VGname>
```

## 8.10 Troubleshooting

Troubleshooting disk hardware, LVM, and file system problems usually require intimate knowledge of the event history leading to the problem. For hardware problems:

Check cabling

Check SCSI terminator

Check SCSI ID jumpers or switch settings

Run diagnostics from the diagnostic diskettes or using `diag`

AIX V3.1 and, to some degree, AIX V3.2 had problems with SCSI disks that auto-spinup when powered on. AIX likes to request spinup as part of identifying the device. Disable the hardware auto-spinup if available.

For LVM related problems, try resynchronizing the ODM and configuration table entries by exporting the problem volume group followed by an import. You can narrow down the problem area by using `lslv` to display logical volume attributes and maps.

If a file system has become corrupted, take the file system off-line and run the `fsck` command. `fsck` will walk the file system structures and identify problem entries or chains. In an emergency situation (no backups), you can use the file system debugger to modify super block and inode entries. Do not try this one unless you are very familiar with these structures.

Occasionally a volume-group-related ODM update may abort, leaving the volume group locked. To unlock a volume group, issue a `getlvodm, putlvodm` sequence using the volume group name as an argument.

```
# putlvodm -K `getlvodm -v rootvg`      Unlock rootvg
```

## 8.11 InfoExplorer Keywords

| | | | |
|---|---|---|---|
| diag | chpv | /etc/vfs | fuser |
| cfgmgr | exportvg | gnodes | df |
| mkdev | importvg | vnodes | mkps |
| PVID | rootvg | inode | rmps |
| VGID | mklvcopy | /etc/filesystem | chps |
| lspv | mklv | JFS | /etc/swapspaces |
| mkvg | mirgratepv | fsck | swapon |
| extendvg | getlvodm | crfs | lsps |
| lsvg | putlvodm | rmfs | slibclean |
| varyonvg | istat | mount | mkszfile |
| varyoffvg | find | umount | mksysb |

## 8.12 QwikInfo

*Disk*

Hardware

External SCSI drives may be added while the system is on-line.

| | |
|---|---|
| `cfgmgr` | Configure disks added after IPL |
| `diag` | Diagnostic, certify, and format routines. May also be invoked from diag diskettes. |

*Volume groups:*

Before a disk may be used, it must have a PVID and be a member of a volume group.

| | |
|---|---|
| mkdev -l <hdisk?> -a -pv = yes | Create a PVID |
| mkvg -f -y <VGname> <hdisk? hdisk?> | Create a VG |
| lsvg | List VG |
| extendvg -f <VGname> <hdisk> | Add to a VG |
| varyonvg/varyoffvg <VGname> | VG on-line/off-line |
| importvg/exportvg <VGname> <hdisk?> | Import/export VG |
| exportvg <VGname> | Export a VG |
| putlvodm -K `getlvodm -v <VGname>` | Unlock a VG |

*Journaled file system:*

File systems may be quickly created from an existing VG by invoking SMIT `crjfs`.

| | |
|---|---|
| smit crjfs | Create JFS |
| /etc/filesystems | File system attributes |
| mount, umount | Mount/unmount file sys |
| fuser, lsof | Locate open files |

*Logical volumes:*

Custom file systems may require that a logical volume first be created using SMIT `mklv`. The file system may then be created in the new logical volume.

| | |
|---|---|
| smit mklv | Create LV |
| lslv | List LV |

*Paging space:*

| | |
|---|---|
| smit mkps | Create page space |
| lsps -a | List page space |
| swapon -a | Active all page space |

Chapter

# 9

# Terminals and Modems

## 9.1 Terminal Types

We've come a long way from the days when the term "TTY" referred to a real teletype device. I remember the satisfaction of finally leaving the card punches behind and getting access to the teletype lab in my undergraduate days. TTY is now loosely used to describe everything from serial cathode ray terminals (CRT) to software-driven pseudo-TTY (PTY) devices. The attributes and configuration options associated with these devices quite often overlap. In many cases, the terminology used to describe these attributes are holdovers from the teletype days. Add to this mix vendor enhancements and you end up with what can be a fairly confusing configuration and management task.

## 9.2 Serial TTY Support

One might think that a well-seasoned specification like RS-232D wouldn't still be causing so much grief. I know that a good deal of my gray hair has come from sweating over a soldering iron and a breakout box in the wee hours of the morning, trying to get those old TTY and modem connections up and running on the new box in town.

### 9.2.1 Cabling

First comes cabling. Common RS-232C interfaces use DB25 or DB9 male and female connectors. Signal direction and the wiring configuration at each end of the cable depend on whether you are connecting to a *data terminal equipment* (DTE) or *data communication equipment* (DCE) device. DTE devices are usually workstations or terminals. DCE devices are most often modems (modulator/demodulator) devices used for dial-up service. Only a subset of the EIA-CCITT definition signals are used in most instances (see Table 9.1).

**TABLE 9.1 EIA CCITT Interface Signals**

| DB25 | DB9 | Abbrev | Name | Direction |
|---|---|---|---|---|
| 1 | | FG | Frame ground | |
| 2 | 3 | TxD | Transmit data | DTE→DCE |
| 3 | 2 | RxD | Receive data | DTE←DCE |
| 4 | 7 | RTS | Request to send | DTE→DCE |
| 5 | 8 | CTS | Clear to send | DTE←DCE |
| 6 | 6 | DSR | Data set ready | DTE←DCE |
| 7 | 5 | SG | Signal ground | |
| 8 | 1 | DCD | Data carrier detect | DTE←DCE |
| 20 | 4 | DTR | Data terminal ready | DTE→DCE |
| 22 | 9 | RI | Ring indicator | DTE←DCE |

Positive voltage = 0, Space
Negative voltage = 1, Mark

If you want to do things strictly by the gospel according to IBM, you can order the following cables, and save yourself a bit of work with the solder gun. The native S1 and S2 ports on the back of vintage RS/6000 system units feature a 10-pin modu interface similar to the IBM RT/PC (see Fig. 9.1).

### 9.2.2 Modem/DCE wiring

AIX assumes a DCE (modem) interface by default. These interfaces require a 10-pin modu to DB25 adapter, PN#59F3740. You can then attach async cable PN#6323741 feature code 2936 or any standard DB25 connector. Newer RS/6000s provide standard DB25 interfaces. This is all you need if you are going to plug in a DCE device—for example, a modem (see Fig. 9.2).

Modem connections have to see DCD. If carrier is lost on the line, they *must* hang up the connection. There are many horror stories of modems not hanging up the line on a long distance call, resulting in phone bills larger than the national debt.

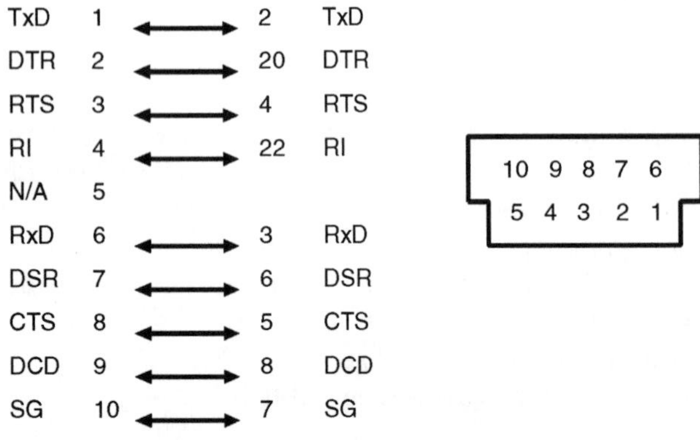


**Figure 9.1** Ten pin modu to DB25 pin-out.

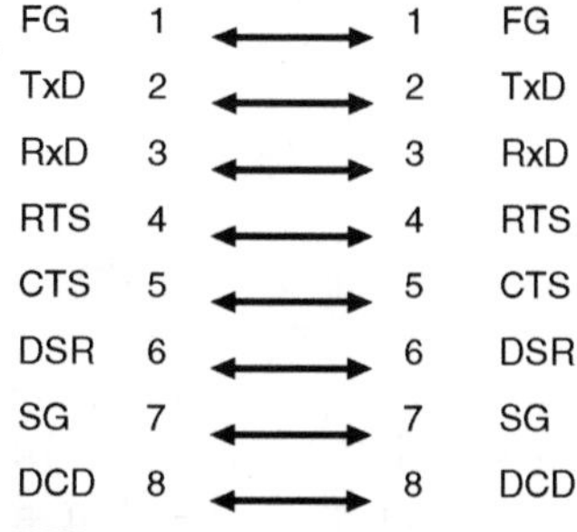


**Figure 9.2** DTE to DCE pin-out.

### 9.2.3 TTY/DTE wiring

A DTE device, like a TTY or printer, will require a *null modem* cable or adapter. IBM calls this a *terminal/printer interposer,* PN#58F2861 feature code 2936. A null modem cable basically connects the transmit line from one end of the connection to the receive line on the other, and vice versa, to support DTE to DTE communication. You may also need to wire hardware flow control lines as well.

Most terminals don't use RTS/CTS handshake signals, although this is not a hard and fast rule. There are some vendors that require an RTS/CTS handshake to jump start connections before commencing data flow. DSR and RI are only useful for modem connections. AIX assumes a DCE port by default. This means the host will expect to see DCD go high (+12v) before it will start sending data. For a terminal connection, the DTE-to-DTE pin-out configuration in Fig. 9.3 will satisfy the DCE DCD/DSR condition by raising these lines when the terminal exerts DTR.

You can reduce the number of signal lines required by using *soft carrier.* Soft carrier is a term referring to software pretending that DCD is present. To use soft carrier, you can add *clocal* to the stty settings defined for the port via SMIT. We will look at SMIT definitions a little later. Using soft carrier, you should be able to run your terminal with the wiring configuration shown in Fig. 9.4.

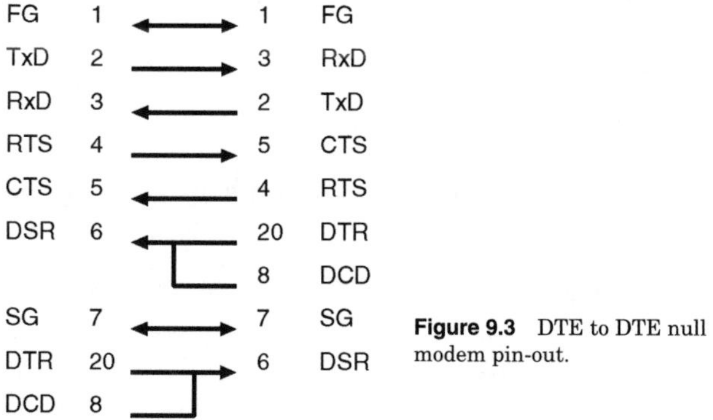


**Figure 9.3** DTE to DTE null modem pin-out.

**Figure 9.4** Four-wire TTY pin-out.

For twisted pair wiring, use one pair for data send, and one pair for data receive. The second wire in each pair should be connected to ground. This will compensate for voltage spikes on the line. For a safe connection, the shield should be connected to frame ground on one end only. If your terminal type requires an RTS/CTS handshake to jump start the connection, bridge the RTS/CTS together on the device end. This configuration works very well with RJ11/RJ45 to DB25/DB9 modular connectors. These modular connectors can then be used with factory-terminated RJ11/RJ45 flat cables. This type of connection will allow you to move things around quickly and easily by unplugging the cable from the adapter without having to remove adapter screws.

### 9.2.4 Serial cable length

How far can these cables be run? According to EIA-232D, cables should not exceed a length of 200 ft, providing they do not exceed a load of 2500 pF (picofarads). The lower the capacitance, the longer the cable. The length is also somewhat dependent on baud rate. As standards tend to be on the conservative side, in practice you can run cables much farther than 200 ft. I've run cables over 500 ft, but if you're nervous about playing fast and loose with standards, you can use a short-haul modem or mux to boost the signals.

### 9.2.5 Port addressing

You may notice some ambiguity concerning port and adapter names. The first planar serial port, marked "S1," is referred to as location "00-00-S1-00," parent adapter "sa0," and port number "s1." The second serial port labeled "S2" follows as location "00-00-S2-00," parent adapter "sa1," and port number "s2."

*TTY location addressing:*

AA.BB.CC.DD

AA: Planar, drawer, or expansion and slot number

BB: Bus and slot number

CC: Adapter connector number

DD: Port number

## 9.3 AIX TTY Definition

Now that the device is cabled and connected to the system unit, define the TTY device characteristics to the operating system. AIX TTY device attributes are stored as ODM objects. The type of information is similar to what you may be used to seeing in the BSD /etc/ttys, /etc/ttytype, and /etc/gettytab files, or the SYSV /etc/inittab, /etc/gettydefs, and /etc/gettytab files. Like SYSV, AIX sets the initial boot state of each TTY in /etc/inittab.

To define or modify TTY attributes, invoke SMIT or use the mkdev command. Considering the number of parameters that must be defined, it will be easier to use SMIT.

If you are adding or updating a large number of devices, add one device via SMIT and then use the $HOME/smit.script file as a boilerplate shell script for defining the remaining devices. Edit the smit.script file and look for the mkdev line used to configure the first device. Remove any old commands and text from previous SMIT runs. Duplicate the mkdev line and update the address information for each new device. Save the file and execute it to configure the remaining devices. This approach is quite useful when configuring terminal servers and concentrators. For best results, make sure the device is powered up during configuration.

```
# smit maktty
# mkdev <options>
```

When updating an existing TTY port, use the SMIT fast path, chgtty. The configuration menu contains the same parameter list as maktty with the exception that the existing port number and location are displayed.

```
# smit chgtty
```

The SMIT menu will display the list of TTY attributes which must be customized for the device type. (See Fig. 9.5.)

You will need to supply the default line speed, data format, terminal type, control characters, line discipline, and login state. SMIT fills in the fields with default information which will assist you in determining the type and format of the data to be supplied.

### 9.3.1 Line speed

Line speed is also called *baud rate*. This is the bits-per-second bandwidth between devices across the wire. Setting this entry is usually straightforward in cases where a single data rate is specified for the device. It gets a little trickier when you want to support multiple data rates for dial-in connections. Supporting multiple data rates is called

```
Add a TTY
                    Type or select values in entry fields.

Press Enter AFTER making all desired changes.

[TOP]                                              [Entry Fields]
TTY type                                     tty
TTY interface                                rs232
Description                                  Asynchronous Terminal
Parent adapter                               sa0
PORT number                                  []                      +
Enable LOGIN                                 disable                 +
BAUD rate                                    [9600]                  +
PARITY                                       [none]                  +
BITS per character                           [8]                     +
Number of STOP BITS                          [1]                     +
TIME before advancing to next port setting   [0]                     +#
XON-XOFF handshaking                         yes                     +
TERMINAL type                                [dumb]
INTERRUPT character                          [^c]
QUIT character                               [^\]
ERASE character                              [^h]
KILL character                               [^u]
END OF FILE character                        [^d]
END OF LINE character                        [^@]
2nd END OF LINE character                    [^`]
DELAYED SUSPEND PROCESS character            [^y]
SUSPEND PROCESS character                    [^z]
LITERAL NEXT character                       [^v]
START character                              [^q]
STOP character                               [^s]
WORD ERASE character                         [^w]
REPRINT LINE character                       [^r]
DISCARD character                            [^o]
INPUT map file                               [none]                  +
OUTPUT map file                              [none]                  +
CODESET map file                             [sbcs]                  +
STTY attributes for RUN TIME                 [hupcl,cread,brkint,icr>
STTY attributes for LOGIN                    [hupcl,cread,echoe,cs8,>
RUN shell activity manager                   no                      +
Optional LOGGER name                         []
STATE to be configured at boot time          [available]             +
[BOTTOM]

F1 = Help        F2 = Refresh     F3 = Cancel      F4 = List
F5 = Undo        F6 = Command     F7 = Edit        F8 = Image
F9 = Shell       F10 = Exit       Enter = Do
```

**Figure 9.5** SMIT add a TTY panel.

*autobaud.* Autobauding allows the port to cycle through a range of baud rates on a time slice basis or when control break is received on the line. Each data rate is tried until the line speed matches that of the connecting device.

To get autobauding working on the RISC System 6000, enter the desired baud rates separated by commas into the `BAUD rate` field. Note that they can be entered in any order. Set the `TIME before advancing to next port setting` to the number of seconds to wait before cycling to the next baud rate in the list. If the user does not enter a login ID before the time slice expires, or sends a control break (ESC), then the next baud rate in the list is tried. The system will continue to cycle through the list until the list is exhausted or the user successfully logs in. If the cycle time is set to "0," manual control breaks are required to cycle through the list.

```
BAUD rate [300,1200,2400,4800,9600]
TIME before advancing to next port setting [6]
```

### 9.3.2 Data format

When characters are sent across the wire, they are framed into sequences of bits which enables the hardware and software to validate the data. Each frame is constructed of the data bits followed by a number of stop bits and parity. The most common selections are

```
PARITY [none] -or- [even]
BITS per character [8]      [7]
Number of STOP BITS[1]      [2]
```

There are also a number of compression and error-checking protocols that may be used to send more data across the wire. These techniques are handled by the hardware and do not require configuring into the operating system.

### 9.3.3 Terminal type

If it is known that a particular terminal type will always be using the port, you may define the terminal name in the `TERMINAL type` field. The name used must match an entry in the SYSV `terminfo` and optionally BSD `termcap` files. Each of these files defines the attribute character strings which are used by AIX to initialize and control terminal attributes.

For modem connections, you may not know the terminal types that will be connecting to the system. I recommend selecting a terminal type of *dumb,* in this instance. This notifies AIX to use very rudimentary terminal control when the connection is established. Use the `tset` command in the `.profile`, `.login`, or shell `.rc` scripts to query the terminal type after the user logs onto the system. `tset` can negotiate most of the common terminal types connecting to your system. In the case that it is baffled, it will prompt the user to enter the terminal type and may also be configured to supply a default suggested type. After terminal type negotiation is complete, `login` stores the type in the `TERM` environment variable for use by the various shells and commands.

The following example can be used in a `.profile` or `.login` script to prompt the user for a terminal type and suggest a default of `vt100` if nothing is entered.

```
tset -m 'dumb:?vt100'
```

AIX interacts with your terminal type based on the characteristics defined in the /usr/lib/terminfo files. Entries in the terminfo are identified by file name descriptors for various vendor terminal devices. Field attributes for a particular terminal type describe the special character sequences used to initialize the terminal, highlight or underline text on the screen, identify function keys, etc.

The terminfo definitions for each terminal type are stored in binary form. Each terminal file is located in a subdirectory under /usr/lib/terminfo based on the first character of the file name.

Terminfo binaries are compiled from source code definition files by using the tic command. The terminfo source may also be extracted from the binary file by using a public domain program like untic or infocmp. Source code for the distribution terminal types is provided in /usr/lib/terminfo. Source files are identified by a .ti suffix in the file name.

*Sample terminfo source:*

```
vt102|vt100p|vt100p-nam|dec-vt100p|dec vt100p,
   am, mir, xenl, xon, cols#80, lines#24, vt#3,
   bel = ^G, blink = \E[5m$<2>, bold = \E[1m$<2>,
   clear = \E[;H\E[2J$<50>, cr = \r, csr = \E[%i%p1%d;%p2%dr,
   cub1 = \b, cud1 = \n, cuf1 = \E[C,
   cup = \E[%i%p1%d;%p2%dH$<10>, cuu1 = \E[A, dch1 = \E[P,
   dl1 = \E[M, ed = \E[J$<50>, el = \E[K$<3>, home = \E[H, ht = \t,
   il1 = \E[L, ind = \n, is2 = \E[1;24r\E[24;1H, kbs = \b,
   kcub1 = \EOD, kcud1 = \EOB, kcuf1 = \EOC, kcuu1 = \EOA,
   kf1 = \EOP, kf2 = \EOQ, kf3 = \EOR, kf4 = \EOS, rc = \E8,
   rev = \E[7m$<2>, rf = /usr/lib/tabset/vt100, ri = \EM,
   rmir = \E[4l, rmkx = \E[?1l\E>, rmso = \E[m, rmul = \E[m,
   rs2 = \E>\E[?3l\E[?4l\E[?5l\E[?7h\E[?8h, sc = \E7,
   sgr0 = \E[m$<2>, smir = \E[4h, smkx = \E[?1h\E= , smso = \E[7m,
   smul = \E[4m,
```

AIX also supplies a rudimentary /etc/termcap file for use with BSD applications. You can also convert termcap definitions into terminfo source using the captoinfo program. The majority of the termcap attribute identifiers map to terminfo identifiers; however, there are some exceptions.

*Sample termcap source:*

```
vt102|vt100p|vt100p-nam|dec-vt100p|dec vt100p:\
   :am:al = \E[L:bl = ^G:bs:cd = 50\E[J:ce = 3\E[K:cl = 50\E[;H\E[2J:\
   :cm = 10\E[%i%d;%dH:co#80:cr = ^M:cs = \E[%i%d;%dr:dc = \E[P:\
   :dl = \E[M:do = ^J:ei = \E[4l:ho = \E[H:im = \E[4h:is = \E[1;24r\E[24;1H:\
   :k1 = \EOP:k2 = \EOQ:k3 = \EOR:k4 = \EOS:kb = ^H:kd = \EOB:ke = \E[?1l\E>: \
   :kl = \EOD:kr = \EOC:ks = \E[?1h\E = :ku = \EOA:le = ^H:li#24:\
   :md = 2\E[1m:mr = 2\E[7m:mb = 2\E[5m:me = 2\E[m:mi:\
   :nd = \E[C:nl = ^J:pt:rc = \E8:rf = /usr/lib/tabset/vt100:\
   :rs = \E>\E[?3l\E[?4l\E[?5l\E[?7h\E[?8h:\
   :sc = \E7:se = \E[m:so = \E[7m:sr = \EM:ta = ^I:ue = \E[m:\
   :up = \E[A:us = \E[4m:vt#3:xn:
```

### 9.3.4 Control characters

The AIX TTY device drivers intercept a set of input control characters defined by the *termio* interface which force execution of various ioctl routines. These routines do things like start and stop screen display, edit characters in the terminal input buffer, etc. You are probably familiar with using CTRL-C to interrupt execution of a process, CNTRL-Z to suspend a process, and CTRL-H to erase characters on the command line. These are examples of the interaction of the termio control characters and the device drivers. In most cases you will want to take the default character set presented by SMIT. These characters can always be overridden on an individual basis from the command line or from login scripts using the `stty` command. The `stty` command allows you to tailor termio behavior for your session. `stty` will be explained further in the following section on *line discipline*.

```
# stty -a            Display current termio setting
# stty erase ^?      Define ctrl-? as erase
```

### 9.3.5 Line discipline

You will need to define the default RUNTIME and LOGIN line discipline options for each TTY port being configured. The LOGIN options are those in effect when a connection is made and during login processing. The RUNTIME options are those which control terminal I/O processing after login is completed, unless overridden by `stty` in the login scripts or from the command line. (See Table 9.2.) In most cases, you can accept the defaults provided by SMIT.

AIX supports layering multiple line disciplines via a stack. POSIX line discipline is used by default. BSD line discipline is also available and may be set as default or added to the stack. There are some problematic BSD options like `cbreak` that don't behave like you would expect. Be advised that most of the AIX applications which control TTY I/O expect POSIX.

```
# stty disp berk     Set BSD line discipline
# stty disp posix    Set POSIX line discipline
# stty add berk      Add BSD line discipline to the stack
```

Like the control characters described here, the line discipline options control how TTY I/O processing is handled. Options are set and queried using the `stty` command.

### 9.3.6 Login state

The `Enable LOGIN` parameter indicates how connections are established to the TTY port after system boot is completed. Use LOGIN

**TABLE 9.2 `stty` Attributes**

| Option | Runtime/Login | Description |
|---|---|---|
| hupcl | R,L | Hang up on close |
| cread | R,L | Enable receiver |
| brkint | R | Signal INTR on break |
| icrnl | R | Map CR to NL character |
| opost | R | Process output options |
| tab3 | R | Horizontal tab style |
| onlcr | R | Map NL to CRNL |
| isig | R | Check for INTR and QUIT characters |
| icanon | R | Canonical input with line editing |
| echo | R | Echo input characters |
| echoe | R,L | Echo erase character |
| echok | R | Echo NL and KILL character |
| echoctl | R | Echo control characters |
| echoke | R | Echo KILL by erase |
| imaxbel | R | Echo bell on input full |
| iexten | R | Recognize other function data |
| cs8 | L | Character size 8 bits |
| ixon | L | START/STOP handshaking on output queue |
| ixoff | L | START/STOP handshaking on input queue |

state to restrict the port to incoming, outgoing, or bidirectional data traffic. This parameter is very important when setting up lines for modem support. LOGIN state values include ENABLE, DISABLE, SHARE, and DELAY.

ENABLE — Use for direct-attach TTY or dial-in-only modem support. AIX starts a *getty* process for each enabled port. The getty process locks the port for exclusive use. An incoming connection negotiates line speed and raises DCD. Upon detecting DCD, getty presents a *login herald* on the connection. The connecting system may now log in to AIX.

DISABLE — Use for dial-out-only support. No getty process is started and the port is available for dial-out applications like `kermit`, `ate`, etc.

SHARE — Use for bidirectional support. AIX starts a `getty -u` on the port which does not lock the port until it sees the DCD signal go high. The port may be locked and opened for use by other processes. When DCD is present, but the port has been locked and in use by another application, the getty process associated with the port loops attempting to lock. If the port has not been locked, getty will lock the port and present a login herald on the line when DCD is asserted.

DELAY — Similar to SHARE. A `getty -r` is started on the line. Rather than relying on the DCD signal to indicate a connection request, getty waits for a character on the input buffer before locking the port and presenting the login herald. The port is available to other processes when not locked for use by getty.

The initial TTY state for each port is defined in `/etc/inittab`. The inittab format is not what you may be familiar with in SYSV UNIX, yet the information supplied is similar.

*Sample* `/etc/inittab` *entry:*

| | |
|---|---|
| `Format: Identifier:run level:Action:Command` | |
| `tty1:2:off:/etc/getty /dev/tty1` | Disable TTY1 at multiuser |
| `tty2:2:on:/etc/getty /dev/tty2` | Enable TTY2 at multiuser. |

## 9.4 Modem Support

In the previous sections describing TTY configurations, options associated with DCE devices have been discussed. However, modems require special attention.

### 9.4.1 Signals

Most modems come from the factory with settings that assume connection to a personal computer. The idea is to either strap signals high or ignore them altogether to make life easier for the novice PC user. Unfortunately these settings can cause real grief to UNIX systems.

Dial-up connections will require that the modem be set for *autoanswer*. For *Hayes* series modems, autoanswer is enabled by setting the `S0` flag to value greater than zero. You will also need to set the TTY port status to ENABLED, SHARED, or DELAY.

`ATS0 = 3` Answer incoming calls on the third ring

If the port state is set to ENABLED or SHARED, the getty process will present a login herald when DCD is raised, due to modem carrier detection on the wire. The modem should also hang up and drop DCD when remote carrier disappears. This interaction requires that the modem DCD signal follows the presence of the remote carrier.

`AT&C1` DCD signal follows remote carrier

If DCD is strapped high on the modem and command echoing is set, this configuration *will* cause a getty race condition when the port is enabled. The getty process sees DCD, so it locks the port and asserts the login herald. The modem echoes back the login herald which is interpreted as an invalid login attempt; thus, getty respawns and a new login herald is asserted. The modem echoes it back. Get the picture? Make certain that DCD follows the carrier as described, and if your applications don't require command echoing, disable it!

`ATE0` Don't echo modem command strings

For you UNIX old-timers who still like to use `tip`, you will need to have the modem always assert DCD. If you intend to use the line for both dial-in and dial-out connections, send the `AT&C0` command string to the modem when you intend to use `tip`.

Modem response strings can also cause problems if they are not set to local only. The RING status sent to the port when an incoming call is detected will be echoed back to the modem. The modem thinks that it has received a command, so it dutifully hangs up on the incoming call.

`ATQ1` Disable command response strings

You want the modem to enable auto-answer and be ready to accept commands when the RS/6000 presents the DTR signal on open(). When DTR dropped on close(), the modem should hang up and reset to accept new connections.

`AT&D3` Hang up at DTR drop, reload default parameters

Making certain that DCD and DTR handshaking is working correctly will reduce the possibility of receiving a phone bill that rivals the national debt.

In most cases, you will want to use hardware handshaking for modem connections. For example, `XON/XOFF` flow control characters will confuse UUCP checksumming. Unfortunately, AIX/6000 has been notorious for dropping `RTS/CTS` hardware flow control settings at each system boot. You can get around this problem by setting hardware handshaking for each TTY port from the boot `rc` scripts. From the command line, use the standard `stty` command.

```
% stty add rts < /dev/ttyN
```

You might think you can just add this command to your boot .rc scripts. You'll want to think again. The `stty` call may block and hang your system! Example code in App. B provides a quick and dirty C program that will set `rts` on the specified TTY device name without blocking. You can get a version that will read a list of TTYs to set from IBM Austin Support.

### 9.4.2 Problems

To debug or test TTY ports, connect the TTY device and enable the port. You should see the login herald displayed on the screen. If the login herald is not displayed, check the cable connections and wiring. If you have a *break-out box,* add it to the cabling between the device and RS/6000. These devices make it much easier to validate signal connections.

If the characters displayed are garbled, validate that the parity and bit definitions for the TTY device are correct. Parity and bits per character may also be a problem if the login herald is displayed but input characters are not recognized.

For modem lines, you could try playing with `ate` or `kermit`, but these applications require a whole level of configuration in themselves. I recommend using the simpler `cu` program. Disable the line if it isn't already disabled. Add the following stanza to the `/lib/uucp/Devices` file for the serial port you are using. In the example, I'll assume `/dev/tty0`, a Hayes modem, and a 2400 baud line speed.

```
Direct tty0 - Any direct
ACU tty0 - 2400 hayes \D
```

After adding the port to `/lib/uucp/Devices`, you should be able to connect to the modem using the `cu` command. Once connected, you can begin sending commands to the modem.

```
# cu -l /dev/tty0 -b2400
```

If you have problems, add the `-d` flag to the `cu` command to start a diagnostic trace on the connection. If you can't connect, then check the cabling and signals with a break-out box. If characters are garbled, check the line speed, parity, data, and stop bits.

## 9.5 High-Function Terminals

*High-function terminal* (HFT) devices are a different sort of beast from the serial-attached TTY devices I have described thus far. AIX treats an HFT as an ASCII pseudodevice or virtual terminal that consists of a combination of display, keyboard, mouse, dials, lighted function keys, and sound devices. These device options provide a wider array of capabilities which must be configured. Primarily these include the *keyboard/display map, national language/locale, display fonts, display color palette,* and *speaker sound level.* There are enough option combinations that you will likely spend more time trying to decide what you want than defining them to the system. Fortunately, you can play with them while the system is on-line. Most of the initial configuration will be done when AIX is installed on the computer.

### 9.5.1 Keyboard

You must define a keyboard map for the type of locally attached keyboard in use on the RS/6000. The keyboard map reflects the location and function of each key on the keyboard. AIX supports three keyboard types: the *101-key keyboard,* the *102-key keyboard,* and the *106-key keyboard.* The keyboard map is a table that defines the ASCII character string transmitted by each key. The keyboard map tables are located in the /usr/lib/nls/loc directory. Entries in the keyboard map table are configurable as required by custom applications. Source files for each keyboard map table are located in the /usr/lib/nls/loc directory and are identified by the .src suffix.

To create or modify a keyboard map, edit the source file as required and execute the genxlt command to compile the code set. See the InfoExplorer document or man page for the genxlt command for a description of the format of the code-set source files.

```
# genxlt < codeset.src > codset.new
```

Keyboard maps are associated with the *locale* in use. The locale defines the language and code set in use (see Table 9.3). Multibyte code sets are not supported for HFT devices. To display the keyboard maps available, use the lskbd command. Note that many of the commands associated with HFT configuration must be entered from the HFT primary device.

```
# lskbd
```

To switch to a new keyboard map, use the mkkbd -n command to make the map available for use, followed by the swkbd -v.

```
# mkkbd -n codeset.name
# swkbd -v codeset.name
```

You can also use the setmaps command to set, display, and debug terminal and code-set maps. AIX-supplied terminal maps are located in the /usr/lib/nls/termap directory.

```
# setmaps                  Display current map and code set
# setmaps -t tty-map       Set TTY map
# setmaps -s code-map      Set code-set map
```

Depending on your typing speed, you may wish to change the default keyboard delay and repetition rate. The default delay rate is 500 ms and the repetition rate is 11 characters/s. The delay rate can be set to 250, 500, 750, and 1000 ms. Repetition rate spans from 2 to 30 characters/s. To alter the delay and repetition rates, use the chhwkbd command.

```
# chhwkbd -d <delay> -r <repetition>
```

You may also turn the keyboard key "click" on or off. I've never understood why vendors enhance keyboard noise. Naturally, the default state is keyboard click on. Use the chsound command to toggle keyboard click.

```
chsound -q      Silence is golden!
```

**TABLE 9.3 AIX Locale and Code Sets**

| Locale | Language | Code set |
|---|---|---|
| Da_DK | Danish, Denmark | IBM-850 |
| da_DK | Danish, Denmark | ISO8859-1 |
| De_CH | German, Switzerland | IBM-850 |
| de_CH | German, Switzerland | ISO8859-1 |
| De_DE | German, Germany | IBM-850 |
| de_DE | German, Germany | ISO8859-1 |
| el_GR | Greek, Greece | ISO8859-7 |
| En_GB | English, Great Britain | IBM-850 |
| en_GB | English, Great Britain | ISO8859-1 |
| En_US | English, United States | IBM-850 |
| en_US | English, United States | ISO8859-1 |
| Es_ES | Spanish, Spain | IBM-850 |
| es_ES | Spanish, Spain | ISO8859-1 |
| Fi_FI | Finnish, Finland | IBM-850 |
| fi_FI | Finnish, Finland | ISO8859-1 |
| Fr_BE | French, Belgium | IBM-850 |
| fr_BE | French, Belgium | ISO8859-1 |
| Fr_CA | French, Canada | IBM-850 |
| fr_CA | French, Canada | ISO8859-1 |
| Fr_FR | French, France | IBM-850 |
| fr_FR | French, France | ISO8859-1 |
| Fr_CH | French, Switzerland | IBM-850 |
| fr_CH | French, Switzerland | ISO8859-1 |
| Is_IS | Icelandic, Iceland | IBM-850 |
| is_IS | Icelandic, Iceland | ISO8859-1 |
| It_IT | Italian, Italy | IBM-850 |
| it_IT | Italian, Italy | ISO8859-1 |
| Ja_JP | Japanese, Japan | IBM-932 |
| ja_JP | Japanese, Japan | IBM-eucJP |
| Nl_BE | Dutch, Belgium | IBM-850 |
| nl_BE | Dutch, Belgium | ISO8859-1 |
| Nl_NL | Dutch, Netherlands | IBM-850 |
| nl_NL | Dutch, Netherlands | ISO8859-1 |
| No_NO | Norwegian, Norway | IBM-850 |
| no_NO | Norwegian, Norway | ISO8859-1 |
| Pt_PT | Portuguese, Portugal | IBM-850 |
| pt_PT | Portuguese, Portugal | ISO8859-1 |
| Sv_SE | Swedish, Sweden | IBM-850 |
| sv_SE | Swedish, Sweden | ISO8859-1 |
| tr_TR | Turkish, Turkey | ISO8859-9 |

### 9.5.2 Display

The RS/6000 supports a number of natively attached displays and graphics adapters. There are some common parameters that may be tailored that span most of these devices. These include the display fonts, color palette for color displays, and cursor shape. You will have to refer to the installation instructions for configuration options specific to the device. I can't keep up with IBM development fast enough to list all the options here!

### 9.5.3 Display fonts

Display fonts are as religious an issue as favorite editors and operating systems. The available HFT fonts are located in `/usr/lpp/fonts`. You can get a list of the available fonts using the `lsfont` command.

```
# lsfont
```

You may define a default font palette which consists of up to eight alternate font identifiers. Available font alternates are identified by a number ranging from 0 through 8. To make a new font available, use the `mkfont -n` command.

```
# mkfont -n fontname.path
```

To list all the font identifiers available in the current font palette, use the `chfont -l` command.

```
# chfont -l
```

You may switch between alternates by invoking `chfont -a`.

```
# chfont -a5        Switch display font to alternate number 5
```

You may also set the display fonts and font palette using SMIT.

```
# smit chfont
# smit chfontpl
```

### 9.5.4 Display palette

Color HFT devices will support a palette of 16 colors from which foreground and background display colors may be selected. Select the color map from SMIT. Each color is represented as an integer from 1 to 16.

```
# smit palettevalues
```

After selecting the palette colors, you may set the foreground (text) and background color using SMIT.

```
# smit backforg
```

You may also select one of six cursor shapes for the display (see Table 9.4).

```
# smit chcursor
```

### 9.5.5 Dials and lighted function keys

*Dial and light programmable function* (LPF) key pads are defined via SMIT. A logical device name is associated with the parent adapter slot and port number used by the device. Port values are either 1 or 2 for a

**TABLE 9.4 Cursor Options**

0 - no cursor
1 - single underscore
2 - double underscore (default)
3 - lower half character cell
4 - midcharacter dash
5 - full character cell

graphics adapter, or s1 and s2 for the standard serial port. You may also add a short text string that identifies the function of the device.

### 9.5.6 Speaker volume

To get a handle on the beeps and honks emanating from the RS/6000, you need to set the speaker volume. Use the chsound command to set the speaker volume level. Volume selections include off, low, medium, and high.

```
# chsound -o        Turn sound off
```

### 9.5.7 Virtual terminals

As I mentioned, an HFT device is a *virtual terminal* interface. The AIX operating system supports up to 16 virtual terminal interfaces per physical display. Each virtual terminal supports all the attributes of an individual physical display. Under AIX, each virtual terminal session controls distinct shells allowing the user to have up to 16 separate application sessions active at one time. The open command is used to initiate each new virtual terminal session. The user switches between the virtual terminal displays using the ALT RIGHT-CTRL keys.

```
# open shell-name
```

To limit the maximum number of virtual terminal sessions allowed, use the chnumvt command.

```
# chnumvt 1-16
```

## 9.6 Console

In most cases, the system console will either be the primary display or tty0. You can redirect console output to another device or file using the chcons and the swcons commands. The chcons command sets the console path for the next system boot. The swcons command redirects console output for the current session.

```
# chcons pathname     Switch output on next boot
# swcons pathname     Switch output now
```

To check the current console path use `lscons`.

```
# lscons
```

### 9.6.1 Console problems

If you are running a system without an attached console or sharing a console between systems, make certain that you have the termio option `clocal` defined for the device. This inhibits console output from blocking if the device is not available. You will end up with multiple `srcmstr` daemons running if console output is blocked. This situation tends to confuse the `srcmstr` as the current state of any subsystem it is controlling. Bad news!

In some instances, an HFT device can become hung or inhibit display output. If the HFT device is also the system console, this can be a nuisance. In many cases, you can free a hung HFT by writing to `/dev/hft`, directing an `stty` command sequence to the device, or using the `tput` command. These techniques may also work with other TTY devices.

*Examples:*

```
# echo "Open Sez-A-Me" > /dev/hft
# stty sane
# tput -Thft clear > /dev/hft
```

Note that it may take around one minute for these commands to take effect.

## 9.7 Pseudo-TTY Devices

It's difficult to decide where to talk about *pseudo-TTY* (PTY) devices. You will see texts discuss PTYs in relation to TCP/IP and X11 applications. I thought it best to discuss them along with other TTY devices, in that they exhibit many of the same characteristics.

A PTY device is represented by a pair of character device drivers in a master/slave pair that implements a pseudo-TTY connection. The master/slave pair may be operating on different systems in a network or on the same computer. The *master,* `/dev/pty` side of the connection sends and receives data like a user at a real TTY. The *slave,* `/dev/tty` side of the connection provides the standard terminal interface to applications such as login shells.

AIX implements two PTY interfaces. The default PTY type is opened as `/dev/ptc`. The operating system allocates both the master PTY and slave TTY devices, which eliminates the need for the application program to test both sides of a PTY connection to determine if it is in use. The number of standard AIX PTYs is limited only by the file table size (see App. B for sample C code to allocate PTY pair).

```
            Change/Show Characteristics of the PTY

Type or select values in entry fields.
Press Enter AFTER making all desired changes.

                                            [Entry Fields]
Number of BSD STYLE symbolic links          [64]            +#
STATE to be configured at boot time         [available]      +

F1 = Help        F2 = Refresh      F3 = Cancel       F4 = List
F5 = Undo        F6 = Command      F7 = Edit         F8 = Image
```

**Figure 9.6** SMIT change TTY panel.

AIX also supports BSD-style PTYs for use with traditional BSD applications. This implementation consists of both master /dev/pty[p0-sf] and slave /dev/tty[p0-sf] special files. You can create up to 64 BSD PTYs via SMIT (see Fig. 9.6). You may also create additional BSD PTYs manually, using chdev.

```
# smit chgpty
# chdev -l pty0 -a "num = 64"
```

## 9.8 DOS TTY Definition

Since many of us are running DOS applications under pcsim on AIX, I thought it would be useful to mention a few configuration options and files involved in supporting modems and TTYs with pcsim. To use pcsim with TTYs via direct connection or dial-in, make sure your terminal key map is defined in the /usr/lpp/pcsim/tty directory. You can take a look at the default key maps supplied by IBM to get a feel for what you need. If you are looking at purchasing TTYs for use with pcsim, check to see if they support *PC scan code*. This allows a TTY to emulate the 25-line monochrome PC screen, and, in many cases, to support AT or PS/2 keyboards. This makes life much easier for users unfamiliar with using key maps. You also need to initialize pcsim for serial ports at boot time.

```
/etc/tty/ttyconf -l pcsim
```

See the lpp.README file in /usr/lpp/pcsim for a description of serial port setup. Finally, to use a serial port as a COM port from pcsim, use the following command when you start a pcsim session. Note that, in this example, /dev/tty0 is the defined serial port.

```
pcsim -com1 /dev/tty0
```

This information should alleviate some of the frustration involved in getting a TTY or modem connection running on your AIX workstation.

At least you'll be able to keep all your hair and keep your family happier about your working hours. If nothing else, I wanted to present enough basic information to get you pointed in the right direction. For more information, go ahead and plow through the InfoExplorer documentation. I would also recommend *UNIX System Administration Handbook,* by Evi Nemeth, Garth Snyder, and Scott Seebass (Prentice Hall). If you have an IBMLink connection, there are a number of good "HOWTO" memos covering TTY and modem topics an all the AIX platforms. Good luck!

## 9.9 InfoExplorer Keywords

| | | | |
|---|---|---|---|
| mkdev | captoinfo | lskbd | chnumvt |
| maktty | stty | swkbd | chcons |
| chgtty | getty | setmaps | swcons |
| terminfo | /etc/inittab | chhwkbd | srcmstr |
| 0termcap | tip | chsound | hft |
| tset | ate | mkfont | tput |
| TERM | cu | lsfont | pty |
| tic | uucp | chfont | ttyconf |
| untic | genxlt | open | pcsim |
| infocmp | | | |

## 9.10 QwikInfo

### TTY

*Serial port settings:*

| | |
|---|---|
| `smit maktty` | Create TTY port |
| `smit chgtty` | Modify TTY port |
| `cu -l /dev/tty0 -b2400` | Test modem port |

*Line states set by* `/etc/inittab` *entry:*

| | |
|---|---|
| ENABLE | getty running on port and login herald presented. |
| DISABLE | No getty running on port. Dedicated dial-out. |
| SHARE | getty `-u` running on port with no lock. Wait for DCD high, then lock and present login herald. |
| DELAY | getty `-r` running on port. Wait for characters on input buffer before presenting login herald. |

*Defining terminal type and attributes:*

| | |
|---|---|
| `/usr/lib/terminfo` | SYSV TTY database |
| `tic, untic, infocmp` | Manage terminfo src |

| | |
|---|---|
| `tset -m 'dumb:?vt100'` | Query TTY type |
| `/etc/termcap` | BSD TTY database |
| `captoinfo` | termcap to terminfo src |
| `ttyconf -l pcsim` | |

*Line discipline:*

| | |
|---|---|
| `# stty -a` | Display port attributes |
| `# stty disp <berk|posix>` | BSD or POSIX line display |

## HFT devices:

| | |
|---|---|
| `chsound -q` | Disable keyboard click |
| `chhwkbd -d <delay> -r <repetition>` | Set keyboard rate |
| `setmaps` | Display/set keyboard map and code set |
| `smit chfont` | Display/set font set |
| `tput -Thft clear > /dev/hft` | Unlock hung HFT |
| `lscons, chcons, swcons` | Console path |

*Virtual terminals:*

| | |
|---|---|
| `open <shell-name>` | Start virtual terminal |
| `chnumvt <1-16>` | Set # virtual terminals |

## PTY devices:

| | |
|---|---|
| `/dev/ptc` | Autoallocate PTYs |
| `smit chgpty` | Set number BSD PTYs |

## PCSIM:

```
ttyconf -l pcsim
```

Chapter

# 10

# Printers

## 10.1 Printing Overview

The AIX printing subsystem provides a rich set of commands and configuration options that goes far beyond the printing facilities offered by many other UNIX implementations. If you are familiar with the traditional BSD or SYSV printing environments, you will find that the AIX printing subsystem is not only interoperable with these environments, but it also involves some significant differences. The printing subsystem in AIX comprises approximately forty commands designed to meet the demands of the distributed printing technologies found in most networked work groups. Many of these commands are provided to support compatibility at the user interface level with BSD, SYSV, and older versions of AIX. Before we can delve into the details of this command set, it will be helpful to understand how AIX manages the print queuing system from a high-level functional viewpoint.

The AIX printing subsystem is made up of the following logical and physical components:

| | |
|---|---|
| *Print device* | Device driver and hardware interface |
| *Queue device* | Holding area for files waiting to be printed on the associated print device |
| *Queue* | Holding area for files waiting for delivery to another queue or queue device |
| *Virtual printer* | Logical abstraction of queue and device based on datastream format |

The normal life cycle of a file in the AIX printing subsystem begins when a user or application submits the file for printing with a specified queue name. When the file's priority in the queue brings it to the top of the list of waiting jobs, the qdaemon determines the next step in processing based on queue definition stanzas in the `/etc/qconfig` file. The device and backend entries in the queue stanza may indicate that this is a virtual printer and the file is to be filtered and passed to a queue device. If these stanza entries indicate that this is a queue device, then the file is directed to the device driver of an available local print device. (Refer to Fig. 10.1.) The stanza may indicate that this is a remote queue and the file is to be routed over the network to a remote `lpd` daemon for further handling.

It is the system administrator's responsibility to tailor the stanzas in `/etc/qconfig` to apply the appropriate filtering and routing to jobs in the queuing subsystem to ensure that they arrive at their destinations with the appropriate attributes for printing. This must be done in a way that hides the complexities of the underlying processing and interfaces from the end users.

`/etc/qconfig` *stanza*

```
lp:
discipline = fcfs
up = TRUE
device = dlp0
dlp0:
file = /dev/lp0
header = never
trailer = never
access = write
backend = /usr/lib/lpd/piobe
```

The following sections will cover the steps required to configure print devices, queue devices, local and remote queues, and virtual printers. Although these procedures will involve tailoring the subsystem interfaces using SMIT, the corresponding stanzas in `/etc/qconfig` are generated automatically by SMIT. You may find that once you have become familiar with the overall process and the format of the

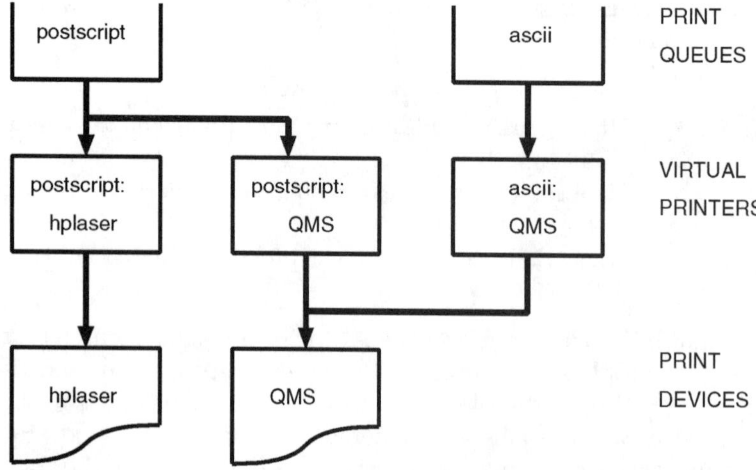


**Figure 10.1** Print queue, virtual printer, device relationship.

qconfig stanzas, you may wish to edit the `/etc/qconfig` file directly and avoid using the SMIT panels. I would recommend that you avoid doing this initially until you feel comfortable with the interaction of all the components in the printing subsystem.

## 10.2 Print Devices

Local printer and plotter devices managed by AIX will usually be attached to a serial RS-232/RS-422 port or parallel port. Access to networked print devices is handled by the remote queuing facilities which will be discussed in a later section. The RS/6000 system planar supports both serial and parallel ports marked `P` and `Sn`, respectively. You may also use multiport serial adapters, available from both IBM and third-party vendors, for connecting additional devices. The planar female DB25 parallel port may require the use of a DB25 to Centronics adapter cable to connect the device to the system. For the planar serial ports, you will need a 10-pin MODU to DB25 or DB9 adapter. The following pin-out diagrams describe the serial DB25 interface for the planar connection and the RJ45 to DB25 interface used by the IBM multiport concentrators (see Fig. 10.2). Note that the RS/6000 expects to see CTS high when the printer is powered up. You can force the CTS signal high by connecting CTS and RTS on the computer side of the interface if the printer does not supply CTS.

Next, carefully review your printer's hardware manual concerning the attributes of the device interface and printing characteristics (see Fig. 10.3). These include things like number of bits per character, parity bits, signal handshaking, lines per page, special control codes, etc. This information will be required to tailor the AIX device driver configuration for the device. Make sure that the device is connected to

| RS/6000 | | | | Printer |
|---|---|---|---|---|
| FG | 1 | ←→ | 1 | FG |
| TxD | 2 | → | 3 | RxD |
| RxD | 3 | ← | 2 | TxD |
| RTS | 4 | → | 5 | CTS |
| CTS | 5 | ← | 4 | RTS |
| DSR | 6 | ← | 20 | DTR |
| | | | 8 | DCD |
| SG | 7 | ←→ | 7 | SG |
| DTR | 20 | → | 6 | DSR |
| DCD | 8 | | | |

| RJ45 | | | | DB25 |
|---|---|---|---|---|
| FG | 1 | ←→ | 1 | FG |
| RTS | 2 | ←→ | 4 | RTS |
| RxD | 3 | ←→ | 3 | RxD |
| DCD | 4 | ←→ | 8 | DCD |
| SG | 5 | ←→ | 7 | SG |
| TxD | 6 | ←→ | 2 | TxD |
| DTR | 7 | ←→ | 20 | DTR |
| CTS | 8 | ←→ | 5 | CTS |

**Figure 10.2** Serial cable pin-out.

```
                         Add a Printer

Move cursor to desired item and press Enter.
  Add a Printer/Plotter
  Configure a Defined Printer/Plotter

F1 = Help        F2 = Refresh       F3 = Cancel       F8 = Image
F9 = Shell       F10 = Exit         Enter = Do
```

**Figure 10.3** SMIT add printer panel.

the system and powered up before beginning the device driver configuration process. Use the SMIT fast path `mkprt` to begin device driver customization.

```
# SMIT mkprt
```

Select the SMIT option `Add a Printer/Plotter`. SMIT will display a set of preconfigured driver selections for various IBM and vendor printers and plotters (see Fig. 10.4). If the device type you are using is not displayed, then select one of the options `Other parallel printer` or `Other serial printer`. If the printer you are adding emulates one of the IBM-supplied devices, it may be easier to select one of these entries if you are not certain of the correct device characteristics required for the driver definition. I have always found that there are fewer headaches involved if you can make one of the standard configurations work. You can always go back later and customize it to meet your requirements.

```
                  Printer/Plotter Type

Move cursor to desired item and press Enter.

[TOP]
2380          IBM 2380 Personal Printer II
2381          IBM 2381 Personal Printer II
2390          IBM 2390 Personal Printer II
2391          IBM 2391 Personal Printer II
3812-2        IBM 3812 Model 2 Page Printer
3816          IBM 3816 Page Printer
4019          IBM 4019 LaserPrinter
4029          IBM 4029 LaserPrinter
4072          IBM 4072 ExecJet
4201-2        IBM 4201 Model 2 Proprinter II
4201-3        IBM 4201 Model 3 Proprinter III
4202-2        IBM 4202 Model 2 Proprinter II XL
[MORE...41]

F1 = Help        F2 = Refresh       F3 = Cancel
F8 = Image       F10 = Exit         Enter = Do
```

**Figure 10.4** SMIT printer/plotter panel.

```
            Printer/Plotter Interface

Move cursor to desired item and press Enter.

parallel
rs232
rs422

F1 = Help          F2 = Refresh        F3 = Cancel
F8 = Image         F10 = Exit          Enter = Do
```

**Figure 10.5** SMIT printer/plotter interface panel.

SMIT will now prompt you for the type of interface you are using (see Fig. 10.5). The screen options displayed will depend on the type of interfaces supported by the previously selected printer model. For example, a preconfigured entry for a parallel printer will not prompt you for a selection of serial port options like bits per character, parity, and number of start/stop bits. If a serial port is selected, SMIT may further prompt you for parent adapter and port number.

After you have selected the interface type, the real work begins. SMIT will display the panel of driver options supported by the chosen device type (see Fig. 10.6). The device driver configuration will determine how the input data stream is interpreted and whether carriage control information is to be generated and/or passed through to the device. For example, a form feed control character can be generated automatically by the device driver and sent to the printer when the input line count exceeds the number specified by `Number of LINES per page` and if `Send FORM FEEDS` is enabled. Remember that you can get into confusing situations when you have a printer jumpered for generating auto-form feeds at the desired number of lines and also have the device driver configured to do the same. Most of the options are self-explanatory, but must be mapped closely to the printer's hardware settings and capabilities.

### 10.2.1 Testing the device and driver

Once you have completed the device driver configuration, you may test the interface by sending a file directly to the printer, bypassing handling by the queuing system. This can be done using an application like the `cat` command to direct a file to the device special file name for the printer.

```
# cat <FileName> > /dev/lp0
```

If you want to disable the translation done by the device driver to test the printer hardware interface and settings, use the `splp` command to enable transparent access to the printer.

```
# splp -p + /dev/lp0        Enable transparent access
```

```
                        Add a Printer/Plotter

Type or select values in entry fields.
Press Enter AFTER making all desired changes.

[TOP]                                              [Entry Fields]
Printer/Plotter type                           2380
Printer/Plotter interface                      parallel
Description                                    IBM 2380 Personal Prin>
Parent adapter                                 ppa0
* PORT number                                  []                      +
Type of PARALLEL INTERFACE                     [standard]              +
Printer TIME OUT period                        [60]                    +#
STATE to be configured at boot time            [available]             +

The following attributes have meaning only when the Printer/Plotter is not used
with a Print Queue:
Number of COLUMNS per page                     [80]                    +#
Number of columns to INDENT                    [0]                     +#
Send all characters to printer UNMODIFIED      no                      +
Send BACKSPACES                                yes                     +
WRAP CHARACTERS beyond the specified width     no                      +
Send FORM FEEDS                                yes                     +
Send CARRIAGE RETURNS                          yes                     +
Send LINE FEEDS                                yes                     +
Add CARRIAGE RETURNS to LINE FEEDS             yes                     +
Convert lowercase to UPPERCASE                 no                      +
EXPAND TABS on eight position boundaries       yes                     +
Return on ERROR                                no                      +
[BOTTOM]

F1 = Help       F2 = Refresh     F3 = Cancel     F4 = List
F5 = Undo       F6 = Command     F7 = Edit       F8 = Image
F9 = Shell      F10 = Exit       Enter = Do
```

**Figure 10.6** SMIT add printer/plotter panel.

```
# cat <FileName> > /dev/lp0       Direct file to the interface
# splp -p ! /dev/lp0              Enable driver translation
```

Another useful tool for testing the device driver and interface is the `lptest` command. `lptest` will produce a ripple pattern of characters which can be directed to the device special file name. You can control the number of columns and lines produced with options on the command line. This is useful when testing line-wrap handling and the generation of auto-form feeds.

```
# lptest <Columns> <Lines> > /dev/lp0
```

Modifications to the printer device driver may be made via SMIT `chgprt`.

```
# smit chgprt
```

The SMIT panel options are similar to the driver options listed when you initially added the device. You may also update device options from the command line using `splp`. If no options are included on the command line, then the current driver settings are displayed. `/dev/lp0` is used as a default if no device name is specified.

```
device = /dev/lp0 (+ yes ! no)
CURRENT FORMATTING PARAMETERS (ignored by qprt, lpr, and lp commands)
Note: -p + causes the other formatting parameters to be ignored.
-p !    pass-through?              -c +   send carriage returns?
-l 66   page length (lines)        -n +   send line feeds?
-w 80   page width (columns)       -r +   carriage rtn after line feed?
-i 0    indentation (columns)      -t !   suppress tab expansion?
-W !    wrap long lines?           -b +   send backspaces?
-C !    convert to upper case?     -f +   send form feeds?
CURRENT ERROR PROCESSING PARAMETERS
-T 60   timeout value (seconds)    -e !   return on error?
```

## 10.3 Print Queues and Queue Devices

Print queues are somewhat like teller lines at the bank. Each file waits its turn in line for the next available printer or queue. Just like preferred customer and short transaction tellers, you may define custom scheduling disciplines for high-priority and quick-job queues. When defining your print queuing topology and scheduling decisions, it will be important to understand the difference between a *queue* and a *queue device.* Basically, a queue device holds files for dispatching to local device drivers, whereas a queue may dispatch to yet another queue or queue device. The procedures for creating both queue types are the same, with the exception of the destination as defined by the `file` = stanza. To create a queue, use the SMIT fast path command `mkque`. (Refer to Fig. 10.7.)

```
# smit mkque
```

### 10.3.1 Local and remote queues

AIX supports both local and remote printer queues (see Fig. 10.8). Local queues are used to feed printers directly attached to the local machine, whereas remote queues are local holding tanks for files

```
                        Add a Queue

Move cursor to desired item and press Enter.
Add a Local Queue
Add a Remote Queue

F1 = Help        F2 = Refresh       F3 = Cancel       F8 = Image
F9 = Shell       F10 = Exit         Enter = Do
```

**Figure 10.7** SMIT add queue panel.

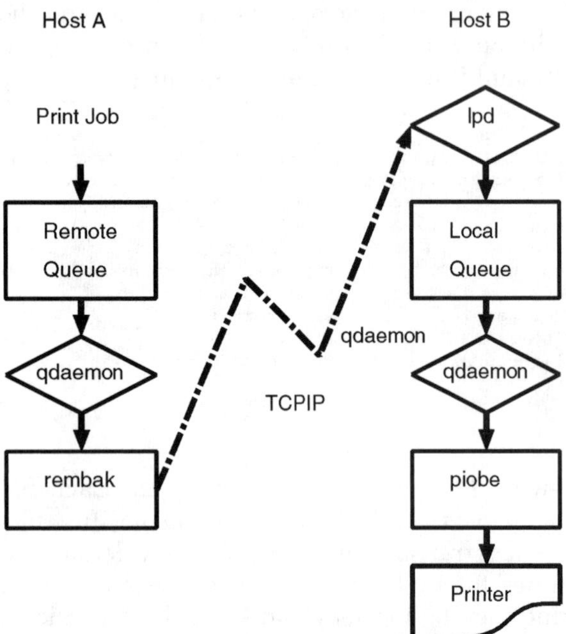


**Figure 10.8** Local remote print queuing.

which are to be transferred over the network to a remote machine. Although both queue types are functionally equivalent, they are configured and handled differently by the queuing subsystem. Common configuration options for local and remote queues require that you supply a queue name, activation state at system boot time, a scheduling discipline, and accounting options. The scheduling discipline defines the priority a job has in relation to other jobs in the queue. Most commonly these are either `Shortest Job Next (SJN)` or `First Come First Serve (FCFS)`. The accounting options will be covered in the chapter on AIX accounting (Chap. 21). You may also specify that the queue is the system default if no queue name is specified on the command line when a job is submitted for printing.

### 10.3.2 Backend programs

The primary differences in how files in local and remote queues are handled are governed by the *backend* program invoked by the qdaemon for each job in the queue. The backend program is responsible for housekeeping chores, data filtering and conversion, and dispatching the file to its destination. For local queues, the backend program is usually `piobe` and for remote queues, the `rembak` program is used. It is also possible to include your own program or shell script as a backend program for custom applications. A simple batch scheduling system may be implemented using the print queuing system to control the dispatching of batch jobs. Backend programs may be used to execute shell scripts submitted by a user with preconfigured resource limits. The queuing system will govern the number of batch jobs executing on the system and delineate priorities based on the scheduling disciplines used.

The default local queue backend, `/usr/lpd/piobe`, creates a pipeline of filters for converting data formats. The output from the filter stream is directed to the printer with header and trailer pages as specified by the configuration options. Whether the configuration defines a queue, queue device, or custom queue will depend on the values supplied for the `backend` = , file = and `access` = stanzas. In the case of a queue device, the output file is normally the device special file name of the printer. If the queue will be used to dispatch files to other local queues, then the name of the destination queue can be used. For custom applications, you can control the access permissions the backend program has to the output file. Normally, access will be defined as write-only or read-write. (Refer to Fig. 10.9.)

Remote queues (see Fig. 10.10) are processed by a `/usr/lpd/rembak`. The `rembak` backend program creates an `lpd` control file for each print job which will be passed along with the data file to a remote `lpd` daemon. These control files contain tag information that specifies the data-stream type, origin information, and handling options as specified when the user submitted the job for printing. When configur-

```
                        Add a Local Queue

Type or select values in entry fields.
Press Enter AFTER making all desired changes.

                                              [Entry Fields]
* NAME of queue to add                      []
ACTIVATE the queue?                         yes                       +
Will this become the DEFAULT queue?         no                        +
Queuing DISCIPLINE                          first come first serve    +
ACCOUNTING FILE pathname                    []
NAME of device to add                       []
BACKEND OUTPUT FILE pathname                []
ACCESS MODE of backend output file          write only                +
* BACKEND PROGRAM pathname                  [/usr/lpd/piobe]
Number of FORM FEEDS prior to printing      [0]                       #
Print HEADER pages?                         never                     +
Print TRAILER pages?                        never                     +
ALIGN pages between files within jobs?      yes                       +

F1 = Help        F2 = Refresh      F3 = Cancel      F4 = List
F5 = Undo        F6 = Command      F7 = Edit        F8 = Image
F9 = Shell       F10 = Exit        Enter = Do
```

**Figure 10.9** SMIT add local queue panel.

```
                         Add a Remote Queue

Type or select values in entry fields.
Press Enter AFTER making all desired changes.

                                                              [Entry Fields]
* NAME of queue to add                                    []
ACTIVATE the queue?                                       yes                    +
Will this become the DEFAULT queue?                       no                     +
Queuing DISCIPLINE                                        first come first serve +
ACCOUNTING FILE pathname                                  []
* DESTINATION HOST for remote jobs                        []
Pathname of the SHORT FORM FILTER for queue status output [/usr/lpd/aixshort]   +/
* Pathname of the LONG FORM FILTER for queue status output [/usr/lpd/aixlong]   +/
* Name of QUEUE on remote printer                         []
NAME of device to add                                     []
* BACKEND PROGRAM pathname                                [/usr/lpd/rembak]

F1 = Help        F2 = Refresh     F3 = Cancel     F4 = List
F5 = Undo        F6 = Command     F7 = Edit       F8 = Image
F9 = Shell       F10 = Exit       Enter = Do
```

**Figure 10.10** SMIT add remote queue panel.

ing the remote queue entry in SMIT, you will need to specify the remote host's domain name and remote queue name. You will also need to specify the short and long filter names to be used to filter the status information passed by remote `lpd` systems. Use the default `aixshort` and `aixlong` filters for remote AIX Version 3 systems and `aix2short` and `aix2long` for AIX Version 2 on remote RTs.

### 10.3.3 Postscript printing

AIX provides support for postscript printing through the use of the Adobe TranScript utilities (see Table 10.1). These utilities are also available in source code from AT&T as part of their *AT&T Tool Kit.* These utilities are primarily filters which may be used as backends to convert from ASCII, troff, plot, Tek4010, and Diablo into Postcript. Postscript header and trailer programs for banner pages are located in the `/usr/lpd/pio/burst` directory.

**TABLE 10.1 Code Conversion**

| TranScript utility | Conversion |
|---|---|
| `escript` | ASCII to Postscript |
| `psc,psdit,psroff` | troff to Postscript |
| `psplot` | plot to Postscript |
| `ps4010` | Tek4010 to Postscript |
| `ps630` | Diablo to Postscript |

### 10.3.4 Custom backends

You may wish to use your own custom shell scripts and programs as queue backends. If your backend application requires access to variables and data handled by the qdaemon, there is a library of routines supplied in `/usr/lib/libqb.a` which will allow you to communicate with the elements of the queuing system. Normally your backend program should write to standard out. `qdaemon` will open and lock the output file specified in the `file =` parameter in the qconfig stanza for you. For a complete list of the routines supported in `/usr/lib/libqb.a`, see InfoExplorer's *Understanding Backend Routines in libqb.a.*

### 10.3.5 BSD and SYSV support

The AIX printing subsystem will interoperate with BSD and SYSV print spooling systems. Many of the standard BSD and SYSV commands are available in AIX to allow users to easily move back and forth between systems in a heterogeneous environment. They don't have to use different commands on each system. As a system administrator, you will find that the AIX printing subsystem is much closer to SYSV than to BSD in the way it handles remote printing. Many of the `lpd` control file tags supported in the BSD environment are not available in AIX. When print jobs are inbound from a remote BSD system, AIX will ignore these unsupported control file tags. The control file tags used by AIX and SYSV are the same in most cases. Use the `bsdshort` and `bsdlong` filter names for remote status queries for BSD systems. Use `attshort` and `attlong` for SYSV status information.

### 10.3.6 Customizing banner pages

If you will be using header and/or trailer pages for a local queue, you can customize their format to match those used by other systems in your environment. The format templates for burst pages are stored in the `/usr/lpd/pio/burst` directory. For each format template, a file name prefix of `H` is used to indicate header definitions and `T` for trailers. There are sample definitions provided for ASCII, plotter, and Postscript banners. The templates consist of program, text, and variable sections. Variables are prefixed with a `%` sign: (Refer to Table 10.2.)

*Example* `H.ascii` *banner:*

```
*##############################################################
* EXAMPLE H.ascii Banner
*##############################################################
* *****************************************************************
%t %T
%p %P
%q %Q
%h %H
```

**TABLE 10.2 Banner Template Variables**

| | |
|---|---|
| %A | Formatting flag values |
| %D | Banner user name |
| %H | Machine name |
| %P | Time printed |
| %Q | Time queued |
| %S | Submitting user name |
| %T | Title |
| %% | Escape for percent sign |

```
%s %S
%d = = = = => %D <= = = = =
*******************************************************************
%a
%A
*******************************************************************
```

You may wish to add your own custom banner definitions to this directory. Use one of the existing header or trailer pages as a template. You can update the associated queue entry via the SMIT fast-path command `chviprt`. You may find it much easier to simply edit the appropriate printer field in the `/usr/sbin/pio/custom` file and build a new memory image of the definition for use by `piobe`. The memory image is built by `/usr/lpd/pio/etc/piodigest`. The memory images are kept as colon files in the directory `/usr/lpd/pio/ddi`. Since the `piodigest` options are a little verbose, you can quickly create a new colon file by executing `/etc/lsvirprt` without any attribute options for the given queue or virtual printer name.

```
# /etc/lsvirprt -d lp0
```

Remember to conserve paper. Only use burst pages when they are needed. You may also specify that a single header and/or trailer page will be used for all of a particular user's queued files by grouping. Encourage your users to recycle and keep recycle bins near your printers and plotters.

## 10.4 Virtual Printers

Virtual printers allow you to direct print jobs to particular queue devices based on the data-stream format of the file. A virtual printer name represents a logical view of the queue, queue device, and printers associated with a print job based on its attributes. When you configure a virtual printer, you will supply all three of these components. To create a virtual printer, use the SMIT fast path `mkvirprt`.

```
# smit mkvirprt
```

## 10.5 Testing and Modifying Printer Configuration

You may test your virtual printer, queue, queue device, and print device combinations with the same tools used when testing the hardware interface and driver. Simply use the virtual printer, queue, or queue device name when using the /usr/bin/cat or /usr/bin/lptest commands.

```
# cat <FileName> > lp
# lptest <Columns> <Lines> > lp
```

It goes without saying that you must verify the operation of the AIX printing subsystem in the same way your end users will interoperate with it. Develop a short suite of print commands and options based on the environments used by your user community to validate the subsystem any time you have made any changes. Depending on your user base, you may need to test all of the AIX, BSD, and SYSV commands.

When you need to display or modify your configuration, it is helpful to remember that AIX uses a two-character command and SMIT fast-path prefix scheme with the unique suffixes that represent virtual printers virprt, queues and queue devices que, and print devices prt. These prefixes are usually mk to add, ls to list, ch to change, and rm to remove a component. For example the fast-path names to make, list, modify and remove a queue are mkque, lsque, chque, and rmque, respectively. This is not always the case, but you may find it a helpful rule that will reduce the time you spend in InfoExplorer. In some cases, you will have to remove the entry and then re-add it to make the desired modification.

## 10.6 qdaemon and /etc/qconfig

The AIX printing subsystem is managed by the master print daemon, /etc/qdaemon. qdaemon is started, refreshed, or stopped similar to other subsystems under AIX with the startsrc, refresh, or stopsrc commands.

| | |
|---|---|
| `# startsrc -s qdaemon` | Start the qdaemon |
| `# refresh -s qdaemon` | Build new /etc/qconfig.bin |
| `# stopsrc -s qdaemon` | Stop the qdaemon |

qdaemon is automatically started and stopped during system boot and shut down when the init state changes as specified in /etc/inittab.

```
qdaemon:2:wait:/bin/startsrc -s qdaemon
```

qdaemon reads the queuing system configuration from a binary copy of the /etc/qconfig file, called /etc/qconfig.bin. The binary copy is automatically created by /usr/lib/lpd/digest when qdaemon is started or refreshed.

Once you have become familiar with the process of configuring the queuing subsystem, you may find it tedious using the SMIT fast-path menus. You can make your modifications by modifying the stanzas in /etc/qconfig with a standard editor. After you have made your changes, refresh qdaemon to bring them into production. Remember that for new printers and plotters you will also need to create the associated device special files.

*Example* /etc/qconfig:

```
*
* PRINTER QUEUEING SYSTEM CONFIGURATION FILE
*
* /etc/qconfig
*
* Local Queue Device
*
lp:
discipline = fcfs
up = TRUE
device = dlp0
dlp0:
file = /dev/lp0
header = never
trailer = never
access = write
backend = /usr/lib/lpd/piobe
*
* Remote BSD Queue
*
rp:
host = daffy.acme.com
s_statfilter = /usr/lpd/bsdshort
l_statfilter = /usr/lpd/bsdlong
rq = applelaser
device = drp0
drp0:
backend = /usr/lpd/rembak
*
* PostScript Queue to Convert ASCII
*
ps:
device = dps
discipline = fcfs
dps:
backend = /bin/enscript
file = lp
*
* Batch Queue for Running Shell Scripts
*
bsh:
device = bshdev
discipline = fcfs
bshdev:
backend = /bin/sh
*
* Custom Queue Backend
*
alw:
device = dalw
```

```
up = TRUE
dalw:
file = /dev/null
backend = /usr/local/etc/lpd2prt
```

## 10.7 `lpd` Daemon

Inbound print requests from a TCP/IP-based network are managed by the `/usr/sbin/lpd` daemon. The `lpd` daemon manages incoming job requests from the network and deposits them into the appropriate queues for subsequent processing by `qdaemon`. Like `qdaemon`, the `lpd` daemon is a subsystem which can be started as part of system boot and shutdown processing by adding it to `/etc/inittab`, or as required from the command line. The `/etc/lpd/locks` file contains the PID of the currently running `lpd` daemon.

```
# startsrc -s lpd
# stopsrc -s lpd
```

To control which remote systems may communicate with `lpd` and access your local queues, you must add the host name of each remote system into the `/etc/hosts.lpd` file. A single "+" in the `hosts.lpd` file indicates that any remote system may have access to your local queues.

*Example* `/etc/hosts.lpd`

```
#
# /etc/hosts.lpd
#
# This file defines which foreign hosts are permitted to remotely
# print on your host. To allow a user from another host to print
# on your host, that foreign hostname must be in this file
#
daffy.acme.com
judy.acme.com
star.acme.com
```

Communication with remote `lpd` daemons is handled by the `writesrv` subsystem. If you have trouble communicating with a remote system that is responding to other network services, make certain that the `writesrv` subsystem is running and that it is listening to a socket.

| | |
|---|---|
| `# lssrc -s writesrv` | Verify subsystem operative |
| `# ps aux \| grep writesrv` | Verify process is running |
| `# netstat -a \| grep writesrv` | Verify socket connection |

## 10.8 Administering Jobs and Queues

Now that you have the print queuing subsystem configured, the real fun begins. This might be analogous to opening a new freeway. You are going to need to define policies as to how the system is to be used and provide tools for your traffic cops to keep things flowing smoothly.

Queue management and administration tasks in AIX can be handled by one command, `/bin/enq`. AIX does provide wrapper programs for `enq` which may be easier to remember, but in most cases they use the same options. Once you have a handle on the option set, it will likely be easier to use `enq`. If you are familiar with the BSD or SYSV print management commands, you may use these in the AIX environment to provide uniformity in a heterogeneous environment. For the sake of this discussion, we will focus on `enq` and its wrapper counterparts. For the weak of heart, you can perform these functions using SMIT. The basic administration responsibilities for the queuing subsystem include starting and stopping access, listing queue jobs and status, promoting jobs in a queue, and removing jobs from a queue. The `enq` command and its associated wrapper programs may focus the action of each of these tasks to all jobs or queues, specific queues, specific users, or specific jobs using the following options:

| **Option** | **Focus** |
|---|---|
| `-A` | All queues |
| `-P printer` | Specific printer |
| `-u user` | Specific user |
| `-# number` | Specific job |
| `-L` | Long-format output |

### 10.8.1 Starting and stopping queues and printers

From time to time you may find you will have to stop a queue due to a device malfunction or to let a backlog of jobs clear out before accepting additional print requests. Use `qadm` or the `enq` command to manipulate the availability of a queue or device. Note that these commands have no effect on remote queues. To stop `qdaemon` from sending more jobs to a queue and let the currently queued jobs print, use:

```
# qadm -D <Printer>
# enq -D <Printer>
```

To keep `qdaemon` from queuing more jobs and to kill the currently printing jobs, use:

```
# qadm -K <Printer>
# enq -K <Printer>
```

To bring the queue and printer back on-line use:

```
# qadm -U <Printer>
# enq -U <Printer>
```

### 10.8.2 Listing print jobs

In order to manipulate jobs in the queuing subsystem or to review their status, you will need to display the contents of each queue. This is done using the `qchk`, `qstatus`, and `enq` commands. The display format of each is similar. To list the print jobs in all queues, enter one of the commands:

```
# qchk -A
# qstatus -A
# enq -A
```

To list the jobs queued to a particular printer, use:

```
# qchk -P <Printer>
# qstatus -P <Printer>
# enq -A <Printer>
Queue   Dev   Status   Job   Files          User   PP #   Blks   Cp   Rnk
-----   ---   ------   ---   -----          ----   ----   ----   --   ---
lp0     lp0   DOWN
              QUEUED   35    smit.script    root          40     1    1
              QUEUED   36    payroll.rpt    izar          20     1    2
```

The display will list the jobs by queue and device, status, job number and file name, the submitting user, percent printed, size in blocks, copy count, and priority. You will use the information listed in these fields to manipulate the jobs in the queue. The status field provides feedback on the state of the queue, device, and current jobs.

| Status | State |
|---|---|
| READY | Printer accepting print requests |
| DOWN | Printer is off-line |
| UNKNOWN | Printer state is unknown |
| OPR_WAIT | Printer waiting operator response |
| DEV_WAIT | Printer not ready |
| RUNNING | Print job being queued or printing |
| QUEUED | Print job is ready for printing |

### 10.8.3 Changing priority

There are times when special circumstances require that you change the priority of jobs in a queue overriding the default queuing discipline. It may be that you want to defer printing a large job, or an impatient user is leaning over your shoulder with that "I needed this yesterday" look. To change the standing of a job in the queue, use the `qpri` or `enq` commands. To move a job up in priority, give it a higher number. You cannot change the priority of jobs in a remote queue. Once the priority is changed, you should see the position relative to other jobs in the queue change by the value in the rank field.

```
# qpri -P <Printer> -# <JobNumber> -a <Priority>
# enq -P <Printer> -# <JobNumber> -a <Priority>
```

### 10.8.4 Removing print jobs

To remove a print job from a queue, use the qcan or enq commands. If the job you wish to remove is printing, you will first have to stop the printer before removing the job.

```
# qcan -P <Printer> -x <JobNumber>
# enq -P <Printer> -x <JobNumber>
```

If circumstances require that you remove all jobs in a queue, use the -X flag.

```
# qcan -P <Printer> -X
# enq -P <Printer> -X
```

## 10.9 ASCII Terminal Printers

Many ASCII terminals support an auxiliary serial port or parallel port for screen print and printing from connected computers. Routing a print job from the remote computer to the auxiliary port on the terminal requires the sending of a special sequence of characters before and after the print job to enable and disable connection to the auxiliary port. It may be the case that when using this printing capability it will temporarily disrupt normal terminal interaction. The IBM 64-port concentrator will allow concurrent printing and terminal interaction via the AIX /etc/tty/stty-lion program. The stty-lion program requires the start and stop auxiliary print sequences to be given, and the priority that printing is to take over terminal activity.

```
# /etc/tty/stty-lion in_xpar <StartAuxSequence> \
lv_xpar <StopAuxSequence> <PriorityNumber> < /dev/ttyNN
```

### 10.9.1 Pass-through mode

A number of public domain applications exist that will send vt100 auxiliary port sequences to a remote terminal or terminal emulation program.

1. Saving TTY state
2. Setting the TTY to raw mode
3. Sending the start aux sequence
4. Sending the file
5. Sending the stop aux sequence
6. Restoring TTY state

Many terminal emulation packages for personal computers support vt100 pass-through mode sequences. These include kermit for direct connect and dial-up access and NCSA telnet for TCP/IP.

### 10.9.2 Ined Prtty

The AIX INed editor provides pass through mode printing support with the prtty command. prtty may be used as a stand-alone command and is configurable to support any auxiliary port print sequence.

```
# prtty -l <Number> <FileName>
```

The -l number option asks prtty to prompt you after number lines have been printed. You define the start and stop auxiliary sequences in the INed /usr/lib/INed/termcap/terms.bin file for each terminal type you intend to support. You must use the INed editor, e, to edit the /usr/lib/INed/termcap/def.trm file. For each terminal type, set the k2 field with the start auxiliary print sequence, and the k3 field with the stop auxiliary print sequence. When you have completed editing, create a new /usr/lib/INed/termcap/terms.bin file by using the INed tdigest command.

```
# tdigest /usr/lib/INed/termcap/def.trm \
/usr/lib/INed/termcap/terms.bin
```

With pass-through mode printing support, you can define AIX queues for routing jobs to terminal-attached printers. Supply the pass-through mode application name as the backend program and the TTY device special file as the output file in the /etc/qconfig stanza for the queue.

/etc/qconfig *TTY stanza:*

```
ttyp0:
device = dttyp0
dttyp0:
file = /dev/tty0
header = never
trailer = never
access = write
backend = /bin/prtty
```

## 10.10 X Station Printers

AIX supports printing to printers attached to IBM X stations. You may also be able to support printing to other vendor X terminals using either lpd or the pass-through mode printing technique described for ASCII terminals. When using the *IBM X Station Manager,* define an X station-attached printer to the queuing subsystem with the mkvirprt command.

```
# smit mkvirprt
```

Select option 2 `Printer or Plotter Attached to Xstation` from the SMIT menu and supply the X station name. You will be asked to supply the interface type, X station model, printer baud rate, parity, bits per character, start/stop bits, and printer model. This is quite similar to the procedure for adding a standard locally attached printer. Refer to the previous sections on Print Devices (Sec. 10.2) and Print Queues and Queue Devices (Sec. 10.3).

The backend program used for IBM X station printing is `/usr/lpp/x_st_mgr/bin/lpx`. The stanza generated by SMIT for the `/etc/qconfig` file should look like the following entry:

`/etc/qconfig` *X station stanza:*

```
*
* Xstation Queue Device
* xceed:
discipline = sjn
up = TRUE
device = dxceed
dxceed:
file = false
header = never
trailer = never
backend = lpx xceed -s 19200,n,8,1
```

## 10.11 OSF *Palladium*

As AIX moves further into the Open Software Foundation (OSF) specifications, it will be helpful to understand how printing will be defined and managed in this environment. The OSF printing system is based on the *Palladium* distributed printing system developed by MIT Project Athena and based on *ISO DP 10175 Document Printing Application* (DPA). The technology was submitted to the OSF and accepted as part of their Distributed Management Environment (DME). *Palladium* was extended to use the OSF Distributed Computing Environment to provide a client/server-based distributed printing system that supercedes the traditional UNIX `lpd` environment. It is designed to be operating system and architecture independent, and to be amenable to being the RPC interface between these unlike entities. A two-level API is defined, which separates human language printing attributes from that of the servers and underlying operating system.

The *Palladium* distributed printing system is made up of four components that interact to provide a seamless print service to the end user. These components are:

- Print clients
- Print servers

- Printer supervisors
- Printers

*Print clients* act as the user agent for submitting and accepting commands to and from the print service. It is made up of both the high-level and low-level APIs. *Print servers* accept requests from application clients and schedule them on print supervisors. *Print supervisors* are responsible for dispatching files for printing on a printer. *Printers* represents the physical printer device and interface. All interactions are based on the DCE RPC.

*Palladium* supports the two notions of *queue* and *logical printer*. These may be thought of as analogous to the AIX constructs of queue device and virtual printer. The queue, as in the AIX printing subsystem, holds jobs destined for physical printers and remote routing. A logical printer represents an abstraction of the attributes a user has requested for their print job. The print servers and supervisors use these attributes to decide how the job will be queued and routed to a destination.

Logical and physical printer names are stored in the DCE name service along with the names of the print servers that provide the access service for each. Typically, commands will resolve to the name of a logical printer server unless only the physical printer server is listed. To improve robustness and reliability in this distributed environment, more than one server will be listed for both logical and physical printers. Clients may then try each server until the request is accepted. DCE name service groups are also supported to provide multiple names for printer and servers.

The following list of *Palladium* user commands represents the four operations defined by the ISO DPA:

| | |
|---|---|
| `pdpr` | Submit a job to a print server for logical printer |
| `pdmod` | Modify attributes of a print job |
| `pdrm` | Cancel a submitted job |
| `pdls` | List attributes of object instances and classes from a server |

The following list of *Palladium* management commands represents the four ISO DPA administrative operations as well as extensions:

| | |
|---|---|
| `pdclean` | Remove all jobs from a server, queue, or printer |
| `pddisable` | Disable server, queue, or printer |
| `pdenable` | Enable server, queue, or printer |
| `pdinit` | Initialize attributes of a server, queue, or printer |
| `pdinterrupt` | Interrupt current job and resume after specified action |
| `pdpause` | Pause a printing job |
| `pdpromote` | Increase priority of a job |
| `pdresubmit` | Resubmit a job |
| `pdresume` | Resume a paused job |

| | |
|---|---|
| `pdset` | Set the attributes of a DPA or Pd object |
| `pdshutdown` | Shut down the specified server, queue, or printer |

## 10.12 InfoExplorer Keywords

| | | |
|---|---|---|
| qdaemon | piobe | enq |
| /etc/qconfig | /lib/libqb.a | qadm |
| lpd | /usr/lpd/pio/burst | qchk |
| mkprt | lsvirprt | qstatus |
| cat | mkvirprt | qpri |
| splp | startsrc | qcan |
| lptest | refresh | /etc/tty/stty-lion |
| chgprt | stopsrc | prtty |
| mkque | lssrc | tdigest |
| rembak | netstat | /usr/lpp/x_st_mgr/bin/lpx |

## 10.13 QwikInfo

*Printers:*

| | |
|---|---|
| `/etc/qconfig` | Printer definitions |
| `smit mkprt` | Create new printer |
| `splp -p + /dev/lp0` | Transparent access |
| `splp -p ! /dev/lp0` | Enable translation |
| `cat <FileName> > /dev/lp0` | Test the interface |
| `lptest <Columns> <Lines> > /dev/lp0` | Print test pattern |
| `startsrc -s qdaemon` | Start qdaemon |
| `/etc/qconfig` | Printer definitions |
| `bsdlong bsdshort` | lpd control file support |
| `piobe` | Local print backend |
| `# startsrc -s lpd` | Start lpd remote print |
| `rembak` | Remote print backend |
| `/usr/lpd/pio/burst` | Banner pages |
| `lsvirprt -d lp0` | Create new colon file |
| `smit mkvirprt` | Create virtual printer |
| `enq <options>` | Admin print subsystem |
| `prtty -l <Number> <FileName>` | INed transparent print |
| `tdigest` | Compile INed termcap |
| `stty-lion` | 64-pt concentrator print |

Part

# 4

# Network Configuration and Customization

# Chapter 11

# TCP/IP

## 11.1 Internet History

Network technologies took form and began to appear in the late 1960s. Much of what was available at the time was housed in research labs and based on many different design models. It was recognized early on that differing network models would ultimately result in roadblocks to information sharing. Standards organizations came into being to address the problem of interoperability and to formulate a common network model. The *Open Systems Interconnect* (OSI) model was proposed by the *International Standards Organization* (ISO) and adopted as the basis for the majority network development over the last 30 years.

### 11.1.1 OSI model

The OSI model is a layered protocol abstraction that is delimited as seven functional interfaces. At the bottom layer, the model defines the hardware interface for transferring data as signals on the physical medium. Higher levels of the protocol specify packet definition, routing, data integrity, and connection authentication. At the highest levels, data formats and user interfaces are defined.

*OSI model:*

| Layer | Description |
|---|---|
| 7 Application | User interface and services |
| 6 Presentation | Application data transformations |
| 5 Session | Connection authentication |
| 4 Transport | End-to-end data ordering |
| 3 Network | Routing and reporting mechanisms |
| 2 Data | Packet format, integrity, and address definition |
| 1 Physical | Physical hardware specification |

A unit of data in the model is based on the *packet* or, in newer protocols, on the *cell*. Packets are of variable length, whereas cells are of fixed length. Each is made up of a header and data component. Depending upon the protocol and layer, header information identifies the type, address, sequence number, and checksum. Each layer in the OSI stack adds or subtracts headers to facilitate end-to-end delivery of the information.

### 11.1.2 ARPANET

Around the same time that the OSI model was being formulated, the Defense Advanced Research Project Agency (DARPA) funded a project to build a national network connecting government and university research labs. The ARPANET was built using an early point-to-point protocol called the *Network Control Program* (NCP) and packet switching minicomputers running a protocol called *1822*. This topology was replaced in the early 1980s with the *CCITT X.25* packet switching protocol and a new protocol developed by Bolt, Baranek, and Newman (BBN) called *Transmission Control Protocol/Internet Protocol* (TCP/IP). The TCP/IP suite was bundled into BSD UNIX 4.2, and, due to popularity and widespread use, became the de facto standard for internetworking.

Internet protocol definitions are based on a *request for comment* (RFC) process. Draft RFCs are presented to the Internet Activity Board for review. RFC draft status is documented quarterly in the *IAB Official Protocol Standards*. RFC documents are available from a number of sites electronically via anonymous FTP.

Network bandwidth and security problems quickly overcame the rapidly growing ARPANET community. In the late 1980s, the ARPANET was divided into the *Defense Research Internet* (DRI) and the *National Science Foundation Network* (NSFNET). DRI took with it the military research labs from the original ARPANET, leaving the NSFNET to provide wider communication support to universities and other research organizations.

### 11.1.3 NSFNET

The National Science Foundation (NSF) funded a phased migration from the ARPANET into a new three-level hierarchical topology. A national backbone would interconnect regional networks. The regional networks provide access to the NSFNET backbone to universities and organizations residing in their areas of service. NSFNET bandwidth has migrated from T1 to T3 service in most locations. NSFNET long distance circuits are provided by MCI and interconnected using IBM-developed nodal switching systems (NSS). Early NSS systems were based on nine IBM RTs which have since been replaced by a single RS/6000. Thus, the early nickname for the NSS, "Nine Small Systems." NSFNET is managed and operated by Merit Inc.

### 11.1.4 CREN

While the evolution of the Internet was taking place, two other popular university-based networks converged to form the Corporation for Research and Education Network (CREN). These original networks were the Computer Science Network (CSNET) and the Because It's Time Network (BITNET), which were originally based on dial-up/X.25 and NJE/BISYNC connections, respectively. CREN is moving toward an IP topology similar to NSFNET. A first step has involved encapsulating NJE in IP for the existing BITNET sites. It's worth mentioning CREN because of the role it played in popularizing network use and the role it will likely play with NSFNET in the future of large-scale networking.

### 11.1.5 Future net—ATM

There is a race going on, involving the telcos, cable companies, computer vendors, and the entertainment industry, to bring full multimedia services into your living room or work place. The telcos have the switching equipment but lack the bandwidth from the curb into your home or office. Cable companies have the bandwidth but lack the switching infrastructure. The computer and entertainment industries hold the applications and products of interest to the consumer community. The result is collaborations and partnerships in an attempt to bring all the pieces together.

To manage the traffic explosion of worldwide interactive audio-video services requires the implementation of a low-overhead network protocol. Such a protocol is Asynchronous Transfer Mode (ATM). ATM is based on small 53-byte fixed-length cells. Not much room to support both header and data! By dynamically multiplexing small cells between multiple paths, ATM eliminates the problem of continuous large-block data like video causing network traffic jams. ATM speeds begin at 155 megabits/s. First-generation switches will run at 2.4 gigabits/s. Gateways to traditional network protocols will be supported to ease migration. Don't be surprised to eventually see ATM-like protocols emerge to manage data within the workstation.

## 11.2 TCP/IP Suite

It's difficult to get a one-to-one mapping between the TCP/IP and OSI models. TCP/IP bundles much of the functionality defined in the OSI model into a smaller number of layers. Rather than attempt to define a TCP/IP to OSI mapping, it is pertinent to this discussion to present a model of the TCP/IP suite.

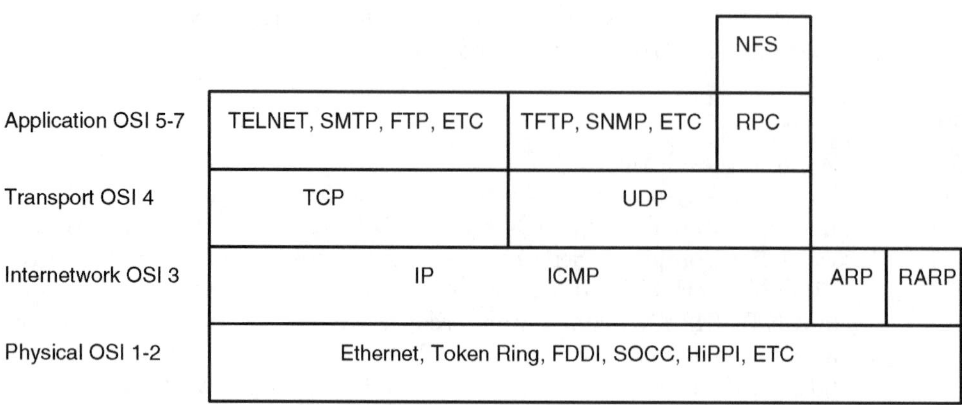


**Figure 11.1** TCP/IP stack.

The *physical layer* represents a conglomeration of hardware interfaces and protocols that interoperate via the conduit defined in the upper layers (see Fig. 11.1). These interfaces employ a wide range of data speeds and physical architectures.

The *internetwork* layer combines the OSI data link layer and a portion of the OSI network layer. The layer is composed of two protocols, *Internet Protocol* (IP) and *Internet Control Message Protocol* (ICMP). IP and ICMP are connectionless datagram protocols that provide the basic data buckets and control in the network.

The *transport layer* defines two protocols, *Transmission Control Protocol* (TCP) and *User Datagram Protocol* (UDP). TCP ensures a reliable ordered transport, whereas UDP service is unreliable and does not ensure delivery. It has been shown that TCP reliability operations cause a significant bottleneck in network throughput on fast processors and networks. The conjecture is that the current network transports are significantly cleaner than those around when the protocol was defined. TCP checksum processing ties up host cycles that could be better used elsewhere. Newer network interface hardware is moving TCP processing into the interface and off of the host processor to improve throughput.

The *application layer* in the TCP/IP suite, like the OSI model, implements the user interface. Client/server protocols are most often defined at the application layer. Common application level services include *Telnet, File Transfer Protocol* (FTP), *Simple Mail Transfer Protocol* (SMTP), *Network File System* (NFS), and the *X11 Window System.*

## 11.3 Planning

Whether you are new to TCP/IP or sport a fair number of stars on your wizard's hat, installing or upgrading your network infrastructure will require some careful planning and plenty of homework. If you aren't considering the implications of the multimedia boom in your bandwidth calculations, then you probably need to increase them by an order of magnitude. Once you turn on the information faucet, your users won't be able to get enough! Have you thought about how you're going to back up all those low cost multi-gigabyte disks populating your workstations? How about telecommuting capability? Fortunately, gateway configurations will allow you to mix and match components to meet most of your connection and bandwidth needs. Notice that I did say *most!*

## 11.4 Hardware Components

The RISC System/6000 supports the gamut of traditional hardware interfaces as well as newer high-speed adapters approaching gigabit/s transfer rates. In the following sections I'll outline the attributes of each of these network interfaces, along with cabling and support hardware.

### 11.4.1 RISC System/6000 Micro Channel

We will begin by looking at the Micro Channel in the RISC System/6000. Latency and buffering problems in the older 40-MB/s Micro Channel bus could only sustain 9 MB/s under the best conditions. Multiple adapters on the bus will degrade throughput during simultaneous transmissions. Thus, the older 40-MB bus was a significant bottleneck for connections requiring speeds beyond basic Ethernet or token ring. The 80-MB/s bus in new systems sustains data rates up to 72 MB/s. Multiple Micro Channel buses are an option on larger systems.

### 11.4.2 Ethernet

*Ethernet* is a 10-MB/s broadcast-based network developed in the early 1980s by Xerox. Ethernet comes in three flavors: *Version 1—1980, Version 2—1982,* and *IEEE 802.3—1983.* It is a broadcast-based protocol that uses collision detection and avoidance to regulate traffic. The *Carrier Sense Multiple Access / Collision Detection* (CSMA/CD) protocol allows any system to start a conversation on the wire, but requires it to back off and wait a pseudorandom period of time if it detects that it has interrupted an existing conversation. The wait-before-retry interval is bounded by a multiple of 51.2 μs. 51.2 μs is the time it takes to transmit a 512-bit packet. Although the specified data rate of Ethernet is 10 MB/s, in reality it will only sustain around 1 MB/s.

The *ether* exists on a segment of cable terminated at each end. The segment terminators absorb signals inhibiting reflections from either

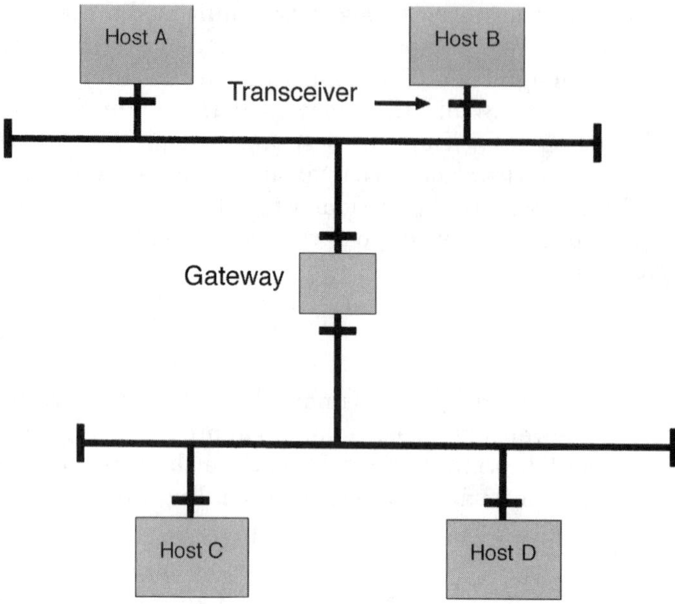


**Figure 11.2** Ethernet network.

end of the wire. Computers and other peripheral equipment are connected to the segment using a *tap* and *transceiver*. Cable segments are bridged together into larger networks using *repeaters*. (See Fig. 11.2.) Ethernet segments are commonly constructed from coaxial or twisted pair cable. The choice of cable will depend on the environment and dictate the cost. As you might expect, twisted pair is the cheapest and easiest medium to install and manage. Newer media options like optical fiber, digital radio, digital microwave, or satellite links may be used between segments to span almost any distance you might have in mind. (Refer to Table 11.1.)

A *transceiver* is used to connect the computer adapter to the Ethernet segment. Internal transceivers located on the adapter card attach to the Ethernet segment using a "T" tap. External transceivers are powered from the segment itself and attach to the adapter via a *drop cable*. Drop cables may be constructed using shielded twisted pair or optical

**TABLE 11.1 Common Ethernet Media**

| Type | Cable | Max seg len | Nodes/segment | Topology |
|---|---|---|---|---|
| 10BASE5 Thickwire* | RG 11 | 500 m | 100 | Bus |
| 10BASE2 Thinwire† | RG 58 | 185 m | 30 | Bus |
| 10BASET Twisted pair | 24 AWG | 100 m | 16 | Star |

*Transceivers 2.3 m apart and segment lengths multiples of 23.4 m.
†Transceivers .5 m apart.

fiber, depending on distance requirements. *Multiport transceivers* may be used to connect multiple machines to a segment using one tap.
*Drop cable DB15 pin-out:*

| Version 1,2 | Pin | IEEE 802.3 |
|---|---|---|
| Shield (ground)* | 1 | Not connected |
| Collision (+) | 2 | Collision (+) |
| Transmit (+) | 3 | Transmit (+) |
| Reserved | 4 | Logic reference (ground)† |
| Receive (+) | 5 | Receive (+) |
| Power return | 6 | Power return |
| Reserved | 7 | Not connected |
| Reserved | 8 | Not connected |
| Collision ( − ) | 9 | Collision ( − ) |
| Transmit ( − ) | 10 | Transmit ( − ) |
| Reserved | 11 | Not connected |
| Receive ( − ) | 12 | Receive ( − ) |
| Power | 13 | Power |
| Reserved | 14 | Not connected |
| Reserved | 15 | Not connected |

*Version 1,2 shields attached to pin 1 and hood.
†IEEE 802.3 inner shield attached to pin 4, outer shield attached to casing.

```
# smit chgenet
```

Figure 11.3 reproduces the SMIT Ethernet adapter panel.

You may want to increase the values of the TRANSMIT and RECEIVE queues. These values represent queues of buffers for incoming and outgoing packets. Values may range from 20 to 150.

Expanding the size of an Ethernet network beyond a single segment requires the use of active devices to recondition packets and to isolate and route traffic. These tasks are performed by *repeaters, bridges,* and *routers,* respectively. Repeaters are used to connect segments separated by distance. Remote repeaters are used in pairs and connected together via optical fiber. Repeaters retime and retransmit packets from one segment to the next. Bridges reconstitute packets similar to repeaters. In addition, they learn the addresses of the machines on each side of the bridge and eventually determine whether to pass traffic from one side to the other based on the addresses of the sender and receiver. Routers determine which segment a particular packet must take to reach its destination. Routers exchange data concerning who their neighbors are to create a picture of the network topology.

New blood is being pumped into Ethernet technology due to the large customer base it currently enjoys. Proposals for 100-MB/s Ethernet are being reviewed by the IEEE. Some of the proposed pro-

```
          Change/Show Characteristics of an Ethernet Adapter

Type or select values in entry fields.
Press Enter AFTER making all desired changes.

                                                   [Entry Fields]
Ethernet Adapter                               ent0
Description                                    Ethernet High-Performa>
Status                                         Available
Location                                       00-06
RECEIVE DATA TRANSFER OFFSET                   [92]                  +#
TRANSMIT queue size                            [30]                  +#
RECEIVE queue size                             [30]                  +#
STATUS BLOCK queue size                        [5]                   +#
Adapter CONNECTOR                              dix                   +
Enable ALTERNATE ETHERNET address              no                    +
ALTERNATE ETHERNET address                     [0x]                  +
Offset to ETHERTYPE field                      [12]                  +#
Offset to 802.3 ETHERTYPE                      [14]                  +#
Apply change to DATABASE only                  no                    +

F1 = Help       F2 = Refresh     F3 = Cancel     F4 = List
F5 = Undo       F6 = Command     F7 = Edit       F8 = Image
F9 = Shell      F10 = Exit       Enter = Do
```

**Figure 11.3** SMIT Ethernet adapter panel.

tocols are already available in the marketplace. Proposals before the IEEE include mechanisms for parallel twisted pair configurations, multiple packet priority, and new multilevel code protocols.

### 11.4.3 Token ring

*Token-ring* networks provide a little bit better throughput than standard Ethernet (see Fig. 11.4). They were originally developed by IBM and later adopted by the IEEE as specification 802.5. Token-ring protocol uses a token passing mechanism to regulate traffic on the ring. A particular workstation on the ring must gain control of a token

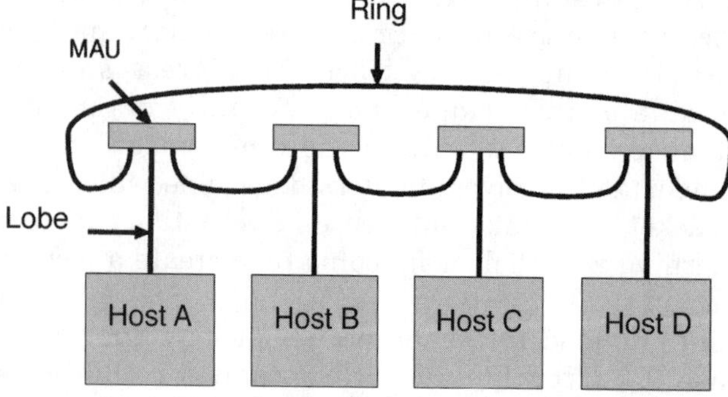


**Figure 11.4** Token-ring network.

before it can transmit data onto the ring. While data is being transmitted on the ring, a token is not available to other stations. A dual-ring topology will provide a degree of fault tolerance. If the ring is broken, the dual paths are used to form a new ring. Token ring supports either 4- or 16-MB/s bandwidth. At the high end, token ring can sustain around 12 MB/s throughput.

Each computer in the ring is configured with an *adapter card.* The adapter is connected to a *multistation access unit* (MAU) with an *adapter cable.* A MAU is a concentrator that supports up to eight station ports along with a *ring-in* and *ring-out* port to interconnect other MAUs. Like Ethernet, repeaters are used to extend distances between MAUs by retiming and retransmitting packets. A repeater may be integrated into a MAU, making it an *active* MAU. MAUs local to the work space can be rack-mounted in a *wiring closet.* A number of cable options are available to fit most environmental, cost, distance, and speed requirements. (Refer to Table 11.2)

A *star ring topology* can be built from a central ring with one or more MAU devices. Dual-pair cables connect each MAU to the ring and represent the *lobes* of the star. For Type 1 cable, lobe lengths can be no more than 100 m, with a maximum of 260 stations on the main ring. Type 3 cable, being unshielded, allows no more than 45 m for each lobe unless active MAUs are used to boost distance. A maximum of 72 stations may be attached to a Type 3 main ring.

Ring traffic control is distributed among all active stations. Each station receives a token or data frame from its nearest neighbor. If the station is not the intended recipient, it retransmits the frame back onto the ring to the next station on the ring. Figure 11.5 displays the SMIT token-ring adapter panel.

```
# smit chgtok
```

### 11.4.4 Fiber Distributed Data Interface (FDDI)

*Fiber Distributed Data Interface* (FDDI), ANSI X3T9.5, is a token passing protocol similar to token ring, but implemented using optical fiber rings. FDDI and its copper-based cousin, *Copper Distributed*

**TABLE 11.2 Token-Ring Media**

| | | |
|---|---|---|
| Type 1 | 22 AWG | 2 shielded pairs |
| Type 2 | 22 AWG | 2 shielded, 4 unshielded pairs |
| Type 3 | 24 AWG | 1 unshielded pair |
| Type 5 | | Solid-core optical fiber |
| Type 6 | 26 AWG | 2 stranded shielded pairs |
| Type 8 | 26 AWG | 2 parallel shielded pairs |
| Type 9 | 26 AWG | 2 solid-conductor shielded pairs |

```
Change / Show Characteristics of a Token Ring Adapter

Type or select values in entry fields.
Press Enter AFTER making all desired changes.

                                                        [Entry Fields]
Token Ring Adapter                        tok0
Description                               Token-Ring High-Perfor>
Status                                    Available
Location                                  00-02
Receive data transfer OFFSET              [92]                      +#
TRANSMIT queue size                       [30]                      +#
RECEIVE queue size                        [30]                      +#
STATUS BLOCK queue size                   [10]                      +#
RING speed                                16                        +
Receive ATTENTION MAC frame               no                        +
Receive BEACON MAC frame                  no                        +
Enable ALTERNATE TOKEN RING address       no                        +
ALTERNATE TOKEN RING address              [0x400050708376]          +
Apply change to DATABASE only             no                        +

F1 = Help       F2 = Refresh     F3 = Cancel     F4 = List
F5 = Undo       F6 = Command     F7 = Edit       F8 = Image
F9 = Shell      F10 = Exit       Enter = Do
```

**Figure 11.5** SMIT token-ring adapter panel.

*Data Interface* (CDDI), support data rates at 100 MB/s. FDDI was designed to be implemented as a network backbone. It has been slow to gain acceptance due to high per-node cost. Although FDDI provides significant bandwidth improvements over standard Ethernet and token ring, it is thought to be too little too late when compared with other emerging technologies.

FDDI, like token ring, operates with distributed control over all stations connected to the ring. Each station receives token or data frames from one neighbor and, if not the recipient, passes them on to the next neighbor. The *media access control* (MAC) layer of the FDDI specification supports tailoring of the token-handling time to reflect the data types generally transmitted over the ring. Low time values provide better interactive response, whereas high values are better for moving large block data.

The RS/6000 supports both single-ring and dual-ring topologies. A *single attach station* (SAS) is used for single-ring configurations. The *dual-attach station* (DAS) adapter provides the ability to support a primary and secondary ring topology. In this configuration, the secondary ring supports traffic flow in the opposite direction from the primary ring. This allows a fail-over ring to be formed in the event the ring is segmented. Note that the secondary ring is available for fault tolerance only and may not be used as a separate network.

It is recommended that 62.5/125-μ multimode optical fiber be used for each ring. You can get away with using other popular fiber sizes

```
            Change/Show Characteristics of a FDDI Adapter

Type or select values in entry fields.
Press Enter AFTER making all desired changes.

                                                      [Entry Fields]
FDDI adapter                                 fddi0
Description                                  FDDI Primary Card, Sin>
Status                                       Available
Location                                     00-07
Receive Data Transfer Offset                 [0]                        +#
Receive Queue Size                           [30]                       +#
Transmit Queue Size (in mbufs)               [30]                       +#
Status Block Queue Size                      [10]                       +#
Enable Alternate Mac/SMT Address             no                         +
Alternate Mac/SMT address                    [0x0]                      +
PMF Password                                 [0x0]                      +
TVX (nsec)                                   [2509200]                  +#
TVX (nsec)                                   [2509200]                  +#
TVX (nsec)                                   [2509200]                  +#
TVX (nsec)                                   [2509200]                  +#
T_REQ (nsec)                                 [10001920]                 +#
T_REQ (nsec)                                 [10001920]                 +#
T_REQ (nsec)                                 [10001920]                 +#
T_REQ (nsec)                                 [10001920]                 +#
USER data                                    []
Receive Beacon Frames                        no                         +
Receive SMT Frames                           no                         +
Receive NSA Frames                           no                         +
Apply change to DATABASE only                no                         +

F1 = Help          F2 = Refresh       F3 = Cancel       F4 = List
F5 = Undo          F6 = Command       F7 = Edit         F8 = Image
F9 = Shell         F10 = Exit         Enter = Do
```

**Figure 11.6** SMIT FDDI adapter panel.

as long as you keep signal loss to a minimum. FDDI concentrators may be connected as lobes in a star ring topology. Fiber distribution panels can be located in wiring closets similar to token-ring MAUs. See Fig. 11.6 for the SMIT FDDI adapter panel.

```
# smit chgfddi
```

### 11.4.5 SLIP/PPP

The RISC System/6000 supports TCP/IP over dial-up lines using *Serial Line Internet Protocol* (SLIP) and *Point-to-Point Protocol* (PPP). The hardware employed by these protocols uses standard serial ports, modems, and switched lines (see Chap. 9).

SLIP is a very simple protocol for framing IP packets on a serial line. It does not support packet addressing or type fields, data compression, or reliability. Only one protocol may be supported on a link at a time. SLIP links must be started manually.

PPP goes further than SLIP by including a *Link Control Protocol* (LCP) for link control and a set of *Network Control Protocols* (NCP) to support multiple protocols at a time. PPP will likely replace SLIP as the standard protocol for serial links.

In most instances, you will want to use links speeds at or above 9600 bits/s.

### 11.4.6 Serial optical channel converter (SOCC)

In the absence of a standard high-speed network solution, IBM supplied a proprietary fiber pipe for the RISC System/6000 called the *serial optical channel converter (SOCC). Although the device is not an IBM strategic direction for networking, it does provide a high-speed option for interconnecting RISC System/6000s.*

SOCC adapters have two half duplex fiber channels each operating at 220 MB/s. The adapters are connected directly to the planar, enabling fast data paths to system memory, bypassing the Micro Channel bus. The architecture can sustain speeds at 18 MB/s in native mode. TCP and UDP are supported at slower rates due to packet processing overhead in the central CPU. SOCC is a point-to-point architecture (see Fig. 11.7). Network Computing Systems markets a DX switch that may be used to interconnect SOCC adapters in a star topology. It also provides gateway adapters for Ethernet, token ring, FDDI, HIPPI, and Hyperchannel.

```
# smit opschange
```

### 11.4.7 High-Performance Parallel Interface (HIPPI)

The *High-Performance Parallel Interface* (HIPPI) standard, ANSI X3T9.3, is based on the *High-Speed Channel* project work, and Cray's *HSX Channel.* HIPPI runs at speeds of 800 MB/s and can be extended

```
Change / Show Characteristics of the Serial Optical Link

Type or select values in entry fields.
Press Enter AFTER making all desired changes.

                                                   [Entry Fields]
* Processor ID number for this machine              [35]        +#
RECEIVE queue size                                  [80]        +#
STATUS BLOCK queue size                             [20]        +#
Apply change to DATABASE only                       no          +

F1 = Help         F2 = Refresh      F3 = Cancel       F4 = List
F5 = Undo         F6 = Command      F7 = Edit         F8 = Image
F9 = Shell        F10 = Exit        Enter = Do
```

**Figure 11.7** SMIT SOCC panel.

to 1600 MB/s. HIPPI uses a copper-cable interface supporting distance of up to 25 m in a point-to-point topology. HIPPI extenders multiplex copper onto fiber to reach distances exceeding 10 k. HIPPI switches and crossbars may be used to interconnect multiple devices.

The RISC System/6000 supports HIPPI connections using the *High-Performance Parallel Interface Driver Group/6000* in conjunction with HIPPI Micro Channel adapters. The driver set supports TCP, UDP, and master/slave IPI-3 (Intelligent Peripheral Protocol). The TCP/UDP protocol set may be used to interconnect to other computers. The IPI-3 protocol is employed for connecting to mass storage systems and devices.

### 11.4.8 Fiber Channel Standard (FCS)

Just around the corner are some interesting technologies being developed for high-speed connections. The *Fiber Channel Standard* shepherded by the HIPPI ANSI group defines a fast fiber pipe operating at 1 gigabit/s to support network protocols. IBM and business partner Ancor are working to define an open architecture based on FCS for clustering RISC System/6000s. The project includes Micro Channel adapter cards and a high-speed FCS switch. FCS will support distances up to 10 km between stations.

### 11.4.9 Asynchronous Transfer Mode (ATM)

In Sec. 11.1.5, I described the emerging Asynchronous Transfer Mode (ATM) protocol, which is the likely candidate for the next nationwide networks. IBM will be marketing ATM adapters for the RISC System/6000 architecture in 1994. Along with ATM adapters, the strategy includes an ATM hub and ATM switch for wide area networks.

## 11.5 TCP/IP Software Configuration

The RISC System/6000 provides a couple of methods for configuring and maintaining TCP services. Like other AIX services, TCP configuration information is stored in the ODM and maintained using SMIT. You may also edit the `/etc/rc.net` script such that it will configure network interfaces and set the host name and routes in the traditional way. Commands are also available to import/export configuration information between the standard tables and the ODM databases.

## 11.6 Addressing

Each computer in the network must be known by a unique identifier. TCP/IP uses three levels of addressing: *hardware address, IP number,* and *domain name.*

### 11.6.1 Hardware address

Manufacturers encode a unique hardware address into each adapter that they produce. You might think that this should satisfy network uniqueness, so why the three levels? Using Ethernet as an example, the hardware address of an interface is a 48-bit number. The first 24 bits identify the manufacturer. The second 24 bits are assigned sequentially to represent each Ethernet adapter produced by the manufacturer. This number is all that is required to identify machines at the physical network layer. These numbers are a bit hard to remember, even when represented in hexadecimal.

### 11.6.2 IP address

A unique IP address is assigned by the network administrator to represent each computer in the network. The IP address abstracts the hardware address to a more general use. At this address level, we aren't concerned with the adapter interface type used on a particular machine. The IP address format is common across the network.

An IP address is a 32-bit number represented as four octets. Each octet is a number in the range of 0 through 255: 255.255.255.255. The address is split into two parts at octet boundaries representing a network address and a host address on that network. The network and host portions represent address classes. There are three address classes: *class A, class B,* and *class C*. See *RFC 1166—Internet Numbers* for a complete description of IP address definition.

*IP address classes:*

| Class | Address | Hosts |
|---|---|---|
| A | N.H.H.H | 16 M* |
| B | N.N.H.H | 64 K* |
| C | N.N.N.H | 254* |

N—network address.
H—host address.
*Numbers 0, 127, 255 are reserved.

Address classes are assigned to organizations depending on the number of machines they project attaching to the network. If the organization represents a number of departments, they may want to request a class A or class B address. This will allow them to assign class B or class C network addresses respectively to each of the departments. The departments may then assign and administer the host addresses available within the network address class.

An example class C network address of 128.99.233 will allow the administrator to assign host addresses in the range of 128.99.233.1 through 128.99.233.254. Numbers 0, 127, and 255 are reserved. The number 0 is used to represent an octet unknown to the local host. The number 127 indicates a loopback or local host address. The number 255 is used for *broadcast.*

Since IP numbers must be unique on the Internet, they are administered by a central authority. *General Atomics / CERFnet, InterNIC* is a Network Information Center sponsored by the National Science Foundation. You can obtain the necessary forms to register your site from InterNIC. Return the completed forms to: hostmaster@internic.net.

General Atomics (U.S. Registration)
P.O. Box 85608
San Diego, CA 92186-9784
(800)444-4345
(619)455-3990 (fax)

info@internic.net

| | |
|---|---|
| rs.internic.net | ftp site for forms |
| is.internic.net | gopher and wais server |

RIPE NCC (European Registration)
Kruislaan 409
1098 SJ Amsterdam
The Netherlands
31-20-592-5065
31-20-592-5090 (fax)

hostmaster@ripe.net

Even if you don't initially intend to connect to the Internet, it is a good idea to have the NIC assign you an address class. The address set assigned will be recorded for your use and will not be assigned to any other organization. You may administer numbers within the class. Later on if you connect to the Internet, it will eliminate the possibility of having to renumber all your host addresses due to address collisions with other sites.

### 11.6.3 Domain address

Although IP addresses uniquely identify computers on the network, they are not easily remembered. This brings us to the third level in the addressing hierarchy, *domain address.*

The simple solution is to map host names to the associated IP numbers. These *host tables* are installed on each machine in the network and provide a directory for host name to IP number address resolution. This works for small networks but immediately breaks down as we scale up to large numbers of systems. Mapping host names to IP numbers is subject to the same scaling problems encountered when mapping given names to phone numbers in a large city. There are far too many name collisions and the phone book is too large for timely incorporation and distribution of updates.

### 11.6.4 Host tables

For small networks, the simplest address resolution method is to record the host name to IP number of all the machines in the network in a table. The table is then distributed to each machine in the network. This method is implemented by the `/etc/hosts` file.

*Example* `/etc/hosts`:

```
#
# IP Number          Host Names
#
127.0.0.1            localhost
128.95.135.13        daffy
128.95.135.24        louie
128.95.142.30        huey
140.27.133.4         donald
```

### 11.6.5 Domain name service

To address the scaling problem, a hierarchical name space methodology was adopted for the Internet community which enforces uniqueness and supports timely distribution of updates. This name space system is a client/server protocol called *BIND Domain Name Service* (DNS).

Computers and organizations in DNS are identified by a *domain name.* A domain name is a name tuple, delimited by "."s, which represents the administrative hierarchy of the name space of which it is a member. Domain names are usually represented in two to four levels. Note that there is no implied mapping of subdomains to IP number octets!

*Domain names:*

```
Format:    hostname.subdomain.subdomain.topdomain
Examples:  dingo.bornes.com
           vnet.ibm.com
```

For large networks, the DNS provides a more efficient and distributed name management and resolution. In the DNS hierarchy, upper-level domains (see Table 11.3) need only record the names of the next lower level in the tree along with the IP numbers of the *name servers* that resolve addresses for that level. A name-resolving protocol called *BIND* is used to recursively query name servers until a domain name is resolved to an IP number. All name servers must know the addresses of the top-level Internet name servers. This system supports local management of the name space and ensures timely information to the network at large. (Refer to Fig. 11.8.)

**TABLE 11.3 Top-Level Domains**

| | |
|---|---|
| EDU | Education |
| GOV | Government |
| MIL | Military |
| ORG | Organizations |
| COM | Commercial |
| NET | Other networks |
| Country code | Two-character international identifier |

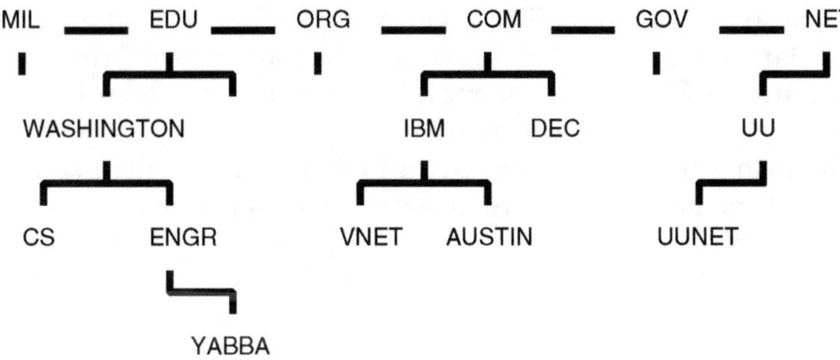


**Figure 11.8** Sample Internet domain subtrees.

Name service for an organization or department is handled by two servers, a *primary* and a *secondary* name service daemon, `named`. You don't need to run `named` on each machine in your network. The `named` daemon obtains local configuration information from a local startup file and table. It caches query data it has received from remote name servers to reduce network traffic. The cached data is time-dependent and is flushed periodically.

At initialization time, the `named` daemon reads `/etc/named.boot` to determine if it is a primary or secondary server, the default domain, zone of authority, and configuration table path.

`/etc/named.boot` *for primary server:*

```
; /etc/named.boot primary
;
directory /etc ; named table path
domain foo.bar.org ; default domain
cache . named.ca ; cache file
primary foo.bar.org primary/named.data ; host info
primary 0.0.127.in-addr.arpa primary/named.rev ; reverse info
```

`/etc/named.boot` *for secondary server:*

```
; /etc/named.boot secondary
;
directory /etc ; named table path
domain foo.bar.org ; default domain
cache . named.ca ; cache file
```

```
secondary foo.bar.org server1 secondary/named.data ; host info
primary 0.0.127.in-addr.arpa primary/named.rev ; reverse info
```

The secondary server will contact the primary server (server1 in the sample) and request a zone transfer of host and reverse pointer information. It will cache local copies of this data in secondary/{named.data named.rev} files. This cached data will allow the secondary server to obtain zone information at startup when the primary server cannot be contacted.

Once named has identified the configuration path, it reads the cache file named.ca, the host data file primary/named.data, and the reverse data file named.rev to obtain the remainder of the configuration data. IBM provides sample configuration tables in the /usr/lpp/tcpip/samples directory.

The cache prime file (/etc/named.ca in the example) defines the IP addresses of the authoritative name servers for root domains.

/etc/named.ca:

```
;
; root cache
;
; Initial cache data for root domain servers.
;
                        999999      IN      NS      NS.INTERNIC.NET.
                        999999      IN      NS      NS.NIC.DDN.MIL.
                        999999      IN      NS      KAVA.NISC.SRI.COM.
                        999999      IN      NS      AOS.BRL.MIL.
                        999999      IN      NS      C.NYSER.NET.
                        999999      IN      NS      TERP.UMD.EDU.
                        999999      IN      NS      NS.NASA.GOV.
                        999999      IN      NS      NIC.NORDU.NET.
;
; Prep the cache (hotwire the addresses). Order does not matter
;
NS.INTERNIC.NET.        999999      IN      A       198.41.0.4
NS.NIC.DDN.MIL.         999999      IN      A       192.112.36.4
KAVA.NISC.SRI.COM.      999999      IN      A       192.33.33.24
AOS.BRL.MIL.            999999      IN      A       192.5.25.82
AOS.BRL.MIL.            999999      IN      A       128.63.4.82
AOS.BRL.MIL.            999999      IN      A       26.3.0.29
C.NYSER.NET.            999999      IN      A       192.33.4.12
TERP.UMD.EDU.           999999      IN      A       128.8.10.90
NS.NASA.GOV.            999999      IN      A       128.102.16.10
NS.NASA.GOV.            999999      IN      A       192.52.195.10
NIC.NORDU.NET.          999999      IN      A       192.36.148.17
```

The host data file primary/foo, identifies table version number, cache refresh and expire times, query retry time, and host to IP number identification data for zone foo. The reverse file, named.rev, is used to supply IP number to host name mapping. Sample awk scripts are supplied to create named.data and named.rev from existing /etc/hosts tables.

```
# hosts.awk /etc/hosts > /etc/named.data
# addrs.awk /etc/hosts > /etc/named.rev
```

Information in the files is represented as fields. The fields, in order, are *NAME, Time To Live* (TTL), *CLASS, TYPE,* and *Resource Data* (RDATA). The NAME field identifies the host name associated with the following data. The TTL field indicates the longevity of the information in seconds. The CLASS field indicates the protocol type, which in our case is *IN,* indicating the Internet. The TYPE and RDATA fields identify descriptive information for the associated NAME. The type of data is based on a set of predefined record types called *resource records* (RR) (see Table 11.4).

`named.data:`

```
; named.data
;
; OWNER        TTL          CLASS  TYPE      RDATA
;
$ORIGIN foo.bar.org.
@                           IN     SOA       server1.foo.bar.org.
(            1.1                             ; serial number for updates
             3600                            ; refresh time seconds
             600                             ; retry time seconds
             3600000                         ; expire time seconds
             86400                           ; minimum
)
;
; Name Servers
;
             99999999       IN     NS        server1.foo.bar.org.
             99999999       IN     NS        server2.foo.bar.org.
server1                     IN     A         123.145.100.1
server2                     IN     A         123.145.100.2
;
; Host Names
;
daffy                       IN     A         128.145.100.13
                            IN     HINFO     "RS/6000-530, AIX 3.2"
                            IN     UINFO     "Jeff Jones, 123-4567"
                            IN     MX        10 mailserver.foo.bar.org
;
donald                      IN     A         128.145.100.30
                            IN     HINFO     "DEC Alpha, OSF1"
                            IN     UINFO     "Jenny Smith, 123-6789"
                            IN     MX        10 mailserver.foo.bar.org
```

`named.rev:`

**TABLE 11.4 Resource Records**

| TYPE | Description |
|---|---|
| A | IP address of the site |
| CNAME | Canonical name—other alias names |
| HINFO | Descriptive host information for the site |
| MX | Preferred mail handler for the site |
| NS | Identifies authoritative name server |
| PTR | Pointer to another part of the name space |
| SOA | Start of zone of authority |
| WKS | Well-known services supported at this site |

```
; named.rev
;
; OWNER      TTL          CLASS  TYPE      RDATA
;
@                         IN     SOA       server1.foo.bar.org.
(            1.1                           ; serial number for updates
             3600                          ; refresh time seconds
             600                           ; retry time seconds
             3600000                       ; expire time seconds
             86400                         ; minimum
)
;
; Name Servers
;
             99999999     IN     NS        server1.foo.bar.org.
             99999999     IN     NS        server2.foo.bar.org.
1                         IN     PTR       server1.foo.bar.org.
2                         IN     PTR       server2.foo.bar.org.
;
; Host Names
;
13                        IN     PTR       daffy.foo.bar.org.
30                        IN     PTR       donald.foo.bar.org.
```

The `named` daemon may also be run as a *caching only* server. In the caching only mode, the server does not supply any preconfigured host data. It only gains data by querying other name servers.

Each machine in the organization that will be using name service must have an `/etc/resolv.conf` file that identifies the default domain name and a list of name servers. When resolving a name to IP address, a query is sent to the first name server in the list. If the timeout period expires before an answer is received, then the second name server is tried.

`/etc/resolv.conf`:

```
; /etc/resolv.conf
;
domain          foo.bar.org         ; default domain
nameserver      123.145.100.1       ; name server
nameserver      123.145.100.2       ; name server
```

## 11.7 Network Routing

It's not enough to know someone's name in the network. In order to send messages to them you have to also know where they are and how to get there. Just like the interstate highway system, in order to navigate a network we rely on information provided by third parties concerning which path to take at each junction. This is called *routing*.

In the previous discussion on hardware, I talked about how *routers* and *gateways* exchange network topology information based on each device's view of their neighborhood. It is this information that we are trusting when we embark on journeys through the network. These devices use a number of tried and true protocols (see Table 11.5) to derive their view of the network at large. These protocols are based

**TABLE 11.5 Routing Protocols**

| | |
|---|---|
| EGP | External Gateway Protocol |
| RIP | Routing Information Protocol |
| IGRP | Internal Gateway Routing Protocol |
| Hello | Initial "Fuzzball" NFSnet Protocol |
| OSPF | Open Shortest Path First Protocol |

on algorithms that maintain *hop count* metrics or compute spanning trees to determine the best route through the network jungle.

Routing information may be determined dynamically by querying the routers for a path from point A to point B, or by the use of static routes configured by the system administrator. Static routes work fairly well for small networks, but as with the name space, they break down as the network size gets large.

### 11.7.1 Static routes

Static routes are set with the `route` command. In most cases, a *default* route is set for all instances to a knowledgeable local router. Additional static routes may be set for networks and individual hosts. Static routing information is normally set as part of the systems tcpip startup procedures. It may be set via SMIT, or by editing the `/etc/rc.tcpip` startup script. When adding a static route, specify the type of route (network, host), IP address of the destination, IP address of the router, and the number of hops.

*Static routes:*

| | |
|---|---|
| `/etc/route add default 123.145.100.10` | Default route |
| `/etc/route add net 123.145.50.0 123.145.50.100` | Route to a net |
| `/etc/route add host 123.145.40.2 123.145.40.33` | Route to a host |
| `/etc/route -f` | Flush all routes |

You may query defined routes using the `netstat - rn` command. The `-r` indicates that `netstat` is to report routes and the `-n` flag specifies not to use name service to determine names. This is much faster and will keep `netstat` from hanging when there are routing problems that inhibit access to name service.

```
# netstat -rn
Routing tables
Destination     Gateway            Flags  Refcnt   Use          Interface
Netmasks:
(root node)
(0)0
(0)0 ff00 0
(0)0 ffff ff00 0
(root node)
Route Tree for Protocol Family 2:
(root node)
```

```
default         128.95.135.100   UG    266     71180277   en0
127             127.0.0.1        U     7       3991       lo0
128.95.135      128.95.135.13    U     191     42439693   en0
(root node)
Route Tree for Protocol Family 6:
(root node)
(root node)
```

### 11.7.2 Dynamic routes

Collecting and/or broadcasting dynamic routing information is the job of the `routed` and `gated` daemons. The `routed` daemon understands the RIP protocol. RIP bases routing data on hop counts. A site with a hop count larger than 16 is deemed unreachable. The `gated` daemon understands RIP, EGP, and Hello protocols. EGP also responds to *Simple Network Monitoring Protocol* (SNMP) queries. The `routed` and `gated` daemons use information configured in the `/etc/gateways` table to identify other network gateways with which to exchange information. If the RIP protocol is used, then known networks are also listed in the `/etc/networks` table. Unless you are setting up a network router, you will want to use `routed` in query-only mode to learn routes from the active routers in the network. When used, the `routed` or `gated` daemons are started with the tcpip subsystem. You may enable them using SMIT or by editing the `/etc/rc.net` startup script.

| | |
|---|---|
| `/etc/routed -q` | Query-only mode |
| `/etc/routed -s` | Announce routes |
| `/etc/routed -t` | Trace packets |
| `# startsrc -s gated` | Start gated daemon |

`/etc/networks:`

```
loop 127 loopback
ethernet 123.145.100
```

`/etc/gateways:`

```
net FOOnet     gateway server1     metric 0     active
```

### 11.7.3 Subnets

*Subnets* are a mechanism that allows an organization with many internal networks to hide the internal structure and routing and announce a single network address to the outside world. A *subnet mask* is used to mask out a portion of the host half of an IP address to be used for routing. Most commonly this is done by using a class B address known to the outside world and masking the third octet as subnet numbers.

When a machine within the organization wants to send a packet to another system, it applies the subnet mask to the destination address to see if the address is on the local network or if it must send it to a router for delivery.

The subnet mask is a four-octet number that indicates which bits in the address are to be masked as the network and subnet portion of the address. The low-order bits of the mask designate the host portion of the address.

| | |
|---|---|
| `netmask 0xfffffff0` | 14 hosts per subnet (0 and 15 excluded) |
| `netmask 0xfffffff8` | 6 hosts per subnet (0 and 7 excluded) |

### 11.7.4 Interface configuration

To begin using the network, the adapter interface must be configured with the local machine IP address, subnet mask, and broadcast address. The interface may be configured using SMIT or by adding an `ifconfig` entry in the `/etc/rc.net` startup script (see Fig. 11.9).

```
# smit chgeth
```

`ifconfig` *parameters:*

```
ifconfig en0 123.145.100.18 netmask 0xffffff00 broadcast 123.145.100.255
```

```
                    Minimum Configuration and Startup

To Delete existing configuration data, please use Further Configuration menus
Type or select values in entry fields.
Press Enter AFTER making all desired changes.

                                                [Entry Fields]
* HOSTNAME                                      [lorrie]
* Internet ADDRESS (dotted decimal)             [123.145.100.18]
Network MASK (dotted decimal)                   [255.255.255.0]
* Network INTERFACE                             en0
NAMESERVER
Internet ADDRESS (dotted decimal)               [123.145.100.1]
DOMAIN Name                                     [foo.bar.org]
Default GATEWAY Address                         [123.145.100.100]
(dotted decimal or symbolic name)
Your CABLE Type                                 dix                  +
START TCP/IP daemons Now                        no                   +

F1 = Help           F2 = Refresh        F3 = Cancel         F4 = List
Esc + 5 = Undo      Esc + 6 = Command   Esc + 7 = Edit      Esc + 8 = Image
Esc + 9 = Shell     Esc + 0 = Exit      Enter = Do
```

**Figure 11.9** SMIT TCP config panel.

The adapter interface can be brought up and down for maintenance or testing using SMIT or, from the command line, using the `ifconfig` command. Note that this will interrupt service to tcpip daemons.

| | |
|---|---|
| `# ifconfig en0 up` | Start Ethernet interface |
| `# ifconfig tk0 down` | Stop token-ring interface |

## 11.8 System Resource Controller

The *system resource controller* (SRC) is a facility that allows the system administrator to easily manage a group of associated daemons and services as a single entity called a *subsystem*. Each of the daemons or services belonging to a subsystem is known as a *subserver*. Subsystems that are related in function can be combined as a *subsystem group*. SRC administration commands allow the system administrator to start, stop, refresh, and trace subsystem groups, subsystems, and subservers as a unit, thus eliminating the complexity of dealing with each component individually.

*SRC commands:*

| | |
|---|---|
| `startsrc/stopsrc [-g] [-s] <subsystem>` | Start/stop a group or subsystem |
| `refresh [-g] [-s] <subsystem>` | Refresh a group or subsystem |
| `traceon/traceoff [-g] [-s] <subsystem>` | Turn trace on or off |
| `lssrc [-l] [-s] <subsystem>` | List subsystem status |

The SRC system master daemon, `/etc/srcmstr`, is started at boot time by an entry in `/etc/inittab`. Subsystems are also started by entries in `/etc/inittab` using the `startsrc` command.

### 11.8.1 TCP/IP subsystem

TCP/IP runs as a *subsystem* under AIX. This means that it is under the control of the *system resource controller* (SRC). The associated daemons that make up the TCP/IP subsystem are known as subservers. Daemons controlled by the master TCP/IP daemon, `inetd`, like `ftpd`, are known as subservers. All services associated with TCP/IP may be started or stopped using the SRC `startsrc` and `stopsrc` commands.

| | |
|---|---|
| `# startsrc -g tcpip` | Start tcpip services |
| `# stopsrc -g tcpip` | Stop tcpip services |

### 11.8.2 Master daemon—`inetd`

Rather than running some of the TCP/IP service daemons continuously, they can be started when a request is made for the service and shut down when the service has been completed. This capability is supported by the `inetd` daemon.

Configuration for inetd is located in the /etc/inetd.conf and /etc/services tables. These tables are mirrored by the InetServ object class in the ODM. Any changes to the table information must be reflected in the ODM. Changes made to these tables through SMIT will automatically be incorporated in the table and the ODM. SMIT updates will also refresh inetd. If you want to maintain the tables using your favorite editor, you may use the inetimp and inetexp commands to copy table information to the ODM and from the ODM respectively.

```
# inetimp    Import inetd.conf and services to InetServ ODM
# inetexp    Export InetServ ODM to inetd.con and services
```

Entries in the /etc/inetd.conf file indicate the service name and startup information. The /etc/service file lists the service name, whether it uses TCP and/or UDP protocols, and the well-known port number associated with the service. Any time updates are made to either of these tables, you will need to refresh inetd. This can be done with the SRC refresh command or by sending a *hangup* signal to the inetd process. Note that some daemons require that the portmap daemon be running.

```
# refresh inetd
# kill -HUP <inetd-pid>
```

/etc/inetd.conf:

```
# inted.conf
#
#                                                                  server
# service   socket   pro-     wait/    user     server          program
# name      type     otcol    nowait            program         arguments
#
echo        stream   tcp      nowait   root     internal
echo        dgram    udp      wait     root     internal
discard     stream   tcp      nowait   root     internal
discard     dgram    udp      wait     root     internal
daytime     stream   tcp      nowait   root     internal
daytime     dgram    udp      wait     root     internal
chargen     stream   tcp      nowait   root     internal
chargen     dgram    udp      wait     root     internal
ftp         stream   tcp      nowait   root     /etc/ftpd       ftpd
telnet      stream   tcp      nowait   root     /etc/telnetd    telnetd
time        stream   tcp      nowait   root     internal
time        dgram    udp      wait     root     internal
bootps      dgram    udp      wait     root     /etc/bootpd     bootpd
tftp        dgram    udp      wait     nobody   /etc/tftpd      tftpd -n
finger      stream   tcp      nowait   nobody   /etc/fingerd    fingerd
exec        stream   tcp      nowait   root     /etc/rexecd     rexecd
login       stream   tcp      nowait   root     /etc/rlogind    rlogind
shell       stream   tcp      nowait   root     /etc/rshd       rshd
talk        dgram    udp      wait     root     /etc/talkd      talkd
ntalk       dgram    udp      wait     root     /etc/talkd      talkd
uucp        stream   tcp      nowait   root     /etc/uucpd      uucpd
comsat      dgram    udp      wait     root     /etc/comsat     comsat
```

The /etc/services file represents the mapping of service name to associated well-known ports.

/etc/services:

```
#
# Network well known services
#
# Service        Port/Protocol  Aliases
#
echo             7/tcp
echo             7/udp
discard          9/tcp          sink null
discard          9/udp          sink null
systat           11/tcp         users
daytime          13/tcp
daytime          13/udp
netstat          15/tcp
qotd             17/tcp         quote
chargen          19/tcp         ttytst source
chargen          19/udp         ttytst source
ftp-data         20/tcp
ftp              21/tcp
arcftp           22/tcp         # unitree auto login
telnet           23/tcp
smtp             25/tcp         mail
time             37/tcp         timserver
time             37/udp         timserver
rlp              39/udp         resource # resource location
nameserver       42/udp         name # IEN 116
whois            43/tcp         nicname
domain           53/tcp         nameserver # name-domain server
domain           53/udp         nameserver
mtp              57/tcp         # deprecated
bootps           67/udp         # bootp server port
bootpc           68/udp         # bootp client port
tftp             69/udp
rje              77/tcp         netrje
finger           79/tcp
link             87/tcp         ttylink
supdup           95/tcp
hostnames        101/tcp        hostname # usually from sri-nic
iso_tsap         102/tcp
x400             103/tcp
x400-snd         104/tcp
csnet-ns         105/tcp
pop              109/tcp        postoffice
sunrpc           111/tcp
sunrpc           111/udp
auth             113/tcp        authentication
sftp             115/tcp
uucp-path        117/tcp
nntp             119/tcp        readnews untp
ntp              123/tcp
ntp              123/udp        # network time protocol (exp)
NeWS             144/tcp
snmp             161/udp        # snmp request port
snmp-trap        162/udp        # snmp monitor trap port
mux              199/tcp        # snmpd smux port
src              200/udp        # System Resource controller
exec             512/tcp
login            513/tcp
who              513/udp        whod
shell            514/tcp        cmd # no passwords used
```

```
syslog          514/udp
printer         515/tcp      spooler # line printer spooler
talk            517/udp
ntalk           518/udp
efs             520/tcp      # for LucasFilm
route           520/udp      router routed
timed           525/udp      timeserver
tempo           526/tcp      newdate
courier         530/tcp      rpc
conference      531/tcp      chat
netnews         532/tcp      readnews
netwall         533/udp      # for emergency broadcasts
uucp            540/tcp      uucpd # uucp daemon
new-rwho        550/udp
remotefs        556/tcp      rfs_server rfs # remote filesystem
rmonitor        560/udp
monitor         561/udp
```

Table 11.6 represents a selection of servers that may be managed by `inetd`. The list is not exhaustive, but represents some of the more common applications.

### 11.8.3 Other network daemons

Not all TCP/IP service daemons run under control of `inetd`. You may also choose to run an `inetd` subserver as a stand-alone daemon to service high traffic loads. This eliminates the overhead involved in restarting the daemon for each service request. Start stand-alone service daemons using an entry in `/etc/inittab` or from a local `rc.local` file (see Table 11.7).

### 11.8.4 Start-up configuration

The TCP/IP subsystem is normally started at system boot via an entry in `/etc/inittab`. The subsystem `/etc/rc.net` and `/etc/rc.tcpip` configuration files contain entries to enable the network interface, set

**TABLE 11.6 `inetd` Subserver Daemons**

| | |
|---|---|
| `ftpd` | File transfer daemon for `ftp` |
| `telnetd` | Network login daemon for `telnet` |
| `rlogind` | Network remote login for `rlogin` |
| `rshd` | Remote shell daemon for `rsh` |
| `rexecd` | Remote command execution daemon |
| `sendmail`* | Network mail daemon |
| `talkd` | Network chat daemon for `talk` |
| `comsat` | Announce incoming mail |
| `fingerd` | Display user information for `finger` |
| `tftpd` | Trivial file transfer daemon for `tftp` |
| `uucpd` | TCP/IP to UUCP gateway |
| `bootpd` | Support `bootp` requests |
| `instsrv` | AIX network installation server |

*Sendmail may run as a subserver of `inetd` or as a stand-alone subsystem.

**TABLE 11.7 TCP/IP Subsystem Daemons**

| | |
|---|---|
| inetd | Master TCP/IP daemon. Listens to ports and launches associated subserver daemon. |
| gated* | Routing daemon supports RIP, EGP, and Hello. |
| routed* | Routing daemon supporting RIP. |
| named | Domain name service daemon. |
| iptrace | Packet tracing support. |
| rwhod | List logged in users on subnet systems. |
| timed | Network time server. |
| syslogd | Log daemon for network services. |

*Make certain that these two daemons are not running at the same time.

the host name, set the default route, start `inetd`, etc. If you want to start tcpip sans SRC and the ODM, comment out the entries in `/etc/rc.net` following the text `Part I—Configuration using the data in the ODM database`. Remove the comments from section `Part II—Traditional Configuration` and tailor the host name, network interface, and default routes per your installation.

*Example* `/etc/rc.net` *Part II:*

```
################################################################## #
# Part II - Traditional Configuration.
###################################################################
#
/bin/hostname lorrie.foo.bar.org                    >>$LOGFILE 2>&1
/usr/sbin/ifconfig en0 inet `hostname` up           >>$LOGFILE 2>&1
/usr/sbin/route add default 123.145.100.10          >>$LOGFILE 2>&1
```

## 11.9 SLIP and PPP

The RS/6000 supports dial-up TCP/IP via *Serial Line Internet Protocol* (SLIP) provided with AIX, and *Point-to-Point Protocol* (PPP) from third-party vendors. SLIP is a very simple encapsulation protocol which will likely be replaced by the more robust PPP. In the following configuration discussion, it is assumed that a serial port has been defined to the system for modem connections. Note also that the standard TCP/IP addressing and routing specifications apply to SLIP. Refer to Fig. 11.10.

The TTY port must be set to DISABLE for SLIP. You cannot use the DELAY or SHARE states.

The dial string is modem-dependent and will be set for either dial-out or auto-answer for incoming connections. The format of the dial string is the same as used by UUCP.

*Sample Hayes Dial String:*

```
"" ATZ OK ATDT123-4567 CONNECT ""
1) ""            Null from modem
```

```
                      Minimum Configuration & Startup

To Delete existing configuration data, please use Further Configuration menus
Type or select values in entry fields.
Press Enter AFTER making all desired changes.

                                                      [Entry Fields]
* HOSTNAME                                           [lorrie]
* Internet ADDRESS (dotted decimal)                  [123.145.50.18]
Destination ADDRESS                                  [123.145.50.10]
Network MASK (dotted decimal)                        [255.255.255.0]
* Activate the Interface After Creating it>          yes
Security Level                                       none
* TTY Port for SLIP Network Interface                [tty0]
Baud Rate                                            [19200]
Dial String                                          []

F1 = Help            F2 = Refresh         F3 = Cancel        F4 = List
Esc + 5 = Undo       Esc + 6 = Command    Esc + 7 = Edit     Esc + 8 = Image
Esc + 9 = Shell      Esc + 0 = Exit       Enter = Do
```

**Figure 11.10** SMIT SLIP config panel.

```
2) ATZ          Send reset to modem
3) OK           Response from modem
4) ATDT...      Send dial command to modem
5) CONNECT      Connection string
6) ""           Done
```

On the system to be dialed into, start SLIP using the `slattach` command.

```
# slattach tty<?>
```

On the dial-out system, start `slattach`. Note that you may include the baud rate and dial string on the command line.

```
# slattach tty<?> 19200 "" ATZ OK ATDT123-4567 CONNECT ""
```

To disable a SLIP connection, send a hangup (`HUP`) signal to the `slattach` process. DO NOT USE `-9 (KILL)`, as this may cause system panics.

PPP goes beyond the simple encapsulation protocol used by SLIP. It provides session negotiation options, link level error detection, compression, and authentication. PPP is available from a number of third-party vendors.

## 11.10 Anonymous FTP

*Anonymous FTP* is a common service available on the Internet that provides public access to repositories of public domain applications and information. Care must be taken when configuring an anonymous FTP server, since you are granting a level of access to your system without password protection. You want to limit the commands and the directory paths that are accessible.

Create an account (ftp) and directory path to be used for anonymous ftp. The `ftpd` daemon provides a level of protection by invoking `chroot(2)` to set the root directory to the directory owned by the ftp account, effectively hiding anything outside that path. Create `bin`, `etc`, and `pub` subdirectories in the ftp account home directory. Copy the `ls` command to the `bin` subdirectory. Install edited copies of `/etc/passwd` and `/etc/group` in the `etc` subdirectory. These files should only contain root, daemon, and ftp accounts. Install software and documents you wish to make available in the `pub` directory. Refer to Table 11.8.

A replacement `ftpd` server that provides additional options for anonymous ftp is available from `wuarchive.wustl.edu`.

## 11.11 Security

*Network security* is often viewed as a contradiction of terms. It is certainly true that you increase exposure to unauthorized access when you permit any outside access to your computing resource. Packet sniffers are publicly available, allowing users to watch all the data traversing the wires. Wiretaps for broadcast networks like Ethernet are easily installed. A workstation in the hands of a hacker can impersonate trusted addresses. The tradeoffs between exposure and additional service must be weighed carefully. Network security is not really the oxymoron that the joke implies. You have the ability to implement security measures; however, as you tighten down the locks, you may lose services and ease of use.

### 11.11.1 Network Trusted Computing Base

AIX supports a set of access control and auditing facilities called the *Trusted Computing Base* (TCB). The TCB system also encompasses

**TABLE 11.8 Anonymous FTP Directory Permissions.**

| | | |
|---|---|---|
| ~ftp | ftp | 555 |
| ~ftp/bin | root | 555 |
| ~ftp/bin/ls | root | 111 |
| ~ftp/etc | root | 555 |
| ~ftp/etc/passwd | root | 444 |
| ~ftp/etc/group | root | 444 |
| ~ftp/etc/pub | ftp | 77* |

*Write access will allow incoming data. You may wish to create a special directory under ~ftp/pub for incoming data.

network support and is known as *Network Trusted Computing Base* (NTCB). Along with TCB user authentication mechanisms, NTCB supplies connection authentication, secure session, auditing of network configuration files and events, and an enhanced security TCP/IP operation mode.

Connection authentication is provided by defining which remote host addresses are allowed to connect to the local system. Security levels may be defined for each network interface to limit the activities that may take place over a given interface.

Secure sessions are enforced through the use of *trusted path, trusted shell* (tsh), and *secure attention key* (SAK). The trusted path and shell limit the applications that may make use of a terminal session. The SAK establishes the environment necessary for a secure session.

The AIX auditing system records changes in permissions, modification times, checksums, and network events.

A full set of security features may be enabled using the `securetcpip` command. `securetcpip` disables untrusted commands and restricts access to interfaces that are not configured at specified security levels. The Berkeley r-commands `rsh`, `rcp`, `rlogin`, and `rsh` are disabled, along with `tftp`. The `ftp`, `telnet`, and `rexec` commands provide additional security checking. Once the `securetcpip` command is invoked, the tcpip lpp must be reinstalled to restore standard operation. Interface security levels are based on the *IP Security* option described in RFC 1038.

### 11.11.2 Traditional security measures

There are some less drastic measures you can take to secure your environment. The first is the judicious use of `.rhosts` and `/etc/hosts.equiv` files. Using these files allows use of the Berkeley r-commands without requiring a password. This eliminates passwords sent in the clear over the net and limits the damage that may be done with PTY sniffer programs. It is true that if these files are compromised they can present a nasty security hole. Care must be taken when implementing their use. Basically these files list the hosts and user names that are allowed to execute r-commands without a password.

Connection authentication can be implemented on a service-by-service basis by implementing a wrapper program for `inetd`. The wrapper program validates and logs the connecting systems address based on an access table. The `tcpd` program available via anonymous ftp from `cert.org` is an example of this type of application. The `tcpd` system controls access by service class as well as by individual service.

Another authentication mechanism gaining popularity is based on an encrypted ticket-granting algorithm authorizing timed access to a service. Tickets are granted by a secure trusted third party. Both the client and server must have the ticket authentication interface incorporated into their respective source code. The *Kerberos* authentication system follows this schema and is being implemented by most vendors. Kerberos is also the authentication system used by OSF technologies.

### 11.11.3 Security information

The *Computer Emergency Response Team* (CERT) based at Carnegie Mellon University tracks and disseminates vendor security information. CERT regularly posts information to the `comp.security.announce` Usenet group. They also support an anonymous ftp site containing security-related documents. Another Usenet security-related discussion group is `alt.security.general.`

*CERT address:*

Computer Emergency Response Team/Coordination Center
Software Engineering Institute
Carnegie Mellon University
Pittsburgh, PA 15213-3890
24hr Hot Line: (412)268-7090
email: cert@cert.org
anonymous ftp: cert.org

## 11.12 Network Management

Implementing and maintaining a smooth-running TCP/IP network requires a similar network of individuals who plan, administer, operate, and troubleshoot the components that make up the system. There are far more models for the assignment of bodies and responsibilities for the people-side of network management than the number of protocols to be managed. Thus, I won't talk about that here. However, to make any management structure work, you need good data collection and alert tools.

A great deal of standards work has gone into defining the *Structure and Identification of Management Information* (*SMI - RFC 1155*), the *Management Information Base* (*MIB - RFC 1156*), and the *Simple Network Monitor Protocol* (*SNMP - RFC 1157*). SNMP has been recommended by the Internet Activities Board (IAB) as a short-term network management tool while the ISO *Common Management Information Protocol* (CMIP) and *CMIP over TCP/IP* (CMOT) protocols are investigated.

SNMP is a protocol which is used to communicate *network element* (NE) statistics and control information to *network management stations* (NMS). The NMS clients may set or query variable information collected by an NE. Asynchronous traps may be generated by an NE and delivered to an NMS client. The standard defines communication based on UDP. Variable types are grouped as objects. RFC 1213 provides a complete list of MIB objects and variable descriptions.

### 11.12.1 AIX SNMP and NetView/6000

AIX V3 provides both SNMP client and agent functions. The client `snmpinfo` application supports SNMP GET, NEXT, and SET functions. The AIX SNMP agent, `snmpd`, supports these MIB-II groups: system, interface, at, ip, icmp, tcp, udp, egp, transmission, and snmp.

An API is provided for application access to MIB data and alerts. MIB variables are stored in the `/etc/mib.defs` and `/etc/mib_desc` files. MIB objects are managed using the `mosy` command. Refer to RFC 1213 for a complete list of MIB-II groups.

The *NetView/6000 Entry* licensed program product can be used to manage and graphically display information of up to 32 snmpd agents. NetView/6000 provides a *dynamic discovery* capability which automatically scopes out and maps your network for management. The Motif based GUI can be used to graphically display network topologies and graph MIB information. For networks larger than 32 nodes, the *SystemView NetView/6000 V2* licensed program product is available. Additional support includes a number of APIs and CMOT support. Refer to Table 11.9.

Configuration data for the `snmpd` agent is specified in the `/etc/snmpd.conf` file. Configuration information includes the path and size of the log file, MIB views, access permissions, traps, and snmpd parameters. Well-known port numbers for *snmpd* network access must be defined in `/etc/services`.

**TABLE 11.9 SystemView NetView/6000 MIB Support**

| | | |
|---|---|---|
| cisco-9.1.mib | rfc1232-DS1 | synoptics-trap.mib |
| fibermux-crossbow.mib | rfc1233-DS3 | ung-bass-asm320-16.7.mib |
| hp-unix | rfc1243-APPLE | ung-bass-suprv-16.7.mib |
| ibm-6611-v1r1.1.mib | rfc1253-OSPF | wellfleet-6.0.mib |
| ibm-alert.mib | rfc1269-BGP | xylogics-annex-7.0.mib |
| ibm-nv6ksubagent.mib | rfc1271-RMON | xylogics-annex.mib |
| ibm-mib | rfc1284-ETHER | xyplex-boot-client.mib |
| net-lwx-r1.mib | rfc1285-FDDI | xyplex-boot-server.mib |
| novell-hubnvle-1.0.mib | rfc1286-BRIDGE | xyplex-bridge.mib |
| novell-hubnvltr-2.0.mib | rfc1289-DECNET | xyplex-character.mib |
| novell-lantern-1.3.mib | rfc1304-SIP | xyplex-decnet.mib |
| novell-nw2snmp-1.0.mib | rfc1315-FRAME | xyplex-ethernet.mib |
| ods-RFCEnBridge.mib | rfc1316-CHAR | xyplex-hub.mib |
| ods-enc.mib | rfc1317-RS232 | xyplex-ieee-hub.mib |
| ods-tr.mib | rfc1318-PARALL | xyplex-internet.mib |
| proteon.mib | suminet-3500-1.0.mib | xyplex-lat.mib |
| rfc1213-MIB-II | synoptics-common.mib | xyplex-mini.mib |
| rfc1229-GINTF | synoptics-ethernet.mib | xyplex-param-client.mib |
| rfc1230-802.4 | synoptics-ieee8023.mib | xyplex-system.mib |
| rfc1231-802.5 | synoptics-tokenring.mib | |

snpd `/etc/services` *ports:*

```
snmp           161/upd
snmp-trap      162/udp
smux           199/tcp
```

`/etc/snmpd.conf:`

```
# smpd.conf
#
# Log attributes
logging file = /var/snmpd/log enabled
logging size = 0 level = 0
#
# MIB views
#
# View name is an arbitrary three integer identifier
#
# view      <view name>      <MIB list>
  view      1.15.7           system
  view      1.15.6           interfaces
#
# Who has access to agent MIB information
#
# Community names defined in /etc/community
#
# community <name>   <address> <netmask>      <permission> <view name>
  community public
  community private daffy     255.255.255.0  readWrite    1.15.7
#
# traps to catch
#
# trap mask:      fe     block no traps
#                 7e     block coldStart trap
#                 be     block warmStart trap
#                 3e     Block both coldStart and warmStart traps
#
# trap     <community name>    <address>     <view name>    <mask>
  trap     public              daffy         1.15.7         fe
#
# snmpd parameters
#
  snmpd maxpacket = 1024 querytimeout = 120 smuxtimeout = 60
```

The `snmpd` daemon can be started and stopped as a subsystem using the SRC `startsrc` and `stopsrc` commands or via SMIT. It can also be started with the tcpip subsystem.

| | |
|---|---|
| `# startsrc -s snmpd` | Start snmpd |
| `# stopsrc  -s snmpd` | Stop snmpd |

## 11.13 Troubleshooting

*If something can go wrong, it will go wrong.* Sounds like Murphy was talking about computer networks! Distributed systems magnify the complexity of stand-alone systems by orders of magnitude. Unfortunately, there isn't much in the way of integrated tools to assist the administrator with troubleshooting problems.

### 11.13.1 Sniffers

Probably the best tool to have handy for medium-to-larger networks is a *sniffer*. A sniffer is a custom computer that attaches to the network to analyze packet traffic. These systems are compact, so they can be taken anywhere and are tuned to keep up with packet rates. Packet types can be filtered and logged to provide statistics over time. For the budget-minded, there are packages available for workstations and PCs which provide many of the same functions.

### 11.13.2 AIX `iptrace`

If portability isn't a problem, the AIX `iptrace` and `ipreport` commands do a very good job at collecting IP traffic traces. The `iptrace` command supports options to record traffic by protocol, host, port, and interface. Protocol types must be defined in the `/etc/protocols` file. Output from `iptrace` is recorded in a file which can later be formatted into a report using the `ipreport` command.

```
# iptrace /tmp/trace.data
# ipreport /tmp/trace.data /tmp/trace.report
```

### 11.13.3 Interface status

The `netstat` command can be used to display interface statistics and connection status for a given workstation or host. An interval flag may be used to record snapshots over time.

*Useful* `netstat flags:`

| | |
|---|---|
| `-i` | Summary packet rates and errors by interface |
| `-a` | Display active connection status |
| `-r` | Display routing table information |
| `-m` | Display mbuf allocation and usage |

### 11.13.4 Reachability

When you want to check reachability, the `ping` command is a useful tool. `ping` sends ICMP echo requests to a remote site. Statistics are gathered and displayed based on the round-trip time and dropped packets. In most cases, reachability problems will be related to routing information or netmask.

```
# ping foo.bar.com
PING foo.bar.com (130.111.58.1): 56 data bytes
64 bytes from 130.111.58.1: icmp_seq = 0 ttl = 252 time = 8 ms
64 bytes from 130.111.58.1: icmp_seq = 1 ttl = 252 time = 3 ms
64 bytes from 130.111.58.1: icmp_seq = 2 ttl = 252 time = 8 ms
64 bytes from 130.111.58.1: icmp_seq = 3 ttl = 252 time = 5 ms
-- foo.bar.com ping statistics --
4 packets transmitted, 4 packets received, 0% packet loss
round-trip min/avg/max = 3/5/8 ms
```

### 11.13.5 Server applications

The `telnet` command can be used to validate the operation of a server application that is listening on a particular port number. Use the port number option with `telnet` to connect to the remote port. Once you have connected, you can interactively initiate a dialog with the application.

```
# telnet daffy.foo.bar.org 25        Telnet to smtp port
```

### 11.13.6 Name service

To validate the operation of your name servers, use the `nslookup` command. `nslookup` can be directed at individual name servers and request specific resource record information. It also supports specifying the query type to use.

```
# nslookup
> daffy.foo.bar.org
Server: <default.server>
Address: 121.91.130.1
Non-authoritative answer:
Name: daffy.foo.bar.org
Address: 121.91.135.14
```

### 11.13.7 mbuf allocation

Large networked multiuser or application server systems often run into the problem of exhausting network buffers called *mbufs*. mbuf structures are used to store data moving between the network and the operating system. Under older versions of UNIX, when you hit the mbuf wall, you had to increase a kernel parameter for mbufs and/or mbclusters, rebuild the kernel, and reboot. This is real bad news for your up-time statistics.

AIX provides an mbuf management facility that dynamically controls the allocation and use of mbufs and mbclusters. The default allocation is based on a low-to-medium packet rate and is somewhat dependent on the number of adapters. The mbuf management facility *netm* controls the minimum and maximum available free space in the pools, and the maximum amount of memory that may be used for the pools. Note that the mbuf and mbcluster pools are pinned in memory. netm increases the pool sizes as network load increases. The mbcluster pool is reduced as load decreases; however, the mbuf pool is never decreased. Each mbuf is 256 bytes in size and each mbcluster is 4096 bytes. (Refer to Table 11.10.)

You don't want netm to be dispatched unnecessarily, and you don't want to overcommit memory to mbuf pools. What you need to do is monitor your packet rates under normal loads and adjust the mbuf parameters at boot time to pin as much memory as you will need and no more. You can modify the following mbuf parameters with the `no`

**TABLE 11.10 Kernel mbuf Variables**

| | |
|---|---|
| lowmbuf | Free mbuf low water mark |
| lowclust | Free mbcluster low water mark |
| mb_cl_hiwat | Max number of free clusters |
| thewall | Max memory available mbufs and clusters |

command. Build a script which is run at boot time to set the parameters and execute a packet spray program or ping in a loop to generate enough network traffic to pin the memory required.

## 11.14 InfoExplorer Keywords

| | | |
|---|---|---|
| TCPIP | traceoff | tftpd |
| chgenet | lssrc | bootpd |
| chgtok | srcmstr | uucpd |
| opschange | /etc/inittab | slattach |
| chgfddi | inetd | chroot |
| named | /etc/inetd.conf | securetcpip |
| awk | /etc/services | /etc/hosts.equiv |
| /etc/hosts | inetimp | tcpd |
| /etc/resolv.conf | inetexp | snmpd |
| route | portmap | SNMP |
| netstat | ftpd | /etc/mib.defs |
| routed | telnetd | /etc/mib_desc |
| gated | rlogind | mosy |
| /etc/gateways | rshd | /etc/snmpd.conf |
| /etc/networks | rexecd | iptrace |
| /etc/rc.net | talkd | ipreport |
| ifconfig | sendmail | /etc/protocols |
| startsrc | comsat | ping |
| refresh | fingerd | nslookup |
| traceon | | |

## 11.15 QwikInfo

**TCPIP**

*Network adapters:*

| | |
|---|---|
| `smit chgenet, chgtok, chgfddi, opschange` | Adptr config fast paths |
| `ifconfig` | Config interface |

*Addressing:*

| | |
|---|---|
| `/etc/hosts` | Static host table |
| `/etc/resolv.conf` | Name servers for address resolution |
| `/etc/named.boot` | Name server config |
| `/etc/named.ca` | Root name server cache |
| `/etc/named.data` | Address listing |
| `/etc/named.rev` | Reverse pointer listing |
| `nslookup` | Query name server info |

*Network routes:*

| | |
|---|---|
| `route` | Administer routes |
| `netstat -rn` | List defined routes |
| `routed` | Routing daemon (RIP) |
| `gated` | Routing daemon (RIP, EGP, Hello) |
| `/etc/gateways` | Known gateways |
| `/etc/networks` | Known networks |

*Services:*

| | |
|---|---|
| `/etc/services` | Well-known ports |
| `/etc/inetd.conf` | inetd subservers |
| `inetimp/inetexp` | Import/export tables to/from ODM |

*TCPIP Group Subsystem:*

| | |
|---|---|
| `/etc/rc.net` | TCPIP startup config |
| `startsrc -g tcpip` | Start all tcpip subsystems |
| `startsrc -s inetd` | Start master Internet |

*Debugging:*

| | |
|---|---|
| `iptrace` | Start packet trace |
| `ipreport` | Format trace output |
| `netstat` | Network statistics |
| `ping` | Check reachability |

*Security:*

Network Trusted Computing Base — Secure TCP

Computer Emergency Response Team /Coordination Center

Software Engineering Institute

Carnegie Mellon University

Pittsburgh, PA 15213-3890
24-hr Hotline: (412)268-7090
email: cert@cert.org
anonymous ftp: cert.org

| | |
|---|---|
| cops | Security checkout package |

# Chapter 12

# UUCP

## 12.1 UUCP Overview

The *UNIX-to-UNIX Copy Program* (UUCP) is almost as old as UNIX itself. It was originally developed by Mike Lesk at Bell Labs around the mid 70s. In the early 80s, it was rewheeled by Peter Honeyman, David Nowitz, and Brian Redman and became *HoneyDanBer UUCP*. UUCP is a simple mechanism which supports remote command execution, file, and e-mail transfer between consenting systems over dial-up and LAN connections. AIX knows UUCP as the *Basic Networking Utilities* (BNU), which are based on the HoneyDanBer version of UUCP. BNU services are part of *BOS Extended Services* lpp.

UUCP provides an ideal avenue for downloading Usenet News or providing Internet e-mail access when you don't want to support a continuous connection to the Internet. Connections may be established from the local site to trusted remote sites within restricted operation parameters. UUCP uses a store-and-forward mechanism to communicate with sites beyond immediate neighbors. Files are transferred from one machine to the next using *hop addressing* and *host tables.* The down side of the store-and-forward nature of UUCP is the extra administration complexity involved in maintaining the host tables.

## 12.2 Using UUCP

A user invokes a UUCP command to transfer a file to a remote site. A work file containing address and control information, and a copy of the file to be transferred, are created in the spool directory. The `uucico` daemon is started, which looks up the name of the first host hop in the `/usr/lib/uucp/Systems` file. The `Systems` file entry identifies a connection device which `uucico` matches to an entry in the `/usr/lib/uucp/Devices` file.

With the connection information in hand, `uucico` attempts to contact the remote system. The connection involves logging in to the `uucp` account on the remote system. Passwords to remote sites are maintained in the local `Systems` file. A successful login starts `uucico` on the remote system. The two `uucico` daemons communicate as a master-slave pair. If permitted by the remote system, the local `uucico` daemon transfers any files destined for the remote site. The remote site, if permitted, may use the connection to transfer files destined for the local site. The connection is dropped once transfers are complete.

In the event that a connection could not be established, or transfer was aborted, the transfer request remains in the uucp spool. Periodically, the `uusched` daemon may be spawned by `cron` to attempt to deliver any queued requests.

### 12.2.1 UUCP addressing

UUCP addresses specify each machine name (hop) in the path from the local to the remote destination. The hop path is read from left to right and terminates with the recipient user name. Each name in the path is delimited by an "!".

```
hop1!hop2!hop3!user
daffy!beaver!jeffries
```

## 12.3 UUCP Configuration

UUCP operation requires that connection information for neighboring remote sites is configured into a set of local tables, and that this information is coordinated with these neighboring UUCP sites. The easiest way to coordinate access with the UUCP community is by joining *UUNET*. UUNET is a large UUCP network that provides access to other UUCP sites and gateways to networks like the Internet and Bitnet. A small connection and use charge is required, which provides access to a large number of network services and topology coordination. For more information on UUNET, contact:

UUNET Technologies Inc.,
Falls Church, Virginia
(703) 204-8000

```
uunet!liaison, liaison@uunet.uu.net
uunet!info, info@uunet.uu.net
ftp.uu.net                              Internet Anonymous FTP Site
```

### 12.3.1 UUCP login ID

As indicated in Sec. 12.2, each system participating in the network must supply access to an account for UUCP connection. The AIX BNU installation process creates a `uucp` account with UID 5, GID 5, home directory `/usr/spool/uucppublic`, and login shell

/usr/lib/uucp/uucico. This account is used to schedule UUCP activities on the system.

```
uucp:!:5:5:unix to unix
copy:/usr/spool/uucppublic:/usr/lib/uucp/uucico
```

To reduce the possibility that a remote site could modify local UUCP configuration tables, create nonprivileged accounts for remote access. Each additional account should be a member of the uucp group, GID 5. Notify each of the remote site system administrators concerning the account name and password that they should use when connecting to your system.

### 12.3.2 Host name

Select a host name that identifies your system to the network. If the number of machines in your network is small, the task is trivial. AIX BNU supports hosts names up to eight characters. If you will be connecting to a large network like UUNET, you will need to coordinate the selection of a host name such that it does not collide with other names in the name space. You can query the local host name with the uuname command.

```
# uuname -l
```

### 12.3.3 Directories and permissions

Special attention should be devoted to verifying the command, configuration files, and spool permissions defined for UUCP. BNU makes use of four directories:

| | |
|---|---|
| /usr/bin | User commands |
| /usr/lib/uucp | Configuration files and daemons; symbolic link to /etc/uucp for configuration files, /usr/sbin/uucp for daemons and administrative commands |
| /usr/spool/uucp | Logs and daemon work space |
| /usr/spool/uucppublic | User directories and UUCP home |

All uucp files and directories other than those owned by users in /usr/spool/uucppublic should be owner and group uucp. Special permissions are as follows:

| | | |
|---|---|---|
| /usr/lib/uucp | 0755 | |
| uucp/System | 0400 | Remote sites and passwords |
| uucp/uucico | 4755 | Master UUCP daemon |
| uucp/uusched | 4755 | Schedule daemon |
| uucp/uuxqt | 4755 | Command execution daemon |
| uucp/{cmds,scripts} | 0755 | Support commands |
| uucp/{files} | 0640 | Other configuration files |

| | | |
|---|---|---|
| /usr/spool/uucp/{subdirs} | 0755 | Log and work directories |
| /usr/spool/uucppublic | 0777 | Public access |

Use the `uucheck` command to validate directory ownership and permissions.

```
# uucheck
```

### 12.3.4 Configuration tables

UUCP makes use of five configuration tables: `Systems`, `Devices`, `Permissions`, `Dialers`, and `Dialcodes`. You can build a functioning UUCP system by modifying the first three and accepting the defaults from the `Dialers` table. The tables may be edited manually or through the use of the `/usr/lib/uucp/uucpadm` command. `uucpadm` is a menu-driven utility that allows you to configure table stanzas similar to SMIT (see Fig. 12.1).

```
# /usr/lib/uucp/uucpadm
```

*Configuration tables:*

| | |
|---|---|
| Systems | Who you will talk to |
| Devices | What interfaces are available for connections |
| Permissions | Permissions supported for each remote system |
| Dialers | Modem handshaking and negotiation |
| Dialcodes | Phone numbers |

#### 12.3.4.1 **/usr/lib/uucp/Systems.**

The Systems table defines who you will talk to. Because the Systems file contains passwords for remote systems, special care must be taken to make certain that it is not accessible by unauthorized users. Each remote system is represented by a stanza that defines:

- System name
- Times when connections are allowed
- Link type

```
            Uucpadm Options:

0) Return to this menu
1) Add/Change UUCP Devices
2) Add/Change UUCP Permissions File
3) Add/Change UUCP Systems
4) Add/Change UUCP Poll File
5) Add/Change UUCP Dialcodes
6) Exit
?) Help

Selection:
```

**Figure 12.1** `uucpadm` panel.

- Link speed
- Phone number
- Login handshaking, user name, and password

*System names* may be represented more than once. Additional entries represent alternate communication links. When a connection is requested, `uucico` will try each entry in turn, attempting to establish the connection.

The *Times* field represents the days of the week and the 24-hour clock representation of the times when connections are supported. Inversely, time intervals outside those represented inhibit connection attempts. Weekdays are represented with the following character codes: `Mo`, `Tu`, `We`, `Th`, `Fr`, `Sa`, `Su`, `Wk`, and `Any`. A connection retry interval in minutes may be specified following the time intervals separated by a ";". Default retry time is five minutes.

*Example time fields:*

| | |
|---|---|
| `Wk2300-0800,SaSu` | Weekdays between 11 PM and 8 AM, any time on Saturday and Sunday |
| `Any` | Access allowed any time |
| `Wk0800-1700;5` | Weekdays from 8 AM to 5 PM with a five-minute retry interval |

The *Type* field represents any device type identified in the `Devices` file and a conversation protocol. The default protocol is `g`. (Refer to Table 12.1.)

*Device types:*

| | |
|---|---|
| ACU | Modem |
| Direct | Direct serial link |
| TCP | TCP/IP connection |

The `Class` field defines the line speed in bits per second. If the line supports any line speed, use the keyword `Any`.

The `Phone` field specifies the full phone number for a dial-up connection. If the entry represents a prefix number that is used in multiple entries, an alphabetic abbreviation may be substituted which represents an entry in the `Dialcodes` file.

**TABLE 12.1 Conversation Protocol**

| | |
|---|---|
| `g` | Used for modem connections. Provides packetizing and checksum functions. |
| `t` | Assumes error-free channel. No packetizing or checksums. |
| `e` | Use for direct BNU connections. Not reliable for modem connections. |

*Example Dialcodes prefix:*

`local5648` "local" Dialcodes 9 = 354

The `Login` field is a short handshaking script that represents the login negotiation for connecting to the remote system. It is a graphic representation of the send and receive character streams that would be used if you were logging in interactively. The remote site sends `login:`. The local site responds with the `user name`. The remote site sends `password:`, and so on. It is sufficient to list only enough of the prompt strings to make them recognizable.

*Example Login script:*

```
"" \r\d\r login:-login: uucp word: Zx&za01
```

## Login Script Special Characters

| | |
|---|---|
| `""` | Expect null string |
| `\N` | Expect null string |
| `EOT` | Send End Of Transmission |
| `BREAK` | Send a BREAK signal |
| `@` | Send a BREAK signal |
| `\K` | Send a BREAK signal |
| `\b` | Backspace |
| `\c` | Suppress new line |
| `\d` | Delay one second |
| `\E` | Start echo checking |
| `\e` | Turn off echo checking |
| `\p` | Pause for .25 to .5 seconds |
| `\n` | New line |
| `\r` | Carriage return |
| `\ooo` | Octal digits |
| `\\` | Backslash |

*Example system entries:*

```
goofy Any ACU 2400 - "" \r\d\r in:-in: uucp word: qrs
venus Any TCP - in:-in: rudy word: 1jx733z
```

**12.3.4.2 `/usr/lib/uucp/Devices`.** The `Devices` file defines the connection device types that are available on the system. They are identified by a `Type` string, followed by `Line`, `Line2`, `Class`, and `Dialer Tokens` (see Table 12.2). Note that the second `Line2` field is a holdover from the old days when modems and dialers were separate devices.

The Type field is commonly:

| | |
|---|---|
| ACU | Modem |
| Direct | Direct connect serial link |
| TCP | TCP/IP connection |

**TABLE 12.2 Devices Fields**

| | |
|---|---|
| Type | Device type identifier |
| Line | Port |
| Line2 | Second port for 801 dialer |
| Class | Line speed |
| Dialer Tokens | Modem identifier |

The Line and Line2 parameters identify the ports used by the connection—for example, tty1. For a TCP connection, use a "-" character as a placeholder.

Class matches the speed parameters specified in the Systems file. It can either be a value representing bits per second or the multispeed parameter Any.

The Dialer Token field represents the name of a modem type listed in the Dialers file. It may be followed by a flag indicating where an associated phone number is located. The \D flag indicates that the phone number is specified in the Systems file. The \T flag specifies the Dialcodes file as the source for the phone number. For TCP/IP connections, use the parameter TCP. For direct connections, specify direct.

*Example* Devices *entries:*

```
ACU tty1 - 1200 hayes \D
Direct tty2 - 9600 direct
TCP -- TCP
```

**12.3.4.3 /usr/lib/uucp/Permissions.** The Permissions file specifies the privileges available to each UUCP login account or machine name. Each entry in the Permissions file specifies the account name, the send/receive permissions, and the commands that are allowed for execution. Be very careful not to include setuid shell scripts as part of the command list. In general, setuid shell scripts are not a good idea anywhere. Note that these permissions do not affect access to non-UUCP login accounts. A user at a remote site may access a non-UUCP login account using ct, cu, or tip and obtain the full set of permissions and command paths available to the account.

Permissions file stanzas are represented as *parameter = value* pairs.

*Permissions parameters:*
Entry:

| | |
|---|---|
| LOGNAME = <LoginID:LoginID ... Options> | UUCP account stanza |
| MACHINE = <MachineName:MachineName ... Options> | System stanza |
| MACHINE = OTHER <Options> | Generic system stanza |

Options:

| | |
|---|---|
| `REQUEST = <yes/no>` | Request to transfer |
| `SENDFILES = <yes/no>` | File transfer allowed |
| `READ = <PathName:PathName...>` | Read paths |
| `NOREAD = <PathName:PathName...>` | Read exception paths |
| `WRITE = <PathName:PathName...>` | Write paths |
| `NOWRITE = <PathName:PathName...>` | Write exception paths |
| `COMMANDS = <Command:Command:...>` | Commands allowed |
| `COMMANDS = ALL` | All commands allowed |
| `VALIDATE = <Name:Name>` | Used with `COMMANDS = ALL` |
| `CALLBACK = <yes/no>` | Callback required |

Once configured, you can validate the format of the `Permissions` file using the `uucheck` command.

```
# uucheck
```

*Example* `Permissions` *Entry:*

```
LOGNAME = vase          \
VALIDATE = jose         \
REQUEST = yes           \
SENDFILES = yes         \
READ = /u1/jose         \
WRITE = /u1/jose        \
COMMANDS = ls:who

MACHINE = goofy         \
REQUEST = yes           \
SENDFILES = yes         \
COMMANDS = ALL
```

UUCP maintains a log of connection attempts by sites not listed in the `Permissions` file. Unauthorized connection attempts are logged by the `remote.unknown` script in the `/usr/spool/uucp/.Admin/Foreign` file.

**12.3.4.4 `/usr/lib/uucp/Dialers`.** In most cases, you can accept the default `Dialers` file as distributed with AIX BNU. The `Dialers` file defines the attributes and command strings required to initialize various modem types. Each modem entry in the file is represented by a *name, dial tone and wait characteristics,* and *initialization and connection sequence.* Add entries to this file when you are using a modem type that is not listed. (Refer to Table 12.3.)

*Default* `Dialers` *File:*

```
# @(#)71 1.3 com/cmd/uucp/Dialers, bos, bos320 6/15/90 23:57:09
#
# COMPONENT_NAME: UUCP Dialers
#
# FUNCTIONS:
#
```

**TABLE 12.3 Dialers Special Characters**

| | |
|---|---|
| = | Wait for dial tone |
| - | Pause |
| "" | Null no wait |
| \d | Delay one second |
| \r | Carriage return |
| \c | New line |
| \p | Pause .25 to .5 seconds |
| \T | Send telephone number |

```
# ORIGINS: 10 27 3
#
# (C) COPYRIGHT International Business Machines Corp. 1985, 1989
# All Rights Reserved
# Licensed Materials - Property of IBM
#
# US Government Users Restricted Rights - Use, duplication or
# disclosure restricted by GSA ADP Schedule Contract with IBM Corp.
#
#
#
# Execute /usr/lib/uucp/uucpadm for on-line uucp configuration help.
hayes       =,-,    "" \dAT\r\c OK \pATDT\T\r\c CONNECT
penril      =W-P    "" \d > s\p9\c )-W\p\r\ds\p9\c-) y\c : \E\DP > 9\c
OK
ventel      =&-%    "" \r\p \r\p-\r\p-$ <K\D%%\r>\c ONLINE!
rixon       =&-%    "" \r\p \r\p-\r\p-$ <K\D%%\r>\c ONLINE!
vadic       =K-K    "" \005\p *-\005\p-*\005\p-* D\p BER? \E\D\e \r\c
LINE
micom       ""      "" \s\c NAME? \D\r\c GO
#
TCP
direct
```

**12.3.4.5 `/usr/lib/uucp/Dialcodes`.** The `Dialcodes` file is basically a phone prefix directory for UUCP. Each prefix number is represented by an alphabetic identifier. The identifiers are used as shorthand for phone numbers in the `Systems` file. Dial tone, " = ," and pause, "-" characters may be used as required in the prefix number.

*Dialcodes format and example:*

| Identifier | Prefix number |
|---|---|
| local | 9 = 356 |
| oregon | 9–1503 |

## 12.4 UUCP Daemons

AIX BNU support is managed by four daemons:

| | |
|---|---|
| `uucico` | Master daemon responsible for connection and transfer control |
| `uusched` | Schedules UUCP requests |
| `uuxqt` | Execute command requests from remote sites |
| `uucpd` | Support UUCP over TCP/IP |

The UUCP master daemon, uucico, establishes connections and transfers files created by the uucp and uux commands. Transfer requests are spooled to the /usr/spool/uucp/<SystemName> directory. uucico records transfer activities and status to the /usr/spool/uucp/.Log/uucico file. The uucico daemon is invoked by uucp, uux, and uusched. It can also be invoked from the command line to debug connections.

The uusched daemon is started periodically by cron using the uudemon.hour command. uusched locates files queued in the /usr/spool/uucp/<SystemName> directory and invokes uucico to attempt delivery. Each request type is identified by a prefix character, C.* (command files), D.* (data files), and E.* (execute files).

uuxqt is invoked periodically like uusched by cron. It scans the /usr/spool/uucp/<SystemName> directory for execution requests from remote systems. The remote execution requests are identified by the X.* prefix.

UUCP over TCP/IP connections are established by the uucpd daemon. uucpd runs as a subserver invoked by inetd. The server uses reserved port number 540 which must be configured in /etc/services.

/etc/services uucpd entry:

```
uucp      540/tcp      uucpd
```

## 12.5 Housekeeping and Logs

UUCP requires periodic housekeeping to ensure a smooth-running facility. The chores include periodically running uusched and uuxqt to handle queued requests and clean up log and work files. These types of activities are handled by cron. The following uucp crontab is supplied as part of the default AIX BNU configuration and can be enabled to take care of UUCP housekeeping chores. To enable cron support, edit the crontab and remove the comments from the schedule lines. Adjust the times per your environment.

/usr/spool/cron/crontabs/uucp:

```
#
# UUCP Crontab - Housekeeping Chores.
#
20,50 * * * * /bin/bsh -c "/usr/lib/uucp/uudemon.poll > /dev/null"
25,55 * * * * /bin/bsh -c "/usr/lib/uucp/uudemon.hour > /dev/null"
45 23 * * * /bin/bsh -c "/usr/lib/uucp/uudemon.cleanu > /dev/null"
48 8,12,16 * * * /bin/bsh -c "/usr/lib/uucp/uudemon.admin > /dev/null"
```

Like most other AIX systems, BNU creates a number of log files that periodically need to be closed and archived. Log files are compacted and cycled by the uudemon.cleanu command. The uudemon.cleanu utility is configured in the default uucp crontab.

## 12.6 Hardware

UUCP connections are supported over serial links and TCP/IP as described in the previous sections. Refer to Chap. 9 and Chap. 11 for detailed descriptions concerning serial and TCP/IP-based interfaces.

## 12.7 UUCP Commands

It's helpful to understand the command set that makes up a service. The combination of user and administrator commands can provide insights into how the service can be used and enhanced.

| | |
|---|---|
| Cvt | Convert non-BNU UUCP files to BNU |
| uucheck | Validate Permissions file |
| uuname | List host names from Systems file |
| uucpadm | Tailor configuration files |
| uuclean | Clean spool directories |
| uucleanup | Clean spool directories |
| uukick | Establish connection with debug support |
| uulog | Display log information |
| uupoll | Poll a remote site |
| uuq | Display scheduled job queue |
| uusnap | Display status |
| uustat | Display statistics |
| uutry | Establish a debug connection overriding retry limits |
| uucp | Transfer a file to a remote site |
| uux | Execute a command on a remote site |
| uuencode | Encode a binary file for text transfer |
| uudecode | Decode a uu-encoded file |
| ct,cu,tip | Establish connection to a remote site |
| uusend | Send a file to a remote site |
| uuto | Copy a file to a remote site |

## 12.8 Troubleshooting

Testing a new or problem connection can be done using uucico or uutry. The uucico debug flag -x<num> will display a connection trace. You control the verbosity of the trace by specifying a <num> value from 1 to 9.

```
# uucico -r1 -x9 -sgoofy
conn(goofy)
Device type goofy wanted
getto ret 6
expect: ("")
got it sendthem (^MDELAY^M)
expect: (login:)
timed out
Call Failed: LOGIN FAILED
conversation complete: Status FAILED
```

You can use this feedback to validate your entry in the `Systems` file for the particular site. You can also use a simple connection command like `cu` to validate that your link is operational. See Chap. 9 for information on testing serial links.

Use the `uucheck` command to validate file permissions and configurations defined in the `Permissions` file. Use `uulog` to display connection histories.

## 12.9 InfoExplorer Keywords

| | |
|---|---|
| UUCP | /usr/lib/uucp/Permissions |
| uucico | /usr/lib/uucp/Dialers |
| /usr/lib/uucp/Systems | /usr/lib/uucp/Dialcodes |
| /usr/lib/uucp/Devices | uucp |
| uusched | uux |
| cron | uuxqt |
| /usr/spool/uucppublic | uucpd |
| /usr/lib/uucp/uucico | inetd |
| uuname | uutry |
| uucheck | cu |
| uucpadm | |

## 12.10 QwikInfo

### UUCP

*Addressing:*

| | |
|---|---|
| host1!host2!user | UUCP store-and-forward hop addressing format |

*Tables:*

| | |
|---|---|
| /usr/lib/uucp | Configurations files |
| /usr/spool/uucppublic | Public spool directory |
| /usr/spool/uucp | Logs and work space |
| /usr/lib/uucp/System | Host table |
| /usr/lib/uucp/Devices | Network interfaces |
| /usr/lib/uucp/Dialcodes | Phone numbers |
| /usr/lib/uucp/Dialers | Modem control and logon handshaking |
| /usr/lib/uucp/Permissions | UUCP login privileges |

*Daemons:*

| | |
|---|---|
| uucico | Master UUCP daemon |

| | |
|---|---|
| `uusched` | UUCP scheduler daemon |
| `uuxqt` | Execute a command |
| `uucpadm` | UUCP configuration tool |
| `uucpd` | UUCP over TCP |

*Commands:*
See Sec. 12.7.
*UUNET:*

UUNET Technologies Inc,
Falls Church, Virginia
(703) 204-8000
uunet!liaison, liaison@uunet.uu.net
uunet!info, info@uunet.uu.net
ftp.uu.net Internet Anonymous FTP Site

Chapter

# 13

# Network File System

## 13.1 Virtual File System

Distributed file systems are made possible by generalizing UNIX file system data structures to provide a common interface to various underlying file system architectures. This open interface is called a *virtual file system* (VFS). Early work by Bell Labs used this VFS abstraction to develop their *remote file system.* Later on Sun Microsystems decided to move the interface abstraction down to the file level to better facilitate a common operation interface. File system architectures supported by VFS are represented in the `/etc/vfs` file.

```
/etc/vfs
cdrfs   5   none                       none
jfs     3   none                       /sbin/helpers/v3fshelper
nfs     2   /sbin/helpers/nfsmnthelp   none                       remote
```

Incore VFS structures allow the kernel to operate on various local file system architectures. VFS structures also provide a switch point for determining local or remote file system operations. The general mount structure for a virtual file system contains an array of operation types supported on the underlying file system. This array is called `vsops`. Likewise, a VFS `inode` abstraction called `vnodes` contains an array of `inode` operation types called `vnodeops`. A `gnode` structure is used to map `inodes` and `vnodes`.

## 13.2 Network File System

To support remote file system operations, a facility is required to trap and reroute file system operations from one machine to another. This must include support for file system operations between machines with different architectures and operating systems. A method is needed to map data formats from one architecture to another. Sun developed a *remote procedure call* (RPC) mechanism which allows a remote

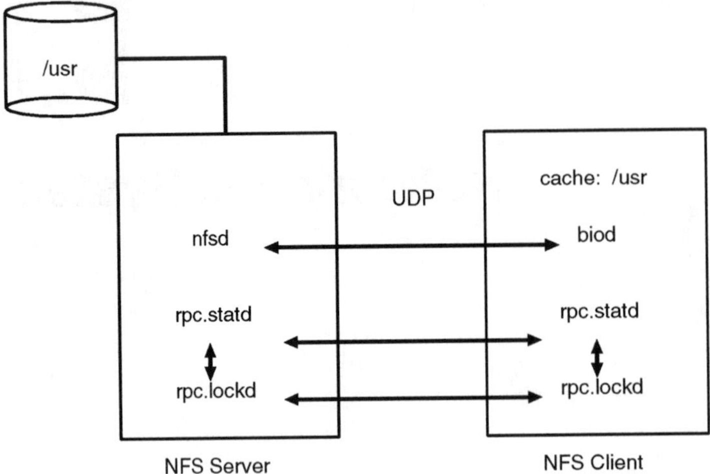


**Figure 13.1** NFS server-to-client interface.

machine to execute functions on behalf of the local system and return the results to the originating process. Sun also provided an *external data representation* (XDR) language that is used to communicate data formats between machines. These specifications along with VFS semantics became the basis of Sun's *Network File System* (NFS). NFS is based on a client/server architecture that enables applications to seamlessly interoperate with files and directories shared between networked machines without regard to their locale (see Fig. 13.1). Sun later placed this architecture in the public domain and it became a de facto standard for distributed file systems.

## 13.3 Starting NFS

NFS is managed as a subsystem by the AIX `srcmstr`. Thus, NFS subserver daemons may be started or stopped as a group, using the `startsrc` and `stopsrc` commands. NFS operation may also be managed from the SMIT `nfs` submenus.

```
# startsrc -g nfs        Start NFS subsystem
# stopsrc -g nfs         Stop NFS subsystem
```

NFS start-up options and daemons are configured in the `/etc/rc.nfs` script. The script begins by starting the NFS block I/O `biod` daemons. If the `/etc/exports` file exists, it is exported using `exportfs -a`, followed by `nfsd` and `rpc.mountd` start-up. The script finishes up by starting the `rpc.statd` and `rpc.lockd` daemons. The `/etc/rc.nfs` script also contains entries for starting NIS and HANFS subsystems and subservers.

NFS may be made the default remote file system type by defining it as the `defaultvfs` in `/etc/vfs`. Uncomment the following lines in the `/etc/vfs` table.

```
%defaultvfs jfs nfs
nfs 2 /etc/helpers/nfsmnthelp none remote
```

## 13.4 NFS Server

The NFS server is designed as a stateless system. This eliminates the need to support recovery operations in the event of a server or client failure. It turns out that this is not entirely true. NFS uses UDP as a transport, and we all know that UDP does not guarantee packet delivery or packet order. To overcome the deficiencies of UDP, NFS servers must maintain a volatile cache of recent RCP handshaking state to avoid duplicate, out-of-order, or lost I/O operation packets. This also means that the server must keep track of who it is talking to. To keep the `nfsd` daemon stateless, additional daemons are used to track machine connections, RPC status, and file locks. IBM's *High Availability Network File System* (HANFS) makes use of the volatile cache state and lock daemon information to support backup NFS servers.

To ensure file integrity, NFS servers use a *write-through* cache, forcing file updates immediately to disk. Data integrity is maintained at the sake of performance. Asynchronous write support is available in some architectures to improve read performance when data integrity is not an issue.

### 13.4.1 NFS server daemons

NFS servers rely on a number of daemons to manage distributed file system services. I/O requests from multiple clients are multiplexed through a configurable number of `nfsd` and `biod` daemons. The `nfsd` daemons manage file I/O operations and the `biod` daemons control block I/O services. The actual number of `nfsd` and `biod` daemons required is based on the client load the server is expected to support. The default configuration starts eight `nfsd` daemons and six `biod` daemons.

Being that NFS is RPC-based, the NFS servers must register themselves with the `portmap` daemon. The `portmap` daemon maintains the available set of RPC applications on a particular machine. Each application is represented as a tuple of application name, version, and port number. Servers register their application data with the `portmap` daemon. Client applications query the `portmap` daemon to learn the port number associated with a known server application name and version. `portmap` listens to a well-known port number listed in /etc/services, thus avoiding the "chicken and egg" problem of determining what portmap's port number is.

The rpc.mountd daemon is used by the server to manage and track client mount requests. Recent RPC operations between clients and servers are cached by the rpc.statd daemon. SYSV advisory file and record locking is supported by the server's rpc.lockd daemon.

*NFS server daemons:*

| | |
|---|---|
| nfsd | NFS server daemon |
| biod | NFS block I/O daemon |
| portmap | RPC program-to-port manager |
| rpc.mountd | NFS mount manager |
| rpc.statd | RPC status manager |
| rpc.lockd | NFS lock manager |

### 13.4.2 Exporting server file systems

Each file system or directory available for remote mounting is identified by an entry in the server's /etc/exports file. Along with the directory path name, the /etc/exports entry controls which machine names are allowed root permissions and write access. If NFS root access is not enabled for a remote NFS client, the root UID of the server is mapped to a default UID of -2 (4294967294), user name *nobody*. This restricts access against the superuser UID on a remote machine.

The /etc/exports is a flat ASCII text file which may be edited or maintained via the SMIT mknfsexp fast path (see Fig. 13.2). Updates to the /etc/exports file must be made known to the server daemons. Update notification is achieved by invoking the /usr/sbin/exportfs command.

```
                     Add a Directory to Exports List

Type or select values in entry fields.
Press Enter AFTER making all desired changes.

                                                         [Entry Fields]
* PATHNAME of directory to export                       []               /
* MODE to export directory                              read-write       +
HOSTNAME list. If exported read-mostly                  []
Anonymous UID                                           [-2]
HOSTS allowed root access                               []
HOSTS & NETGROUPS allowed client access                 []
Use SECURE option?                                      no               +
* EXPORT directory now, system restart or both          both             +
PATHNAME of Exports file if using HA-NFS                []

F1 = Help         F2 = Refresh      F3 = Cancel       F4 = List
F5 = Undo         F6 = Command      F7 = Edit         F8 = Image
F9 = Shell        F10 = Exit        Enter = Do
```

**Figure 13.2** SMIT NFS exports panel.

*Example* /etc/exports:

```
/usr/lpp/info/En_US -ro,access = alph,lisa
/home -rw,root = alph,access = alph,lisa,armada
# /usr/sbin/exportfs -a
# smit mknfsexp
```

## 13.5 NFS Clients

To improve performance, the NFS clients implement clientside data caching. This requires that some level of cache consistency be maintained between multiple NFS clients and the server. A time stamp expiration mechanism is used to allow the clients to update cache information when it becomes stale.

Each client runs multiple copies of the NFS biod block I/O daemon. Clients also run the portmap daemon. portmap is queried to identify RPC services and bind port connections to NFS servers.

NFS RPC mechanisms allow clients to block applications in the event of a server failure. I/O operations continue when access to the server is restored. A retry limit is provided such that client applications do not wait forever in the case of long-term server failures. Sun also added hard and soft mount options so that a client could be interrupted when server access is blocked.

*NFS client daemons:*

| | |
|---|---|
| biod | NFS block I/O daemon |
| portmap | RPC program-to-port manager |

### 13.5.1 Importing file systems

Client NFS file system definitions are configured as stanzas in the /etc/filesystems file. The stanza is similar to a local file system definition with the addition of the remote owning site name listed in the nodename = parameter. The dev = parameter defines the directory path on the remote machine to be mounted. /etc/filesystems entries may be edited directly or managed using the SMIT mknfsmnt fast path (see Fig. 13.3).

```
# smit mknfsmnt
```

*Example* /etc/filesystems *NFS stanza:*

```
/usr/spool/news/nn/NN:
dev      = /news/nn/NN
vfs      = nfs
nodename = news
mount    = true
type     = nfs
options  = ro,bg,soft,intr,nosuid
account  = false
```

```
Add a File System for Mounting

Type or select values in entry fields.
Press Enter AFTER making all desired changes.

                                                                        [Entry Fields]
[TOP]
* PATHNAME of mount point                                                []          /
* PATHNAME of remote directory                                           []
* HOST where remote directory resides                                    []
Mount type NAME                                                          []
* Use SECURE mount option?                                               no          +
* MOUNT now, add entry to /etc/filesystems or both?                      now         +
* /etc/filesystems entry will mount the directory on system RESTART.     no          +
* MODE for this NFS file system                                          read-write  +
* ATTEMPT mount in background or foreground                              background  +
NUMBER of times to attempt mount                                         []          #
Buffer SIZE for read                                                     []          #
Buffer SIZE for writes                                                   []          #
NFS TIMEOUT. In tenths of a second                                       []          #
Buffer SIZE for writes                                                   []          #
NFS TIMEOUT. In tenths of a second                                       []          #
Internet port NUMBER for server                                          []          #
* Mount file system soft or hard                                         hard        +
Allow keyboard INTERRUPTS on hard mounts?                                yes         +
Minimum TIME, in seconds, for holding attribute cache after file modification        [3]    #
Maximum TIME, in seconds, for holding attribute cache after file modification        [60]   #
Minimum TIME, in seconds, for holding attribute cache after directory modification   [30]   #
Maximum TIME, in seconds, for holding attribute cache after directory modification   [60]   #
Minimum & Maximum TIME, in seconds, for holding attribute cache after any modification []   #
The Maximum NUMBER of biod daemons allowed to work on this file system   [6]         #
* Allow execution of SUID and sgid programs in this file system?         yes         +
* Allow DEVICE access via this mount?                                    yes         +
* Server supports long DEVICE NUMBERS?                                   yes         +

F1 = Help        F2 = Refresh       F3 = Cancel       F4 = List
F5 = Undo        F6 = Command       F7 = Edit         F8 = Image
F9 = Shell       F10 = Exit         Enter = Do
```

**Figure 13.3** SMIT NFS mount panel.

The `type = nfs` parameter may be added to the stanza definitions to identify NFS file systems as a group. This way they can be mounted or unmounted as a group using the `-t` option of the `mount` and `umount` commands.

```
# mount -t nfs
# umount -t nfs
```

## 13.6 Secure NFS

NFS suffers from a few security holes. These security problems are primarily due to collisions in the UID and GID name space, and the lack of authentication in the RPC. For example, UID 1234 might be user *sleepy* on one machine and user *tulip* on another. If the file system with sleepy's home directory is NFS-mounted on tulip's machine, then tulip will have owner permissions over sleepy's files.

To solve these problems, Sun implemented a distributed file management and authentication system called *Yellow Pages* (YP) or

*Network Information System* (NIS). AIX provides secure NFS services using the Sun YP management tools. Since the YP prefix is used for most NIS commands and daemons, I'll use YP when referring to secure NFS tools in the following sections. Yellow Pages is the older and probably better-known terminology.

AIX also supports *access control lists* (ACL) over NFS. This feature is an add-on function to the RPC and does not alter NFS protocol. AIX ACL support is only available to AIX V3 NFS clients.

### 13.6.1 Yellow Pages

The Yellow Pages system uses a master server, and one or more slave servers, to distribute a common set of system configuration files to a collection of client machines under the jurisdiction of the *YP domain.* Each file in the distribution set is converted into ndbm database format and stored as a *YP map* file in the server /etc/yp/<DomainName directory. YP maps are created from text files using the makedbm command. The maps are then distributed using the yppush command. A common ndbm Makefile, /etc/yp/Makefile, is used to create YP maps. Collectively the YP map files make up the YP database as created by the ypmake command. A YP database may be transferred to another domain using the ypxfr command.

### 13.6.2 YP name space

The YP domain name and the set of participating machine names are defined using the /bin/domainname command. The domain defines the area of administrative control available to the servers.

```
# /bin/domainname <DomainName>
```

*YP Netgroups* define collections of machines that are identified for special configuration and administration requirements. A netgroup does not necessarily correspond to a particular domain. It might be that a subset of machines in the domain are configured with a different /etc/hosts.equiv file from the rest of the domain. The netgroup definition file, /etc/netgroups, identifies each *netgroup name* followed by participant tuples. Each tuple is enclosed in parentheses and identifies the *machine, user,* and *domain* name of the netgroup participant.

/etc/netgroups *format:*

```
netgroupname1     (host,user,domain) (host,user,domain) ...
netgroupname2     (host,user,domain) (host,user,domain) ...
```

Users within domains and groups are identified by a *net name.* A net name is a concatenation of the *operating system name, user name,* and *Internet domain name.* Net names are maintained in the /etc/yp/<DomainName>/netid.byname YP map.

*Net name format and example:*

```
Operating System Name . User Name @ Domain Name
unix.janice@fido.net
```

Net names incorporate the primary host name entry from the /etc/hosts table. Sites that use domain name service must also have /etc/hosts tables available which match name service entries.

### 13.6.3 YP file classes

The YP versions of the distribution files for the domain use the same format as their local system counterparts. What differs is how they are used. Three classes of files govern the behavior of client machines in the YP domain: *local, global,* and *optional.* Local files override YP copies of the same information. For example the local /etc/passwd file takes precedence over /etc/yp/yppasswd. Global files override their local counterparts. Examples would include files like /etc /hosts and /etc/networks. Optional files override local copies if the local copy contains a netgroup identifier or the magic YP "+" character. The "+" prefix to a table entry indicates that the YP-equivalent information should be used.

All the distribution files may be updated on the server, then pushed to the slave servers and clients. Local client updates are possible in some instances through the use of YP update commands. For example, the YP version of the passwd file, yppasswd, can update global password information if the user changes the password using the yppasswd command.

### 13.6.4 YP servers and clients

To create a YP master server, YP slave server, or YP client, invoke the SMIT fast paths mkmaster, mkslave, or mkclient, respectively. Servers may be initialized by invoking ypinit from the command line. (See Fig.13.4.)

| | | |
|---|---|---|
| `# smit mkmaster` | `# ypinit - m` | Initialize a master |
| `# smit mkmaster` | `# ypinit - s` | Initialize a slave |
| `# smit mkclient` | | Initialize a client |

### 13.6.5 Public key authentication

NFS authentication is implemented through the use of *DES Public Key* services. Users in the YP domain must have their own public and private encryption key entries in the /etc/publickey file. The system administrator defines new user entries in the file via the newkey command. Users update their public keys using the chkey

```
                Configure this Host as a NIS Master Server

Type or select values in entry fields.
Press Enter AFTER making all desired changes.

                                                              [Entry Fields]
HOSTS that will be slave servers                                []
* Can existing MAPS for the domain be overwritten?              yes        +
* EXIT on errors, when creating master server?                  yes        +
* START the yppasswdd daemon?                                   no         +
* START the ypupdated daemon?                                   no         +
* START the ypbind daemon?                                      yes        +
* START the master server now, at system restart, or both?      both       +

F1 = Help          F2 = Refresh       F3 = Cancel       F4 = List
F5 = Undo          F6 = Command       F7 = Edit         F8 = Image
F9 = Shell         F10 = Exit         Enter = Do
```

**Figure 13.4** SMIT NIS master server panel.

command. The `/etc/publickey` file is then YP mapped to `/etc/yp/publickey.byname`. Users' entries are identified in the files by their net names.

| | |
|---|---|
| `# newkey -u username` | Create user public key entry |
| `# newkey -h hostname` | Create root public key entry |
| `# cd /etc/yp; make publickey` | Build YP publickey.byname |

The `keyserv` daemon encrypts the public keys and stores them as private keys in the `/etc/keystore` file. A separate file, `/etc/.rootkey`, is used to hold the superuser private key. This avoids problems when private keys are wiped clean during a system reboot following a crash. To initialize the `keyserv` server, invoke the SMIT `mkkeyserv` fast path or the `/usr/etc/yp/mkkeyserv` command.

```
# smit mkkeyserv
# /usr/etc/yp/mkkeyserv -B
```

The `keylogin` command is used to decrypt a user's secret key, which is stored by the `keyserv` server for secure RPC operations. `keylogin` can be added to the default system login profile. A `keyserv` entry is required to access file systems flagged with the `-secure` option in `/etc/exports` and `/etc/filesystems`. Note that this mechanism requires synchronized clocks between participating machines. System time is used to create and expire keys stored in the server. The default secure NFS expiration is 30 minutes.

### 13.6.6 Starting YP (NIS) services

Like NFS, YP is managed as a subsystem under AIX. YP daemons are started using the SRC `startsrc` and `stopsrc` commands. The

/etc/rc.nfs script contains code to start up YP services before bringing up NFS.

```
# startsrc -g yp
# stopsrc -g yp
```

*YP daemons:*

| | |
|---|---|
| ypserv | YP server daemon |
| ypbind | YP server binding manager |
| yppasswdd | YP passwd update daemon |
| ypupdated | YP map update invoked by inetd |
| keyserv | Public key server daemon |
| portmap | RPC program-to-port manager |

### 13.6.7 Automounter

The automount daemon can be run in a large YP network to simplify NFS file system access. The automount daemon will automatically mount a file system whenever a file or directory in the file system is opened. Files and directories associated with an automount file system are kept in a YP map. Automount forks child processes that appear as NFS clients which monitor file systems based on the information in the maps. The daemons umount file systems that have not been accessed in the last five minutes. The master automount map file is auto.master.

| | |
|---|---|
| /usr/sbin/automount | Automount daemon |

## 13.7 Troubleshooting

Complex distributed services like NFS and NIS present a real debugging puzzle when things run amuck! Based on the symptoms and error messages associated with the problem, begin examining each component of the system. Refer to Chap. 12 for details on debugging network problems.

Begin troubleshooting problems by listing and verifying the current set of client mounts known to the server. The client mount list is recorded in /etc/rmtab and displayed using the showmount command.

```
# showmount -a
asimov:/usr/local/gnu
asimov:/usr/local/bin
asimov:/usr/local/lib
softy:/n0
softy:/n1
```

The showmount command can also be used to verify the list of exported directories as recorded in the /etc/xtab file. This information should match up with the entries in /etc/exports. If the data doesn't match, invoke exportfs -a to refresh /etc/xtab.

```
# showmount -e
/usr/lpp/info/En_US        alph, lisa
/n1                        softy
/n0                        softy
/usr/local/gnu             asimov
/usr/local/lib             asimov
/usr/local/bin             asimov
```

NFS I/O statistics can be reset and displayed using the nfsstat command. Statistics include the number and success of RPC and NFS calls for both servers and clients.

```
# /usr/sbin/nfsstat
```

*Server rpc:*

```
calls        badcalls     nullrecv     badlen     xdrcall
10341661     0            0            0          0
```

*Server nfs:*

```
calls    badcalls
8492917 0
null     getattr   setattr    root       lookup       readlink read
0 0%     821190 9% 23522 0%   0 0%       4641837 54% 2884 0%  932979  10%
wrcache  write     create     remove     rename       link     symlink
0 0%     608394 7% 15528 0%   13485 0%   4400 0%      940 0%   2059 0%
mkdir    rmdir     readdir    fsstat
832 0%   592 0%    996294 11% 427981 5%
```

*Client rpc:*

```
calls       badcalls      retrans     badxid      timeout     wait      newcred
329686      13            1255        73          1249        0         0
```

*Client nfs:*

```
calls      badcalls     nclget       nclsleep
304494     7            304494       0
null       getattr      setattr      root        lookup      readlink   read
0 0%       55533 18%    54 0%        0 0%        96869 31%   213 0%     100873 33%
wrcache    write        create       remove      rename      link       symlink
0 0%       53 0%        36 0%        27 0%       19 0%       0 0%       9 0%
mkdir      rmdir        readdir      fsstat
2 0%       0 0%         35008 11%    15798 5%
```

RPC errors like Application Not Registered are related to the portmap daemon. Check to see that the portmap daemon is running on both the local and remote system. You can also verify the application, version, protocol, and port data maintained by local and remote portmap daemons using the rpcinfo command.

```
# rpcinfo -p daffy

program     vers      proto      port
100000      2         tcp        111       portmapper
100000      2         udp        111       portmapper
100001      1         udp        1060      rstatd
100001      2         udp        1060      rstatd
100001      3         udp        1060      rstatd
100012      1         udp        1061      sprayd
100003      2         udp        2049      nfs
100005      1         udp        810       mountd
100005      1         tcp        812       mountd
100024      1         udp        824       status
100024      1         tcp        826       status
300082      1         udp        829
300082      1         tcp        831
100021      1         tcp        906       nlockmgr
100021      1         udp        908       nlockmgr
100021      3         tcp        911       nlockmgr
100021      3         udp        913       nlockmgr
100020      1         udp        916       llockmgr
100020      1         tcp        918       llockmgr
100021      2         tcp        921       nlockmgr
300049      1         udp        681
300049      1         tcp        683
```

Verify that the `srcmstr` daemon is aware of the current NFS and NIS subsystems and subservers states. Erratic behavior will occur if the SRC environment is out of sorts. Subsystem and subserver states can be displayed using the `lssrc` command.

```
# lssrc -g nfs
```

| Subsystem | Group | PID | Status |
|---|---|---|---|
| biod | nfs | 8417 | active |
| nfsd | nfs | 13324 | active |
| rpc.mountd | nfs | 15908 | active |
| rpc.statd | nfs | 12851 | active |
| rpc.lockd | nfs | 18499 | active |

Since small deltas in client/server response times can add up quickly for large NFS environments, you may want to closely monitor traffic between systems. You can easily collect statistics with network sniffers or using a public domain package like `nfswatch`.

## 13.8 Highly Available NFS Servers

Those of you who have been dealing with IBM for any number of years have surely heard of *Reliability, Availability, and Serviceability* (RAS). To remain competitive in the glass-house environments, UNIX must provide the same 7 by 24 availability that has been the hallmark of operating systems like MVS. The proliferation of X stations and diskless workstations in departmental computing environments means that there are a whole lot of folks out there who are depending on those RS/6000 servers to be ready whenever they are.

Like anyone else, I hate any system interruptions. Whenever a system or service drops out of sight, I want that service back as quickly as possible. The sooner it is back up and running, the happier I am going to be. A *highly available* system should be able to survive a single point of failure and impose only the minimum required delay while service recovery transitions occur.

### 13.8.1 High Availability Network File System/6000

One of the problems with NFS is that when the NFS server goes down, so do all your applications and diskless workstations that were depending on the servers' file systems. High Availability Network File System/6000 (HANFS) provides an extension to standard NFS services that allows a second RS/6000 to act as a backup NFS server should the primary NFS server fail. HANFS can be configured such that each RS/6000 may be acting as primary NFS servers for distinct file systems while acting as backup servers for the other, the primary requirement being that they share physical connections to external SCSI disks and additional network adapters (see Fig. 13.5). Note that the shared disks volume groups are only online to the primary NFS server, and that internal disks are not supported.

HANFS makes use of the server's RPC cache information along with the *journaled file system* (JFS) logs to enable NFS server recovery on the backup system. The primary server's NFS RPC cache information is recorded in the JFS logs and is read by the backup server to reconstruct the cache.

During normal operation, the HANFS servers periodically exchange *alive messages*. When the primary NFS server fails, the backup server takes over the volume groups and checks their consistency. It rebuilds the duplicate cache from the information stored in the JFS logs and begins impersonating the failed server's network IP address. NFS locks are then resynchronized by stopping the

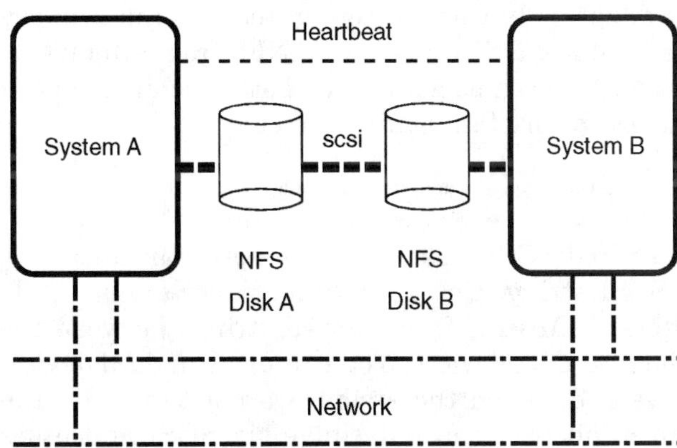


**Figure 13.5** HANFS interface diagram.

rpc.lockd daemon from accepting new locks while the rpc.statd daemon requests all NFS clients to reclaim their locks. After a grace period, the rpc.lockd daemon begins to accept new lock requests. Other than the notification to reclaim file system locks, remote NFS clients only experience a short delay while server recovery procedures are completed. Recovery time after a server failure is somewhere in the neighborhood of 30 to 300 seconds.

HANFS also supports the automatic reintegration of the primary server once the problem failure has been rectified and the system is back on line. Basically the procedure described in the previous paragraph is reversed and the servers go back to doing their old jobs. Note that no changes to standard NFS client software is required to make use of HANFS services. HANFS will work fine with your Sun, HP, DEC, and other standard (grain of salt here) NFS clients and servers.

### 13.8.2 Configuring HANFS

HANFS requires that each system have three network interfaces, the primary interface, a secondary interface that will be used in takeover mode, and a slip interface for the exchange of aliveness messages. These interfaces can be configured using the SMIT hanfs_mktcpip_prm, hanfs_mktcp_sec, and hanfs_mktcp_ter fast paths.

```
# smit hanfs_mktcpip_prm      Primary network interface
# smit hanfs_mktcpip_sec      Secondary takeover interface
# smit hanfs_mktcpip_ter      Tertiary aliveness interface
```

Set the alternate hardware address of the secondary adapters to match the hardware address of primary adapters.

```
# lscfg -l ent0 -v        Display hardware address
# smit hanfs_chgenet      Set alternate Ethernet address
# smit hanfs_chgtokn      Set alternate token-ring address
```

Once the network adapters have been configured, set the primary adapters to the detach state. This prevents HANFS from attempting to access the network with the same address on both machines. Verify that all network connections are functioning correctly.

```
# smit hanfs_chdev      Set primary net adapter to detach
```

Next, connect the shared SCSI disk strings to both machines, one on each end of the SCSI string. Use *pass-through terminator* (PTT) cables and terminators (IBM #2915) on shared strings between the host adapters and the first disk devices. You can use standard device-to-device cables between disks on the string. Do not terminate the PTT cables. Keep in mind that you only have six SCSI addresses available for disks. SCSI IDs 6 and 7 are used by the host adapters on each end of the chain. Configure the adapter SCSI IDs on each machine using the SMIT `hanfs_chscsi` fast path.

```
# smit hanfs_chscsi        Set SCSI adapter addresses
```

Power up the primary machine and verify that the disks on the string are in the `Available` state.

With the hardware configuration completed, you're ready to configure HANFS software. Begin by tailoring the HANFS configuration table on each system. Once again you can use SMIT to complete this task. The configuration table identifies adapter addresses, host names, and default HANFS parameters.

```
# smit hanfs
```

Create or `varyon` the shared volume groups and file systems on the primary server. The default NFS exports file identified by the HANFS configuration file is `/etc/exports.hanfs`. Update this file with the new shared file systems or the existing NFS export information from `/etc/exports`.

```
# smit mknfsexp        Configure exports
```

Start the HANFS daemons on each system.

```
# smit hanfs_starthanfs
```

### 13.8.3 High Availability Cluster Multiprocessor/6000

*High-Availability Cluster Multiprocessor*/6000 (HACMP/6000) goes beyond HANFS by providing configurable recovery and restart capabilities for critical applications on the backup server during a system failure. HACMP/6000 is essentially a small cluster of up to four loosely coupled RS/6000s (see Fig. 13.6), each of which may be custom-tailored to support application-specific recovery procedures in the event of a failure on the primary server.

HACMP/6000 operates in one of three modes. A mode 1 operation involves using RS/6000s as an idle standby system. The standby system will take over support of the shared SCSI devices and network services in the event of the primary systems failure. A mode 2 operation permits independent use of all RS/6000s connected in the cluster. All systems are running independent workloads as well as acting as backup servers for each other. Should either system fail, critical applications and devices may be recovered and restarted on the surviving system. You will take a performance hit on the survivor due to increased load. Mode 3 operation will allow concurrent shared disk access by the same application running on all processors, as well as providing the same backup recovery facilities in modes 1 and 2.

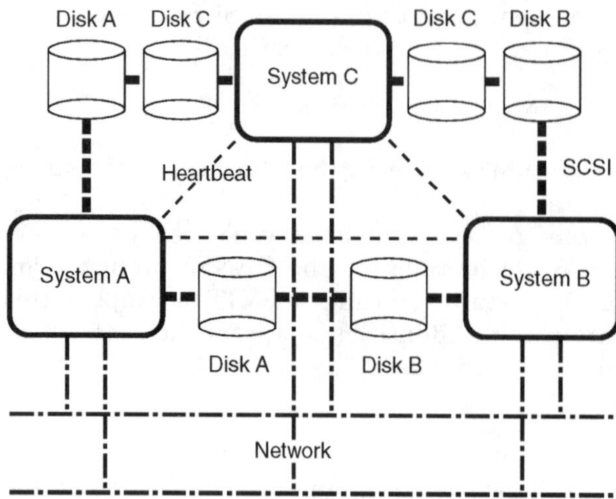


**Figure 13.6** HACMP interface diagram.

Applications developed to make use of mode 3 operation will remain available during recovery and restart processing.

## 13.9 High-speed NFS

There are several bottlenecks that contribute to slow NFS throughput. You begin with limited network bandwidth. At only 10 megabits/s, a moderately loaded Ethernet can cause significant delays for NFS traffic. The 10-ms wait for collision detection and avoidance in Ethernet is also significant overhead for frequent low-cost NFS operations. NFS server CPU cycles and memory must be shared between all operating system components. Network processing, file system buffering and control, kernel scheduling, and other OS daemons are all competing for the same resources. Finally, device interfaces are not optimized for network file system serving. NFS synchronous disk writes block other NFS traffic on the device. This all adds up to *slow* NFS response.

### 13.9.1 Prestoserv

To improve NFS performance, Legato *Prestoserv* software and hardware support is available for RS/6000 NFS servers. Prestoserv accelerates NFS performance by caching synchronous write activity to memory rather than directly to disk. Data is saved in battery-backed nonvolatile memory to ensure integrity in the event of a failure.

### 13.9.2 7051 network dataserver

To support high-speed NFS traffic between a large number of clients, consider the IBM *7051 POWER Network Dataserver*. The 7051 is a

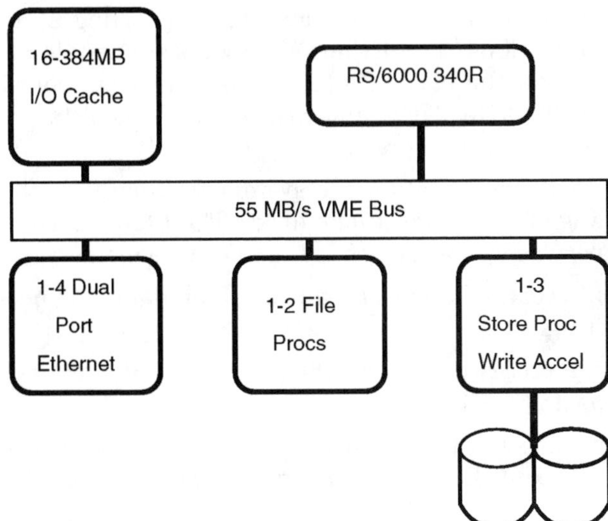


**Figure 13.7** Dataserver architecture.

hybrid multiprocessor architecture that is dedicated to NFS server operation. The 7051 can exceed and sustain data rates at 2000 NFS I/O operations per second. A fully configured 7051 can easily support over 200 NFS clients.

The 7051 is based on technology developed by Auspex. The *functional multiprocessing* (FMP) architecture implements intelligent processors, running in parallel on a VME bus, that control each piece of the server framework (see Fig. 13.7). The network, file system, and storage management functions are removed from the host processor and embedded in dedicated 32-bit intelligent processors. Note that these FMP processors DO NOT run UNIX. This complex of processors is then supported by a large dedicated I/O memory cache. The I/O cache is use to coalesce random NFS data into sequential blocks for the storage servers. The cache also maintains inode and indirect block information that might otherwise be repeatedly written to disk. Transient network packets may also be found in the I/O cache. All message passing and I/O processing between the server processors and the cache flow over the VME bus and do not interrupt the host processor.

*7051 components:*

- RS/6000-340R host processor. The host processor supports NFS mount requests, account management, and system backups. It may be used to run other AIX applications as required. The 340R's Micro Channel slots may be used to connect other devices. Supported devices include token-ring adapter, FDDI adapter, SCSI controller, BMX channel adapter, and ESCON control unit adapter.

- A maximum of four dual-port Ethernet adapters supporting up to eight Ethernet connections. The Ethernet processors handle all network processing on the card. Protocols supported on-board include IP, UDP, RPC, XDR, NFS, and SNMP. NFS requests are passed directly to the file processors.
- One or two *file processors* maintain file system metadata for the file systems residing on the dataserver's disks. The file processors support local memory as well as access to the I/O cache memory.
- 16-MB to 384-MB I/O cache handles data block, metadata, and network packet buffering.
- One to three storage processors control the array of SCSI disk used for file system support.
- One to three write accelerators with nonvolatile storage. These optimize host processor disk activity for dumps, and improve NFS throughput.
- One or two storage racks, depending upon the model. The storage racks may contain a combination of hot pluggable 2-MB or 2.4-MB disk and 4-mm or 8-mm tape devices. The model 840 rack provides from five to twenty slots for up to 48 GB of on-line storage. The model 800 rack adds five to forty slots for an additional 96 GB. Combined, they total 144 GB of NFS served storage.

The dataserver's *virtual partition manager* (VMP) allows you to dynamically allocate disk partitions on the fly. The storage processors support mirroring and striping to give you RAID 0 + 1 performance. Partitions may span physical devices. Fragmented partitions may be concatenated to reclaim space. A performance monitor is also available to assist you in managing the storage space and to identify problem areas.

To improve availability and integrity during backup processing, you can create a mirror of an active partition. Detach the mirrored partition from active use, then back up the mirrored image. Backups may be directed to SCSI-attached, rack-mounted, or networked tape devices. Optical and tape jukeboxes are supported.

## 13.10 Andrew File System

In order to impose additional levels of authentication and administration and to improve the scalability of NFS, Carnegie Mellon University developed the *Andrew File System* (AFS). AFS, now a product of Transarc Corporation, uses a remote procedure call mechanism called `RX` to support client/server interactions. AFS uses the Kerberos authentication system to validate client access to remote file systems. AFS introduces the notion of a `cell`, which defines the administrative domain over file systems in the shared space. A consistent view of the shared file system space is provided using a common root tree /afs. Subtrees for each cell follow the root, using the cell name /afs/cell-name/. Note that no restriction is placed on mount points or naming under NFS. AFS cells are identified by a database called CellServDB.

AFS security is further enhanced through the use of *access control lists* (ACL). ACLs extend the standard UNIX file permissions to provide a finer degree of granularity on access rights. AFS uses the first four UNIX permission bits to define *read, lookup, insert, write, delete, lock,* and *administer* (rliwdka) permissions. Note that AFS ACLs only apply to the directory levels of a file system. AFS also uses a UserList to define access rights and mapping. Users gain access to the AFS shared file space via the klog command which grants them a Kerberos ticket for access, and then they release their rights via the unlog command. Under AFS, the standard path can no longer be used to access files on the server.

Another important enhancement for distributed file systems is that AFS separates the logical file system structure from the disk blocks used to contain the file system. AFS *volumes* may contain one or many file system hierarchies. The volumes are made up of *partitions* that are collections of disk blocks identified by the special name, vicepnn, n = a,b,c,.... AFS also improves client cache consistency using a call-back mechanism to invalidate data blocks which have been modified. Release-level file system replication is also supported by AFS.

## 13.11 OSF Distributed File System

The Open Software Foundation selected a design based on AFS V4 from Transarc Corporation for their Distributed Computing Environment (DCE) *Distributed File System* (DFS). Conceptually, DFS is quite similar to AFS. The major differences involve the integration of DFS with the other DCE services, and the underlying *DCE local file system.* Thus, DFS requires a larger number of support daemons than normally used with AFS. Users who are familiar with AFS will be able to adapt to the DFS semantics easily. System administrators will require a little more homework in order to configure and activate all the DCE services on which DFS depends, as well as DFS configuration itself.

Like AFS, DFS uses a Kerberos based authentication system, and cell administrative domains. Users gain access to DFS using the dce_login command, and release access with the kdestroy command. Cell and DFS administrative information is served to DFS participants by DCE directory services. DFS shared file system trees are also similar to AFS in that a common root is identified with the next level delimited by cell name. The DFS shared root is named /... and cell subdirectories follow as /.../cellname/.

ACLs are also used in DFS, and they apply to both directories and files. DFS modifies the standard UNIX file permission bits to support *read, write, execute, control, insert,* and *delete* (rwxcid) permissions. The UNIX permission bits reflect the ACL permissions when viewed with standard commands like `ls`. DFS users are identified uniquely and globally to the DCE environment, such that problems with UID and GID collisions are eliminated.

Interaction between DFS clients and servers is controlled by the Network Computing System (NCS) protocol developed by Hewlett-Packard and Apollo. DFS client cache consistency is maintained via a token-passing mechanism. The DFS server controls the rights to file access tokens, which must be acquired by a client. The cache manager pulls a large *chunk* (64K) of data when a file is opened. This mechanism supports a high number of clients to servers. DFS also supports both scheduled and release file system replication.

DFS can export any VFS that has been enhanced to support DCE VFS+. DFS also provides an NFS protocol exporter for access by NFS clients. The protocol exporter does not support authentication. AFS and DFS may also be used independently on a file server. Any DFS user may export locally owned files into the shared file system space. These capabilities allow DCE DFS to be easily integrated into existing NFS and AFS environments.

### 13.11.1 DCE local file system

In order to gain the full benefit of DFS services and access control, you must use the DCE local file system architecture. File systems structures are separated from the physical disk storage which hold them similar to AFS. A DCE *fileset* is analogous to the AFS *volume,* and represents the unit of file system administration. Likewise, disk storage sets are called *aggregates* and map to the AFS concept of *partitions.* Files within the file system are allocated in structures called *containers.* Containers are built from disk blocks and may grow and shrink dynamically as required. Containers provide three modes of storage: *in-line mode,* which uses extra space in an *anode* to store small amounts of data; *fragment mode,* which combines small containers in a single disk block; and *blocked mode,* used to build large files. The anode tables are analogous to UNIX inodes. Each aggregate of storage is described by three types of containers: a *bitmap container* maps logged and unlogged fragments in the aggregate; a *file table container* supplies an array of anodes for each fileset; and a *log container* holds the aggregate transaction log.

The DCE local file system is a log-based file system similar to the AIX journaled file system (JFS). All file system metadata updates are grouped and logged as atomic transactions. Groups of transactions against a single object are also grouped into an equivalence class to facilitate recovery. The transaction equivalence class ensures that either all or none of the updates will be applied during system recovery.

Filesets may be moved between aggregates while maintaining on-line access via a procedure called *fileset cloning*. Space must be available in the partition to build a copy of the fileset. The cloned fileset is marked "read-only" and kept up to date via copy-on-write procedures until the move is complete. This facility, along with logging and dynamic container sizing, provides a highly available file system that is quite easy to administer.

## 13.12 InfoExplorer Keywords

| | | | |
|---|---|---|---|
| /etc/vfs | rpc.lockd | YP | mkclient |
| jfs | defaultvfs | makedbm | ypinit |
| cdrfs | HANFS | yppush | /etc/publickey |
| nfsmnthelp | startsrc | ypmake | newkey |
| inode | stopsrc | ypxfr | chkey |
| vnodes | exportfs | domainname | keyserv |
| gnode | portmap | netgroup | /etc/keystore |
| NFS | /etc/services | /etc/netgroups | /etc/.rootkey |
| srcmstr | mknfsexp | yppasswd | mkkeyserv |
| /etc/exports | mount | /etc/networks | keylogin |
| nfsd | umount | /etc/hosts | showmount |
| biod | ndbm | mkmaster | nfsstat |
| rpc.mountd | NIS | mkslave | rpcinfo |
| rpc.statd | | | |

## 13.13 QwikInfo

**NFS**

*Tables:*

| | |
|---|---|
| /etc/exports | Exported file systems |
| /etc/filesystems | File system mount info |
| /etc/vfs | File system type info |

*Daemons:*

| | |
|---|---|
| startsrc g nfs | Start nfs subsystem |
| nfsd | Server I/O mux daemons |
| biod | Client I/O mux daemons |
| rpc.lockd | File lock daemon |

| | |
|---|---|
| `rpc.statd` | Status daemon |
| `rpc.mountd` | Track mount requests |
| `portmap` | RPC port mapping daemon |

### *Yellow Pages:*

| | |
|---|---|
| `startsrc -g yp` | Start YP services |
| `/etc/yp/Makefile` | Create YP maps |
| `domainname` | Define hosts in YP domain |
| `/etc/netgroups` | Collection of hosts for admin purposes |
| `/etc/yp` | YP maps |
| `/etc/yp/yppasswd` | YP password file |
| `smit mkmaster, ypinit -m` | Make YP master server |
| `ypinit -s` | Initialize YP slave |
| `smit mkclient` | Make YP client |
| `keyserv` | YP encryption daemon |
| `/etc/keystore` | Private key file |
| `/etc/.rootkey` | Root private key |
| `/usr/etc/yp/mkkeyserv` | Initialize keyserv |

## High Availability NFS:

| | |
|---|---|
| `smit hanfs_mktcpip_{prm sec ter}` | Define interfaces |
| `smit hanfs_chg{enet tokn}` | Set alternate adapter |
| `smit hanfs_chscsi` | Set SCSI addresses |
| `smit hanfs_starthanfs` | Start HANFS |

### *Debugging:*

| | |
|---|---|
| `showmount` | Display client mounts |
| `nfsstat` | NFS statistics |
| `rpcinfo` | RPC port accessibility |

Chapter

# 14

# Network Computing System

## 14.1 NCS Overview

The *Network Computing System* (NCS) is a set of remote procedure call based tools that support distributed processing and data manipulation in a networked environment. NCS is a component of the *Network Computing Architecture* developed by APOLLO. The NCS RPC should not be confused with Sun RPC. NCS uses an object-oriented approach to access and manipulate network resources. Network resources are identified as objects by class or category. The interface used to access a network object is defined by the operation set associated with the the object class. NCS objects may be replicated in the network.

NCS consists of a *network computing kernel* (NCK) and a *network interface definition language* (NIDL). The network computing kernel consists of the *RPC run-time library* and a *location broker*. These components are used to build NCS-based applications.

## 14.2 NCS Remote Procedure Call

NCS RPC uses BSD sockets and UDP to create client/server connections (see Fig. 14.1). An NCS client application invokes an operation on a network object via an RPC without any knowledge of the interface implementation. The RPC request is passed to the *client stub* which uses the RPC run-time library to pass the operation request to the NCS server application. The operation request indicates the desired network object. Three types of operation requests are supported:

| | |
|---|---|
| Unbound | No server or host information is included in the request. The request is broadcast on the network and accepts the first server response. |
| Bound-to-host | The operation request specifies a host identifier. The request is sent to the location broker on the host to resolve the server port address. |

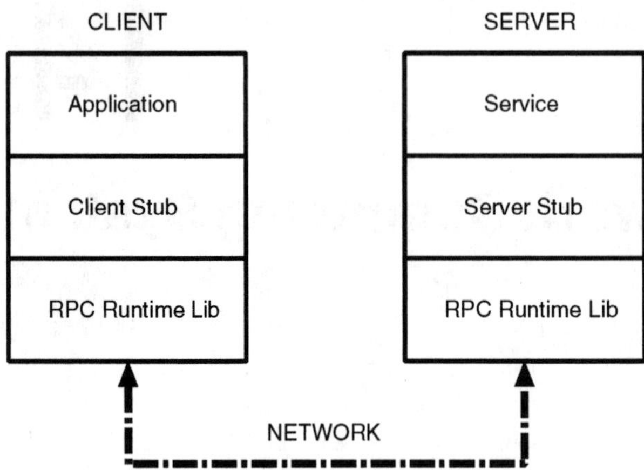


**Figure 14.1** NCS RPC interface.

Bound-to-server  The operation request identifies server port and host.

The NCS server hierarchy is similar to that of the NCS client. The server application uses a *server stub* to access the RPC run-time library routines.

## 14.3 Network Interface Definition Language

The NCS *Network Interface Definition Language* (NIDL) is used to define the interface stubs and the RPC operations supported. The NIDL compiler creates two stub files defining the interface. One is linked with the client and the other with the replicated server. The NIDL compiler generates C and Pascal syntax. Each stub controls data transfer, conversion, and connection binding.

## 14.4 Location Broker

The NCS *location brokers* register server data and respond to queries from NCS RPC clients. (Refer to Table 14.1.) Location brokers are accessed via a set of callable routines called *location broker agents.* A

**TABLE 14.1 Location Broker Database Entries**

| | |
|---|---|
| Object UUID | 128-bit object identifier |
| Type UUID | Object type |
| Interface UUID | Interface operation set |
| Flags | Global or local information |
| Annotation | Text description of service |
| Socket address len | Socket field length |
| Socket address | Server location |

location broker may either be a *local location broker* (LLB), which supports a local host, or a *global location broker* (GLB), which registers server applications for the network at large. Location brokers may be replicated. Consistency between brokers is maintained via a *data replication manager.*

## 14.5 Configuring NCS

NCS local and global location brokers are started via the `/etc/rc.ncs` script. NCS is managed as an SRC subsystem, and, as such, is started or stopped using the SRC `startsrc` and `stopsrc` commands. (See Fig. 14.2.)

```
$ startsrc -g ncs          Start NCS subsystem
$ startsrc -s llbd         Start local location broker
$ startsrc -s nrglbd       Start global location broker
```

## 14.6 Resource License Manager

The IBM *resource license manager* (RLM) is an NCS subserver that is used to provide concurrent license access to applications available over network. RLM will grant access until the concurrent license limit is reached for a particular application.

RLM regulates access in one of two methods: *node locking* and *site licensing.* Node locking permits invocation of the application only on

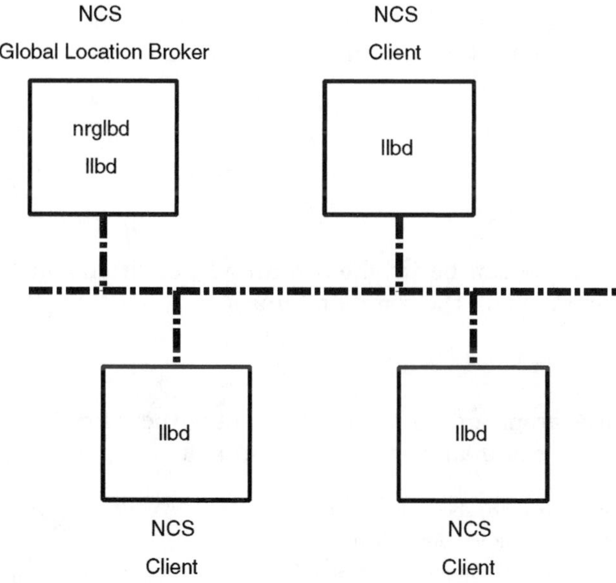


**Figure 14.2** NCS network.

the specified node. Site licensing provides unrestricted access to any of the machines at the site. See /usr/lpp/rlm/db/nodelock.README.

*Sample* /usr/lpp/rlm/db/nodelock *file:*

```
# Vendor ID       Password

38241e850000.0d.00.00.da.b4.00.00.00 87thcmbc4474eeamascqaaa
28221f850000.0d.00.00.bd.14.00.00.00 k7tvcmnc4884bvvmasccgaz
```

To manage application licenses, one or more RLM servers run under NCS on networked systems at the site. Each server maintains its own license database and is responsible for a portion of the licenses available. The RLM servers respond to license access requests from client applications. RLM components include a GUI and command line administration interfaces, the license server, database, security access configuration, and a logging facility.

*RLM components:*

| | |
|---|---|
| rlm | Motif-based administration GUI |
| rlmd | License server |
| rlmadmin, | |
| rlmstat, | |
| rlmrpt | Command line administration interfaces |
| /usr/lpp/rlm/db/lic[fru.5]db | Vendor product license database |
| /usr/lpp/rlm/db/user | User access control |
| /usr/lpp/rlm/db/logfile | License server event file |
| /usr/lpp/rlm/db/nodelock | Node locked license registration file |

RLM is started along with NCS as defined in /etc/rc.ncs. The rlmd subserver can also be started from the command line using the startsrc command.

```
$ startsrc -s rlm
```

## 14.7 Using RLM

The RLM Motif interface can be invoked in an X11 environment by entering the rlm command on the command line.

```
$ rlm
```

To use RLM services from an ASCII display, enter the rlmadmin, rlmstat, and rlmrpt commands at the shell prompt.

```
Add Vendor ACME Software to the RLM Database
$ rlmadmin        Add x3270 license for node tulip
$ rlmstat -i      Display server license information
$ rlmrpt -l       List license events
```

## 14.8 InfoExplorer Keywords

| | | |
|---|---|---|
| NCS | nrglbd | rlmd |
| startsrc | nidl | rlmadmin |
| stopsrc | ncs | rlmstat |
| llbd | rlm | rlmrpt |

## 14.9 QwikInfo

### NCS:

| | |
|---|---|
| /etc/rc.ncs | NCS Configuration |
| startsrc -g ncs | Start NCS subsystem |
| startsrc -s llbd | Start local location broker |
| startsrc -s nrglbd | Start global location broker |

*Resource license manager:*

| | |
|---|---|
| /usr/lpp/rml/db | Configuration files |
| rlm | Motif admin tool |
| rlmadmin, rlmstat, rlmrpt | Line mode admin tools |
| rlmd | License server |

Chapter

# 15

# System Network Architecture

## 15.1 Introduction to SNA

*System Network Architecture* (SNA) is a layered proprietary network architecture developed by IBM for interconnecting systems. To fully address SNA configuration and operation requires an understanding of a large set of SNA program and hardware components spanning a number of operating system environments. This subject is beyond the scope of this book. The following discussion will concentrate on how the RISC System/6000 can be incorporated into the SNA environment and the services it provides. To provide a level set for those new to SNA, I'll begin by defining basic SNA *lingo,* along with a diagram of a logical SNA network.

## 15.2 SNA Overview

Each system participating in an SNA network is known as a *node* (see Fig. 15.1). Nodes are interconnected to other nodes via *links.* Nodes are classified based on the services they provide as either *boundary nodes* or *peripheral nodes.* Boundary nodes manage routing and address translation for the global network. Peripheral nodes have a local view of the network and support limited routing and addressing capability. They rely on the boundary nodes to hide the structure of the global network. Nodes are also further broken down into *types* based on the interfaces they support.

Each node contains a set of resources called *network addressable units* (NAU). An NAU can be either a *physical unit* (PU), a *logical unit* (LU), or a *control point* (CP). A PU controls real physical resources like links, storage, and I/O hardware. An LU provides transparent network access to the end user. An end-user LU is either a program or device. A CP manages a node. A master CP, called the *system services control point* (SSCP), manages all the nodes defined

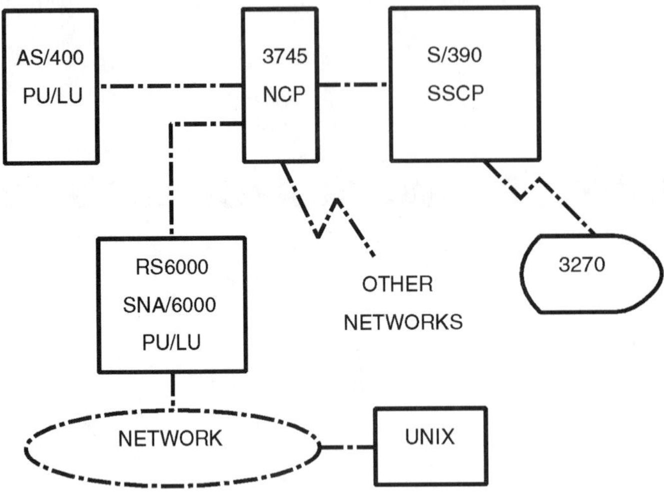


**Figure 15.1** SNA network.

within its domain. Multiple SSCPs may exist on a network, interconnecting their domains in a peer-to-peer relationship. Like nodes, NAUs are also broken down into types based on their characteristics and legacy.

*Physical unit types:*

*PU type 2.1.* Peripheral node with limited addressing and routing control. Provides multiple links and multiple LU sessions.

*PU type 4,5.* Boundary node providing address translation and routing control. PU type 5 contains the domain SSCP.

*Logical unit types:*

*LU type 0.* Primary and secondary LU support via API access for point-of-sale devices.

*LU type 1.* LU support for input/output devices (printers, punches, storage devices, console).

*LU type 2.* LU emulation of 3270 data streams.

*LU type 3.* LU emulation of 3270 printer streams.

*LU type 6.2.* Advanced Program-to-Program Communication (APPC) between LUs on a peer-to-peer basis vs. primary-to-secondary.

Information exchange between NAUs on remote nodes involves creating paths at each layer of the protocol (see Fig. 15.2). At the physical layer, an *attachment* must be started in either outgoing *call* or

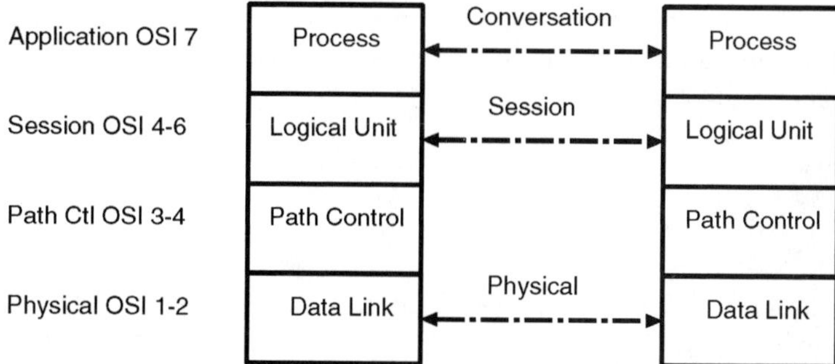


**Figure 15.2** SNA protocol stack.

incoming *listen* mode. The attachment represents the hardware and driver programs that interface the node to the network.

A *connection* is created between the nodes. The connection describes the network path between the nodes. This includes the attachments, addresses, and application descriptions.

A *session* must be established between the two NAUs. Sessions are long-lived paths that may be used serially by a number of applications.

At the top level, the LUs coordinate information transfer via a *conversation*. A *resource id* (rid) is returned when a conversation is started to identify the conversation. A conversation description clearly identifies the send and receive application roles.

## 15.3 AIX SNA Services/6000

The RISC System/6000 can be incorporated into an SNA network through the facilities provided by the *AIX SNA Services/6000* licensed program product. AIX SNA Services/6000 implements a set of programs, C library routines, device drivers, and configuration files that provide LU and PU application transaction support. AIX SNA Services/6000 *does not* provide PU type 4 or 5 boundary node support.

SNA services run as subsystems under the *system resource controller* (SRC). The SNA *system resource manager* (SRM) interacts with SRC to coordinate LU sessions and conversations. SRM is responsible for starting and stopping connections and sessions, and maintains secure conversations.

Applications access SNA network services via a set of library routines which interact with a multiplexed device driver, `/dev/sna`. The library routines resident in `/lib/libsna.a` manage network interaction and data flow work through the equivalent AIX operating system calls. AIX standard I/O library calls are supported by the SNA device driver. This allows applications and standard AIX commands to interact with SNA network services just like any I/O device. A *con-*

*nection identifier* name may be used as an extension to the /dev/sna device special file name to indicate the remote service to be used with the application.

```
# cat file-name > /dev/sna/<connection-identifier>
```

### 15.3.1 Physical interface

AIX SNA Services/6000 supports Ethernet (standard and IEEE 802.3), token ring, X.25, and synchronous data link control (SDLC) protocols. SDLC is a synchronous packet protocol which supports serial data over switched and nonswitched point-to-point and multipoint links. SDLC protocol is available for EIA232D, EIA422A, X.21, V.25, and V.35 physical links. SNA and TCP/IP may coexist on a single Ethernet or token ring adapter.

### 15.3.2 Defining the network

SNA configuration data is defined via SMIT and stored as structured objects in a database. Access to configuration profiles is controlled via subroutine calls to a data manager. Under AIX 3.1, profile information is located in /usr/lpp/sna/objrepos. In keeping with the file system tree restructuring in AIX 3.2, the profiles have been moved to /etc/objrepos/sna. Profiles describe the characteristics and attributes of all network interactions.

*Profiles descriptions:*

| | |
|---|---|
| SNA | Defines attributes and environment of SNA SRM and SRC. |
| Attachment | Defines network link characteristics. May be referred to by multiple connection profiles. Related hierarchically to lower-level control point, logical link, and physical link profiles. |
| Control point | Describes local PU. May be referred to by multiple attachment profiles. |
| Logical link | Defines the protocol used by an attachment. |
| LU address reg | Generic LU addresses. |
| Physical link | Defines physical interface hardware type. |
| Connection | Defines characteristics of the network link. |
| Local LU | Local LU definition associated with a TPN. May be referred to by multiple connection profiles. |
| TPN list | Lists all transaction programs that may access a connection. |
| TPN | Defines a transaction program. |
| RTPN list | Lists all remote transaction programs that may access a connection. |
| RTPN | Defines remote transaction program. |

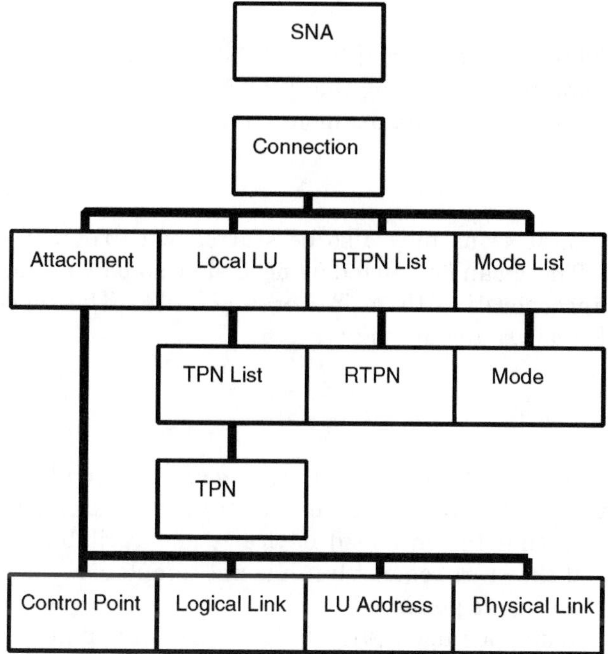


**Figure 15.3** Profile hierarchy.

| | |
|---|---|
| Mode list | Lists all mode rule profiles associated with a connection. |
| Mode | Defines a rule set that governs interaction on a connection. |

You may have noted that the profile descriptions indicate that they are related hierarchically (see Fig. 15.3). When defining a new service, configure the associated profiles from the bottom level of the profile to the top. This will make configuration procedures easier, since higher-level protocols refer to lower-level names. Select a connection name for the service and use it to name the other related profiles. SMIT will append profile-specific suffixes to this name.

After installing AIX SNA Services/6000, you will be prompted to configure your network interfaces along with the local and remote applications that will communicate over the link. The configuration information is applied by completing the profiles associated with each level of the service. Since some of this information is defined by remote sites and the domain SSCP, you will want to collect this data before running the initial configuration. Sample profile forms are supplied in *AIX Communication Concepts and Procedures, Vol 2, GC23-2203* in the section entitled "AIX SNA Services Customization Forms." The `peu` command is used to create the profiles which are verified by the `verifysna` command. These are invoked automatically by the installation procedures, but may be invoked later if required.

### 15.3.3 Starting and stopping services

AIX SNA Services/6000 may be started at each boot by editing the `/etc/rc.sna` script and uncommenting the SRC `startsrc -s sna` command. You may also start the `sna` daemon manually or via SMIT.

```
# startsrc -s sna
```

Attachments and connections may also be started with the SRC `startsrc` command. These can be started as needed or as part of the boot procedures by incorporating them in `/etc/rc.sna`. The type and name are included as arguments to `startsrc`.

```
# startsrc -t attachment -o name
# startsrc -t connection -o name
```

Once started, the resource state may be *active, inactive,* or *pending.* The active state indicates that the resource is available for use. The inactive state indicates that the intended device is not available. If the server has received the start request but has not completed start-up processing, then the state is pending.

SNA services may be stopped using the SRC `stopsrc` command or via SMIT. Three types of stops are supported as selected by the associated `stopsrc` flag: *normal, forced,* or *cancel.* A normal shutdown waits for application activity to complete. A forced shutdown does not wait for application completion, but informs the remote stations that the link is being dropped. Cancel is similar to forced, but no notification is sent. Stopping attachments and connections requires the specification of the type and the name.

| | |
|---|---|
| `# stopsrc -s name` | Normal shutdown |
| `# stopsrc -f name` | Forced shutdown |
| `# stopsrc -c name` | Cancel shutdown |

## 15.4 SNA Security

Secure communications on the network are enabled through the use of two passwords, a *communication authority password* and a *BIND password.* If the configuration profile database is not secured, then a communication authority password is not required. The communication authority password is required on secured systems to change configuration profiles. You may set the communication authority password using the `mksnapw` command from the command line or via SMIT. To change the password, use the `chsnapw` command or SMIT. To remove the password, setting the security level to unsecured, use `rmsnapw` or SMIT.

```
# mksnapw
# chsnapw
# rmsnapw
```

BIND passwords may be required for LU 6.2 sessions. Specify the password when configuring the profile for the LU. The password is requested from the remote system when a connection is requested. You can generate cryptic BIND passwords using the *security keys* facility. This can be done via SMIT or using the genkeys command. Specify the encryption phrase and number of keys as arguments.

```
# genkey -n <number> <encryption phrase>
```

The BIND password may be updated via SMIT or using the chsnaobj command.

```
# chsnaobj -t connection -u lu6.2 -v no <name>
```

## 15.5 Network Management

SNA network management procedures are implemented and operated from *NetView* running on the domain SSCP. The RISC System/6000 can be configured to pass topology and alert information from attached networks and local applications to the central NetView manager on the SSCP. This is implemented using an SSCP-PU connection between the SSCP NetView and an AIX network manager application.

Network management applications have been a moving target over the lifetime of AIX V3. Initially *AIX Network Manager / 6000* was used to manage SNMP information on TCP/IP-based networks. This product has been replaced by *NetView / 6000 Entry* for networks up to 32 SNMP agents. *SystemView NetView / 6000 V2* is used for networks larger than 32 SNMP agents. The NetView/6000 Entry manager provides all the necessary communication support to interchange data with the central SSCP. The SystemView NetView/6000 V2 manager requires both SNA Services/6000 and AIX NetView Service Point to communicate with the central SSCP. See Chap. 11 concerning SNMP.

## 15.6 Troubleshooting

Since SNA resources are initiated by SRC, you can display limited status information using the SRC lssrc command or via SMIT.

```
# lssrc -l -s sna                        Display general link status
# lssrc -l -t connection -o name         Display connection status
# lssrc -l -t attachment -o name         Display attachment status
```

SNA links may also be traced using the trace facility. Specify the trace level and associated name to the `traceson` and `tracesoff` commands. Flags and options are similar to the `lssrc` command. Use `trcrpt` to generate a report. As always, tracing can also be managed from SMIT. Trace output is located in `/usr/lpp/sna` for AIX 3.1 and `/var/sna` for AIX 3.2.

| | |
|---|---|
| `# traceson -l -t type -o name` | Start a trace |
| `# tracesoff -t type -o name` | Stop a trace |
| `# trcrpt /var/sna/name` | Generate a report. |

API level traces may be managed using the `trace` and `trcstop` commands or using SMIT. Reports are generated using `trcrpt`.

| | |
|---|---|
| `# trace -a -j 271` | Start an API trace |
| `# trcstop` | Stop an API trace |
| `# trcrpt -d 271` | Generate a report |

SNA events and errors are logged to an internal error log called `/usr/lpp/sna/snalog.*` under AIX 3.1 and `/var/sna/snalog.*` at AIX 3.2. You can interrogate the error log using your favorite pager. Remember to periodically clear the log using `errclear`.

| | |
|---|---|
| `# more /var/sna/snalog.*` | Display log entries |

## 15.7 InfoExplorer Keywords

| | |
|---|---|
| /lib/libsa.a | rmsnapw |
| /dev/sna | genkeys |
| SNA | chsnaobj |
| SSCP | lssrc |
| LU | startsrc |
| PU | traceson |
| peu | tracesoff |
| verifysna | trcrpt |
| /etc/rc.sna | trace |
| mksnapw | trcstop |
| chsnapw | snalog |

## 15.8 QwikInfo

**SNA:**

| | |
|---|---|
| `/lib/libsna.a` | SNA C I/O library |

| | |
|---|---|
| `/dev/sna` | SNA multiplexed device |
| `peu` | Create SNA profiles |
| `verifysna` | Verify profiles |
| `startsrc -s sna` | Start SNA subsystem |
| `startsrc -t attachement -o <name>` | Start SNA attachment |
| `startsrc -t connection -o <name>` | Start SNA connection |
| `mksnapw, chsnapw, rmsnapw` | Connection authority pw |
| `genken` | Gen encryption key |
| `chsnaobj` | Update SNA config |

Part

# 5

# System Services and Resources

Chapter

# 16

# Process Management

## 16.1 Process Overview

A group of processes executing under AIX is analogous to the generations of a family tree. Child processes are begotten by parent processes. Processes are born, live out their life's avocation, then pass away. Process id 1, `init,` is the great-grandparent from which all process generations owe their being. Like a loving grandparent, `init` takes in the orphan processes that have lost their parents. Each process gets its turn to execute on the CPU. Like little children, they require the guidance of the scheduler so that everyone is ensured a fair share of the CPU. The system administrator represents the grand overseer over the process universe, wielding ultimate control over the lives of all processes. A benevolent and all-seeing system administrator will learn the ways of process life in the AIX world in order to maintain tranquillity and peace.

## 16.2 Process Attributes

A process consists of an executing program and its address space. Each process is named by a positive integer number called the *process identifier* (PID). The PID is a vector index in the kernel process table. PIDs are unique and are allocated in a somewhat random fashion. Process table entries point to per-process kernel data structures. The `proc` data structures define the attribute values associated with the process. See `/usr/include/sys/proc.h.` The global AIX process table can support up to 131,071 PIDs. Let's see you get that many running on one machine!

*Sampling of process attributes:*

Process identifier

Process group identifier

Process parent identifier

Process owner

Effective and real user and group identifiers

Priority

Controlling terminal

Address space

Size in pages

Paging statistics

Resource utilization

Process state

### 16.2.1 Displaying process attributes

Active process attributes can be interrogated from the command line using the ps command. You can also use SMIT to invoke ps, but you may find that using ps from the command line is faster. AIX supports two flavors of ps: SYSV and BSD. The SYSV personality is used when the command line arguments are preceded by the "-" character, otherwise the BSD format is used.

```
# ps -elk                                        SYSV process display format

F       S  UID  PID   PPID  C   PRI NI ADDR  SZ  WCHAN    TTY   TIME      CMD
b03     S  0    0     0     120 16  -- 4008  8   -        -     7:37      swapper
202803  S  0    1     0     0   60  20 2004  244 -        -     22:02     init
303     R  0    514   0     120 127 -- 4809  12           -     67063:23  kproc
303     S  0    771   0     0   39  -- 2805  16           -     18:55     kproc
303     S  0    1028  0     0   36  -- 580b  16           -     0:00      kproc
40a01   S  0    1286  0     0   60  20 58cb  24           -     65:33     kproc
240801  S  0    1611  3097  0   60  20 e13c  108 12ce960  -     0:00      qdaemon
40a01   S  0    2140  1     0   60  20 d01a  16           -     0:00      kproc
240801  S  0    2781  1     0   60  20 f89f  52  5a55358  -     8:10      syncd
240801  S  0    2888  1     0   60  20 8130  148          -     10:18     cron
260801  S  0    3097  1     0   60  20 b0d6  180          -     0:00      srcmstr
42801   S  0    3551  1     0   60  20 78af  248 cc18     -     0:00      errdemon
240801  S  0    3834  1     0   60  20 2a25  236 597557c  0     0:00      tsm
40201   S  0    3956  1     0   60  20 f81f  16           -     0:00      kproc
260801  S  0    4131  3097  0   60  20 e8dd  148          -     0:08      syslog
260801  S  0    4390  3097  0   60  20 b0f6  232          -     0:00      sendmail
240801  S  0    4686  1     0   60  20 2945  36  3f0a8    -     0:00      uprintfd
260801  S  0    4908  3097  0   60  20 2104  128          -     0:00      portmap
260801  S  0    5167  3097  0   60  20 3106  176          -     0:00      inetd
240801  S  4084 12615 11846 1   60  20 12c2  112          pts/0 0:00      ksh
```

```
# ps auxw                                        BSD process display format

USER  PID   %CPU %MEM SZ   RSS  TTY  STAT STIME   TIME      COMMAND
root  0     0.0  0.0  8    8    -    S    Jul 13  7:36      swapper
root  1     0.0  1.0  244  132  -    S    Jul 13  22:00     /etc/init
root  514   0.5  0.0  12   8    -    R    Dec 31  66978:43  kproc
root  771   0.0  0.0  16   16   -    S    Dec 31  18:53     kproc
root  1028  0.0  0.0  16   16   -    S    Dec 31  0:00      kproc
root  1286  0.1  0.0  24   24   -    S    Jul 13  65:33     kproc
root  1611  0.0  0.0  108  72   -    S    Jul 13  0:00      /etc/qdaemon
```

```
root     2140   0.0  0.0  16   8    -     S   Jul 13    0:00    kproc
root     2781   0.0  0.0  52   28   -     S   Jul 13    8:09    /etc/syncd 60
root     2888   0.0  1.0  148  192  -     S   Jul 13    10:17   /etc/cron
root     3097   0.0  0.0  180  12   -     S   Jul 13    0:00    /etc/srcmstr
root     3551   0.0  0.0  248  12   -     S   Jul 13    0:00    /usr/lib/errdemon
root     3956   0.0  0.0  16   8    -     S   Jul 13    0:00    kproc
root     4131   0.0  0.0  148  60   -     S   Jul 13    0:08    /etc/syslogd
root     4390   0.0  1.0  232  196  -     S   Jul 13    0:00    /usr/lib/sendmail
root     4686   0.0  0.0  36   12   -     S   Jul 13    0:00    /etc/uprintfd
root     4908   0.0  0.0  128  12   -     S   Jul 13    0:00    /usr/etc/portmap
root     5167   0.0  1.0  176  168  -     S   Jul 13    0:00    /etc/inetd
deroest  12615  0.0  2.0  112  384  pts/0 S   11:52:25  0:00 -  ksh
```

The COMMAND and CMD columns represent the program being run in the process address space. A special set of kernel processes, kprocs, are represented to collect accounting data for system overhead. You may notice that one kproc process collects *very high* amounts of CPU. There is no cause for alarm. This kproc entry collects the system wait and idle time and represents it in the CPU field.

### 16.2.2 Process identifiers

Along with its PID, each process records the integer ID of its parent and its group membership, *parent process identifier* (PPID), and *process group identifier* (PGID). Process groups are collections of one or more processes. The group leader has a PGID equal to its PID and each member has a PGID that matches the leader. Unless reset by a setpgrp() call, a process inherits the PGID of its parent. Process groups provide a mechanism for signaling all processes within the group using the PGID. This eliminates the need to know each member's PID. The PID, PPID, and PGID are the primary handles used by the system administrator for controlling process behavior.

### 16.2.3 Effective and real UID and GID

Processes are associated with an owning *user identifier* (UID) and *group identifier* (GID). The UID and GID name space are maintained as part of the system account management and are recorded in the /etc/passwd and /etc/group files (see Chap. 21). The *real UID* and *real GID* numbers identify process owners for accounting and process control purposes. An *effective UID* (EUID) and *effective GID* (EGID) are assigned to each process and represent the permissions and privileges available to the process during its lifetime.

### 16.2.4 Controlling terminal

Processes other than system daemons are usually associated with a *control terminal.* The control terminal represents the default device for standard input, output, and error channels and for sending signals via keyboard control characters. The control character to signal mapping is user-customizable and recorded in the termio structure.

See Chap. 9 for details on keyboard mapping. The controlling terminal is identified in the `ps TTY` column.

### 16.2.5 Resource utilization and priority

AIX uses a priority-based set of run queues to allocate CPU resources among active processes. Priorities values range from 0 to 127, each of which is represented by a run queue. Lower-numbered queues are scheduled more often than higher-numbered queues. Processes in a run queue level are scheduled in a round robin fashion. Each process's queue priority is calculated from the sum of its short-term CPU usage (0 to +100), its nice value (0 to 40), and the minimum user process level (40). The priority value increases for processes that execute frequently and decreases for those that are waiting for execution. Processes with a priority value exceeding 120 will execute only when no other process in the system requires CPU resources. Process short-term CPU usage, priority, and nice value are displayed in the `PRI`, `C`, and `NI` fields using the SYSV `ps -l` option.

The *nice* value is an integer that represents coarse priorities between processes. AIX supports both the BSD nice value range of 20 to −20, and the SYSV range of 0 to 39. The larger the number, the lower the scheduling priority. The two-value ranges are mapped such that BSD −20 corresponds to SYSV 0 for highest priority, and BSD 20 to SYSV 39 for lowest priority.

New processes inherit the nice value of their parents. The nice value may be altered dynamically during the process lifetime. The owning UID for a process can lower the process nice value. Only the superuser can improve nice priority. The nice value can be set from the command line using the `nice` command.

```
# nice -n <value> <command>
```

Process owners and the superuser can modify existing process nice values by using the `renice` command.

```
# renice <value> -p <PID>
```

Be aware that the BSD `#CPU` field represents the percentage of CPU resources that a process has used in its lifetime. You may see short-lived processes shoot up to very high `#CPU` numbers. A better gauge for identifying CPU crunchers or runaway processes is the `TIME` column.

### 16.2.6 Process state

The scheduler parcels out CPU time slices at a frequency that makes it appear as if all processes are executing at the the same time. In fact,

**TABLE 16.1 Process States Displayed by `ps`**

| | |
|---|---|
| O | Nonexistent |
| S | Sleeping |
| W | Waiting |
| R | Running |
| I | Intermediate |
| Z | Canceled |
| T | Stopped |
| K | Available kernel process |
| X | Growing |

they are being scheduled one at time, except in the case of multiprocessor systems. When a process isn't executing on the CPU, it may be waiting on a resource or lock, sleeping on an event, suspended, or moving through some dispatch or scheduler state. The process state is maintained as part of the `proc` structure information. The process state is displayed by `ps` in the `STAT` column when the BSD `l` or SYSV `-l` flag is used (see Table 16.1). For processes that are flagged *Waiting,* the `WCHAN` column identifies the address of the event being waited on.

## 16.3 Parent-Child Inheritance

A parent process creates a new child process by invoking the `fork()` system call. The kernel reserves a vacant PID for the child and copies the attribute data associated with the parent into the child's `proc` structure. The child is a clone of the parent until either the child, the parent, or a privileged authority modifies the child's attributes via a system call. The most common method of modifying a child's `proc` attributes is by invoking a new program via the `exec()` system call.

## 16.4 Controlling Processes

In Sec. 16.2.5, I talked about using the `nice` and `renice` commands to coarsely control the scheduling priorities between processes. What do you do when process management requires a heavier hand? You use `kill`!

The command name `kill` sounds much more ominous than it in fact is. What `kill` does is send a specified signal to a process. The signal does not necessarily cause process termination. Note that `kill` is a built-in command for some shells—for example, `/bin/csh`. The behavior of the shell version of `kill` and `/bin/kill` may be different.

```
# kill [-Signal] [PID PID PID …]
```

| | |
|---|---|
| `PID > 0` | Send signal to specified PIDs |
| `PID = 0` | Send signal to PIDs which have PGIDs equal to the sender |
| `PID = -1` | Send signal to all PIDs with EUID equal to the sender |

| | |
|---|---|
| `PID < -1` | Send signal to all PIDs with a PGID equal to the absolute value of the specified PID |

If you want to send a signal to all your processes except the sending process, use the `killall` command.

```
# killall [-signal]
```

To display the set of supported signals, use the `-l` argument to `kill`.

```
# /bin/kill -l
NULL HUP INT QUIT ILL TRAP IOT EMT FPE KILL BUS SEGV SYS PIPE ALRM
TERM URG STOP TSTP CONT CHLD TTIN TTOU IO XCPU XFSZ MSG WINCH PWR
USR1 USR2 PROF DANGER VTALRM MIGRATE PRE GRANT RETRACT SOUND SAK
```

AIX signals are based on the SYSV implementation; however, some BSD signals are mapped to their SYSV counterparts, and BSD signal system calls are available. (Refer to Tables 16.2 and 16.3.) When writing or porting programs that use BSD signals and calls, be aware that signals are not automatically reset after being caught. They must be specifically reset to the required behavior in the signal handler routine.

### 16.4.1 Rules of thumb

It seems to be a common practice to use the `KILL (9)` signal to terminate a process. I recommend that you do this only as a last resort after first trying `HUP (1)` and `ABRT (6)`. The latter two signals allow a process to terminate gracefully. In the case of `ABRT`, a core file is produced which may be used for debugging. The `KILL` signal basically attempts to yank the process out of the process table without permitting any cleanup activities.

```
# kill -1 <PID>      First try HUP
# kill -6 <PID>      Then try ABRT
# kill -9 <PID>      KILL if all else fails
```

Occasionally, a user may try out some ingenious bit of C code that contains a statement along the lines of

```
while(1) fork();
```

I'm not insinuating that this is done on purpose, but it can be a pain in the neck to stop. New processes are being created as fast as you can kill them. One little trick you can try is to kill them by PGID. Use the formatted output, `-F`, option with SYSV `ps` to display the PGID. Then send a signal to the negative PGID.

```
# ps -el -F pgid,runame = <procname>
# kill -6 -<pgid>
```

**TABLE 16.2 Signal Names and Numbers**

| | | |
|---|---|---|
| SIGHUP | 1 | Hang up at terminal disconnect. |
| SIGINT | 2 | Interrupt. |
| SIGQUIT | 3 | Quit. |
| SIGILL | 4 | Illegal instruction. |
| SIGTRAP | 5 | Trace trap. |
| SIGABRT | 6 | Abort process and core dump. |
| SIGEMT | 7 | EMT instruction. |
| SIGFPE | 8 | Floating-point exception. |
| SIGKILL | 9 | Kill process. Can't be caught or ignored! |
| SIGBUS | 10 | Bus error. |
| SIGSEGV | 11 | Segmentation violation. |
| SIGSYS | 12 | System call bad argument. |
| SIGPIPE | 13 | Write on a pipe with no one reader. |
| SIGALRM | 14 | Alarm clock timeout. |
| SIGTERM | 15 | Termination signal. |
| SIGURG | 16 | Urgent condition on I/O channel. |
| SIGSTOP | 17 | Stop. Can't be caught or ignored! |
| SIGTSTP | 18 | Interactive stop. |
| SIGCONT | 19 | Continue. Can't be caught or ignored! |
| SIGCHLD | 20 | Sent to parent on child stop or exit. |
| SIGTTIN | 21 | Background read attempted from control terminal. |
| SIGTTOU | 22 | Background write attempted to control terminal. |
| SIGIO | 23 | I/O possible or completed. |
| SIGXCPU | 24 | CPU time limit exceeded. |
| SIGXFSZ | 25 | File size limit exceeded. |
| SIGMSG | 27 | Input data is in the HFT ring buffer. |
| SIGWINCH | 28 | Window size changed. |
| SIGPWR | 29 | Power-fail restart. |
| SIGUSR1 | 30 | User-defined signal 1. |
| SIGUSR2 | 31 | User-defined signal 2. |
| SIGPROF | 32 | Profiling time alarm. |
| SIGDANGER | 33 | System crash imminent; free page space! |
| SIGVTALRM | 34 | Virtual time alarm. |
| SIGMIGRATE | 35 | Migrate process (Locus TCF). |
| SIGPRE | 36 | Programming exception. |
| SIGVIRT | 37 | AIX virtual time alarm. |
| SIGGRANT | 60 | HFT monitor mode granted. |
| SIGRETRACT | 61 | HFT monitor mode should be relinquished. |
| SIGSOUND | 62 | HFT sound control has completed. |
| SIGSAK | 63 | Secure attention key. |

**TABLE 16.3 Signal Compatibility Mapping**

| | |
|---|---|
| SIGIOINT SIGURG | Printer to backend error signal. |
| SIGAIO SIGIO | Base lan I/O. |
| SIGSIGPTY SIGIO | PTY I/O. |
| SIGSIGIOT SIGABRT | Abort process. |
| SIGSIGCLD SIGCHLD | Death of child. |
| SIGLOST SIGIOT | BSD signal ?? |

### 16.4.2 Ignoring hangup

A common problem is starting a command in the background or as a daemon from the command line of a login shell only to find that the command exits when you log out. This is because a *hangup* (HUP) signal is sent to the process when your terminal connection has been broken. You can specify that these commands are to ignore HUP by using the nohup command.

```
# nohup <command> &        Background process ignoring hangup.
```

## 16.5 Scheduled Processes—cron

The UNIX cron utility provides a basic means for scheduling jobs to be run at a particular time of the day or on a periodic basis. cron can be used to take care of regular system housecleaning tasks like sync'ing disk writes, cleaning out /tmp, and running accounting programs. These types of periodic tasks may be tailored through the use of crontabs. A crontab is a list of commands and scripts with designated run times that will be invoked by cron under the EUID of the owner. cron reports any errors or output information to the owning user after the commands are executed. cron logs errors to a log file, /var/adm/cron/log, and if AIX auditing is enabled, produces audit records.

### 16.5.1 crontab

To create a crontab, use your favorite editor and create a table with the following format:

minutes hours day month weekday command

Each of the time-associated fields may be represented as a comma-separated list. A "*" may be used to represent all possible times. For example, if I wanted to display uptime statistics every half hour on the system console, I would add the following line to my crontab file.

```
0,30 * * * * /bin/uptime > /dev/console
```

Once you have your crontab file tailored to your liking, hand it off to cron by invoking the crontab command.

```
# crontab <YourCrontabFile>
```

All crontabs are stored in /var/adm/cron/crontabs under the owning user name.

*User* adm Crontab:

```
# (C) COPYRIGHT International Business Machines Corp. 1989,1991
# All Rights Reserved
# Licensed Materials—Property of IBM
#= = = = = = = = = = = = = = = = = = = = = = = = = = = = = = = = = =
# SYSTEM ACTIVITY REPORTS
# 8am-5pm activity reports every 20 mins during weekdays.
# activity reports every an hour on Saturday and Sunday.
# 6pm-7am activity reports every an hour during weekdays.
# Daily summary prepared at 18:05.
#= = = = = = = = = = = = = = = = = = = = = = = = = = = = = = = = = =
# Daily summary prepared at 18:05.
#= = = = = = = = = = = = = = = = = = = = = = = = = = = = = = = = = =
0 8-17 * * 1-5 /usr/lib/sa/sa1 1200 3 &
0 * * * 0,6 /usr/lib/sa/sa1 &
0 18-7 * * 1-5 /usr/lib/sa/sa1 &
5 18 * * 1-5 /usr/lib/sa/sa2 -s 8:00 -e 18:01 -i 3600 -ubcwyaqvm &
#= = = = = = = = = = = = = = = = = = = = = = = = = = = = = = = = = =
# PROCESS ACCOUNTING:
runacct at 11:10 every night
# dodisk at 11:00 every night
# ckpacct every hour on the hour
# monthly accounting 4:15 the first of every month
#= = = = = = = = = = = = = = = = = = = = = = = = = = = = = = = = = =
10 23 * * 0-6 /usr/lib/acct/runacct 2>/usr/adm/acct/nite/accterr
>/dev/null
0 23 * * 0-6 /usr/lib/acct/dodisk > /dev/null 2>&1
* * * * /usr/lib/acct/ckpacct > /dev/null 2>&1
15 4 1 * * /usr/lib/acct/monacct > /dev/null 2>&1
#= = = = = = = = = = = = = = = = = = = = = = = = = = = = = = = = = =
```

The system administrator can enforce access controls on who may use `cron` services by listing user names, one per line, in the `/usr/adm/cron/{cron.allow,cron.deny}` files. `cron` checks these files' authorizations, before invoking a user's `crontab` file. The default is to allow access to all users.

### 16.5.2 Ad hoc jobs

Suppose you want to run a job off-hours, but don't want to create a `crontab` entry for it. It may be a one-time-only run. You can do this using the `at` and `batch` commands. Note that `batch` is just a script that invokes `at`. Execute `at`, specifying the time and the input stream of commands. The job stream is copied to the `/usr/spool /cron/atjobs` directory. `cron` then executes the job stream at the specified time. Authorization to run `at` jobs is controlled like `crontab` by listing user names in the `/usr/adm /cron/{at.allow, at.deny}` file. The default is to allow access to all users.

| | |
|---|---|
| `# at <time> input <Ctrl-D>` | Start a job at time |
| `# at -r jobnumber` | Remove a job |
| `# atq <username>` | List scheduled jobs |

If a more sophisticated batch scheduling system is required, see Chap. 27.

### 16.5.3 Managing cron activities

In active batch environments, you might want to place some limits on cron scheduling. The /usr/adm/cron/queuedefs file can be configured to limit the number of concurrent jobs by *event type,* set the default nice value, and set the retry limit. Event controls are listed one per line in the queuedefs file.

queuedefs *format:*

```
e.[j#][n#][w#]
```

| | |
|---|---|
| e | Event type |
| j | Max number of concurrent jobs |
| n | Nice value |
| w | Retry wait in seconds |

queuedefs *events types:*

| | |
|---|---|
| a | at events |
| b | batch events |
| c | crontab events |
| d | sync events |
| e | ksh events |
| f | csh events |

The queuedefs file is shipped empty. Default values for all event types support 100 concurrent jobs, at nice value 2 with a 60-second retry limit.

*Example* queuedefs *entry:*

| | |
|---|---|
| c.2j2n90v | 2 crontab jobs, nice value 2, retry every 90 seconds. |

## 16.6 System Resource Controller

AIX provides a mechanism for controlling and managing sets of programs that function collectively as a unit. This mechanism is called the *system resource controller* (SRC). SRC provides simple command interfaces to display status, refresh, start, and stop system services as a single entity. These interfaces reduce the operation and administration complexity of managing all the daemons and programs that make up a particular service.

The collection of programs that make up an SRC service unit are called subsystems. The daemons that make up a subsystem are known as subservers. Subsystems may be grouped by the overall service they provide and are identified as subsystem groups. For example, the ftpd daemon is a subserver of the inetd subsystem. The inetd subsystem is a group member of the TCPIP subsystem group.

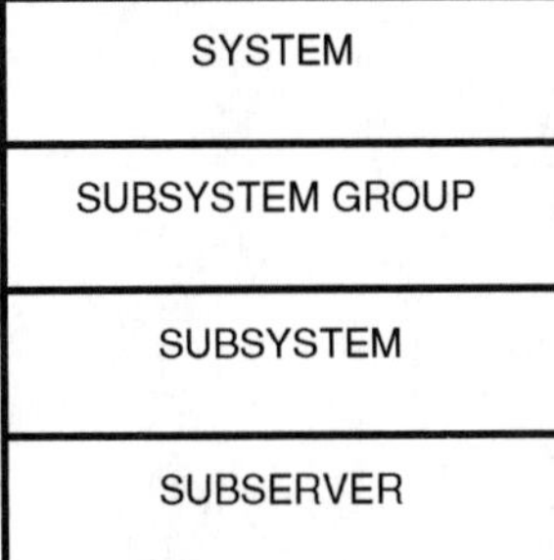


**Figure 16.1** SRC hierarchy.

SRC allows the operator or administrator to operate on a service at the subserver, subsystem, or subsystem group level (see Fig. 16.1).

### 16.6.1 SRC components

Overall SRC is provided by the `srcmstr` daemon. `srcmstr` is started at boot time by an entry in `/etc/inittab`.

```
srcmstr:2:respawn:/etc/srcmstr       # system resource controller
```

`srcmstr` identifies subsystem components from definition in ODM object classes `/etc/objrepos/{SRCsubsys,SRCnotify`. Subsystems and subserver configuration information is managed through the use of the `{mk,ch,rm}server` and `{mk,ch,rm}ssys` commands. In most cases, the subsytems and subservers are predefined for each product at installation time.

Once a subsystem group, subsystem, or subserver is configured into the ODM, it may be operated on using the following commands:

| | |
|---|---|
| `startsrc` | Start a subsystem |
| `stopsrc` | Stop a subsystem |
| `refresh` | Restart or refresh a subsystem |
| `trace{on,off}` | Trace a subsystem |
| `lssrc` | Display subsystem status |

Subsystems may be started at boot time following the `srcmstr` by invoking the `startsrc` command as part of a boot rc script or directly from `/etc/inittab`.

*SRC command examples:*

| | |
|---|---|
| `# startsrc -g tcpip` | Start the TCPIP subsystem group |
| `# stopsrc -s qdaemon` | Stop the qdaemon subsystem |

To display the status of all defined subsystems, use the `lssrc` command. Note that subsystem control may also be invoked via the SMIT `subsys` and `subserver` fast paths.

```
# lssrc -a
```

| Subsystem | Group | PID | Status |
|---|---|---|---|
| syslogd | ras | 4484 | active |
| lpd | spooler | 5511 | active |
| routed | tcpip | 6296 | active |
| portmap | portmap | 5820 | active |
| inetd | tcpip | 6091 | active |
| biod | nfs | 8417 | active |
| nfsd | nfs | 13324 | active |
| rpc.mountd | nfs | 15908 | active |
| rpc.statd | nfs | 12851 | active |
| rpc.lockd | nfs | 18499 | active |
| qdaemon | spooler | 12627 | active |
| writesrv | spooler | 13157 | active |
| infod | infod | 19063 | active |
| iptrace | tcpip | | inoperative |
| gated | tcpip | | inoperative |
| named | tcpip | | inoperative |
| rwhod | tcpip | | inoperative |
| timed | tcpip | | inoperative |
| sendmail | mail | | inoperative |
| snmpd | tcpip | | inoperative |
| keyserv | keyserv | | inoperative |
| ypserv | yp | | inoperative |
| ypbind | yp | | inoperative |
| ypupdated | yp | | inoperative |
| yppasswdd | yp | | inoperative |
| llbd | ncs | | inoperative |
| nrglbd | ncs | | inoperative |

## 16.7 InfoExporer Keywords

| | | |
|---|---|---|
| init | renice | atq |
| process | kill | subsystems |
| ps | signal | subservers |
| kproc | nohup | /etc/inittab |
| setpgrp | cron | srcmstr |
| /etc/passwd | at | startsrc |
| /etc/group | crontab | stopsrc |
| termio | batch | lssrc |
| nice | atjobs | killall |

## 16.8 QwikInfo

**Process management:**

*Process control:*

| | |
|---|---|
| /usr/include/sys/proc.h | Process attributes |
| ps -<options> | Display running process information (SYSV) |
| ps <options> | Display running process information (BSD) |
| nice | Lower process priority |
| renice | BSD admin process cntrl |
| kill | Send process a signal |
| kill -l | List signals |
| killall | Kill all your processes |
| nohup | Ignore hangup signal |

### *Batch support:*

| | |
|---|---|
| cron | System job scheduler |
| /var/spool/cron/crontabs | cron job tables |
| /usr/adm/cron/{cron.allow,cron.deny} | Authorize cron use |
| at | Batch job support |
| /usr/adm/cron/queuedefs | cron job limits |

### *Subsystems:*

| | |
|---|---|
| srcmstr | Subsystem master daemon |
| startsrc, stopsrc, refresh | Manage subsystems |
| lssrc | List subsystem state |

Chapter

# 17

# Electronic Mail

## 17.1 Mail System Overview

It is with mixed feelings that I write this chapter on configuring and managing electronic mail—the reason being that electronic mail is addictive! Don't try to tell me it's not. It's one of those things that once you have it, you can't live without it. Everyday my mailbox receives close to a hundred mail files. I find myself sneaking an e-mail fix throughout the day, in the evenings, on weekends, after church! I feel like I'm pushing an uncontrolled substance!

Seriously, electronic mail provides avenues of collaboration that are changing the way we do business, research, and interact with each other. Electronic mail is informal. People who have never been introduced feel at ease to discuss almost any topic via electronic mail. The impromptu nature of electronic mail seems to allow people to express their views and feelings honestly (sometimes beyond their better judgment).

It's our duty as administrators to support this kind of interaction. After all, information sharing is what this industry is all about. With a little feeding and care, the electronic mail system can be a controlled substance that is good for everyone.

The electronic mail (e-mail) system is conceptually, if not physically, divided into two components: the *user agent* (UA) and the *mail transport agent* (MTA).

*Mail components:*

| | |
|---|---|
| `/bin/mail or /usr/ucb/mail` | User agent |
| `/usr/sbin/sendmail` | Mail transfer agent |

### 17.1.1 Mail user agents

The mail user agent provides the user interface to the mail system. The UA presents incoming mail to the user for reading and archiving.

Editor facilities for composing, forwarding, or replying are managed by the UA. A great deal of *human factors* research is being invested in UA design. Sure, make it even more addictive!

The ATT and BSD mail programs provide all the basic elements of a good UA. No frills, but they get the job done. For naive users, these probably aren't good UAs to use. Full-screen menu-oriented UAs like `elm` or `pine` are probably a better choice. Because this is an administrator's text, I won't spend time on the pros and cons of the various UAs. It's a religious issue best left to the practitioners. Since I am employed by the University of Washington, I will at least say that you can obtain a copy of `pine` via anonymous ftp from `ftphost.cac.washington.edu`. You can find `elm` and other user-friendly UAs from a number of ftp sites on the network. Use `archie` to find the ftp site nearest you. See App. A.

In the following sections, when referring to a UA, assume basic ATT or BSD mail functionality and options.

The system administrator is responsible for setting the default UA configuration options. The default options are defined in the `/usr/lib/.Mail.rc` file. Each user may override the global defaults by resetting the options in a local `$HOME/.mailrc` file.

*Configuration file for UA:*

```
# /usr/lib/Mail.rc
#
# Options
#
set ask askcc dot save keep crt
#
# Don't display the following header lines
#
ignore Received Message-Id Resent-Message-Id
ignore Status Mail-From Return-Path Via
```

### 17.1.2 Mail transport agents

The MTA is responsible for receiving and delivering mail. At a minimum, the MTA must be able to accept mail from UAs and the network, decipher addresses, and deliver the message to a local user mailbox or to a remote MTA. Better MTAs will be able to detect e-mail loops, route a single mail message for multiple recipients at the same site, support privacy, and route problem mail to a site postmaster. Common MTAs include BSD `sendmail`, `mmdf`, `smail`, and `mhs`. In the following sections, I will discuss `sendmail` configuration and administration.

### 17.1.3 Addressing and headers

In order for a mail message to traverse from user A to user B, an addressing mechanism that is understood by the MTAs must be used. From the discussion in Chap. 11 concerning the domain name space, you might think that this is a simple issue. However, e-mail gateways to other networks involving other addressing protocols can make address resolution an AI-hard problem (artificial intelligence).

The most common UNIX mail formats involve Internet domain addressing and UUCP addressing.

| | |
|---|---|
| `user@domain-address` | Internet address |
| `host1!…!destination!user` | UUCP address |

Two types of mail headers are attached to each mail message that defines the attributes of the message. The *Simple Mail Transfer Protocol* (SMTP RFC 821) provides a command syntax that MTAs use to negotiate mail transfer from one MTA to the next.

*Example SMTP header:*

| | |
|---|---|
| `HELO daffy.foo.bar.edu` | Introduce yourself to the MTA |
| `MAIL From: raphael@park.foo.edu` | Indicate the originator |
| `RCPT To: rachael@lite.house.com` | Announce the recipients |
| `DATA` | Supply the data |
| `… email message …` | |
| `QUIT` | Exit |

The second type of mail header is the RFC 822 header. It is used by both the MTA and UA. The RFC 822 header identifies the path the mail message has traveled, date, originator, recipients, subject, etc.

*Example mail header:*

```
Received: from mailer.foo.edu
by lite.house.com id AA03037;
Tue, 16 Jun 89 15:07 PST
Received: from park.foo.edu
by mailer.foo.edu id aa12242;
Tue, 16 Jun 89 15:01 PST
Date: Tue, 10 Aug 93 14:59:10 PST
From: raphael@park.foo.edu
To: rachael@lite.house.com
Subject: Meeting Wednesday

Rachael:
Can we meet on Wednesday to discuss mailer
configuration for the department workstations.

Raphael
```

The ordering of the received lines indicates the MTA path that the mail message has traveled. This path can be used to debug routing problems and loops.

### 17.1.4 How mail is sent

When a user composes a mail message, the UA attaches a header envelope to the message separated by a blank line. The UA then hands the message off to the sendmail MTA. A new sendmail daemon is forked to process the new message. Sendmail passes each of the addresses associated with the mail message through address translation rule sets. The rule sets parse the address line and determine if the message destination is local or remote. If the message is destined for a remote site, name service may be queried to determine if a preferred mail exchange site is requested for the remote site (name service MX record). If the remote site is running a sendmail MTA, the message is transferred to the remote site using the SMTP protocol described previously. At the remote site, sendmail runs the addresses through the rule sets again to determine if the recipient is local or remote. If the recipient is local, the headers are rewritten and the message is spooled to the recipients mail inbox.

## 17.2 Sendmail Configuration

The *sendmail* MTA is probably the most common MTA in use. Unfortunately, it is one of the most difficult to configure. Sendmail was originally written by Eric Allman at the University of California at Berkeley at a time when mail traffic was sparser than what we experience today. It is to Eric's credit that sendmail has proven to be general enough to evolve with the traffic requirements. Sendmail has gone through many changes since its inception and as a result has become quite complex. Successfully configuring a `sendmail.cf` file can certainly be considered one of the rites of passage to UNIX wizardom.

*Sendmail data files:*

| | |
|---|---|
| `/etc/sendmail.cf` | Sendmail configuration file |
| `/etc/sendmail.cfDB` | Compiled sendmail configuration file |
| `/etc/sendmail.nl` | Sendmail national language rules |
| `/etc/sendmail.nlDB` | Compiled national language rules |
| `/etc/aliases` | Mail aliases |
| `/etc/aliases{DB, DB.pg}` | Compiled alias file |
| `/etc/sendmail.pid` | PID of sendmail daemon |
| `/etc/sendmail.st` | Mail statistics |

*NOTE:* These files are accessed via symbolic links from `/usr/lib`.

### 17.2.1 `sendmail.cf`

The sendmail configuration file, `/etc/sendmail.cf`, contains the majority of the options and rules required by sendmail to deliver e-mail. The `sendmail.cf` file maintains three sets of configuration data:

- Options, variables, and parameters
- Address rewriting rule sets
- Mailer identification and delivery

The best way to start configuring a new sendmail.cf file is to obtain a copy of one that works. AIX V3 supplies a boilerplate sendmail.cf file that can be used with minimal changes if your e-mail environment is not complex. By complex, I mean that you have a number of mail gateways to other networks or a hierarchy of MTAs. You can tailor the sendmail.cf file using your favorite editor or using the AIX /usr/lib/edconfig command. edconfig provides a menu-oriented approach to editing sendmail.cf components. For those of you new to sendmail, it focuses your attention on the option being changed. It's easy to get confused when working with the whole file in an editor. The edconfig command (see Fig. 17.1) may become confused with custom sendmail.cf files. Use it only with the AIX-supplied sendmail.cf.

```
# /usr/lib/edconfig /etc/sendmail.cf
```

Commands and definitions begin in column 1 in the sendmail.cf file. Comments begin with a "#" character. Blank lines are ignored. Due to the number of special characters used, you need to be careful when adding address types like DECNETS "::" node delimiters. A set of predefined character symbols is used to indicate the definition of new symbols, classes, options, macros, or rules. Using a "$" sign with a macro or variable name indicates the *value* of the variable or macro. A "?" indicates a boolean test. In the following discussion, I'll define the symbols used in each section of the sendmail.cf file and provide an example.

**17.2.1.1 Options and definitions section.** The first section of the sendmail.cf file identifies the run-time options and variables. These include definition of the host or domain name, if name service mail exchange is supported, message precedence, etc.

```
Classes:

 0) Return to this menu
 1) Exit without writing edited configuration file
 2) Write edited configuration file and exit
 3) Edit Host Name Information
 4) Edit Domain Name Parts
 5) Edit Configuration Options
 6) Set the configuration file level
 ?) Help

Selection:
```

**Figure 17.1** edconfig panel.

*Option symbols:*

| | | |
|---|---|---|
| "D" | Defines a symbol from text or a built-in variable.<br>*Example:* `DSfoo.bar.com` | Defines subdomain as var "S." |
| "C" | Defines a class from a list<br>*Example:* `CFhost1 host2 host3` | Defines a host list as var "F." |
| "F" | Defines a class from a file<br>*Example:* `FF/usr/local/lib/hosts` | Obtains list "F" from hosts file. |
| "H" | Defines header formats<br>*Example:* `D?P?Return-Path: <$g>` | Defines return-path format. |
| "O" | Sets sendmail run-time options<br>*Example:* `OA/etc/aliases`<br>`OK ALL` | Defines alias file path.<br>Supports all nameservice mail exchange records and host table lookups. |
| "T" | Sets trusted users<br>*Example:* `Tusername1 username2` | These users may invoke sendmail and masquerade as other users. |
| "P" | Sets message precedence<br>*Example:* `priority = 100`<br>`junk = −100` | Indicates delivery priority if `Precedence:` header field is found. Negative numbers do not return mail on error. |

**17.2.1.2 Address rules.** The address rewriting rules are where the apprentices are separated from the wizards. The `sendmail` daemon uses the rule sets to parse the address lines from the mail header to determine how the mail message should be delivered.

Each rule set is made up of three parts: *left hand side* (LHS), *right hand side* (RHS), and *optional comment* (C). Each part is separated by a TAB. In general, if an address matches the LHS rule, then the RHS rule is applied to the address. The rule sets are applied in order until a failure occurs (see Table 17.1). Any number of rule sets can be defined (see Table 17.2).

To deliver a mail message, the rule sets must resolve to a (*mailer, host, user*) tuple.

*Example: Rule Set 7 Parses Domain String*

```
S7
#Domain addressing (up to 6 level)
R$+@$-.$-.$-.$-.$-.$-      @$2.$3.$4.$5.$6.$7
R$+@$-.$-.$-.$-.$-         @$2.$3.$4.$5.$6
R$+@$-.$-.$-.$-            @$2.$3.$4.$5
R$+@$-.$-.$-               @$2.$3.$4
R$+@$-.$-                  @$2.$3
R$+@$-                     @$2
```

**TABLE 17.1 Default `sendmail.cf` Rule Sets**

| Rule set | Description |
|---|---|
| 3 | Applied first and is responsible for canonicalizing the address to internal form. |
| 2 | Rewrite recipient address. |
| 1 | Rewrite sender address. |
| 0 | Applied last and determines delivery. Address must be resolved to a (*mailer, host, user*) tuple. |
| 4 | Final rewrite of canonical internal form to external form. |

**TABLE 17.2 Rule Set Symbols**

| | | |
|---|---|---|
| *LHS Tokens:* | | |
| | `$*` | Match 0 or more tokens |
| | `$+` | Match 1 or more tokens |
| | `$-` | Match exactly 1 token |
| | `$ = X` | Match any token in class X |
| | `$X` | Match any token not in X |
| *RHS Tokens:* | | |
| | `$n` | Use token `n` from LHS |
| | `$>n` | Call ruleset `n` |
| | `$#mailer` | Resolve to mailer |
| | `$@host` | Specify host to mailer |
| | `$:user` | Specify user to mailer |
| | `$[host$]` | Get host from resolver |
| | `$@` | Terminates ruleset |
| | `$:` | Terminates current rule |

**17.2.1.3 Mailer delivery.** The last section of the `sendmail.cf` file identifies the mailers to be used to deliver the mail message. Each mailer is identified by a name, a program used to transfer the messages to the mailer, the set of program flags, the send and receive rules, and the argument set.

*Mailer identification format:*

```
M<mailer> P = <prog> F = <flags> S = <send-rule> F = <receive-rule> A =
<arguments>
Example local and OSIMF X.400 RFC 987 Mailer Definition
Mlocal, P = /bin/bellmail, F = lsDFMmn, S = 10, R = 20, A = mail $u
M987gateway, P = /usr/lpp/osimf/etc/x400mailer, F = sBFMhulmnSC, S = 15,
R = 25, A = gateway -f /etc/x400gw.cfg $f $u
```

Sendmail accesses configuration file information from a compiled version of the `/etc/sendmail.cf` table. To compile a new version of the database use the sendmail `-bz` flag.

```
# /usr/lib/sendmail -bz              Compile a new sendmail.cf database
```

### 17.2.2 sendmail.nl

The AIX-supplied `sendmail` daemon also obtains national language rule sets from the `/etc/sendmail.nl` file. The national language rules are regular expressions that may be used to identify country names or country codes to support language translation. If the country is identified in the list of NLS code sets, the message is converted to the correct code set.

*AIX-supplied* `/etc/sendmail.nl`:

```
# aix_sccsid[] = "com/cmd/send/sendmail.nl, bos, bos320 AIX 6/15/90
23:25:54"
#
# COMPONENT_NAME: CMDSEND sendmail.nl
#
# FUNCTIONS:
#
# ORIGINS: 10 26 27
#
# (C) COPYRIGHT International Business Machines Corp. 1985, 1989
# All Rights Reserved
# Licensed Materials—Property of IBM
#
# US Government Users Restricted Rights—Use, duplication or
# disclosure restricted by GSA ADP Schedule Contract with IBM Corp.
#
# Created: 03/24/89, INTERACTIVE Systems Corporation
# ######################################################################
#
# This file contains lists of regular expressions which are
# compared against the destination address when sending out
# mail to other systems. Each comma-separated list is preceded
# by either "NLS:" or "8859:". Addresses which match an item
# in these lists will have the body of the mail item encoded
# as either NLS escape sequences or ISO 8859/1 characters,
# respectively.
#
# Before each address is compared with these lists it is passed
# through ruleset 7, which normally strips the user information
# from uucp-style addresses and route and user information from
# domain-style addresses.
#
# The following example lists shows how this file might look:
#
# #list the nls compatible systems
# NLS: ^@.*madrid\.,
# ^@rome,
# ^@.*italy\.europe$,
# !nagasaki!$,
# lisbon!,
# munich,
# berlin
#
# #list the ISO-8859 compatible systems
# 8859: .*vienna!$,
# ^@bangkok\.thailand,
# ^@tangiers,
# ^@kinshasa
```

```
#
# Note that all dots "." in an address must be escaped with
# a backslash "\". All standard regular expression rules apply.
# Several of the above examples are not recommended for actual
# use but are shown to give some idea of the flexibility that
# is allowed. For example, the first example "madrid" will match
# any domain-style address which has this name as a subdomain.
# A more likely example of this type is "italy.europe" which will
# match all domains that are in that subdomain. The examples
# "munich" and "berlin" are not recommended forms either since they
# will match a variety of addresses.
#
# This file must be compiled using the "-bn" option before sendmail
# can use it. It is recommended that this file be tested against
# common addresses using the "-br" option to verify that addresses
# are being interpreted correctly.
#
######################################################################
```

### 17.2.3 Aliases

The sendmail *alias* database provides a mechanism for forwarding mail to one or more users when mail is addressed to the alias name. In particular you will want to set up aliases for the site `postmaster` and `MAILER-DAEMON` ids. The postmaster account is a standard used by the network at large for requesting mail help and information for a site. The MAILER-DAEMON account is used by sendmail to route problem mail.

*Example* `/etc/aliases`:

```
##
# Aliases in this file will NOT be expanded in the header from
# Mail, but WILL be visible over networks or from /bin/mail.
#
# >>>>>>>>>> The program "newaliases" must be run after
# >> NOTE >> updating this file before any changes
# >>>>>>>>>> show through to sendmail.
##
# Alias for mailer daemon
MAILER-DAEMON:root
# The following alias is required by the new mail protocol, RFC 822
postmaster:root
# Aliases to handle mail to msgs and news
msgs: "|/usr/ucb/msgs -s"
nobody: "|cat>/dev/null"
# Alias for uucp maintenance
uucplist:root
### These are local aliases ###
trouble: root
root: deroest
```

Sendmail accesses alias information from a dbm version of the `/etc/aliases` table. To compile a new version of the `/etc/aliases` table, use the `/usr/lib/newaliases` command or `/usr/lib /sendmail -bi`.

`# /usr/lib/sendmail -bi`   Create new alias database

### 17.2.4 Mail logs

It's a good idea to keep logs of sendmail activity. They are very helpful in diagnosing problems, identifying slow mail loops, and sleuthing connections from remote sites. Sendmail logs activities using `syslogd`. The default log file location per `/etc/syslog.conf` is the `/var/spool/mqueue/syslog` file.

*Example* `syslog`:

```
Aug 9 13:19:01 daffy sendmail[146022]: AA146022: message-id =
<9308092018.AA05836 @mx1.cac.washington.edu>
Aug 9 13:19:01 daffy sendmail[146022]: AA146022: from =
<MAILER@UWAVM.U.WASHINGTON.EDU>, size = 1731, class = 0, received from
mx1.cac.washington.edu (140.142.32.1)
Aug 9 13:19:02 daffy sendmail[51047]: AA146022: to =
<deroest@daffy.cac.washington.edu>, delay = 00:00:02, stat = Sent
```

Because the log file tends to grow rapidly, you need to periodically close it and archive it. This procedure can be handled via `cron` and the `/usr/lib/smdemon.cleanu` script. The script closes the syslog file and copies it to a `log.` file for archiving. The default `root` crontab contains an entry for `smdemon.cleanu`. However, it is commented out. Remove the comment and replace the crontab to activate log file cleanup.

*Crontab for* `smdaemon.cleanu`:

```
45 23 * * * ulimit 5000; /usr/lib/smdemon.cleanu > /dev/null
```

## 17.3 Starting and Stopping Sendmail

Sendmail is invoked as a subsystem from the `/etc/rc.tcpip` script. The AIX sendmail automatically compiles the `/etc/aliases` and `/etc/sendmail.cf` files when it is started. If you are running a non-IBM-supplied sendmail, you may need to force a compile of these files as part of the start-up.

| | |
|---|---|
| `# /usr/lib/sendmail -bi` | Compile /etc/aliases |
| `# /usr/lib/sendmail -bz` | Compile /etc/sendmail.cf |
| `# /usr/lib/sendmail -bn` | Compile /etc/sendmail.nl |

You can also use the `/etc/newaliases` command to compile the alias file. If you update any of the configuration information while sendmail is running, compile the files and refresh the sendmail subsystem by issuing an SRC `refresh` command or sending the daemon a SIGHUP.

```
# refresh -s sendmail
# kill -1 'cat /etc/sendmail.pid'
```

The basic start-up flags for sendmail should invoke sendmail as a daemon and specify the time in minutes between mail queue scans for postponed messages. These flags are `-bd` and `-q<time>`.

```
# /usr/lib/sendmail -bd -q30m       Start and scan mail queue every 30 minutes
```

To stop the `sendmail` daemon, use the SRC `stopsrc` command or send a SIGABORT to the daemon.

```
# stopsrc -s sendmail
# kill -6 'cat /etc/sendmail.pid'
```

## 17.4 Debugging

The simplest way to test sendmail is to use the `-v verbose` flag with `/usr/bin/mail`. It provides feedback on the interaction between MTAs.

```
# /usr/bin/mail -v bart@krusty.fun.com
Subject: test
test mail body
.
bart… setsender: uid/gid = 4084/0
bart@krusty.fun.com… Connecting to krusty.fun.com.tcp…
bart@krusty.fun.com… Connecting to krusty.fun.com (tcp)…
220 krusty.fun.com Sendmail 5.65/Revision: 2.28
ready at Mon, 9 Aug 93 12:40:42 -0700
>>> HELO mobius.bank.org
250 krusty.fun.com Hello mobius.bank.org, pleased to meet you
>>> MAIL From:<doogie@mobius.bank.org>
250 <doogie@mobius.bank.org>… Sender ok
>>> RCPT To:<bart@krusty.fun.com>
250 <bart@krusty.fun.com>… Recipient ok
>>> DATA
354 Enter mail, end with "." on a line by itself
>>> .
250 Ok
>>> QUIT
221 krusty.fun.com closing connection
bart@krusty.fun.com… Sent
```

Test rule sets by invoking sendmail with the `-bt` flag. Sendmail will prompt for the rule sets to be invoked and the address. Separate each rule set number with a comma.

```
                  # /usr/lib/sendmail -bt -C/usr/lib/sendmail.cf
                  ADDRESS TEST MODE
                  Enter <ruleset> <address>
                  > 2,4,0 deroest@washington.edu
rewrite:  ruleset  2  input:    "deroest"      "@"    "washington"  "."   "edu"
rewrite:  ruleset  2  returns:  "deroest"      "@"    "washington"  "."   "edu"
rewrite:  ruleset  4  input:    "deroest"      "@"    "washington"  "."   "edu"
rewrite:  ruleset  4  returns:  "deroest"      "@"    "washington"  "."   "edu"
rewrite:  ruleset  0  input:    "deroest"      "@"    "washington"  "."   "edu"
rewrite:  ruleset  0  returns:  "^V" "local"   "^X"   "deroest"     "@"   "daffy"
                  >
```

The sendmail command supports a number of debugging and trace levels. They can be activated using the start-up option `-d<nn>.<mm>`, where <nn> and <mm> define the debug and trace levels. You'll want to redirect the output to a file as it can be *very* verbose. The IBM AIX `sendmail` daemon only supports a value of `21.`<mm> where <mm> can be any positive integer. If you are running a current copy of sendmail, refer to the source code for debug and trace values.

```
# /usr/lib/sendmail -bd -q30m -d20.1
```

Check the logs, mail queue, and stats files periodically for stalled mail or loops. You can list the pending delivery queue using the `mailq` command.

```
# mailq
Mail Queue (1 request)
-QID—Size——Q-Time——————Sender/Recipient————
AA49872 (no control file)
```

Files in the mail queue are identified by a QID. The first character of the QID designates the type of queue file.

| | |
|---|---|
| "d" | Message data file |
| "l" | Lock file |
| "n" | Backup file |
| "q" | Control file |
| "t" | Temp file |
| "x" | Transcript file |

The `/etc/sendmail.st` file can be checked using the `/usr/lib /mailstats` command.

```
# mailstats
Mailer      msgs_from      bytes_from      msgs_to      bytes_to
local       123            8450            57           2780
```

To reset mail statistics, invoke `mailstats` with the `-z` flag.

```
# mailstats -z
```

## 17.5 Managing Mail Queues

As administrators, it's our responsibility to inform users when mail arrives and pester them to get rid of old unwanted mail. Since the latter is a difficult job at best, I'll start with the easy one of informing users when mail arrives.

The `comsat` daemon, when prompted by `sendmail,` informs users that new mail is waiting. This feature is supported by the `MAIL` and `MAILMSG` variables defined in the default `/etc/profile.`

| | |
|---|---|
| `MAIL = /var/spool/mail/$LOGNAME` | Path to incoming mail |
| `MAILMSG = "[YOU HAVE NEW MAIL]"` | Mail waiting message |

The `comsat` daemon must also be defined in `/etc/inetd.conf`

```
comsat      dgram      udp      wait      root      /etc/comsat comsat
```

It's also a good idea to inform users when mail is waiting at login time. This can be accomplished by checking the mail from the default login scripts for each shell. See Chap. 21 for details on setting up systemwide default login scripts.

*Sample login mail check:*

```
#! /bin/sh
#
if [ -s "$MAIL" ]
then echo "$MAILMSG"
fi
```

Without being heavyhanded with your user community, it is difficult to encourage users to keep up with incoming mail. The best policy is to use regular reminders and track queue usage using disk utilization commands like `du`.

| | |
|---|---|
| `# du -s /var/spool/mail` | Disk usage for mail queue |
| `# du -s /var/spool/mail/*` | Mail queue usage by user |

## 17.6 OSIMF/6000

Chapter 11 described the Open Systems Interconnection (OSI) reference model for networking. Besides the reference model, there exist OSI standards for transport, file transfer, and electronic mail services. For sites interested in providing OSI protocol support, the *OSIMF/6000* licensed program product is available for the RISC System/6000 which provides the protocols listed previously. OSIMF/6000 will coexist with the TCP/IP protocol stack on a single system. This allows you to implement a protocol gateway between OSI and TCP/IP.

For the purposes of this electronic mail discussion, X.400 MTA to SMTP gateway support is defined by RFC 987 and can be configured using OSIMF/6000. In this environment, you may elect to use either RFC 822 style UAs or the X.400 UA provided by OSIMF/6000.

Since a complete description of X.400 protocol and components is beyond the scope of this book, I'll briefly outline the steps in defining an X.400 gateway.

1. After installing OSIMF/6000, edit the `/usr/lpp/osimf/etc/loadmhs` script and include the local presentation address of the

MTA. The presentation address is the MAC-level address of the adapter.

2. Next, edit the MTA configuration file, `/etc/mta.cfg`, and include the O/R names (originator/recipient), UAs, and MTA/UA routing information. Edit the X.400/SMTP gateway file `/etc/x400gw.cfg` to define O/R name mapping attributes. Check the mailer section of `/etc/sendmail.cf` to see that OSIMF/6000 gateway support is defined.
3. Invoke `/usr/lpp/osimf/etc/makemhs` to build a new X.400 MTA.

### 17.6.1 Starting and stopping the gateway

OSIMF/6000 start-up parameters are specified as arguments to the `/etc/rc.osimf` command. To invoke X.400 mail support, use the `-mhs` argument.

```
# rc.osimf -mhs        Start X.400 mail support
```

To stop OSIMF/6000 protocols, use the `osimf.clean` command.

```
# osimf.clean -mhs        Stop X.400 mail support
```

## 17.7 InforExplorer Keywords

| | |
|---|---|
| /usr/lib/.Mail.rc mail | /usr/lib/smdemon.cleanu |
| .mailrc | mailq |
| sendmail | mailstats |
| mmdf | comsat |
| smail | MAIL |
| mhs | MAILMSG |
| /etc/sendmail.cf | /etc/profile |
| /etc/aliases | /etc/inetd.conf |
| edconfig | inetd |
| /etc/sendmail.nl | du |
| postmaster | OSIMF |
| /etc/syslog.conf | osimf |
| syslogd | makemhs |
| cron | |

## 17.8 QwikInfo

### Electronic mail

*Mail user agent:*

| | |
|---|---|
| `/bin/mail` or `/usr/ucb/mail` | User agent |
| `/usr/lib/Mail.rc` | Global options |
| `/home/$USER/.mailrc` | User options |

*Mail transfer agent:*

| | |
|---|---|
| `/usr/sbin/sendmail` | Mail transfer agent |
| `/etc/sendmail.cf` | Sendmail configuration |
| `/etc/sendmail.cfDB` | Compiled sendmail.cf |
| `/etc/sendmail.nl` | Sendmail NLS rules |
| `/etc/sendmail.nlDB` | Compiled NLS rules |
| `/etc/aliases` | Mail aliases |
| `/etc/aliasesDB` | Compiled alias file |
| `/etc/sendmail.pid` | PID of sendmail daemon |
| `/etc/sendmail.st` | Mail statistics |
| `/var/spool/mail/$USER` | Incoming mail |
| `/var/spool/mqueue` | Queued mail |

*Mail subsystem:*

| | |
|---|---|
| `sendmail -bi` | Build new alias DB |
| `sendmail -bz` | Build new sendmail DB |
| `sendmail -bn` | Build new NLS DB |
| `sendmail -bd -q30m` | Start sendmail |
| `mailq` | List queued mail |
| `mailstats` | List mail statistics |

*Debugging:*

| | |
|---|---|
| `mail -v <user@address>` | Verify delivery |
| `telnet <host>` | 25 Telnet to SMTP port |
| `sendmail -bt -C/usr/lib/sendmail.cf` | Test rewrite rule sets |
| `sendmail -d20.1` | Run sendmail in debug |
| `/var/spool/mqueue/syslog` | Sendmail log |

Chapter

# 18

# News

## 18.1 Read All About It

Usenet News is a network-based bulletin board system that reaches hundreds of thousands of users via Internet and UUCP connections. Users interact in electronic discussion groups called *newsgroups* using interfaces called *news readers*. The news reader clients present an interface that resembles electronic mail user agents. Usenet topics range from serious research discussions to humor, hobbies, politics, just about anything you can think of. News is another one of those addictive network services. Providing news service is a carrot that will assist in getting the hard sell folks to use your computers. However, "Once you giveth you canst taketh away!"

## 18.2 News Resources

Any system on the network can host a bulletin board and accept or provide *news feeds* with other interested sites. Depending on the feeds a site is willing to accept, a news server can receive tens of megabytes of news information a day. Dedicated spool space is required to house news data. Control over who you accept feeds from, the news groups you will accept, and setting expiration policies for old news allow you to manage the disk resources required. It is a good idea to house news in a file system of its own.

Network bandwidth is another important consideration. Sites receiving news feeds via dial-up UUCP connections will want to run transfers during off hours and implement high-speed modems with data compression.

For very active news sites, the news server will require sufficient memory and CPU to support the connection daemons and search processing resources required by news reader connections. Using server software that supports *threaded* searches will reduce search CPU requirements.

## 18.3 News Server

The news server machine receives and transmits news feeds and accepts client connections using the *Network News Transfer Protocol* (NNTP). The NNTP protocol is described in RFC977 along with the general overview of how network news functions. NNTP represents a basic protocol that supports a limited set of commands and responses allowing for the selection and identification of news groups and articles (see Table 18.1). The protocol is similar to that employed by electronic mail *Simple Mail Transfer Protocol* (SMTP).

There are a number of news software packages available via anonymous ftp. Packages like `nntp` and `inn` provide the server support for reader/poster clients, transfer clients for news feeds, and administration tools for controlling resource utilization. News server daemons can be run stand-alone or they can be invoked by inetd. The choice will depend on the traffic levels to be supported. The server forks a daemon for each client connection which maintains the dialog for news articles located in `/usr/spool/news`. Note that most of the server software comes as a base package and then a large number of patches are available. Make sure you get the whole set of patches when installing a particular release.

Servers can restrict client access and posting by identifying trusted sites in the `/usr/lib/news/nntp.access` file. Trusted sites are identified by address, access rights, post allowed, and news groups. A host address may be either the host name, domain name, network name, or IP address. Wild cards are supported using the "`*`" character. Negation is implemented using the "`!`" character.

`/usr/lib/news/nntp.access:`

```
#
# Example nntp server access file
#
# Address   Access   Post    Newsgroups
default     xfer     no
```

**TABLE 18.1 NNTP Commands**

| Command | Description |
|---|---|
| `ARTICLE, BODY, HEAD` | Return news article, body, or header |
| `STAT` | Set current article pointer |
| `GROUP` | Return first and last group article numbers |
| `LIST` | Return list of news groups |
| `HELP` | Return command summary |
| `IHAVE` | Identify article number to server |
| `LAST` | Set article pointer to previous article |
| `NEWGROUPS` | New groups created since date and time |
| `NEWNEWS` | List of message IDs of new articles |
| `NEXT` | Set article pointer to next article |
| `POST` | Request posting to a group |
| `QUIT` | End connection with server |
| `SLAVE` | This connection is to a slave server |

```
ibm-competator      read    post    !comp.unix.aix
daffy       no      no
*.whatsamata.edu    no      no
128.239.2.110       read    no
```

Although these packages provide their own NNTP protocol support under the `nntpxmit` program, additional software like *nntplink* can be incorporated to improve performance and provide time-based news updates.

Your best bet is to take a look at all the server packages and pick one that represents your sites requirements. Be sure to review the documentation supplied with the server software carefully. Other server sites with which you interact are depending on the coordination of feeds. Subscribe to the administration and new user news groups for additional information.

*News-related news groups:*

```
news.sysadmin
news.software.b
news.software.nntp
news.software.readers
news.newsites
news.announce.newusers
news.announce.newgroups
```

## 18.4 News Readers

Like cars on the highways, there are a number of news reader packages to choose from (see Table 18.2). Most sites end up supporting more than one news reader. "Different strokes for different folks!"

The news readers are responsible for user interaction with the news groups. They perform functions like news group subscription, archiving, searching, reading, and posting. Each user's news interaction state is kept in a `$HOME/.newsrc` file. The `.newsrc` file indicates which groups a user has subscribed to and the identification number of the last article read.

`$HOME/.newsrc:`

```
alt.activism! 1-27300
alt.angst! 1-2052
```

**TABLE 18.2 News Readers**

| | |
|---|---|
| rn | Read News |
| trn | Threaded Read News |
| xrn | X11 Read News |
| nn | No News is Good News |
| tin | Threaded Internet News |
| gnus | Gnu Emacs News Macros |
| pine | Email User Agent with News Support |
| NewsGrazer | Macintosh News Reader |

```
alt.aquaria! 1-12683
alt.atheism! 1-28722
alt.bbs! 1-10369
alt.beer! 1-5058
alt.books.technical! 1-953
alt.brother-jed! 1-1075
alt.callahans! 1-19131
alt.cd-rom! 1-2789
alt.co-ops! 1-464
alt.cobol! 1-781,785-786
alt.config! 1-8285
```

It goes on and on.

Some news readers incorporate their own posting software, yet there are posting packages that may be added which provide additional features and improved header checking. In general, the posting software validates the news header, appends a user-supplied `.signature` file, and transfers the file to the news server.

## 18.5 News Groups

The last time I looked at my `.newsrc` file there were 2380 different news groups. Mind you, I don't subscribe to them all. On the average, I have noticed about five new news groups coming on-line each day. Sites may add local groups as they see fit. Networkwide groups must go through a balloting procedure before the group becomes public. Many electronic mail discussion lists are forwarded into news groups. A number of the Bitnet Listserv discussions are represented in news groups under the `bit.listserv` classification (see Table 18.3).

News groups that are related to AIX and UNIX administration are listed as follows. You likely won't be able to follow them regularly, but they are worth checking out.

**TABLE 18.3 News Group Classifications**

| | |
|---|---|
| alt | Alternative topics |
| bionet | Genetics and biology topics |
| bit.listserv | Bitnet Listserv discussion topics |
| biz | Vendor topics |
| clari | Newspaper |
| comp | Computer-related topics |
| gnu | Gnu freeware topics |
| k12 | Elementary and secondary education topics |
| misc | Miscellaneous topics |
| news | Usenet administration and use |
| rec | Recreation topics |
| sci | Scientific topics |
| soc | Social topics |
| talk | General topics |
| vmsnet | VMS topics |
| * | Various local groups |

| | |
|---|---|
| `comp.unix.aix` | AIX and RS/6000 discussion |
| `comp.unix.wizards` | UNIX wizards Q&A |
| `comp.unix.sources` | Public domain sources |
| `comp.unix.large` | Large and distributed UNIX systems |
| `comp.unix.osf.misc` | OSF general discussion |
| `comp.unix.osf.osf1` | OSF/1 discussion |
| `bit.listserv.aix-l` | Bitnet AIX e-mail discussion |
| `bit.listserv.sp1-l` | Bitnet POWER Parallel SP1 discussion |
| `bit.listserv.ll-l` | Load Leveler batch discussion |
| `bit.listserv.power-pc` | POWER PC discussion |
| `bit.listserv.dqs-l` | Distributed Queuing System discussion |

## 18.6 News Software Sites

The AIX public domain software repository at UCLA has both source and binary news server and news reader packages. See App. A for information on obtaining software from public servers.

## 18.7 QwikInfo

*NEWS:*

| | |
|---|---|
| `nntp` | News daemon |
| `nntpxmit` | News transfer |
| `nntplink` | News transfer |
| `/var/spool/news` | News spool |
| `/usr/lib/news/nntp.access` | Restrict nntp access |
| `rn, trn, xrn, nn, tin, gnus` | News readers |
| `$HOME/.newsrc` | News group state |

Chapter

# 19

# DOS Services

## 19.1 DOS Under AIX

*WARNING: The topic of this chapter may be offensive to hardened UNIX afficionados.* That's right, it's about MS-DOS. *Gasp!* As hard as it is to believe, the majority of computer users *don't run UNIX.* Alas, its true. Have no fear, the tools described will show you how MS-DOS and AIX can coexist and interoperate peacefully on the same hardware.

## 19.2 DOS Tools

Basic DOS file import and export capability is provided under AIX, using the `dosformat`, `dosdir`, `dosread`, `doswrite`, and `dosdel` commands. These commands are useful when sharing text files between the two operating systems. `dosformat` uses an RS/6000 diskette drive to DOS format 3.5-in diskettes. The `dosread` and `doswrite` commands move files between AIX and DOS media with selectable line end NL to CR-LF mapping and Ctrl-Z end of file insertion. `dosdir` displays DOS diskette directory contents. `dosdel` removes a file from the diskette media.

```
# dosformat                              Format a diskette
# dosdir                                 Display disketted directory
# dosread [-a] <DOSFile> <AIXFile>       Copy a DOS file to AIX
# doswrite [-a] <AIXFile> <DOSFile>      Copy an AIX file to DOS
# dosdel <DOSFile>                       Delete a DOS file
```

Pacific Microelectronic's *Common-Link* software can be used to include Macintosh disk formats. The program supports both DOS and Mac file transfer via diskette with easy-to-use menus.

## 19.3 Intel Emulation

DOS emulation packages provide the next level of DOS functionality under AIX. Packages like IBM's *Personal Computer Simulator/6000* (pcsim) and Insignia's *SoftPC* emulate the Intel hardware environment on top of AIX. Device support and application response may suffer due to the multiple layers of emulation required and limited device access. It's common to see a 10 × degradation in application throughput and up to 20 × degradation for graphics display control under software emulation.

| | |
|---|---|
| Layer 6 | Application |
| Layer 5 | Windows |
| Layer 4 | DOS |
| Layer 3 | Intel Emulation |
| Layer 2 | AIX |
| Layer 1 | RS/6000 Hardware |

## 19.4 Personal Computer Simulator/6000

AIX *Personal Computer Simulator/6000* (pcsim) emulates an Intel 80286 PC hardware environment under AIX. The Intel emulation doesn't support multitasking environments like Windows 3.1 or OS/2, and there is no support for protected mode applications. *Officially,* pcsim runs MS-DOS 3.30. MS-DOS 4.0 and 5.0 will work within limits. You can run Windows 3.0 in real mode, but I question why you would want to do this, even on a real 286 machine. pcsim shares display, disk, and diskette resources with AIX; however, there is no direct control or access provided to RS/6000 devices or the Micro Channel.

### 19.4.1 Installing DOS on pcsim

The first problem many people run into after installing pcsim is that they forget to install MS-DOS. You execute the `pcsim` command, DOS isn't found, so you're thrown into the BASIC interpreter. *Sigh!* The following procedure will fix you up.

1. Create a file for the emulated C drive

```
# touch /usr/lpp/pcsim/Cdrive
```

2. Start pcsim with DOS diskette inserted

```
# pcsim -A 3 -C /usr/lpp/pcsim/Cdrive -save
```

3. Create DOS partitions

```
C> A:\FDISK
```

4. Install DOS

```
C> A:\SELECT C: 001 US
```

5. Exit pcsim and set permissions

```
# chmod 444 /usr/lpp/pcsim/Cdrive
```

### 19.4.2 Multiuser pcsim

pcsim supports a limit of five users in a multiuser environment. The shared DOS OS and application base reside in the read-only `C:` drive, `/usr/lpp/pcsim/Cdrive`. A shared read-write data drive may be set up as drive `D`. Create a directory called `/usr/lpp/pcsim/Drive` with permissions set to 777. Make sure that this drive is defined in the default pcsim profile. Each pcsim user may also have local directories as drives `E` through `Z`. Only one user at a time will have access to diskette drives.

In a multiuser environment, if you have to kill pcsim sessions from AIX, remember that they are using shared memory that must be freed. Look for `x495043` in the ipcs list. Remove each entry, last to first, using the `ipcrm -m` command. Remember to consider the pcsim resource requirements on your system when planning a multiuser environment.

### 19.4.3 Running pcsim

You can tailor your pcsim environment using command line flags at each invocation, or using a static configuration profile called `simprof`.

*Example pcsim command line:*

```
% pcsim -A 3
        -C /usr/lpp/pcsim/Cdrive
        -D /usr/lpp/pcsim/Drive
        -E /home/user/DOS/Edrive
        -dmode V
        -lpt1 lp
        -mouse com1
        -refresh 50
```

*Example* `simprof` *profile:*

```
Adiskette     : 3
Cdrive        : /usr/lpp/pcsim/Cdrive
Ddrive        : /usr/lpp/pcsim/Ddrive
Edrive        : /home/user/Ddrive/DOS/Edrive
dmode         : v
lpt           : lp
mouse         : com1
refresh       : 50
```

Note that you can't use shell environment variables in the profile.

You can create a simprof profile based on the command line flags by adding the -save flag when invoking pcsim. A default system profile is located in /usr/lpp/pcsim/samples directory. When pcsim is started, it will look for simprof profiles in the current directory, your home directory, and the system default directory. Options in each of these profiles will be accumulated for the session. To exit pcsim, type <ESC>pcsim.

### 19.4.4 pcsim features

**19.4.4.1 Display.** pcsim emulates both monochrome and VGA displays. Monochrome emulation of Code Page 437 is available for HFT, aixterm, and TTY sessions. VGA is supported from AIXwindows and may be sized to full screen. Default VGA resolution is 720x480 with 256 colors. IBM Xstations must be configured for 256 colors for full VGA compatibility. The display type is selected using the dmode command line flag or profile parameter.

Most of the performance problems experienced under pcsim are related to refreshing the display. Each screen update requires a complete refresh of the display. You can set the screen refresh rate using the refresh flag or profile parameter. Refresh rate may range from 20 to 500 ms. When pcsim is updating a remote AIXwindows session, network performance can be a bottleneck. Each screen refresh will result in a burst of screen data based on the following formula. Monochrome mode will provide better performance if graphics are required.

$$\text{Height} \times \text{Width} \times \text{BitDepth} \times \text{RefreshRate} = \text{BytesPerSec}$$

Screen attributes for a given terminal type are the result of a combination of *terminfo* and *pcsim/TTY* definitions. I'll cover pcsim terminal attributes further in the next section. If your terminal definition does not support a 25-line screen, you can use the F12 key to shift the display between the first and 25th screen lines.

**19.4.4.2 Keyboard.** Like terminal screen attributes, keyboard maps are based on information in the /usr/lib/terminfo and /usr/lpp/pcsim/tty configuration files. pcsim TTY definition files are named like their terminfo counterparts identifying the desired emulation. Custom key definitions can be set up by editing the section labeled HARDCMD in the appropriate pcsim TTY file. If you aren't certain what sequence a particular key on your terminal transmits, use vi in input mode and enter the sequence ctrl-V *your-key*. You should see the sequence of characters sent by *your-key* displayed on the screen. Remember that some keys transmit a CR/NL sequence. Make sure you include this in your definition. The following commands are useful when setting and verifying your key map definition.

| | |
|---|---|
| /usr/lpp/pcsim/samples/simXkeymap | Set key maps |
| /usr/bin/setmaps | |
| /usr/bin/editty | Check syntax |

**19.4.4.3 Mouse.** Mouse support under AIXwindows is available using *grab mode* or *free mode*. Grab mode attaches the mouse to the pcsim window and is no longer available to other AIXwindows clients. To select grab mode, define the mouse using `Com1` or `Com2`. *Note that capital letters are significant in the* `ComN` *identifiers.* Free mode allows you to share the mouse with other AIXwindows clients. The mouse is only active under pcsim when it is within the window. Configure free mode using `com1` or `com2`. For best results use the Microsoft or PS/2 mouse drivers, and a screen refresh rate of 50. To keep AIXwindows and pcsim mouse acceleration in synch, specify `-wrap` when starting X.

**19.4.4.4 Disk.** DOS disks may be emulated within an AIX file, or provided via access standard AIX file system directories. The latter facilitates sharing files between AIX and DOS and will work in NFS and AFS environments. When accessing an AIX directory as a hard disk, remember to create a `.doslabel` file if you intend to label the disk with the DOS `LABEL` command. To access lowercase file names in the AIX directories, specify the `case` command line flag or profile parameter. Emulated disks are created within an AIX file using the DOS `FDISK` command. Multiple logical drives may be created within a single emulation file. Drive letters are mapped to files, directories, or devices using command line flags or profile parameters. Standard convention is to use letters `C` and `D` for emulated disks and `E` through `Z` for AIX directories.

RS/6000 diskette drives may be shared between AIX and one pcsim session. The diskette drives are identified using drive letters `A` and `B`. The `dtime` command line flag indicates idle time when the diskette drive is available to one side or the other. CD-ROM is also accessible as a DOS disk as long as it formatted in *High Sierra* or *ISO9660*.

**19.4.4.5 Printers.** Printer support is provided by mapping the DOS LPT1, LPT2, and LPT3 print devices to standard AIX print queues. Specify the AIX queue name after each of the LPTn command line flags or profile parameters, where *n* represents device 1, 2, or 3. DOS print jobs are passed to AIX as files and then passed to the appropriate qdaemon queue using `enq -q`. Since pcsim and AIX must communicate when an individual print job file should be closed and printed, the `ptime` flag is provided to indicate device idle state.

**19.4.4.6 COM devices.** Access to RS/6000 serial ports is defined using `comN` to `/dev/ttyP` mapping from command line flags or profile entries. `N` indicates the com port number and `P` the TTY device.

Applications that are timing-dependent on com port control may exhibit unpredictable results due to AIX device buffering. To make RS/6000 serial ports available to pcsim, complete the following procedure.

```
1. % cp pcsim/lib/pcsimdd /etc/tty/pcsimdd
2. % ln /etc/tyy/pcsimdd /etc/drivers/pcsimdd
3. Configure the serial port using SMIT
4. Add "/etc/tty/ttyconf -l pcsim" to /etc/rc
```

**19.4.4.7 Memory.** *Conventional* and *extended* memory are supported by pcsim. *Expanded* memory is not supported. Conventional memory is the first 640 KB of DOS memory. The Intel 80286 processor introduced the ability to address memory beyond 640 KB. DOS did not have this capability, so expanded memory managers were developed to open a small window in conventional memory, within which to address the upper memory blocks. Extended memory managers came along later that allowed direct addressing of the upper regions of memory. Use the `xmemory` parameter to define from 1 MB to 15,875 MB of extended memory. Allocation units are in 1-KB units. For performance reasons, you should note that pcsim is designed to stay resident in memory and not be paged out. Remember that you are basically dedicating memory to each pcsim session to support DOS conventional, extended, and video memory requirements.

**19.4.4.8 Coprocessor.** Intel 80287 coprocessor emulation is available using the `i287` command line flag. I have heard reports that the 287 emulation is either faster or slower under pcsim than the real McCoy. You'll have to decide this one for yourself. One thing to watch out for is that floating-point numbers are represented in 80-bit format in memory and 64-bit IEEE format when expressed in registers.

### 19.4.5 pcsim AIX communication

pcsim does not provide any default communications mechanism between DOS and AIX. You can hack a communication channel by using print queues with a custom backend to trap and interpret incoming commands from pcsim. It will work, but it is NOT elegant. A cleaner solution can be found in the `/usr/lpp/pcsim/samples` files. Example applications are provided which allow you to send commands and signals to AIX processes from within pcsim. An AIX process may also attach to the simulator's shared memory to provide a communications channel.

## 19.5 Binary Interfaces

To improve response and device support, vendors like Insignia and Sun Microsystems SunSelect division are implementing application binary interfaces on top of the UNIX kernel. The *Windows Application Binary Interface* (WABI) from SunSelect is getting the most press in this area.

WABI is a reverse-engineered set of Windows application subroutines. These routines provide the interface glue between a Windows application and the base X11 and UNIX kernel routines. This removes some of the emulation overhead and improves response. WABI delivers 486 response under current RISC platforms.

| | |
|---|---|
| Layer 4 | Application |
| Layer 3 | WABI |
| Layer 2 | AIX |
| Layer 1 | RS/6000 Hardware |

IBM has endorsed WABI and will be supporting it on the PowerPC and RS/6000 platforms. Sun would like to see other UNIX vendors bundle WABI with their base operating system offerings. This work has been done without the blessing or assistance of Microsoft.

### 19.5.1 Microkernel personalities

Further improvements in speed, device support, portability, and available OS personalities are being realized using *microkernel* technology. Microkernel operating systems like Carnegie Mellon's *Mach* modularize many traditional kernel functions and move them outside the kernel into user space. What's left is a very small streamlined kernel with standard interfaces to portable file system, device driver, scheduler, and pager modules.

IBM has been working with microkernel technology in the design of their *WorkplaceOS* operating system. WorkplaceOS packages virtual memory management, task and thread management, interprocess communication, I/O processing, interrupt handling, and hardware interfaces into a base kernel. At the next level, modular *Personality Neutral Services* (PNS) like file system support, naming services, device drivers, scheduler, pager, and network services are added. Operating system personalities are layered on top of the PNS layer. This architecture defines a standard open interface for layering operating system personalities like UNIX, DOS, Macintosh, Taligent, etc. Since some layered services may not fit the PNS model, a dominant personality is used to manage non-PNS services in a multipersonality environment.

| | |
|---|---|
| OS layer | UNIX, DOS, Mac, etc. |
| PNS layer | File system, device, naming, pager, scheduler, network |
| Kernel layer | VMM, IPC, Threads, I/O, Interrupt, Hardware |
| Hardware layer | Intel, PowerPC |

See Fig. 19.1 for a microkernel block diagram.

| Operating System Personalities |
|---|
| Personality Neutral Services<br>File System, Device, Naming, Pager, Scheduler, Network |
| Microkernel<br>VMM, IPC, Threads, I/O, Interrupt, Hardware |
| Hardware Architectures |

**Figure 19.1** Microkernel layers.

The microkernel design provides additional functionality, such as parallelism, not normally associated with personal computers and workstations. Multiple OS personalities will allow the user to mix and match applications and share data. WorkplaceOS will be available on Intel and PowerPC architectures.

## 19.6 Remote DOS Services

In the near term, most of us are going to get the best DOS response running native on real Intel or clone architectures. An AIX server can be used to enhance the native DOS environment by providing file system, application, and printing services. The good news is that two common remote DOS file system and print server packages are provided as part of the base AIX operating system, the *PC NFS* authenticator `pcnfsd` and the *AIX Access for DOS* (AADU) server `pci` (see Fig. 19.2).

### 19.6.1 PC NFS

PC NFS server support is provided by the standard AIX NFS services with the addition of authentication and spooling services provided by `/usr/sbin/rpc.pcnfsd`. Authentication services provide a login mechanism allowing PC NFS users to gain privileges by identifying themselves to the AIX server. Users may access NFS file systems without authentication, but their privileges are mapped to user `nobody`. NFS services may be accessed over Ethernet, token-ring, or slip connections. If you are using slip, you will want to use error-correcting modems, as NFS is based on UDP, which does not provide any error-checking or checksum support.

`pcnfsd` may be run as a subserver under the `inetd` subsystem or as a stand-alone server. To run `pcnfsd` as a subserver under `inetd`, add the following entry to the `/etc/inetd.conf` file:

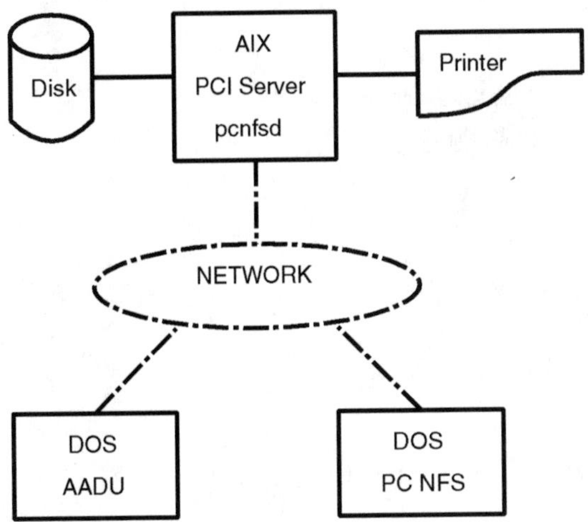


**Figure 19.2** Remote DOS services.

```
pcnfsd sunrpc_udp udp wait root /usr/sbin/rpc.pcnfsd pcnfsd 150001 1
```

You may want to run `pcnfsd` as a stand-alone daemon to alter the location of the spooling directory. Remove any existing `pcnfsd` entries from `/etc/inetd.conf`, and add the following lines to `/etc/rc.tcpip`:

```
if [ -f /usr/sbin/rpc.pcnfsd ]; then
/usr/sbin/rpc.pcnfsd -s <SpoolDirPath>; echo 'pcnfsd\n'
fi
```

### 19.6.2 DOS server for AADU

File system, print spooling, and UNIX application access are also provided by Locus Computing Corporation's *PC-Interface* (PCI), more commonly known to the AIX community as AADU. PCI uses a proprietary protocol to provide access to these services over Ethernet, token-ring, and dial-up connections.

The AIX `pci` server is started by invoking the `/etc/rc.pci` script from an `/etc/inittab` entry. The `inittab` entry should read:

```
rcpci:2:wait:/etc/rc.pci > /dev/console 2>&1
```

`pci` supports print spooling via the `/usr/pci/bin/pciprint` script. You can direct default LPT1 spooling to a particular AIX print queue by editing `pciprint` and specifying the default queue name. For example:

```
exec /bin/enq -P LaserJet
```

## 19.7 InfoExplorer Keywords

| | |
|---|---|
| DOS | simXkeymap |
| dosformat | setmaps |
| dosdir | editty |
| dosread | enq |
| doswrite | ttyconf |
| dosdel | pcnfsd |
| pcsim | /etc/inetd.conf |
| ipcrm | inetd |
| simprof | /usr/sbin/rpc.pcnfsd |
| /usr/lib/terminfo | /etc/inittab |
| /usr/lpp/pcsim/tty | /usr/pci/bin/pciprint |
| vi | pci |

## 19.8 QwikInfo

### DOS

*Tools:*

| | |
|---|---|
| dosformat | Format a diskette |
| dosdir | Display disketted dir |
| dosread [-a] <DOSFile> <AIXFile> | Copy a DOS file to AIX |
| doswrite [-a] <AIXFile> <DOSFile> | Copy an AIX file to DOS |
| dosdel <DOSFile> | Delete a DOS file |

Personal Computer Simulator/6000:

| | |
|---|---|
| /usr/lpp/pcsim | Product and config dir |
| pcsim | Start PCSIM |
| $USER/simprof | Start up profile |
| /etc/tty/ttyconf -l pcsim | Add serial port access |
| /usr/lpp/pcsim/samples/simXkeymap | Set key maps |
| editty | Edit key map |
| /usr/lpp/pcsim/samples | Sample programs |
| ipcrm -m | Remove shared mem segment from failed pcsim |

*Remote PC services:*

| | |
|---|---|
| rpc.pcnfsd | PC NFS daemon |
| pci | PC Interconnect (AADU) |

Chapter

# 20

# X11 Administration

## 20.1 Windows on the World

Using almost any operating system from a single-window ASCII display is becoming a thing of the past. Why is this so? Windowing systems like X Windows, Microsoft Windows, and the OS/2 Presentation Manager are springing up everywhere and redefining the overall human interface to computing. Once you have windows, you can't live without them!

## 20.2 AIXwindows Overview

The *AIXwindows / 6000* system is the IBM variant of the X11 release 4 and release 5 distribution. The X Windows System was developed by a group of vendors and researchers at MIT collectively known as the X Consortium. The consortium was formed in January of 1988 to build upon the windowing system developed by the MIT computer science department and MIT *Project Athena.* Consortium membership is open to any organization as either an *affiliate* or *member-at-large.* For more information contact:

MIT X Consortium
Laboratory for Computer Science
545 Technology Square
Cambridge, MA 02139

X Windows uses a reverse client/server mechanism based on *Widget* and *toolkit* libraries to manage a display either locally or over a network connection using RPC. The reason I call it "reverse client/server" is that commonly in the X environment, the clients are the remote entities that are communicating with the local X server which controls the local display. The X Consortium code is freely available and will build on most UNIX architectures, including AIX.

Like most windowing systems, X Windows incorporates the use of a mouse and cursor to provide *point-and-click* management of clients displayed on the screen. Window managers provide the ability to *drag and drop* displayed clients to any location on the screen. The window manager also provides customization of the display environment, including menu interfaces used to invoke X clients.

*Common X Windows components:*

| | |
|---|---|
| `X` | Server controlling a local display device. |
| `mwm` | Motif window manager. One of many that assist in managing the screen environment. |
| `xterm, aixterm` | Emulated terminal connection to a system using master slave PTY devices. |
| `xclock` | Analog or digtal clock icon. |
| `xbiff` | Icon alert for electronic mail delivery. |
| `xeyes` | Icon used to watch your screen cursor position. |
| `xrdb` | Manage X resources like color map, font paths, and client attributes. |
| `xdm` | X display manager primarily used with X Stations. |

The AIXwindows base product includes:

- X Windows Version 11 Release 4 or 5
- OSF/Motif Version 1 Release 1 or 2
- National language support
- 24-bit color
- AIXwindows Desktop Environment
- Display Postscript for HFT devices

Additional products are available to provide SGI Graphics Library, PHIGS, Graphical Kernel System (GKS), and PEX support.

## 20.3 X Windows Administration

There are more than enough texts available concerning generic X Windows administration under the X Consortium code. I would recommend the "X Window System" texts by O'Reilly & Associates. For the sake of this discussion, I'll focus on defining the default X start-up configuration, window manager defaults and X Station management using the *AIX X Station Manager/6000.*

## 20.4 Product Locations

The AIXwindows product is installed and resides in `/usr/lpp/X11`. Symbolic links are used to map access to the programs and libraries stored in the `lpp` directory to the standard paths, `/usr/bin/X11` and `/usr/lib/X11`.

*X Windows paths:*

| | |
|---|---|
| `/usr/bin/X11 -> /usr/lpp/X11/bin` | Executables |
| `/usr/lib/X11 -> /usr/lpp/X11/lib` | Libs and Defaults |
| `/usr/lib/<Xlibs> -> /usr/lpp/lib/X11/<Xlibs>` | Tool and Widget libs |
| `/usr/lpp/X11/Xamples` | Contributed X tools |
| `/usr/include/X11` | Include files and bit maps |
| `/usr/lib/X11/fonts->/usr/lpp/X11/lib/X11/fonts` | X fonts |
| `/usr/lib/X11/app-defaults` | Resource defaults |

## 20.5 Start-up Defaults

You may want to tailor the start-up files used by the X server, xdm, and the window managers. Default start-up files are supplied in the `/usr/lpp/X11/custom` and `/usr/lpp/X11/lib` directories.

| | |
|---|---|
| `System.xinitrc` | Default `xinit start-up file.` |
| `System.mwm` | Default Motif Window Manager start- up file |

In most cases, you will have to provide a number of different window managers for your user base. Window managers like editors and shells are a religious matter whose choice is best left up to the practitioner. The following sections describe some of the common window managers with sample configuration files.

## 20.6 Fonts

Default AIXwindows fonts are located in the `/usr/lpp/X11/lib /X11/fonts` directory. A symbolic link is provided so that they may be accessed using the standard font path, `/usr/lib/X11/fonts`. *Display Postscript* fonts for HFT devices are located in `/usr/lpp /DPS/fonts/afm`. *Bit-map distribution format* (`*.bdf`) and *server normal format* (`*.snf`) are available with the X11R4 format. The conversion programs `bdftosnf` and `snftobdf` can be used to interchange formats. Note that the `snf` fonts are compressed due to size. The AIXwindows X11R5 distribution uses the *portable compiled font* (`*.pcf`) format. The `pcf` fonts take up less space and are readable across different machine architectures.

Both `100dpi` and `75dpi` font sets are provided in subdirectories by the same name, `fonts/100dpi` and `fonts/75dpi`. Each of these subdirectories contain two index files, `fonts.dir` and `alias.dir`, that are referenced by X clients and servers to locate particular font names. These index files are built by invoking the `mkfontdir` command.

| | |
|---|---|
| `# cd /usr/lib/X11/fonts/100dpi` | |
| `# mkfontdir` | Create `fonts.dir` and `alias.dir` for 100-dpi fonts. |
| `# cd /usr/lib/X11/fonts/75dpi` | |
| `# mkfontdir` | Create `fonts.dir` and `alias.dir` for 75-dpi fonts. |

The `alias.dir` file is used to reference long logical font names using a short alias. The logical font name is created from the font attributes, which include, *foundary, font family, weight, slant, width, style, pixels, points, horizontal dpi, vertical dpi, spacing, average width, owner,* and *code set.*

*Example logical name mapping:*

| Font file | Logical name |
|---|---|
| Bld17.snf.Z | -ibm—bold-r-block- -23-16-100-100-c-110-ibm-850 |
| Bld17.iso1.snf.Z | -ibm—bold-r-block- -23-16-100-100-c-110-iso8859-1 |
| Bld17.iso2.snf.Z | -ibm—bold-r-block- -23-16-100-100-c-110-iso8859-2 |
| Bld17.iso3.snf.Z | -ibm—bold-r-block- -23-16-100-100-c-110-iso8859-3 |
| Bld17.iso4.snf.Z | -ibm—bold-r-block- -23-16-100-100-c-110-iso8859-4 |
| Bld17.iso5.snf.Z | -ibm—bold-r-block- -23-16-100-100-c-110-iso8859-5 |
| Bld17.iso7.snf.Z | -ibm—bold-r-block- -23-16-100-100-c-110-iso8859-7 |
| Bld17.iso9.snf.Z | -ibm—bold-r-block- -23-16-100-100-c-110-iso8859-9 |
| Bld14.snf.Z | -ibm—bold-r-bold- -20-14-100-100-c-90-ibm-850 |
| Bld14.iso1.snf.Z | -ibm—bold-r-bold- -20-14-100-100-c-90-iso8859-1 |
| Bld14.iso2.snf.Z | -ibm—bold-r-bold- -20-14-100-100-c-90-iso8859-2 |
| Bld14.iso3.snf.Z | -ibm—bold-r-bold- -20-14-100-100-c-90-iso8859-3 |
| Bld14.iso4.snf.Z | -ibm—bold-r-bold- -20-14-100-100-c-90-iso8859-4 |
| Bld14.iso5.snf.Z | -ibm—bold-r-bold- -20-14-100-100-c-90-iso8859-5 |
| Bld14.iso7.snf.Z | -ibm—bold-r-bold- -20-14-100-100-c-90-iso8859-7 |
| Bld14.iso9.snf.Z | -ibm—bold-r-bold- -20-14-100-100-c-90-iso8859-9 |

## 20.7 Window Managers—Take Your Pick

What does a window manager do for you? As the name implies, you use a window manager to dynamically arrange the layout of windows and objects on your display. It stylizes frame and title decoration, imparting a common look and feel to all the objects displayed. It is the window manager that allows you to click and drag objects on the screen, shuffle windows up and down, and customize pull-down menus. Without a window manager you don't have any way to manipulate or move overlapping objects or alter their size. It is quite easy to see just how much you depend on your window manager by trying to run your X environment without using one.

Although I won't cover each of the window managers in Table 20.1, it is worthwhile listing a FEW of them to give you a feel for the variety that is available. They are not listed in any particular order, since the development history tends to be very blurry due to the interbreeding and building on previous work that is common with popular applications. It seems that just when I think I have heard of them all, someone mentions a new one. I do want to mention some of the

**TABLE 20.1 Window Managers**

| | |
|---|---|
| awm | Ardent Window Manager |
| uwm | A Window Manager for X |
| swm | Solbourne Window Manager |
| dxwm | DECwindows Window Manager |
| twm | Tab Window Manager |
| tvtwm | Tom's Virtual Tab Window Manager |
| aixwm | AIX 1.2 Window Manager |
| mwm | OSF Motif Window Manager |
| olwm | Open Look Window Manager |
| tekvm | Tektronix Window Manager |
| m_swm | Sigma Window Manager |
| gwm | Generic Window Manager |

unique features available in a couple of these. The first is *Tom's Virtual Tab Window Manager*—tvtwm. This window manager provides a virtual root window which may be defined larger than the physical screen size. This allows users with a small display to move windows and objects that are not in use out of the field of view. A small map of your virtual root window is displayed to map where objects are located on the virtual root window. You can use your mouse to drag the root window around to move objects in and out of the field of view. The second one worth noting is the *Generic Window Manager*—gwm. This is a lisp-based system which may be used to prototype new window managers or emulate existing ones. It also has a nice interface to *emacs.* On the down side, gwm is quite large, which is often the case with many lisp-based applications.

### 20.7.1 Window manager configuration

The window manager is usually started last in your X start-up configuration file. It may either be started in foreground or background, depending on the particular window manager. Starting the window manager last allows you to configure your environment such that you can exit the X server when you exit the window manager. If you start your X session with the `xinit` or `startx` commands, then the window manager is usually the last entry in your `.xinitrc` file. If you are using xdm, then it will be last in your `.xsession` file.

Window managers, like all well-behaved X clients, provide a mechanism to allow users to customize the appearance, interaction, and behavior via resource files. A start-up rc configuration file used in conjunction with the X resource information defined in the `.Xdefaults` file can be modified to tailor the window manager to meet your needs. For the purpose of limiting the scope of this discussion, I will focus on the start-up rc configuration files. If you are interested in the options supported in `.Xdefaults`, these are listed in the man page for the particular window manager.

**TABLE 20.2 Window Manager Functions**

| | |
|---|---|
| `f.exec` | Start a command or shell script |
| `f.kill` | Kill the selected client |
| `f.menu` | Display a menu |
| `f.title` | Display a menu title |
| `f.separator` | Display a separator bar in menus |
| `f.raise` | Bring client to the front |
| `f.resize` | Resize a client |
| `f.move` | Move a client |
| `f.minimize` | Reduce client to an icon |
| `f.maximize` | Restore icon to an open client |
| `f.restart` | Restart the window manager |

The configuration file will generally allow you to define actions and menus, which are bound to a mouse button or key for activation. Although formats do differ for each window manager, they tend to follow the following format:

```
LABEL/TITLE                      FUNCTION     # Define Menus and Actions
KEY/BUTTON       CONTEXT         FUNCTION     # Bind Keys/Buttons to Actions
```

The `CONTEXT` describes where the button or key action is active. For example, you may want to use a button to display a menu only when the cursor is on the root window. Window manager functions are called by defining the `f.function-name` in the configuration file entry. Common function names include those listed in Table 20.2.

You may also define default background and foreground colors and default fonts to be used for title bars, menus, and icons. However, it may be more convenient to define these kind of resources in the `.Xdefaults` file along with resource definitions for other X clients. A good place to start your window manager configuration testing is to make a copy of the system default configuration file and modify it to your liking. These are most commonly found in the `/usr/lib/X11/` subdirectories. Consult the window manager man page for the exact location. Since you may be overwhelmed by the bulk of information in the system default configuration file, I will provide some simple example rc files for the more commonly used window managers.

### 20.7.2 Motif Window Manager

We will begin our brief foray into the world of window managers with the *Motif Window Manager*—mwm. mwm is the window manager most of us are familiar with ala AIXwindows. The Motif Window Manager was the first technology to hit the streets from the Open Software Foundation. Its 3-D look and feel is based on the development work done by Hewlett-Packard and Microsoft. It is quite similar in look and feel to the Microsoft Presentation Manager and Microsoft

Windows. The default configuration file used by mwm is `/usr/lib/X11/system.mwmrc`. Your local copy is called `.mwmrc`. In the example that follows, I have defined a primary menu called `RootMenu` which will be displayed when button 1 on the mouse or the SHIFT-ESC key sequence is pressed with the cursor on the root window. I can also restart or quit mwm from the menu, or select a submenu called *Applications.* From the Applications menu I can start an *AIX PC Simulator* window.

```
# SAMPLE .mwmrc
# Menus and Functions
Menu RootMenu
{
      "Root Menu"       f.title
      no-label          f.separator
      "Appls"           f.menu Applications
      "Restart..."      f.restart
      "Exit mwm"        f.quit_mwm
}
Menu Applications
{
      "Applications"    f.title
      no-label          f.separator
"Dos Window"            f.exec "pcsim -dmode v &"
}
# Key and Button Bindings
Keys DefaultKeyBindings
{
      Shift<Key>Escape      root      f.menu      RootMenu
}
Buttons DefaultButtonBindings
{
      <Btn1Down>      root      f.menu      RootMenu
}
```

I lied when I said I wasn't going to discuss resource entries for the `.Xdefaults` file. Since mwm is being used by many AIX users, it is worth diverting a moment to describe a short example. In the example listed, I have specified the use of the *icon box,* defined menus to use black lettering on a light blue background and to use rom14 as my default font.

```
# Sample .Xdefaults Mwm Resources
Mwm*useIconBox: true
Mwm*menu*foreground: black
Mwm*menu*background: lightblue
Mwm*fontList: rom14
```

### 20.7.3 OPEN LOOK Window Manager

Next on the list of window managers is Motif's rival, the *OPEN LOOK Window Manager*—olwm. olwm was developed by Sun Microsystems and AT&T. OPEN LOOK tends to dictate much of the look and feel provided by the window manager, and thus has a very simple configuration file, `.olwmmenu`, for defining menus. One nice aspect of OPEN LOOK is its ability to pin a menu to the display. This means you don't have to hold the mouse button down to keep the menu displayed on the screen. The example configuration file defines a menu called *root menu* with a subtitle *WINDOWS* that will allow the user to start an *xterm* or *tn3270* connection to a remote host and query the *uptime* information for a system using the `rsh` command.

```
# Sample .olwmmenu
TITLE "root menu"
"Clients"         MENU
  TITLE           "WINDOWS"
  TITLE           "XTERM"
     "milton"     "xterm -display $DISPLAY -sb -tn xterms -title milton &"
  TITLE           "TN3270"
     "oly"        "xterm -display $DISPLAY -title oly -e tn3270 oly &"
  TITLE           "UPTIME"
     "byron"      "rsh byron uptime &"
END
"Exit"            EXIT
```

### 20.7.4 Tab Window Manager

Probably the most commonly used public domain window manager is what was called *Tom's Window Manager* in X11V3, and is now the *Tab Window Manager*—twm. twm does not have the 3-D look and feel that are the signatures of Motif and OPEN LOOK. twm goes much further to allow you to define resource information like color and font options in the `.twmrc` configuration file. In the example that follows there are some default resource definitions for title bars, icons, and menus. It defines the menu and key/button bindings in a fashion similar to the window managers previously listed. It also demonstrates defining a user function called *de- raise-n-focus,* which is activated by the F1 key. This user function is built using the window manager functions f.deiconify, f.raise, and f.focus. The default configuration file is `/usr/lib/X11/twm/system.twmrc`.

```
# Sample .twmrc
# Resources
Color
{
BorderColor "MidnightBlue"
BorderTileForeground "Black"
{
"xterm" "CornflowerBlue"
}
MenuForeground "white"
IconForeground "black"
}
TitleFont "8x13"
IconManagerDontShow
{
```

```
"xdspclock"
}
# Menus and Functions
menu "Appls"
{
"Applications" f.title
"byron" ("Wheat":"SlateGray") !"xterm -e rlogin byron &"
"lock"                        !"xlock -mode qix -nice 5 &"
"move"                        f.move
}
# Button and Key Bindings
Button1  =        : frame      : f.menu "Stuff"
"F1"  =           : frame      : f.function "de-raise-n-focus"
Function "de-raise-n-focus"
{
   f.deiconify
   f.raise
   f.focus
}
```

### 20.7.5 A Window Manager for X

No discussion of window managers would be complete without including *A Window Manager for X*—uwm. uwm is basically a no-frills window manager held over from the X10 days and is included with most vendor and MIT Consortium X distributions. Note that the initial sequence, *resetbindings, resetvariables,* and *resetmenus* listed in the example `.uwmrc` is the common practice for configuring uwm. Like twm, you can define window manager and client resources in the configuration file. The default configuration file is `/usr/lib/X11/uwm/system.uwmrc`.

```
# Sample .uwmrc
# Resource
resetbindings
resetvariables
resetmenus
background = Wheat
bordercolor = Red
menufont = fixed
# Menus
menu = "WindowOps" {
RefreshScreen:      f.refresh
Redraw:             f.redraw
Move:               f.move
Exit:               f.exit
}
# Button and Key Bindings
f.menu =      :root:      middle down : "WindowOps"
```

## 20.8 Tools and Tips

If you don't have executable versions of these window managers built, but do have the MIT X Consortium source code, you can find the some of the public domain window managers in the following locations:

```
Standard      ./mit/clients
X11R4         ./contrib/windowmgrs
X11R5         ./contrib/clients
```

There are also some X clients that make it much easier choosing font and color combinations for your environment. *xfontsel* allows you to dynamically select font options in a window and display an example character set using the font on your screen. For color selection, there is an X11R5 contrib client called *xcolors* that will display a color palette on your screen and allow you to select foreground and background color combinations. *xwininfo* can be used to select initial positioning geometry for a client at start-up. Using *xwininfo,* you can position and click on a client to display its positional information on the screen.

## 20.9 IBM Xstation Administration

Xstations provide a very cost effective alternative to providing fully equipped workstations as platforms for X Windows. Using one or more workstations as servers, Xstations provide all the functionality of a complete X Windows-based workstation. Xstations also reduce many of the administration headaches for both the system administrator and end user.

Most environments support a number of different vendor Xstations and would like to manage them as a group from central servers under `xdm`. At EPROM level +1.5 for the Xstation 120 and using the IBM Xstation Manager at version 1.3 or above, all models of the IBM Xstation can be supported alongside the rest of your Xstation menagerie under `xdm`. You can also obtain boot server code from *Advanced Graphics Engineering* (AGE) which will allow the use of UNIX systems other than an RS/6000 or PS/2 as a boot server. Take a look at the IBM Red Book *IBM Xstation 120/130,* GG24-3695 for more details. This book is a little dated; however, most of the information is still relevant.

## 20.10 Xstation Hardware

For those of you who might not remember the IBM Xstation 120, it was IBM's entry offering in the Xstation market. The IBM Xstation 120 is configured with two processors. An 8-Mhz Intel 80186 is used for I/O and communications, and a 50-Mhz Texas Instruments 34010 processor handles video graphics. It supports 512 KB to 8.5 MB of system memory, *DRAM,* and 512 KB to 2 MB of video memory, *VRAM.* There is 512 KB of RAM and two 128-KB ROM sections used for the I/O subsystem, diagnostics, and boot support. Ethernet, 10base5 (thick), and 10base2 (thin) are supported along with a token-ring adapter slot. Serial and parallel slots are standard for a local printer and/or plotter. If you are using X11R4 and the IBM Xstation

Manager 1.2 or 1.3, you will need a minimum of 1.5 MB of system memory for the X server code, fonts, etc. The amount of video memory required will be dependent on the resolution and color bits of the monitor. You can select from a variety of monitors. A keyboard and mouse are included.

The IBM Xstation 130 is similar to the model 120, but is beefier. Webster's defines *beefier* as "heavily and powerfully built, substantial, sturdy, full of beef." I like the part about "full of beef." The model 130 comes with a 12.5-MHz Intel 80C186 and a 32-MHz Texas Instruments 34020. Thus, 32-bit graphics capability is available over the 16-bit support in the model 120. You may select from 1 to 16 MB DRAM and 1 to 2 MB VRAM. Two ROM sections have been upgraded to 256 KB each. A PS/2 dual-port asynch adapter may be included to bring the total number of serial ports up to four. A second Ethernet or token-ring adapter may be added. Finally, an optional 30-MB hard disk may be used to store portions of the X server code, backing store pixmaps, fonts, etc. This disk space is not accessible for standard applications. The extra disk space may be thought of as additional system memory.

The Xstation 150 tops the IBM Xstation line, delivering a very impressive 115,000 Xstones. The 150 incorporates 64-bit RISC using a Motorola 88110 processor. The system comes with 6 MB of system memory that can be expanded to 22 MB. 2 MB of video memory is standard, along with 2 MB of flash memory containing X11R5 server code and diagnostics. Flash memory can be upgraded to 4 MB. 10BaseT Ethernet support has been added to 10Base5, 10base2, token ring, and SLIP. Four serial ports at up to 38.4 Kbps may be configured into the system. The IBM Xstation 150 supports local X11 clients. Simple Network Management Protocol (SNMP) agent code is available.

### 20.10.1 Configuration and boot

When you flip on the power switch, the Xstation performs a *power-on self-test* (POST). Once POST is passed, it will optionally direct or broadcast a `bootp` request packet attempting to find a boot server. Once contact is made, the information received determines the IP addresses of the Xstation and the server, and the name of the boot configuration file. Since this information can be configured into the Xstation, you may opt to bypass the `bootp` step for normal operation. To configure address information into the Xstation, access the network configuration menu by pressing the F12 key after POST has completed. These configuration screens allow you to set the IP address information for the terminal, server, and gateway, and disable the `bootp` process. Similar information may be configured for token-ring connections. The model 130 and 150 also support IP over a serial link using SLIP. To configure the model 130 or 150 for a serial TTY connection, press the F11 key after POST has completed.

Once the boot server has been contacted, the Xstation will tftp a copy of the bootfile /usr/lpp/x_st_mgr/bin/bootfile from the server. The bootfile and configuration file downloaded, inform the Xstation which fonts, key map, rgb database, and server code should be requested from the server.

During the bootp and tftp steps, the Xstation display provides some diagnostic information concerning the terminal/server packet exchanges. The two lines of interest are:

```
BOOTP 0000 0000 0000 0000
TFTP 0000 0000 0000 0000 0000
```

The first column of numbers indicates the number of packets sent from the Xstation. The second column indicates the number of packets received from the server. The third column is the count of bad packets received. The fourth column displays the number of timeouts that have occurred. The fifth column on the TFTP line displays the final error code for the transaction. You may access further diagnostic and test information by simultaneously pressing CTRL-break after POST has completed.

## 20.11 AIX Xstation Manager/6000 Configuration

The AIX Xstation Manager/6000 program product provides the boot services for IBM Xstations. As I mentioned earlier, you may also get the Xoftware product from AGE, if you wish to provide boot support from other than an RS/6000 or PS/2. Once the Xstation Manager is installed, verify that its services are defined in the following tables:

```
/etc/rc.tcpip
/usr/lpp/x_st_mgr/bin/x_st_mgrd -b \
/usr/lpp/x_st_mgr/bin/x_st_mgrd.cf -s x_st_mg

/etc/services
bootps        67/udp      # bootp server port
bootpc        68/udp      # bootp client port
x_st_mgrd     7000/tcp    #ibm X terminal

/etc/inetd.conf
bootps dgram udp wait root /etc/bootpd bootpd /etc/bootptab
```

You may then define your network type, bootfile, and bootfile directory via the Xstation selection from the SMIT Devices menu. You may also specify whether the server is a primary or secondary server. It is a good idea to support two boot servers if possible. The Xstations may then be configured to try each server in sequence at start-up time.

Once you have defined your network type, you may define each of the Xstations being supported. You need to identify each Xstation's network type, the hardware address of the adapter, whether xdm services will be used, and the initial application to be started. You may also define local printer support for Xstations equipped with printers via the SMIT Printer/Plotter menu.

## 20.12 X Windows Display Manager—xdm

As of release 1.2 of the AIX Xstation Manager/6000, the *XDM Control Protocol* (XDMCP) is supported at the X11R4 level. This means you can use the full services provided by `xdm` (X Windows Display Manager) to manage your start-up clients and restrict access to your Xstation. You can tailor your initial X11 environment by editing entries in your `$HOME/.Xsession` file, much the same way you do with `$HOME/.xinitrc`. Default parameters for `xdm` are defined in `/usr/lib/X11/xdm/Xsession`. You will also want to define some of your shell environment variables in your `$HOME/.Xsession` file, since `xdm` circumvents standard shell start-up procedures.

One of the main advantages of using `xdm` is that it provides user-based authentication for access to your Xstation. It is common practice—or should be—to restrict access to your X11 environment by using the `xhost` command. However, `xhost` only authenticates at the host level. Anyone on a time-shared host that you have permitted via `xhost` has access to your X11 server. `xdm` uses an access control mechanism called the *MIT-MAGIC-COOKIE,* which is controlled by file access permission. Basically `xdm` writes a random number code (the magic cookie) into your `$HOME/.Xauthority` file, and shares this number with your X11 server. X11 clients must then authenticate themselves to the server by presenting the code when connecting to the server. You may share this magic cookie with other machines, from which you may start clients using the `xauth` program. A combination of `xhost` and `xauth` mechanisms will go a long way to securing your Xstation. X11R5 adds two more authentication protocols called *XDM-AUTHORIZATION-1* and *SUN-DES-1,* respectively. These are both based on the Data Encryption Standard (DES).

It is possible to use magic cookies with the standard `xinit` start-up used by AIXwindows. Basically, you need to generate some kind of random number from your `$HOME/.xinitrc` file and store it in your `$HOME/.Xauthority` using `xauth`. I haven't tried this with IBM Xstations, but it will work with standard servers.

## 20.13 InfoExplorer Keywords

| | |
|---|---|
| `AIXwindows` | `tftp` |
| `mwm` | `x_st_mgrd` |
| `xinit` | `/etc/inetd.conf` |

| | |
|---|---|
| X11 | /etc/services |
| xdm | XDMCP |
| X | .Xsession |
| xterm | xhost |
| aixterm | xauth |
| xclock | aixdt |
| xbiff | bdftosnf |
| xrdb | snftobdf |
| bootp | mkfontdir |

## 20.14 QwikInfo

### X11

*AIXwindows, X11 components:*

| | |
|---|---|
| /usr/bin/X11 | X11 programs |
| /usr/lib/X11/fonts | Font directory |
| /usr/lib/X11/app-defaults | Application defaults |
| /usr/lib | X11 libraries |
| /usr/lpp/X11 | AIXwindows |
| /usr/lpp/X11/Xamples | Samples and contribs |

*Clients and server:*

| | |
|---|---|
| X | X server |
| .Xdefaults | Application defaults |
| xdm | X display manager |
| $HOME/.Xauthority | xdm magic cookie |
| mwm | Motif window manager |
| aixterm, xterm | X terminal emulator |
| .xinitrc | Start-up file |
| System.xinitrc | X11 system defaults |
| .mwmrc | mwm configuration |
| System.mwmrc | mwm defaults |
| .Xsession | xdm start-up file |
| mkfontdir | Create fonts directory and alias files |

*AIX Xstation Manager/6000:*

| | |
|---|---|
| /usr/lpp/x_st_mgr | AIX Xstation Manager |
| x_st_mgrd | Xstation daemon |

Part

6

# Users and Security

Chapter

# 21

# Managing the User Environment

## 21.1 User Administration Policy

"User" is a four-letter word! If you administer multiuser systems and haven't taken care to define default environment policies or to streamline account management, there are likely many other four-letter words in our vocabulary. A large user base can dominate a system administrator's time with trivial tasks like adding and expiring accounts, setting passwords, juggling home directories, fixing UID collisions, etc. The list goes on and on, and so do the requests. Just remember that it's users that keep us employed!

The default environment policies can be thought of as a contract for basic services and resources. Whether it is formally stated or implied, your user base assumes some level of support. There will be less confusion for both your users and user support communities if the basic rules of the road are formally stated and documented. A simple way to disseminate this type of information is to make it available as a man page or help file. You can also provide a default policy statement as a `msg` file that is displayed the first time a user logs on to the system.

First you need to define what the policies are and how they will be implemented. What are the requirements for establishing an account? What basic resources are provided with an account? What does the default shell environment look like? How long does an account last?

*Resource policies:*

Physical resources

Resource limits

Account access rights

Account environment

## 21.2 Physical Resources

Let's start out by making sure we don't promise more than we can deliver. What are the workload characteristics of your user base? How much disk, tape, memory, and CPU resources will be required to support your expected total number of users and the expected concurrent user sessions? In an existing environment, you can construct a fairly good profile by sifting through old accounting information. It's also worthwhile to benchmark your application mix. Push the system to the limit. Stress the CPU, paging, and I/O subsystems. This will give you a feel for what to expect during spikes in load.

### 21.2.1 User file systems

After you have determined the resource level you can offer, structure the physical resources such that they can be managed easily under software control. Begin by segregating user home directory file systems from the rest of the operating system. This isolates these file systems from operating system upgrades and maintenance. Set up user file systems on different physical disks and volume groups. This will facilitate moving them between machines if circumstances require. Use a naming convention for user file system mount points that are easy to remember and easy to identify. A possible method would be to use the `/u<number>` scheme on AIX. In a distributed or clustered environment you might use the first character of the machine name which owns the file system followed by an integer. Don't make them too long!

To reduce the impact of managing user home directories in multiple user file systems, use symbolic links to link the top-level user directories in each file system to a common `/home` directory. No matter where a particular user's home directory physically resides, it can be accessed via the `/home/<user name>` path. Specify the symbolic link path name for the home directory field in the `/etc/passwd` file. This will allow you to move user directories around in your user file systems to balance utilization without requiring each user to learn a new home directory path.

```
# ln -s /u6/stimpy /home/stimpy
stimpy:!:1234:30:Stimpson Cat:/home/stimpy:/bin/ksh
```

You will also need to size your user file systems. If large files are not heavily used, then multiple small file systems may be preferred. Small file systems (less than 1 GB) reduce backup and restore times. They can be easily moved and will partition your user community such that a file system catastrophe won't effect your entire user base.

## 21.3 UID Space and Groups

User account names are, in fact, a matter of human convenience in identifying users under UNIX. The AIX operating system identifies a particular user by an unsigned long integer called the *UID*. The UID is mapped to the user name in the `/etc/passwd` file. UIDs are used on other UNIX systems, but may be represented under other integer formats. Traditionally, the UID space was limited to 32 k, but this has proved to be too small for large time-sharing UNIX systems.

It's a good idea to segregate your user UID space from the UIDs used by system daemons administrative accounts. This simplifies the task of identifying privileged accounts for accounting and security applications. Pick a number like 1000 to define the bottom of your user UID space for allocation. In a distributed environment where users may have accounts on different systems, or if you are using *Network File System* (NFS), you will want to ensure that UIDs are unique across systems. By "unique," I mean that if user "stimpy" is UID 1234 on host A, then the same UID is reserved for stimpy on any other system. Ownership and permission problems can arise if the same UID represents different users in distributed environments. Remember, the operating system identifies users by UID.

While you define your UID space, it's also a good idea to plan your *Group ID* (GID) space. Groups provide a coarse mechanism for sharing information between users. In Chap. 22, file and directory permissions are described which permit *read, write,* and *execute* permissions for *world, group,* and *owner.* AIX and other UNIXs assume a limited group set to implement access privileges. What needs to be decided is whether you want to implement other GID sets for specific work groups or collaborators. If your user base is small, this can be done relatively easily. For large numbers of users, managing GID sets can be a big chore.

AIX provides a much better solution to sharing information through *access control lists* (ACLs). ACLs supply a finer granularity of control and user management. ACLs will be discussed in Chap. 22.

### 21.3.1 `/etc/group` and `/etc/security/group`

GID mapping is maintained in the `/etc/group` and `/etc/security/group` files. The `/etc/group` file lists each group name and GID followed by the list of members. The `/etc/security/group` file contains a stanza for each group name in the `/etc/group` file and indicates whether the group may be administered by users other than root and identifies the administrators by user name. Groups and their associated attributes are managed via SMIT or from a series of group management commands.

| | |
|---|---|
| mkgroup | Create a new group |
| chgroup | Change group attributes |
| lsgroup | List groups and attributes |
| chgrpmem | Change administrators or members of a group |
| setgroup | Reset the current group set for a user |
| newgrp | Set the group ID for session |
| rmgroup | Remove a group |

*Example* /etc/group:

```
system:!:0:root,ops
daemon:!:1:
bin:!:2:root,bin
sys:!:3:root,bin,sys
adm:!:4:bin,adm,kenm,root
uucp:!:5:uucp
mail:!:6:
security:!:7:root
cron:!:8:root
staff:!:10:root,ren,stimpy,daffy,huey,dewey
:user:!:30:luge,acadmus,gwyneira,bungi
```

*Example* /etc/security/group:

```
system:
   admin = true
daemon:
   admin = true
bin:
   admin = true
sys:
   admin = true
adm:
   admin = true
uucp:
   admin = true
mail:
   admin = true
security:
   admin = true
cron:
   admin = true
staff:
   admin = false
   adms = ren,stimpy
user:
   admin = false
```

## 21.4 Resource Limits

How much of the pie are you going to give each user? How you do make sure each user gets no more than his or her fair share? Profiling the application mix with estimated concurrent users will give you some ballpark figures. AIX provides the capability to enforce limits on each user's slice of the available system resources through operating system controls. Limits can be defined for CPU, memory, and disk utilization on a per-process basis. Total number of concurrent processes per user is capped by kernel configuration parameter. Aggregate file system usage can be governed through activating disk quotas at user and group levels.

### 21.4.1 /etc/security/limits

The kernel manages per-process limits using the `setrlimit()`, `getrlimit()`, and `vlimit()` system calls. Each process has an associated `rlimit` structure that indicates soft and hard ceilings for each resource type. The `rlimit` structure is defined in `/usr/include/sys/resource.h`. Default and resource limits for the system and users are specified in the `/etc/security/limits` file. Each user defined to the system is represented by a stanza identified by user name. System defaults are active for each user that does not have an overriding parameter under the user's stanza. When a process exceeds one of the specified limits, it is killed.

`/etc/security/limits:`

```
* limits
*
* Sizes are in multiples of blocks, CPU time is in seconds
*
* fsize - maximum file size in blocks
* core - maximum core file size in blocks
* cpu - per process CPU time limit in seconds
* data - maximum data segment size in blocks
* stack - maximum stack segment size in blocks
* rss - maximum real memory usage in blocks
*
* NOTE: a value less than or equal to zero implies "unlimited"
*

default:
   fsize = 2097151
   core = 2048
   cpu = -1
   data = 262144
   rss = 65536
   stack = 65536

root:

stimpy:
   fsize = 10240
   cpu = 3600
```

The kernel limits the maximum number of processes per user as specified by the kernel configuration parameter *maxuproc*. The default value of 40 indicates that up to 40 processes may be running concurrently for a given user. The value may not be exceeded by logging into the system multiple times. The maxuproc value may be altered via SMIT or with the `chdev` command. (See Fig. 21.1.)

```
# chgdev -l sys0 -a maxuproc = 80
# smit chgsys
```

```
                 Change / Show Characteristics of Operating System

Type or select values in entry fields.
Press Enter AFTER making all desired changes.

                                                               [Entry Fields]
Maximum number of PROCESSES allowed per user               [80]                 +#
Maximum number of pages in block I/O BUFFER CACHE          [20]                 +#
Maximum Kbytes of real memory allowed for MBUFS            [2048]               +#
Automatically REBOOT system after a crash                  false                +
Continuously maintain DISK I/O history                     true                 +
HIGH water mark for pending write I/Os per file            [33]                 +#
LOW water mark for pending write I/Os per file             [16]                 +#
Enable memory SCRUBBING                                    false                +
Amount of usable physical memory in Kbytes                 524288
Primary dump device                                        /dev/hd7
Secondary dump device                                      /dev/sysdumpnull
Error log file size                                        1048576
State of system keylock at boot time                       normal
Size of data cache in bytes                                64K
Size of instruction cache in bytes                         32K

F1 = Help         F2 = Refresh      F3 = Cancel      F4 = List
F5 = Undo         F6 = Command      F7 = Edit        F8 = Image
F9 = Shell        F10 = Exit        Enter = Do
```

**Figure 21.1** SMIT operating system parameter panel.

*Disk quotas* limit the maximum number of blocks a user or group may consume on participating file systems. The AIX implementation of disk quotas is based on BSD quotas. User and group quota limit are set by the system administrator using the `edquota` command. Quota limits for disk blocks and inodes are specified by three parameters: *soft limit, hard limit,* and *grace period.*

The value of the soft limit indicates at what point the user or group begins receiving warnings that their soft limit has been exceeded and that they are approaching the hard limit. Warnings are delivered at login time and at each close that exceeds the specified limit. The hard limit specifies at what point the user or group will no longer be able to allocate additional disk space or inodes. The grace period defines a period of time that the user or group has to reduce their utilization below the soft limit value. If utilization is not reduced before the grace period expires, the soft limit is enforced as a hard limit.

To implement disk quotas on a file system, edit the stanza entry in `/etc/filesystems` associated with file system name. Add the parameter `quota = <userquota>,<groupquota>` to the stanza. The `userquota` and `groupquota` values indicate the quota types to be enforced. The quota limits for each user or group are recorded in files in the top-level directory named `quota.user` and `quota.group`, respectively. You may override these file names with your own by including `userquota = <pathname>` and `groupquota = <pathname>` parameters in the file system stanza.

```
/etc/filesystems:

/u1:
   dev = /dev/lv43
   vfs = jfs
   log = /dev/loglv00
   mount = true
   check = true
   options = rw
   quota = userquota
   userquota = /u1/user.quota
```

If the quota limit files do not exist on the file system, you can create them using `touch`.

```
# touch /u1/quota.user
```

Use the `edquota` command to create a user quota for one of the users on the system. These values will be used as a template for setting the limits for other users on the system. The `edquota` command will invoke the default editor and display the quota values for update.

```
# edquota stimpy
Quotas for user stimpy:
/u1: blocks in use: 50, limits (soft = 80,  hard = 100)
     inodes in use: 11, limits (soft = 120, hard = 150)
/u2: blocks in use: 0,  limits (soft = 80,  hard = 100)
     inodes in use: 0,  limits (soft = 120, hard = 150)
```

After setting the soft and hard limits for the default user, invoke `edquota -p <default-user> <new- user>` to set the default limits for each additional user in the system.

```
# edquota -p stimpy ren
```

Enable the quota system by executing the `quotaon` command. As part of the nightly system housekeeping, update the information in the quota files by running the `quotacheck` command. You can use the `-a` flag to indicate all quota file systems.

*Quota update commands:*

```
quotaoff -a
quotacheck -a
quotaon -a
```

The quota limits for a user or a summary can be displayed using the `quota` and `repquota` commands, respectively.

```
# quota ren
```

Disk quotas for user `ren` (uid 4084):

```
Filesystem  blocks  quota  limit  grace  files  quota  limit  grace
/u1         11836*  5120   6144   none   363    1000   2000

# repquota
```

```
                        Block limits                          File limits
User          used      soft    hard    grace       used    soft    hard    grace
root     –    31448     0       0                   700     0       0
bin      –    57700     0       0                   2037    0       0
sys      –    4         0       0                   1       0       0
news     –    4         0       0                   1       0       0
bilbro   –    16        0       0                   4       0       0
```

## 21.5 User Account Access Rights

Who gets an account and how long can they keep it? Access and expiration policies might not seem like a big deal for small work groups; however, the less ambiguity the better. There are also legal implications that can be avoided if these policies are formalized and made public. Expiring and cleaning up accounts on large user base systems can be automated easily if expiration policies are clearly defined. AIX provides a mechanism for expiring accounts and performing the cleanup housekeeping. By providing both facilities, AIX allows you to implement grace periods between when an account expires and when it is actually removed from the system. This can be incorporated into a *last-use* policy. Chapter 22 covers expiration procedures.

## 21.6 User Account Environment

What face will the system present to new users? As system administrator, you are charged with setting up the default environment for each new account. You want to maintain some level of control over environment parameters, yet allow users the freedom of tailoring their own work spaces. Shells, editors, terminal definitions, and the like, are religious issues best left to the faithful! You can't keep everyone from shooting themselves in the foot. You also don't want to open the flood gates to more shell environments than you can support. You can provide a simple, modular login environment that simplifies recovery for the adventurous user when shell experimentation goes awry.

Begin by defining the default environment variables which will be set for all users (see Table 21.1). Environment variables are *name* = *value* pairs that are read by shells and commands to set values or determine behavior. For example, the environment variable `EDITOR` indicates what editor is to be invoked by applications like `mail` or `rn`. Environment variables may be command- or shell-specific, and they may be modified by the end user.

### 21.6.1 `/etc/environment` and `/etc/profile`

AIX provides two files which are used to set default environment variables for the system. The `/etc/environment` file contains default variables set for each process by the `exec()` system calls. The `/etc/profile` file contains the set of environment variables and

**TABLE 21.1 Common Environment Variables**

| | |
|---|---|
| PATH | List of directory paths to search for commands and files |
| LIBPATH | List of library paths to search for binding |
| PAGER | Default full screen pager |
| EDITOR | Default editor |
| TZ | Time zone |
| TERM | Terminal type |
| MAIL | Incoming mail path |
| MAILMSG | Message text prompt when new mail arrives |
| LANG | Locale name in effect for NLS |
| LOCPATH | Directory containing locale file |
| NLSPATH | Full path to NLS catalogs |
| USER | User name (csh) |
| LOGNAME | User name |
| TNESC | Telnet escape key sequence |
| HOME | Home directory path |

commands that will be invoked when a user logs into the system. The contents of these files are read before local shell start-up files and they are best kept non-shell-specific. The AIX-supplied `/etc/environment` and `/etc/profile` files provide a good boilerplate for tailoring your own defaults.

*System* `/etc/environment` *variables:*

```
PATH = /usr/bin:/etc:/usr/sbin:/usr/ucb:/usr/bin/X11:/sbin
TZ = PST8PDT
LANG = C
LOCPATH = /usr/lib/nls/loc
NLSPATH = /usr/lib/nls/msg/%L/%N:/usr/lib/nls/msg/prime/%N
ODMDIR = /etc/objrepos
```

`/etc/profile:`

```
# (C) COPYRIGHT International Business Machines Corp. 1989, 1990
# All Rights Reserved
# Licensed Materials—Property of IBM
#
# US Government Users Restricted Rights - Use, duplication or
# disclosure restricted by GSA ADP Schedule Contract with IBM Corp.
#
################################################################

# System wide profile. All variables set here may be overridden by
# a user's personal .profile file in their $HOME directory. However,
# all commands here will be executed at login regardless.

trap "" 1 2 3
readonly LOGNAME

# Automatic logout, include in export line if uncommented
# TMOUT = 120

# The MAILMSG will be printed by the shell every MAILCHECK seconds
# (default 600) if there is mail in the MAIL system mailbox.
MAIL = /usr/spool/mail/$LOGNAME
MAILMSG = "[YOU HAVE NEW MAIL]"
```

```
# If termdef command returns terminal type (i.e. a non NULL value),
# set TERM to the returned value, else set TERM to default hft.
TERM_DEFAULT = hft
TERM = `termdef`
TERM = ${TERM:-$TERM_DEFAULT}

export LOGNAME MAIL MAILMSG TERM

trap 1 2 3
```

### 21.6.2 /etc/security/environ

Individual user environment variables may also be defined in the /etc/security/environ file. This file contains a stanza for each user in the system, identified by user name followed by a list of environment variables and the associated value. The environment *variable = value* pairs are separated by commas. Those variables specified as usrenv are set at login. To protect environment variables from being reset by unprivileged applications, use the sysenv specification.

*Example* /etc/security/environ *stanza:*

```
stimpy:
   usrenv = "TNESC = 35,PAGER = /bin/more,EDITOR = /bin/vi"
   sysenv = "HOME = /home/stimpy"
```

Next, define the default shell and shell environment variables. The default shell and start-up files are set by the /etc/security /mkuser.sys script and /etc/security/mkuser.default file. The mkuser.sys script reads the mkuser.default file and creates the home directory, sets permissions, and copies the default shell start-up file from /etc/security into the new home directory. The mkuser.sys script is invoked each time the mkuser command is executed by SMIT or from the command line to add a new account.

/etc/security/mkuser.default:

```
user:                    # General user defaults

   group = staff
   groups = staff
   prog = /bin/ksh
   home = /u/$USER

admin:                   # Administrative user defaults

   group = system
   groups = system
   prog = /bin/ksh
   home = /u/$USER
```

*Shell start-up files:*

| | |
|---|---|
| sh | .profile |
| ksh | .profile, .kshrc (If indicated by ENV) |
| csh, tcsh | .login, .cshrc, .logout |

The default behavior of mkuser.sys is to copy a complete shell start-up file into the user's home directory. This can be a problem should you decide to change some part of the default shell environment later on. You will need to incorporate the change into each user's start-up files without destroying any customizations added by the user.

A simple solution is to create a skeleton shell start-up file that contains a single line which sources or invokes a read-only system default shell start-up file. The skeleton file is copied to the user's home directory at account creation time. Users may append lines to their local copy of the skeleton file which overrides or adds to the environment variables, commands, and aliases specified in the system default start-up file. The system administrator maintains the shell environment data in the system defaults files. Default start-up would include things like displaying the message of the day file, /etc/motd, or invoking the msgs command to display system update information at login time. Skeleton and associated system defaults start-up files are created for each supported shell. The skeleton shell files should be available for copy should a user decide to change their default shell.

*Example skeleton and system* csh *start-up files:*

```
# /usr/local/skel/.cshrc
#
# Skeleton .cshrc file copied to the users home
# directory at account creation.
#
# Source system csh defaults
#
source /usr/local/lib/std.cshrc
#
# Local user changes are added after this line.

# /usr/local/skel/.login
#
# Skeleton .login file copied to the users home
# directory at account creation.
#
# Source system csh defaults
#
source /usr/local/lib/std.login
#
# Local user changes are added after this line.

# /usr/local/lib/std.cshrc
#
# System default csh startup environment. (read only)
#
if !($?prompt) goto NOPROMPT
set prompt = "_`hostname`% "
set history = 30
```

```
set savehist = 30
alias a alias
alias h history
umask 022
NOPROMPT:

# /usr/local/lib/std.login
#
set ignoreeof
setenv PATH "/usr/local/bin:/usr/bin/X11:/usr/ucb:/usr/bin:/bin:"
setenv EXINIT "set shell = /bin/csh"
stty dec crt
stty -tabs ff1
setenv TNESC 35
msgs -f
```

You can further break the system start-up file hierarchy down to support a start-up file which sets the PATH environment for all shells. That way, modifications to search path only involves updating one file. You might also want to separate aliases from environment variables, or TTY settings.

Depending on the shell, you will also need to be aware of how the start-up files are handled by other commands. For example, the remote shell command, rsh, does not invoke $HOME/.login for csh users. Thus, important csh environment information should be maintained in the std.cshrc file rather than the std.login file.

### 21.6.3 /etc/security/login.cfg

Even with simple schemes like this, many of us don't want to have to support every shell that might be built by a user. You can restrict the shells supported on the system by specifying the shell path in the /etc/security/login.cfg file. Edit the usw: stanza and list the path name of each supported shell, separated by commas after the shell = parameter.

/etc/security/login.cfg supported shells:

```
usw:
shells = /bin/sh,/bin/bsh,/bin/csh,/bin/ksh,/bin/tsh,/usr/bin/sh,
         /usr/bin/bsh,/usr/bin/csh,/usr/bin/ksh,/usr/bin/tsh,
         /usr/mbin/sh,/usr/mbin/bsh,/usr/mbin/csh,/usr/mbin/ksh,
         /usr/mbin/tsh,/usr/local/bin/tcsh
```

The /etc/security/login.cfg file also defines the default login heralds, alternate authorization programs, and passwd profile. Stanzas associated with these facilities will be discussed in Chap. 22.

## 21.7 Managing User Accounts

System administrators can't escape the ongoing stream of account management requests that come from an active user community. The good news is that AIX automates the task of adding, updating, and removing user accounts by providing a set of tools that take care of updating all the appropriate tables and file systems. It's not the perfect world, but it beats doing it by hand!

### 21.7.1 Adding a user account

To add a new user to the system, execute the `mkuser` command either from the command line or by using SMIT. Due to the number of parameters involved, I suggest using SMIT unless you are accepting system defaults. In the event that you are adding a large number of users, you can add the first using SMIT, then duplicate the `mkuser` command in the `smit.script` file for each subsequent account to be created. (See Fig. 21.2.)

```
                          Create User

Type or select values in entry fields.
Press Enter AFTER making all desired changes.

[TOP]                                        [Entry Fields]
* User NAME                                  []
ADMINISTRATIVE User?                         false          +
User ID                                      []             #
LOGIN user?                                  true           +
PRIMARY group                                []             +
Group SET                                    []             +
ADMINISTRATIVE groups                        []             +
SU groups                                    [ALL]          +
HOME directory                               []
Initial PROGRAM                              []
User INFORMATION                             []
Another user can SU to user?                 true           +
User can RLOGIN?                             true           +
TRUSTED PATH?                                nosak          +
User can RLOGIN?                             true           +
TRUSTED PATH?                                nosak          +
Valid TTYs                                   [ALL]
AUDIT classes                                []
PRIMARY authentication method                [SYSTEM]
SECONDARY authentication method              [NONE]
Max FILE size                                [2097151]      #
Max CPU time                                 [-1]           #
Max DATA segment                             [262144]       #
Max STACK size                               [65536]        #
Max CORE file size                           [2048]         #
Max physical MEMORY                          [65536]        #
File creation UMASK                          [022]
EXPIRATION date (MMDDhhmmyy)                 [0]
[BOTTOM]

F1 = Help        F2 = Refresh       F3 = Cancel      F4 = List
F5 = Undo        F6 = Command       F7 = Edit        F8 = Image
F9 = Shell       F10 = Exit         Enter = Do
```

**Figure 21.2** SMIT create user panel.

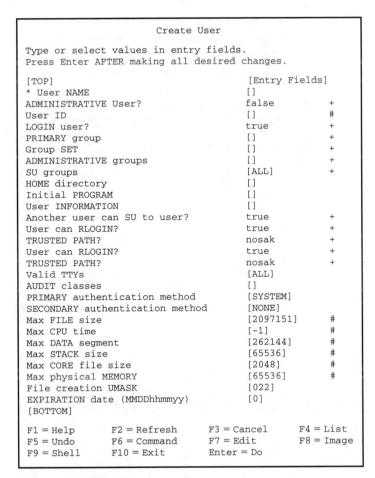

**TABLE 21.2 `mkuser` Fields**

| | |
|---|---|
| User NAME | Up to 8-character user name. Should not be upper case or use special characters. |
| ADMINISTRATIVE USER | Administrative privileges. |
| User ID | Unique integer. May need to be altered if you are using unique UIDs across multiple systems. |
| LOGIN User | Can the user login to the system? |
| PRIMARY Group | Default group at login. |
| Group SET | Other group membership. |
| ADMINISTRATIVE Groups | User is an administrator of these groups. |
| SU Groups | Groups that may issue the `su` command. |
| HOME Directory | Home directory path `/u/<user name>`. |
| Initial PROGRAM | Login shell program. |
| User INFORMATION | User full name, phone, etc. for `GECOS` field in `/etc/passwd` file. |
| Another user can SU to user | Can this UID be accessed with `su`? |
| User can RLOGIN | Can the user use `rlogin` to access the system? |
| TRUSTED PATH | Trusted path status. |
| Valid TTYs | TTY ports that may be used to login to this UID. |
| AUDIT Classes | Audit classes representing this UID. |
| PRIMARY Authentication Method | Authentication program used to validate this user to the system. Default SYSTEM represents standard user name and passwd. |
| SECONDARY Authentication Method | Secondary authentication program. If it fails, it does not deny access. |
| Max FILE size<br>Max CPU time<br>Max DATA segment<br>Max STACK size<br>Max CORE file size<br>Max physical MEMORY | Resource limits for the user. |
| File creation MASK | Default `umask` for the user. |
| EXPIRATION Date | Expiration date and time for this account. |

```
# smit mkuser
```

For most general user accounts, you can select a user name and accept the supplied defaults. (See Table 21.2.)

See the following Chap. 22 on *Security* for more information concerning primary and secondary authentication methods as well as passwd support.

### 21.7.2 Updating user accounts

You can modify existing user accounts by invoking the `chuser` command from the command line or via SMIT. In most cases, only a small number of fields are changed, so using chuser from the command line does not involve a large number of arguments. You may also update system account tables directly with an editor in some cases. Care should be taken that stanza format and permissions are not compromised.

```
# smit chuser
```

You can list the current set of attributes defined for a user using the lsuser command.

```
# lsuser stimpy
stimpy id = 4084 pgrp = system groups = system,security,staff,user,bitnet
home = /u/stimpy shell = /bin/ksh gecos = Stimpson Cat login = true
su = true rlogin = true daemon = true admin = true sugroups = ALL
admgroups = ALL tpath = nosak ttys = ALL expires = 0 auth1 = SYSTEM
auth2 = NONE umask = 22 fsize = -1 cpu = -1 data = -1 stack = -1 core = -1
rss = -1 time _last_login = 744387016
time_last_unsuccessful_login = 743980324 tty_last_login = pts/6
tty_last_unsuccessful_login = pts/34 host_last_login = daffy.foo.bar.org
host_last_unsuccessful_login = cs11.foo.bar.org unsuccessful_login_count = 0
```

### 21.7.3 Removing user accounts

To remove users from the system, use the rmuser command (see Fig. 21.3). It can be invoked from the command line or using SMIT. The rmuser command takes care of removing the user from the system tables and deleting the home directory from the file system. You also have the option of retaining user data in the /etc/security /passwd file.

```
# rmuser -p stimpy
# smit rmuser
```

To automate the process of removing accounts from the system, you can use cron to run a nightly process that looks for expired accounts and invokes rmuser. See Chap. 16 concerning using cron.

```
                 Remove a User from the System

Type or select values in entry fields.
Press Enter AFTER making all desired changes.

                                              [Entry Fields]
* User NAME                                   [stimpy]      +
Remove AUTHENTICATION information?            Yes           +

F1 = Help        F2 = Refresh      F3 = Cancel      F4 = List
F5 = Undo        F6 = Command      F7 = Edit        F8 = Image
F9 = Shell       F10 = Exit        Enter = Do
```

**Figure 21.3** SMIT remove user panel.

### 21.7.4 Restricting access

If it is necessary to restrict access to the system for a particular user, you may deny access from a number of mechanisms, depending on the situation. Login access can be restricted by setting the `LOGIN User` and `User can RLOGIN` fields to `false`. You may also restrict access by resetting the date in the `EXPIRATION` field. If you wish to send the user an informative message concerning account status to the user, create a script or program to write the message to stdout and add the program name to the `Initial PROGRAM` field for the user. After the user supplies a user name and passwd at login time, the message is displayed and the user is logged off. Use the `chuser` command to enable the desired level of access restriction.

## 21.8 Password Files

All the information injected by the AIX account management tools end up as entries in a number of account support tables. I have discussed the structure that some of these files provide in the previous sections. There are three other files that are primarily responsible for identifying an account to the operating system and application set. These are the `/etc/passwd`, `/etc/security/passwd`, and `/etc/security /user` files.

### 21.8.1 `/etc/passwd`

The `/etc/passwd` file uses the standard password file format available on most UNIX systems, the only exception being the use of a shadow password file. *Shadow password* support removes the encrypted password from the world-readable `/etc/passwd` file and places it into another file with restricted access. A place holder, `!`, is inserted into the password field in `/etc/passwd`. Each field in the `/etc/passwd` file is separated by a colon.

`/etc/passwd` *fields:*

```
USER NAME:!:UID:GID:GECOS:HOME DIRECTORY:SHELL
root:!:0:0:System Overseer:/:/bin/ksh
daemon:!:1:1::/etc:
bin:!:2:2::/bin:
sys:!:3:3::/usr/sys:
adm:!:4:4::/usr/adm:
uucp:!:5:5::/usr/lib/uucp:
stimpy:!:4084:30:Stimpson Cat:/u1/stimpy:/bin/ksh
```

AIX commands and applications that must resolve user information query `/etc/passwd` through the use of library calls like `getpwnam()`. Parsing large password files can cause significant delays in command response time. To improve response time, AIX supports building a structured `dbm` database from the `/etc/passwd` information. The mkpasswd command reads /etc/passwd and creates a keyed directory file, /etc/passwd.dir, and a data file, /etc/passwd.pag. Password dbm support is not required, but is provided as an option for sites with large user communities.

| | |
|---|---|
| `# mkpasswd /etc/passwd` | Create new passwd dbm database |

### 21.8.2 /etc/security/passwd

Shadow password support is provided by the /etc/security/passwd file. Each user account is represented by a user name stanza. The stanza contains the encrypted password, time of last update, and the update flag. The update flag is either NULL or one of the following values.

| | |
|---|---|
| ADMIN | Only root may change this password |
| ADMCHG | A member of the security group reset this password so it must be changed at next login |
| NO_CHECK | None of restrictions set in the /etc/security/login.cfg file are enforced for this account |

*Example* /etc/security/passwd *stanza:*

```
stimpy:
   password = dWe3asfZpuoJ6
   lastupdate = 722287867
   flags = NO_CHECK
```

### 21.8.3 /etc/security/user

The /etc/security/user file contains the extended attributes defined for the user. Each user is identified by a user name stanza followed by each attribute and value. A default: attribute set follows the header comments in the file. Each user entry may override a default attribute by specifying a local value.

*Example* /etc/security/user *stanzas:*

```
default:
   admin = false
   login = true
   su = true
   daemon = true
   rlogin = true
   sugroups = ALL
   ttys = ALL
   auth1 = SYSTEM
   auth2 = NONE
   tpath = nosak
   umask = 022
   expires = 0

stimpy:
   login = false
   rlogin = false
```

## 21.9 InfoExplorer Keywords

| | |
|---|---|
| msg | touch |
| /etc/passwd | quotaon |
| /etc/group | quotacheck |
| /etc/security/passwd | repquota |
| /etc/security/group | /etc/environment |
| mkgroup | /etc/profile |
| chgroup | /etc/security/environ |
| lsgroup | /etc/security/mkuser.sys |
| chgrpmem | /etc/security/mkuser.default mkuser |
| setgroup | /etc/motd |
| newgrp | msgs |
| rmgroup | /etc/security/login.cfg |
| /etc/security/limits | su |
| rlimit | chuser |
| edquota | rmuser |
| /etc/filesystems | cron |
| quota | mkpasswd |
| groupquota | /etc/security/user |
| userquota | |

## 21.10 QwikInfo

### User Administration

*Passwords:*

| | |
|---|---|
| /etc/security/passwd | Secure passwd entries |
| /etc/passwd | Unsecure passwd entries |
| /etc/passwd.{pag dir} | DBM passwd files |
| mkpasswd | Create DBM files |

*Groups:*

| | |
|---|---|
| /etc/group | Group numbers and lists |
| /etc/security/group | Group configuration |
| mkgroup, chgroup, lsgoup | Manage groups |
| chgrpmem | Change administrators or members of a group |
| setgroup | Reset the current group set for a user |
| newgrp | Set the group ID for session |

### *System defaults:*

| | |
|---|---|
| `/etc/security/limits` | Resource limits |
| `/etc/security/user` | User authorization and configuration |
| `/etc/security/login.cfg` | System authorization, heralds, shells |
| `chgdev -l sys0 -a <attribute>` | Set kernel attributes |
| `smit chgsys` | Set kernel attributes |

### *Disk quotas:*

| | |
|---|---|
| `/<file-system>>/quota.user` | User quota/file system |
| `/<file-system>/quota.group` | Group quota/file system |
| `/etc/filesystems` | Set quota attributes |
| `edquota` | Edit user quota limits |
| `quotaon/quotaoff` | Enable/disable quotas |
| `quotacheck` | Set quotas/file system |
| `quota, repquota` | Report quota, usage |

### *User environment:*

| | |
|---|---|
| `/etc/environment` | System environ defaults |
| `/etc/profile` | System login defaults |
| `/etc/security/environ` | User environ defaults |
| `/etc/security/mkuser.defualt` | User environ defaults |
| `/etc/security/mkuser.sys` | System environ defaults |
| `smit mkuser,chuser,lsuser,rmuser` | Manage user accounts |
| `$HOME/.login` | User login defaults |
| `$HOME/.profile` | User profile defaults |
| `$HOME/.<shell>rc` | Shell start-up defaults |

Chapter

# 22

# Auditing and Security

## 22.1 Security Overview

This age of worldwide communications is bringing us all closer together. Its also means a world of new and unsuspecting targets for the cracker community. It doesn't matter whether your system is stand-alone or tapped into a large network superhighway, it doesn't pay to leave the key under the mat. Sadly enough, this is true for friends as well as enemies. Loose lips sink ships! Corny but true!

Consider that the standard login security based solely on user name and password is in need of improvement. Password expiration is unpopular with users and is rarely enforced. Passwords are often easily guessable words that are quickly cracked, given the processing speed that is widely available at a modest cost. In many cases, it doesn't even require the use of sophisticated cracking programs. Users tend to write passwords down and share them with colleagues. In some cases, additional levels of security are required that are not easily compromised by user insensitivity to security.

Even if you don't think you have anything that anyone would want, your system could be a stepping stone to others. Useful information to system hackers comes in forms like *network address tables, e-mail addresses,* and *modem dial-up numbers.* Physical resources like tape, disk, and CPU time can be exploited to store information or crack passwords. System intruders may be curiosity seekers just poking around or they might be professionals up to serious mischief. Hackers make their way through the back roads of the network, exploiting numerous *known* security holes because administrators are not staying informed. What do you do?

## 22.2 Defining a Security Policy

Before you pack up your computer and store it in a bank vault, consider the benefits of defining and implementing a formal security policy. By setting down and enforcing some simple rules and implementing regular system auditing, you can protect yourself from the majority of attacks. It may not be perfect, but it can go a long way toward peace of mind.

When defining your security policy, keep in mind that there is a tradeoff between level of security and level of usability. Unless you're charged with securing national secrets, try to remember that AIX is an *open system*—open, as in *ease-of-use* rather than *no-locks-supplied.* Make sure that the policy is distributed to your user community and that they understand that their responsibility is protecting resources. The policy should consider maintaining:

- User privacy
- System integrity
- Authorized availability
- Ease of use
- Auditing and accountability

## 22.3 Passwords

What makes a good password? It has to be easy to remember, but not a plain text word or phrase like your mother's name or words from the dictionary. It MUST NOT be shared among users. Who has access to privileged passwords like the root password? Who has access to the table of encrypted passwords?

These are questions and policies that must be implemented to ensure a basic level of security. AIX provides tools that address some of these issues. Others simply require changes in the way we use the system. Sometimes old dogs have to learn new tricks or someone will take all the bones!

### 22.3.1 Shadow password files

One of the biggest problems with traditional UNIX password implementations is that the `/etc/passwd` contains the encrypted password for each user and it is world-readable. Although the `passwd` command uses one-way encryption, crack programs can encrypt common strings and compare the results against the encrypted password in `/etc/passwd`. In the 1960s, this was deemed to be an algorithm that would take hundreds or thousands of years of CPU time to compare all the possibilities. By using dictionaries and common password patterns, faster `crypt()` routines, and the higher-speed processors available today, you can crack most common passwords in reasonable periods of time.

How do you fix this problem? You move the encrypted passwords into a secure table and directory and require the use of secure setuid subroutines to access the information. This is what IBM has implemented on AIX V3. A place-holder character, "!", is inserted in the passwd field of the /etc/passwd file. A secure shadow password file, /etc/security/passwd, contains the encrypted passwd for each user.

/etc/passwd—*mode 644:*

```
root:!:0:0:Almighty Overseer:/:/bin/ksh
```

/etc/security/passwd—*mode 600:*

```
root:
   password = asldfi0237xa0
   lastupdate = 728707306
   flags =
```

### 22.3.2 Password restrictions

Users are not inclined to use esoteric passwords and they do not like to change their password more than once a lifetime. Unfortunately, this breaks the first law of account security. AIX allows the system administrator to remind them somewhat forcefully that it's time for a change, and that they need to be somewhat imaginative in what they choose. You don't want to be a nag, so don't require changes too often and don't require them to be so cryptic that they have to write them down. Tailor password aging and character restrictions in the pw_restrictions stanza in the /etc/security/login.cfg file. Restrictions are applied systemwide. Once the maxage limit is passed, users are required to select a new password at next login.

*Password restrictions*—/etc/security/login.cfg:

```
                 Def  Max  Rec
pw_restrictions:
   maxage =       0   52   8   Max weeks before update enforced
   minage =       0   52   1   Min weeks before update allowed
   minalpha =     0    8   4   Min number of alpha characters
   minother =     0    8   2   Min number of nonalpha characters
   mindiff =      0    8   3   Min chars different from old password
   maxrepeats =   8    8   1   Max number of repeats for any character
```

### 22.3.3 Resetting users' passwords

It doesn't seem to matter whether a password is cryptic or a common word. Users always seem to forget them. A common complaint from system administrators is that AIX requires root's password to reset a user password. In fact, AIX does require root's password if you are not a member of the *security* group, and if you don't use the pwdadm command or SMIT to update passwords. As a member of the security group, you are required to enter your own password to validate who you are.

```
# pwdadm sleepy
<your> Password:
Changing password for "sleepy"
sleepy's New password:
Re-enter sleepy's new password:
```

### 22.3.4 Superuser access

Care should be taken on who has access to root's password and how it is used. Users with access to privileged accounts should log in using their own nonprivileged account and use the `su` command to setuid to privileged accounts. The `su` command logs all invocations to the `/var/adm/sulog` file. This provides an audit trail on who, when, and success of access.

Shell aliases mapping `su` to the full path name, `/bin/su`, will limit the possibility of a *trojan horse* `su` command from being used on a compromised account. A trojan horse copy of `su` will usually act as you would expect, except that it will record passwords in a file monitored by the perpetrator.

AIX provides an additional level of `su` security by defining whether an account can be accessed via `su`, and which groups are permitted `su` access to the account. These restrictions are applied on a per-user basis in the `/etc/security/user` file.

`su` *restrictions*—`/etc/security/user`:

| | |
|---|---|
| `robin:` | |
| `su = <true/false>` | Users may `su` to this account |
| `sugroups = <ALL\|list>` | Groups that may `su` to this account |

### 22.3.5 Auditing passwords

Even when you are enforcing password controls, it is a good idea to periodically audit passwords on your system. It is often a good idea to keep abreast of password cracking tools used by the hacker community. Check out anonymous ftp archives like `wuarchive.wustl.edu` and `ftp.uu.net` for password cracking tools like *Crack* and *killer cracker.*

The COPS package available from CERT contains various security tools along with password crackers. The COPS package and Crack are available via anonymous ftp from `cert.org`.

AIX provides its own set of password validation tools. These tools are part of the larger security system called the *Trusted Computing Base* (TCB). An important piece of the TCB system is the table validation tools. These tools may be invoked individually or as part of the overall system validation from the `tcbck` command.

*TCB password validation commands:*

| | |
|---|---|
| `pwdck` | Checks consistency of the `/etc/passwd` and `/etc/security/passwd` files |
| `grpck` | Checks consistency of the `/etc/group` and `/etc/security/group` files |
| `usrck` | Validates entries in the `/etc/security/user` file |

### 22.3.6 Converting password files from other sources

If you are moving a large user community from another UNIX platform onto AIX, fear not, AIX provides a means for converting standard UNIX `/etc/passwd` files into the various AIX password files. The same tools used to audit password file consistency can be used to convert password files from other systems.

First, copy the password file into the AIX `/etc/passwd` path. Once the password file is available, execute the `pwdck` command to create `/etc/security/passwd` entries.

```
# pwdck -y ALL
```

Next, create user stanza entries for each user in the `/etc/security/limits` file and `/etc/security/user` files, using the `usrck` command.

```
# usrck
```

Finally, update `/etc/group` with any GIDs and group members that existed on the old system. Once updates have been completed, execute the `grpck` command to create `/etc/security/group` entries.

```
# grpck
```

## 22.4 Trusted Computing Base

AIX V3 has an integrated security system called the Trusted Computing Base (TCB). TCB validates and audits both hardware and software components of the RISC System/6000 and AIX V3. TCB is made up of kernel interfaces, configuration tables, and *trusted setuid/setgid* programs, which monitor system consistency.

### 22.4.1 `tcbck` command

The system administrator may add *trusted* applications to the TCB system using the `tcbck` command. It is the administrator's responsibility to guarantee the security of any new application added to TCB.

| | |
|---|---|
| `# tcbck -a <pathname> [attrib = value]` | Mark application as trusted |
| `# tcbck -d <pathname>` | Remove trusted status |

The attributes of trusted components of the TCB system are recorded in the `/etc/security/sysck.cfg` table. The `tcbck` command reads the information recorded in `sysck.cfg` when auditing the security state of the system. The `tcbck` command can be run periodically using `cron`, or interactively from the command line. The latter is useful when you suspect the possibility of the system having been compromised.

```
# tcbck -p ALL
```

You can use `tcbck` to check the integrity of all file system files in the event that they may have been compromised. During a file system scan, `tcbck` validates that files with setuid root and administrative setgid bits preexist in the `/etc/security/sysck.cfg` file. If they do not exist, then the privileged bits are cleared. The same is true for device special files, links to trusted files, and files with the tcb attribute. Note that this can take a significant amount of time.

```
# tcbck -t tree       Invoke file system check.
```

### 22.4.2 /etc/security/sysck.cfg

Trusted applications are identified by stanza entries in the `/etc/security/sysck.cfg` file bearing the path names. Each stanza is followed by a set of parameters defining the attributes of the trusted application. Refer to Table 22.1.

*Example* `/etc/security/sysck.cfg` *stanza:*

```
/usr/bin/acledit:
   owner = bin
   group = bin
   mode = TCB,555
   type = FILE
   oldpath = /bin/acledit
   class = apply,inventory,bos.obj
   size = 5010
   checksum = "44904 5 "
```

### 22.4.3 Trusted communication path

For applications that require a secure interface between the application and the user's terminal, AIX provides the concept of a *trusted*

**TABLE 22.1 TCB `/etc/security/sysck.cfg` Parameters**

| | |
|---|---|
| class | Identifier that is used to group a set of applications. Applications identified by a class may be checked as a unit by `tcbck`. Multiple class names may be specified for an application. |
| owner | File owning user name. Must match directory owner value. |
| group | File group name. Must match directory group value. |
| mode | Specifies one of SUID, SGID, SVTX, or TCB followed by the file permissions. Permissions may be specified as an octal value (ex 644) or a 9-character value (ex. rw-r—r—). |
| links | List of path names that are hard links to this file. Entries in the list are separated by commas. |
| symlinks | List of path names that are symbolic links to this file. Entries in the list are separated by commas. |
| program | Program path name and arguments that may be invoked to check the application. |
| acl | The access control list value for the file. If the ACL value does not match that of the file, `tcbck` applies the value listed in stanza ACL parameter. The value must be consistent with the SUID, SGID, and SVTX value listed in the `mode` parameter. |
| source | The source file name that is to be copied for checking. |

*communication path.* Trusted communication paths allow only TCB trusted programs and devices to interact with the user's terminal. This limits the possibility of trojan horse or eavesdropping applications from opening file descriptors associated with a TTY port.

A trusted communication path is invoked by pressing a *secure attention key* (SAK). The SAK key sequence, `ctrl-x ctrl-r`, is enabled by the system administrator in the `/etc/security/login.cfg` file. SAK support may be set for individual TTY ports.

A secure login session begins by pressing the SAK prior to typing in your user name and password. After the SAK sequence has been entered, `init` revokes all previous opens on the port. A `getty` is started on the port and a new login herald is displayed. After entering your user name and password, TTY port permissions are restricted to your account and the *trusted shell* (tsh) is invoked. The `tsh` shell is akin to the *Korn shell* (ksh), and will only allow execution of trusted applications (those marked with the tcb bit). It is a good idea to initiate a trusted path when working as root or setting passwords.

## 22.5 Access Control

Access control defines the who and how of access to system resources. Traditional UNIX access control is based on user and group ownership of a resource and associated mode bits that define read, write, execute, setuid, and setgid access. Read, write, and execute permissions are set individually for the resource owner, group, and other (everyone). The setuid mode bit indicates that, when the resource is invoked, the resulting process takes on the *effective UID* permissions of the resource owner. The setgid mode bit indicates that *effective GID* permissions will be enabled for the process.

The `chown`, `chgrp`, and `chmod` commands are used to set the owner, group, and mode for a resource. A three-digit octal mask called the `umask` may be set by each user to set the default mode bits automatically when new files are created.

| | |
|---|---|
| `# chown <user name> <path name>` | Set user ownership |
| `# chgrp <group name> <path name>` | Set group ownership |
| `# chmod <mode> <path name>` | Set mode permissions |
| `# umask <mask>` | Set creation mask |

To list the ownership and mode permissions for a file use the `ls` command.

```
# ls -alF /home/deroest
total 880
drwx---      13   deroest   system    1536   Sep 13 08:02   ./
drwxr-xr-x   10   bin       bin        512   Sep 14 22:00   ../
-rw----       1   deroest   system      27   Jan 11 1993    .forward*
-rw----       1   deroest   system    1499   Dec 23 1992    .kshrc*
-rw----       1   deroest   system     315   Nov 20 1992    .login*
```

```
-rw----      2  deroest  system  61765  Aug 31 09:07  .newsrc
-rw----      1  deroest  system    273  Nov 20 1992   .profile*
-rw----      1  deroest  system     33  May 17 09:14  .rhosts*
drwx---      2  deroest  system    512  Dec 24 1992   Mail/
drwx---      2  deroest  system    512  Dec 24 1992   News/
drwxr-x--    2  deroest  system   1024  Apr 14 13:22  bin/
drwxr-xr-x   3  deroest  system    512  Sep 16 22:08  doc/
drwxr-xr-x   4  deroest  system    512  Apr 02 09:58  info/
drwxr-x--    2  deroest  system    512  Jun 14 10:48  src/
```

Using entries in `/etc/group` to support file sharing does not scale well in large multiuser environments. Discretionary access rights should be controlled by the owner of the resource and not require intervention by the system administrator.

### 22.5.1 Access control lists

To address the requirement for extra discretionary access privacy under users' control, AIX V3 provides *access control lists* (ACL). ACLs have been used on a number of other operating systems for many years. ACLs work in conjunction with AIX groups and group lists. They provide a finer granularity of control over access rights within groups.

ACLs are made up of sets of *access control entries* (ACE), which define the access rights to system objects. There are three sections to an ACL. The first defines the file *attributes,* for example, SUID permission. The second section defines the traditional UNIX *base permissions:* owner, group and other ids, and modes. The third section defines the *extended permissions* for the file. This section provides finer control over access rights to the file.

*Example ACL:*

```
attributes:             SUID                          Section 1
base permissions                                      Section 2
  owner (gilbert):      rwx
  group (user):         r-x
  others:               --
extended permissions                                  Section 3
  enabled
  permit                r-     u:jill                 ACE
  deny                  -w-    g:staff                ACE
  specify               r-x    g:user, g:ops          ACE
```

Extended permission ACEs use the format *action access-mode users/groups.* The ACE action field must be one of the following: `permit`, `deny`, or `specify`. The `permit` and `deny` actions add to or remove the access mode from the standard mode value. The `specify` action means to use the exact access mode for the user/group set that follows. This overrides the standard modes defined for the file. Multiple user/group sets specified by `u:user name` and `g:group name`, respectively, indicate that a particular user must be identified by each value in the list before the access mode applies to the user.

Access rights or restrictions are based on the logical union of the representative ACEs for a particular user or group and the traditional UNIX access modes. You have to be very careful managing both ACLs and traditional UNIX permissions. AIX will resolve contradictions between multiple ACLs and standard permissions. Note that using the `chmod` command with octal permission arguments will remove any ACL associated with a file. This can be a problem if you're like me and prefer to use the numbers (sigh).

To create an ACL use the `acledit` command. A default ACL is opened for update in the editor specified by the `EDITOR` environment variable. Tailor the ACL to fit the access rights you have in mind. Set the `disabled` field to `enabled` and save the file. The application will ask you whether you want to apply the ACL on exit.

```
# acledit
```

Use the `aclget` and `aclput` commands to display or apply ACL information for a file.

```
# aclput acl-name file-name        Apply an ACL to a file
# aclget file-name                 Display ACL information
```

In cases where you want to define a set of ACLs which are to be applied to a set of files, use `acledit` to create and save the ACLs to generic file names. You can then use `aclput` to apply each ACL type to the desired files.

## 22.6 Authentication Methods

The designers of the AIX TCB system thought about these issues and provided an interface that allows you to add to, replace, and apply system authentication mechanisms on an individual basis. What's more, it doesn't require modifications to the default authentication code, `/bin/login@ -> /usr/sbin/tsm`, or alteration of the password file format as understood by the command set. Sounds real nice? It is real nice!

The facility is simple to understand and easy to use. The TCB system passes the user name to be authenticated to your local application as an argument. Your code takes whatever action is appropriate to authenticate the user and returns 0 if authentication is successful or 1 if it has failed. Login processing will proceed or abort based on this return code.

### 22.6.1 Authentication tables

Defining your authentication code to the system requires an entry in the `/etc/security/login.cfg` file. As superuser and using your favorite editor, edit the login.cfg file and look for the comment line that contains auth_method:. For each authentication program you want to add, enter a stanza of the form:

```
method_name:
   program = your_program
```

*Example 1:*

```
TOKcheck:
   program = /usr/local/etc/validateTOK
```

The method name you choose will be used to identify the authentication program in the /etc/security/user file. Supply a stanza for each authentication method you intend to use.

Next, you identify which user names will use these methods in the /etc/security/user file. As superuser, edit the user file. The user file header explains the use of the two authorization parameters, auth1 and auth2. The auth1 stanza identifies the primary authentication methods to be employed for each user. If this method set fails, login is denied. The auth2 stanza defines a secondary set of methods that is invoked after the auth1 methods are run. If these methods fail, login is not denied. These secondary methods could be used to provide extra authorization to access secure system resources.

The format of the auth parameters is:

```
auth1 = method<,method...><;username>
auth2 = method<,method...><;username>
```

Supply each method name to be invoked delimited by commas. The default action is to pass the invoking *user name* to the method. You can override this by providing the user name to be used after the method list, delimited by a semicolon. The special method names, SYSTEM and NONE, specify that either the standard password check or no authentication method is to be run, respectively.

To indicate that a method set is to be run for all users unless it is specifically overridden, use the default: stanza located after the header in the /etc/security/user file. In Example 2, the *TOKcheck* method that we identified earlier in the /etc/security/login.cfg file will be run after the standard password check for all users.

*Example 2:*

```
default:
   admin = false
   login = true
   su = true
   daemon = true
   rlogin = true
   sugroups = ALL
   ttys = ALL
```

```
auth1 = SYSTEM,TOKcheck
auth2 = NONE
tpath = nosak
umask = 022
expires = 0
```

In the case that we want to override the default authentication for a particular user, include local auth1 and auth2 parameters after the stanza identifying the user name.

*Example 3:*

```
operator:
   auth1 = SYSTEM,TOKcheck
   auth2 = OPScheck;operator

ops1:
   auth1 = SYSTEM,TOKcheck
   auth2 = OPScheck;operator

ops2:
   auth1 = SYSTEM,TOKcheck
   auth2 = OPScheck;operator

opsmgr:
   auth1 = SYSTEM,TOKcheck
   auth2 = OPScheck;operator
```

In Example 3, we have identified a secondary method called *OPScheck* that might give access to a particular set of commands or resources to system operators. Note also that the user name *operator* is passed to the method program. This will allow the addition of new operator account names without having to identify each one explicitly in the OPScheck source code.

### 22.6.2 Smart card authentication

In the previous section, the examples referred to a sample method called *TOKcheck.* In addition to requiring a user name and password for authorization, add a *token* that uniquely identifies each user. There are a number of *smart cards* and *key cards* on the market that can be used to provide unique authentication tokens. A token card is given to each user and is identified by a unique string that is stored with the user name in a secure central database.

An application called TOKcheck can now be installed, which will generate a random string and display it as output. The user keys the string into the personal token card, which then DES encrypts the string and outputs it to the cards display. The user types this encrypted string back into the TOKcheck application on the terminal. TOKcheck also encrypts the original string using the unique DES key associated with the user's token card in the database. It compares the result with that supplied by the user.

There are automated smart cards available that periodically cycle through encryption strings on both a server and the smart cards. The cards and the server are synchronized by clocks. Using automated smart cards, the user need only enter the current string displayed on the smart card display when the token is requested by an application.

This scheme ensures that the user must be in possession of the correct token card, as well as the correct user name and password. What's more, the encryption string is only valid for a short period of time and cannot be reused by anyone eavesdropping on the wire.

### 22.6.3 Kerberos—trusted third party

Another authentication mechanism that is used in the Open Software Foundation's Distributed Computing Environment (DCE) and Distributed Management Environment (DME) is the *Kerberos* authentication system. Kerberos was originally developed at M.I.T. and is based on the *trusted third party* model. The original design is described in a series of papers presented at the 1988 USENIX Winter Conference.

Kerberos assumes that everything is untrustworthy except the authentication server itself. The authentication server acts as an intermediary between the client and the desired services. The client must authenticate itself to the Kerberos authentication server to gain a ticket, which grants the rights to access distributed services. You only need validate yourself once to the server rather than once for each service you wish to access. The access rights tickets are also valid for a given period of time. The Kerberos ticket mechanism eliminates the need to transmit passwords over network in clear text. Client and server passwords are known by the authentication server. Refer to Fig 22.1.

Whenever access to services is requested by an unauthenticated client, a message is sent to the authentication server that contains client name and the Kerberos ticket-granting service name. The authentication server looks up the names and obtains the *encryption key* for the client and the ticket server. The encryption key is known only to the owning agent and the authentication server. The encryption key can be a one-way DES encrypted password. A message is constructed by the authentication server containing the client and ticket server names, address, and a random *session key,* which it encrypts using the client's encryption key. The message is called a *ticket* and is sent to the client. The client uses its encryption key to decrypt the the ticket and stores the ticket for the duration for which it is valid. The session key is used to encrypt ticket communication with the Kerberos ticket service to gain access to other services and resources.

When access to a service is requested, the ticket service provides a new session key along with a ticket encrypted with the service's encryption key from the authentication server's database. The client

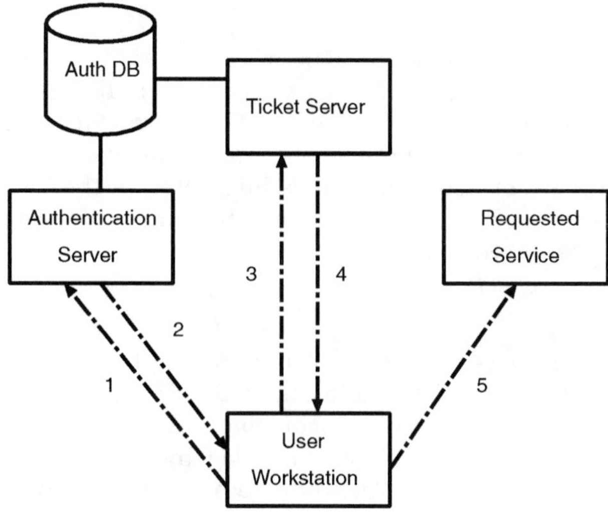


1. Request authentication for user and service
2. Return TS session key and identifiers
3. Request ticket using sealed authenticator
4. Return ticket for requested service
5. Connect to service with authenticator ticket

**Figure 22.1** Kerberos ticket flow.

uses the new session key to create an *authenticator* ticket, which identifies the client, and sends it along with the encrypted service ticket to the new service. The service decrypts the ticket using its encryption key. The service ticket contains the session key, which is then used to decrypt the authenticator ticket. Now the client and service know about each other and real work can begin.

It may seem like a lot of hand waving to inhibit clear text passwords and authentication information from being broadcast over the network. On the other hand, it is extremely easy to eavesdrop on the wire. All this negotiation is taking place under the covers, so it is not visible to the end user. Kerberos won't restrict access to someone who has already compromised another user's login ID and password.

## 22.7 Network Security

AIX TCB also encompasses network interfaces and applications. The network component of TCB is called the *Network Trusted Computing Base* (NTCB). Security issues related to the various network interfaces and protocols are covered in detail in the chapters related to networking. Refer to these chapters for specific information.

## 22.8 System Auditing

When talking about security breaches, it is often not sufficient to periodically check to see if someone left the barn door open. It's much better to be informed when the door is opened. AIX TCB provides an auditing system that supports *event detection, data collection,* and *report processing.* TCB event detection code is integrated in the kernel and trusted programs. Event detection may be enabled for the entire system or for local processes only.

### 22.8.1 Audit logging

The TCB event detection code reports event information to an *audit logger.* The audit logger constructs the audit trail for events. The audit trail includes the type of event, responsible UID, date, time, status, and any event-specific information. Audit logging can be done in either user state or kernel state. The audit records are logged in one of two types of log modes:

BIN — Audit information is logged to a series of files (bins). Data may be compressed and filtered.

STREAM — Audit records are written to a circular buffer that is read synchronously through a pseudodevice. STREAM mode provides real-time event monitoring.

### 22.8.2 Event types

The AIX audit system allows you to configure both event detection and audit trail recording. Event detection can be selected on a per-user basis. Care should be taken to audit those events that are of most interest for your environment. Auditing too many event types can cause significant threats to be lost in the noise. Too few event types may miss important events. Event selection may be *per-process* or *per-object.*

**Event types.**
*Security policy events:*

- Subject events

  process creation

  process deletion

  process attribute changes

- Object events

  object creation

  object deletion

object open
object close
object attribute changes

- Import/export events

  importing/exporting an object

- Accountability events

  updating password tables
  updating group tables
  user login
  user logoff
  updating use authentication data
  updating trusted path configuration
  authentication configuration
  auditing configuration and updates

- General system administration events

  privilege use
  file system configuration
  device configuration
  system parameter configuration
  boot and shutdown
  RAS configuration
  other system configuration

- Security violation events

  access permission refusals
  privilege failures
  diagnostic detected system errors
  attempted alteration of TCB

### 22.8.3 Audit configuration

To configure the AIX TCB auditing system, begin by selecting the event types to be collected. Event types are defined in the `/etc/security/audit/events` file. Using an editor, add or remove event types and the associated output formats.

Group related event types into *audit classes*. Audit classes are one of three types:

general Alterations in the authentication and access controls of the system

system Account modifications and installation

init Init process events, login, cron, etc.

Record each audit class in the /etc/security/audit/config file. If the audit class is to be assigned to individual users, add the class to the users stanza.

/etc/security/audit/config:

```
start:
binmode =    on
streammode = off
bin:
trail =      /audit/trail
bin1 =       /audit/bin1
bin2 =       /audit/bin2
binsize =    10240
cmds =       /etc/security/audit/bincmds

stream:
cmds =       /etc/security/audit/streamcmds

classes:
general =    USER_SU,PASSWORD_Change,FILE_Unlink,FILE_Link,FILE_Rename
objects =    S_ENVIRON_WRITE,S_GROUP_WRITE,S_LIMITS_WRITE,S_LOGIN_
             WRITE, S_PASSWD_READ,S_PASSWD_WRITE,S_USER_WRITE,AUD_
             CONFIG_WR
SRC =        SRC_Start,SRC_Stop,SRC_Addssys,SRC_Chssys,SRC_Delssys,
             SRC_Addserver,SRC_Chserver,SRC_Delserver
kernel =     PROC_Create,PROC_Delete,PROC_Execute,PROC_RealUID,
             PROC_AuditID,PROC_RealGID,PROC_AuditState,PROC_AuditClass
             , PROC_Environ,PROC_SetSignal,PROC_Limits,PROC_SetPri,
             PROC_Setpri,PROC_Privilege
files =      FILE_Open,FILE_Read,FILE_Write,FILE_Close,FILE_Link,
             FILE_Unlink,FILE_Rename,FILE_Owner,FILE_Mode,FILE_Acl,
             FILE_Privilege,DEV_Create
svipc =      MSG_Create,MSG_Read,MSG_Write,MSG_Delete,MSG_Owner,
             MSG_Mode,SEM_Create,SEM_Op,SEM_Delete,SEM_Owner,SEM_Mode
             , SHM_Create,SHM_Open,SHM_Close,SHM_Owner,SHM_Mode
mail =       SENDMAIL_Config, SENDMAIL_ToFile
cron =       AT_JobAdd,AT_JobRemove,CRON_JobAdd,CRON_JobRemove
tcpip =      TCPIP_config,TCPIP_host_id,TCPIP_route,TCPIP_connect,
             TCPIP_data_out,TCPIP_data_in,TCPIP_access,TCPIP_set_
             time, TCPIP_kconfig,TCPIP_kroute,TCPIP_kconnect,TCPIP_
             kdata_out, TCPIP_kdata_in,TCPIP_kcreate

users:
root =       general
```

Audit classes assigned to objects must be configured into the /etc/security/audit/objects file. Log mode, BIN, or STREAM is also defined in this file. Tailor the binmode or streammode stanzas to enable data collection. Any programs used to filter audit records must be defined in /etc/security/audit/{bincmds,streamcmds}.

/etc/security/audit/objects:

```
/etc/security/environ:
```

```
   w = "S_ENVIRON_WRITE"

/etc/security/group:
   w = "S_GROUP_WRITE"

/etc/security/limits:
   w = "S_LIMITS_WRITE"

/etc/security/login.cfg:
   w = "S_LOGIN_WRITE"

/etc/security/passwd:
   r = "S_PASSWD_READ"
   w = "S_PASSWD_WRITE"

/etc/security/user:
   w = "S_USER_WRITE"

/etc/security/audit/config:
   w = "AUD_CONFIG_WR"
```

```
/etc/security/audit/{bincmds,streamcmds}:
```

```
audit,auditpr,auditselect,auditstream
```

## 22.9 Security Tools and Information

I've talked about setting security policies, enforcing access controls, and auditing different aspects of system authentication and authorization. Is this enough to protect your system? The problem is that hackers are busy bees that won't stop prying and testing just because you have put a few access controls in place. You have to keep informed and continue looking for problem areas in the system.

### 22.9.1 virscan

AIX provides a *virus*-scanning application called `virscan`. The `virscan` command reads a set of know virus signatures from the `/etc/security/scan/{virsig.lst,addenda.lst}` files. The signatures are known virus bit strings that may be found in system files and executables. You can add new signatures to the `addenda.lst` file. If `virscan` finds a signature in a file, it records it to the `positive.vir` file.

| | |
|---|---|
| `# virscan <PathName>` | Invoke `virscan` on a directory tree |

### 22.9.2 COPS

In the previous section concerning password cracking, I mentioned the COPS packages from the Computer Emergency Response Team (CERT) at Carnegie Mellon University. COPS will audit system files, look for setuid/setgid programs, writable device files, etc. You can obtain a copy of the COPS package via anonymous ftp to `cert.sei.cmu.edu`.

### 22.9.3 Information sources

CERT regularly posts security advisory memos to the Usenet group, `comp.unix.security`. The memos are also available in their anonymous ftp archive. Report any security problems to CERT. They can be reached at:

Computer Emergency Response Team/Coordination Center
Software Engineering Institute
Carnegie Mellon University
Pittsburgh, PA 15213-3890
(412)268-7090
cert@cert.org
anonymous ftp: cert.org

## 22.10 InfoExplorer Keywords

| | |
|---|---|
| `/etc/passwd` | `/etc/security/sysck.cfg` |
| `passwd` | `cron` |
| `crypt` | `ACL` |
| `/etc/security/passwd` | `SAK` |
| `/etc/security/login.cfgq` | `tsh` |
| `pwdadm` | `chown` |
| `security` | `chgrp` |
| `su` | `chmod` |
| `/var/adm/sulog` | `umask` |
| `/etc/security/user` | `acledit` |
| `TCB` | `aclget` |
| `tcbck` | `aclput` |
| `pwdck` | `audit` |
| `grpck` | `auditpr` |
| `usrck` | `auditselect` |
| `/etc/group` | `auditstream` |
| `/etc/security/group` | `virscan` |

## 22.11 QwikInfo

### Security

*User passwords:*

| | |
|---|---|
| `/etc/security/passwd` | Secure passwd file. |
| `/etc/security/login.cfg` | Set passwd restrictions. |
| `pwdadm` | Reset user passwords. Should be a member of security group. |

### *Superuser access:*

| | |
|---|---|
| `su` | Set user command. |
| `/var/adm/sulog` | Log of `su` activity. |
| `/etc/security/user` | Set `su` restrictions. |

### *Password auditing:*

| | |
|---|---|
| `pwdck` | Checks `/etc/passwd, /etc/security/passwd` consistency. |
| `grpck` | Checks `/etc/group, /etc/security/group` consistency. |
| `usrck` | Validate entries in `/etc/security/user.` |

### *System auditing:*

| | |
|---|---|
| `tcbck` | Manage auditing system. |
| `/etc/security/sysck.cfg` | System audit config. |
| `/etc/security/audit/events` | Audit event types. |
| `/etc/security/audit/config` | Audit class config. |
| `/etc/security/audit/objects` | Audit object config. |
| `audit, auditpr, auditselect, auditstream` | Manage audit system. |

### *Authorization and access:*

| | |
|---|---|
| `SAK` | Secure attention key. |
| `tsh` | Trusted shell. |
| `/etc/securit/user: auth1 auth2` | Define alternate login authorization routines. |
| `chown, chgrp, chmod` | Set standard UNIX access permissions. |
| `umask <mask>` | File creation mask. |
| `acledit` | Edit access control lists. |
| `aclget, aclput` | Assign ACLs. |

### *Virus detection:*

| | |
|---|---|
| `virscan <PathName>` | Invoke `virscan.` |
| `/etc/security/scan/{virsig.lst,addenda.lst}` | Virus signatures. |
| `/etc/security/scan/positive.vir` | Virus found log. |

Chapter

# 23

# System Accounting

## 23.1 Accounting Overview

Let's see, that's 22 minutes of CPU, 3 MB of disk space, and 9 hours of connect time. Will you be putting this on a credit card, cash, or check? Nothing in life is free! Especially computer resources.

Even if you don't *chargeback* for system resources, it's a good idea to regularly monitor utilization. By collecting accounting data, you get a reasonable profile of how your system is being used. Who are the big resource hitters? How soon are you going to need that extra 2 GB of disk space? Maybe you need to justify the resources to a higher authority.

The AIX accounting system is very SYSV in flavor. For those of you with a BSD inclination, there is a set of the standard BSD accounting system management commands bolted onto the SYSV environment. Sites that write their own accounting programs and scripts will find that AIX provides the tools and accounting data formats that will facilitate porting an existing system from other UNIX environments. For the less adventurous, AIX supplies all the commands and scripts required to manage system accounting data. The accounting system is based on a set of three components:

- Data collection
- Management and reporting commands
- Periodic data management scripts

Data collection takes place automatically when accounting is enabled. Management and commands allow you to start and stop the accounting system, manage the data files, and generate reports. The data management scripts are invoked through cron to automate closing out data and generating general summary information.

## 23.2 Data Collection

Data collection begins when system accounting is turned on and stops when it is turned off. AIX samples and records process utilization and session data for each user in the system. The collected information represents connect time, process resources, commands, disk usage, and print queuing utilization.

### 23.2.1 Connect time

Connect time data is accumulated in the `/var/adm/wtmp` and `/etc/utmp` files. Each time you log in to AIX, the `login` process writes a record to `wtmp` and `utmp`. The data indicates the user name, date, time, port, and connecting address. A similar record is written by the `init` process when you exit the system. This data represents the duration of your connection to the system.

Combinations of `rsh` and X11 clients make connection data a bit fuzzy in environments where there is heavy X11 usage. The `xterm` terminal emulation client provides a flag indicating whether or not an `/etc/utmp` record should be written. `xterm` also has a nasty habit of trashing the `/etc/utmp` file. You'll notice the latter problem when your `uptime` statistics look too good to be true.

The `acctwtmp` command records system boot and shutdown times in the `/var/adm/wtmp` file. This data provides an audit trail concerning the comings and goings of users on your system.

### 23.2.2 Process resource usage

Resource utilization information for each process run by the operating system is recorded in the `/var/adm/pacct` file at process exit. The bad news is that no information is run for processes that don't exit! A process accounting record indicates the UID, GID, user name, elapsed wall clock time, CPU time, memory use, character I/O total, and disk block I/O totals.

### 23.2.3 Command usage

A nice side effect of process data is an audit trail of command and application usage. This data provides a profile of application use and may assist in tracking security problems. Be aware that experienced hackers tend to fix up accounting information before leaving the scene. See Chap. 22 for secure system auditing details.

### 23.2.4 Disk usage

You can periodically collect disk usage information for the system and store it in the `/var/adm/dtmp` file. Collecting disk usage data can cause a bit of a load on the system, so it's a good idea to run it during an off-hour shift. AIX assigns disk usage data to users based on the files they own in the file system and any links to files they may have created. The usage statistics for a file are distributed evenly among the users with links to the file.

It is also possible to track disk usage and regulate limits on usage by user and/or group. This is done through the *disk quota* system. See Chap. 21 concerning details on the disk quota system.

### 23.2.5 Print usage

Print queuing system utilization statistics are recorded by the `enq` command and the `qdaemon` process. `enq` writes a record for each print job it handles. The record indicates the print job owner, job number, and the file name. When the file is printed, `qdaemon` writes another record that includes this information plus the number of pages that were printed. There are public domain backends for postscript queues that will supply accounting records for postscript conversion and attributes.

### 23.2.6 Accounting files

Accounting records are stored in a set of files located in the `/var/adm` directory.

`/var/adm` *accounting files:*

| | |
|---|---|
| pacct | Active process data |
| Spacct.<mmdd> | Daily active process data (runacct) |
| qacct | Print usage data |
| ctmp | Connect session data |
| dtmp | Disk usage data |
| wtmp | Active process data |

## 23.3 Accounting Configuration

To configure the accounting system, begin by creating file name stubs with the correct permissions for each of the data collection files. This must be done with `adm` authority. The file name stubs can be created by `touching` the file name or running the `nulladm` command. `nulladm` creates the file names supplied as arguments and sets the correct permissions.

### 23.3.1 Setup collection files

```
# touch /var/adm/{wtmp,pacct}
# chown adm /var/adm/{wtmp,pacct}
# chgrp adm /var/adm/{wtmp,pacct}
# chmod 644 /var/adm/{wtmp,pacct}
# /usr/sbin/acct/nulladm wtmp pacct
```

### 23.3.2 Identifying shifts

Configure the /etc/acct/holidays file to reflect your prime time shift and scheduled holidays. The first line in the file indicates the year and the starting and ending times for prime shift. Subsequent lines indicate the date and description of each holiday scheduled over the year. Each holiday entry indicates:

Integer day of the year

Three-character month name

Integer day of the month

Text string holiday description

/etc/acct/holidays:

```
* (C) COPYRIGHT International Business Machines Corp. 1989 *
All Rights Reserved
* Licensed Material - Property of IBM
*
* Prime/Nonprime Table for AIX Accounting System
*
* Curr Prime Non-Prime
* Year Start Start
*
1990 0800 1700
*
  1     Jan 1     New Year's Day
 50     Feb 19    Washington's Birthday (Obsvd.)
148     May 28    Memorial Day (Obsvd.)
185     Jul 4     Independence Day
246     Sep 3     Labor Day
326     Nov 22    Thanksgiving Day
327     Nov 23    Day after Thanksgiving
359     Dec 25    Christmas Day
365     Dec 31    New Years Eve
```

### 23.3.3 Disk accounting—/etc/filesystems

If you will be collecting disk usage information, add an account = true entry in the stanza for each file system you intend to monitor in the /etc/filesystems table.

*Sample* filesystems *entry:*

```
/home:
dev          = /dev/hd1
vfs          = jfs
log          = /dev/hd8
mount        = true
check        = true
vol          = /home
free         = false
account      = true
```

### 23.3.4 Print accounting—/etc/qconfig

Print usage records will be saved if an account file destination path is identified by the acctfile = file-name parameter for each queue stanza.

*Sample* /etc/qconfig *entry:*

```
acctfile = /var/adm/qacct
```

Rebuild the /etc/qconfig.bin file by refreshing the qdaemon subsystem.

```
# refresh -s qdaemon
```

### 23.3.5 Report directories

Make sure the report summary subdirectories, nite, fiscal, and sum exist with adm permissions in /var/adm/acct.

```
# cd /var/adm/acct
# mkdir nite fiscal sum
# chown adm nite fiscal sum
# chgrp adm nite fiscal sum
# chmod 644 nite fiscal sumπ        375     375
```

### 23.3.6 crontab entries

Remove the comments from the adm and root crontab files. Edit the crontab files using crontab -e.

adm crontab:

```
#= = = = = = = = = = = = = = = = = = = = = = = = = = = = = = = =
# PROCESS ACCOUNTING:
# runacct at 11:10 every night
# dodisk at 11:00 every night
# ckpacct every hour on the hour
# monthly accounting 4:15 the first of every month
#= = = = = = = = = = = = = = = = = = = = = = = = = = = = = = = =
10 23 * * 0-6 /usr/lib/acct/runacct 2>/usr/adm/acct/nite/accterr >
/dev/null
0 23 * * 0-6 /usr/lib/acct/dodisk > /dev/null 2>&1
0 * * * * /usr/lib/acct/ckpacct > /dev/null 2>&1
15 4 1 * * /usr/lib/acct/monacct > /dev/null 2>&1
#= = = = = = = = = = = = = = = = = = = = = = = = = = = = = = = =
```

### 23.3.7 Work unit fees

The chargefee command can be used to add work unit entries for each user on the system into the /var/adm/fee file. This data is later merged with other accounting files by acctmerg. chargefee can be incorporated into the system accounting scripts to implement a chargeback system.

## 23.4 Accounting Commands

As I mentioned in the introduction, AIX offers both SYSV and a subset of the BSD accounting commands. These commands allow you to display, manage, generate reports, and record charge fees from the collected accounting information.

### 23.4.1 Starting and stopping accounting

Start the accounting system by invoking one of the `startup`, `runacct`, `turnacct`, or `accton` commands.

```
# startup
# runacct 2> /var/adm/acct/nite/accterr &
# turnacct on/off
# accton /var/adm/pacct
```

Stop system accounting by using the `shutacct`, `turnacct`, or `accton` commands.

```
# shutacct
# turnacct off
# accton
```

Add a command entry to the `/etc/rc` script to start accounting at boot time.

### 23.4.2 Displaying statistics

At any time, you can take the pulse of your system or look back through accounting history from the command line. You can also create ad hoc reports by directing stdout to a file.

A general summary of data stored in the `/var/adm/pacct` can be displayed using the `sa` command. The `sa` command supports a number of flags that can be used to filter and restrict the output. Two of the most useful flags are the `-m` flag, which summarizes by user, and the `-s` flag, which summarizes by command. The `-s` flag can also be used to merge the summary with an existing history file.

```
# sa -m
root        1038      0.97cpu     8688904tio      9412563k*sec
daemon        34      0.06cpu     1005455tio      6494k*sec
uas            5      0.01cpu      194494tio      2626k*sec
info           1      0.00cpu           6tio      0k*sec
ops          212     30.65cpu     7768811tio      12002184533k*sec

# sa -s
   2     2295.47re      28.11cpu        88544avio      41k      xhm
   3     2069.41re       3.40cpu     92088832avio     106k      xlock
  18      251.81re       2.17cpu       303992avio      65k      vi
```

```
   4     115.28re    0.43cpu    234688avio   218k   aixterm
  94     162.88re    0.24cpu     19148avio     1k   rsh
   6      66.91re    0.21cpu    435008avio    30k   rn
 343       0.26re    0.16cpu      2927avio     0k   mount
  99       1.56re    0.15cpu     10412avio     3k   sendmai*
 374    3553.89re    0.15cpu       152avio     0k   sh
  21      12.79re    0.13cpu     23194avio    11k   csh
   6      22.60re    0.12cpu     71467avio    46k   xterm
   2    1480.58re    0.11cpu    221680avio   128k   twm
```

Connection histories can be displayed using the BSD `ac` and `last` commands or the SYSV `acctcon1` and `lastlog (SYSV)` commands. The `ac` and `acctcon1` commands can tally connection times by day or for the interval of time covered by the `/var/adm/wtmp` file. The `last` and `lastlog` commands can be used to display the login times for all users or an individual user.

```
# ac -p
duane          0.46
deroest      264.16
donn         487.54
noyd        9961.55
ops         1453.22
fox            5.45
root           0.09

# ac -d
Sep 01      total       269.68
Sep 02      total       613.75
Sep 03      total       914.32
Sep 04      total      1110.79
Sep 05      total      1103.98
Sep 06      total      1058.19
Sep 07      total      1060.23
Sep 08      total       933.98
Sep 09      total       944.53

# last -20
ops       pts/92    xtreme.sar.washi    Fri Sep 17 10:41    still logged in
donn      pts/86    xceed.bnn.washin    Fri Sep 17 10:07    still logged in
kenm      pts/75                        Fri Sep 17 10:00    - 10:22 (00:21)
davidw    pts/56    redy.aal.washing    Fri Sep 17 08:23    still logged in
```

Exhaustive command usage information can be generated using the BSD `lastcomm` command. Like `sa`, this command supports a large number of flags to filter the output. Be aware that it will also use significant system resources when invoked!

```
# lastcomm
sh           S     root        __      0.01 secs Fri Sep 17 10:58
umount       S     root        __      0.02 secs Fri Sep 17 10:58
rlogin             deroest     pts     0.02 secs Fri Sep 17 10:57
rlogin       F     deroest     pts     0.01 secs Fri Sep 17 10:57
sendmail     F     root        __      0.01 secs Fri Sep 17 10:58
sendit             csandahl    __      0.08 secs Fri Sep 17 10:58
sendmail     F     root        __      0.05 secs Fri Sep 17 10:58
sendmail     F     root        __      0.11 secs Fri Sep 17 10:58
sendmail     F     root        __      0.01 secs Fri Sep 17 10:58
```

```
sendmail   F   root   —   0.03 secs Fri Sep 17 10:58
sendit         grcm   —   0.16 secs Fri Sep 17 10:58
sh         S   root   —   0.02 secs Fri Sep 17 10:58
sh         S   root   —   0.02 secs Fri Sep 17 10:58
umount     S   root   —   0.01 secs Fri Sep 17 10:58
nfsmnthe   S   root   —   0.01 secs Fri Sep 17 10:58
```

### 23.4.3 Summary reports

A standard set of reports is produced at intervals by the `runacct` and `monacct` commands. These commands are run by the default `adm` and `root` crontabs. The summaries and reports are recorded in the following `/var/adm` subdirectories:

| | |
|---|---|
| `nite` | Daily files used by `runacct` |
| `sum` | Daily summaries created by `runacct` |
| `fiscal` | Monthly summaries created by `monacct` |

Reports and data files of interest include:

| | |
|---|---|
| `nite/lineuse` | Line usage statistics for serial ports |
| `nite/dacct` | Daily disk accounting records |
| `nite/reboots` | List of system reboot times |
| `sum/tacct` | Total accounting summary |
| `sum/cms` | Command use summary |
| `sum/loginlog` | Last use time for user accounts |
| `sum/rprt<mmdd>` | Daily summary report |
| `fiscal/cms<n>` | Fiscal command summary |
| `fiscal/tacct<n>` | Fiscal total accounting summary |

## 23.5 Periodic House Cleaning

Turning on system accounting is a little like opening the flood gates. On an active multiuser system, accounting can generate a large amount of data that must be filtered and archived as part of your regular housecleaning activities. The default accounting procedures specified in the `adm` and `root` crontabs periodically close and rename accounting files to assist in managing the data. It is left up to the system administrator to implement procedures to archive and clean up the old data files. It is a good idea to restart the accounting system daily to keep accounting files from becoming to large to manage.

What information should be saved for posterity? You can take the conservative approach and save everything, reports and data files, or throw caution to the wind and delete the files on a daily basis. Moderation suggests that it might be wise to periodically compress and archive the summary files and keep a copy of the previous day's data files on-line for short-term history queries.

## 23.6 InfoExplorer Keywords

| | |
|---|---|
| wtmp | init |
| pacct | uptime |
| nulladm | acctwtmp |
| startup | dtmp |
| runacct | enq |
| turnacct | qdaemon |
| accton | /etc/acct/holidays |
| shutacct | /etc/filesystems |
| sa | cron |
| ac | crontab |
| last | chargefee |
| lastcomm | /var/adm/fee |
| utmp | acctmerg |
| | monacct |

## 23.7 QwikInfo

### Accounting

*Data collection and configuration files:*

| | |
|---|---|
| /var/adm/wtmp | User, system events |
| /etc/utmp | User access times |
| /var/adm/pacct | Process account file |
| /var/adm/dtmp | Disk usage |
| /var/adm/Spacct.<mmdd> | Daily active process data from runacct |
| /var/adm/qacct | Print usage data |
| /var/adm/ctmp | Connect session data |
| /etc/holidays | Define accounting shifts |
| /var/adm/acct/{nite fiscal sum} | Accounting summaries |
| /var/spool/cron/crontabs/adm | Accounting crontab |

*Collection and reporting:*

| | |
|---|---|
| runacct, turnacct on, accton | Start system accounting |
| shutacct, turnacct off, acctoff | Stop system accounting |
| sa | Filter account data |
| ac, last, lastcom | History data |

Part

# 7

# System Tuning and Recovery

Chapter

# 24

# Backup and Copy Utilities

## 24.1 System Backups

How much is your time and your data worth to you? How many times have you erased what you thought was an unnecessary file only to discover a week later that it contained some vital piece of information? Even the most meticulously maintained system will be subject to disk failures. A regular schedule for system backups will significantly reduce the cost and frustration related to data loss problems. Believe me, you will rest easier each night!

## 24.2 Backup Strategies

When defining a backup strategy, tradeoffs must be made between the time and cost of performing the backups and the level of data recovery that is required. For single-user workstations, the workstation owner has a good idea when a backup should be made to protect critical data. Even in the single-user environment, it's a good idea to develop a discipline for performing regular backups. Large multiuser systems have very dynamic file update characteristics which make it difficult to perform backups on an as-needed basis. Careful thought must be devoted to implementing backup policies that meet the needs of a large and diverse user base.

*Backup policy considerations:*

- Which file systems are backed up and how often
- Backup while file systems are mounted or unmounted
- Full and incremental dump schedules
- Size of file systems
- Media types
- Media rotation schedule

- Backup verification schedule
- Off-site storage
- Bandwidth considerations for network-based backups
- Backup program and format to be used
- Restore procedures
- Data protection and privileges

### 24.2.1 What and when

With the price of storage at one dollar a megabyte and falling, it is awfully easy to keep throwing disk packs at storage bottlenecks. The problem is that you end up spending all your time backing up this proliferation of disks. Vendors don't want you to stop buying disks, so you need to take a harder look at which file systems actually need to be dumped.

Root file systems, like `/usr` and `/`, tend to be static in nature and may be replicated on a number of machines. Thus, they may not require dumping as often as dynamic file systems, such as those containing user home directories and work areas.

### 24.2.2 Mounted or unmounted

To guarantee data integrity, a file system should be `sync'd` and unmounted during backup. Environments that require 24-hour by 7-day-a-week availability may find this procedure difficult to live with. You can perform dumps while a file system is mounted and in use; however, you run the risk of missing data block updates in progress during the dump. A number of shops, including my own, run dumps on live file systems. For the most part, we have not experienced a large number of problems. As a rule, it is not a good practice to dump a live file system if you can avoid it. There are some commercial backup packages available that perform a checksum on each file during a live backup to ensure data integrity. Fancier storage servers, like the IBM 7051 Dataserver, also allow you to copy or mirror a file system, take the copy off-line, then back it up. High file system availability requirements mean that you either spend a little more money for duplicate storage or you cross your fingers and hope that a missed block isn't yours.

### 24.2.3 Sizing

Tune your file system sizes to match the backup media and time constraints. Very large file systems require frequent manual intervention to mount new media and thus more time to dump. It also means more media must be scanned when doing a restore. You know, the file you wanted restored is always the very last one of a 20-reel backup set.

Consider using devices that provide hardware data compression or use a compression program like `compress` or `pack` to compact data on the media. Software compression will take additional time, but the additional time may be offset by media utilization costs.

### 24.2.4 Full and incremental dumps

Time and money always being the deciding factor, it's not practical to run a full file system dump every day. What you really want is to run a periodic full dump followed by daily incremental dumps of the changes made against the full dump. Most UNIX backup commands implement this feature using a set of dump levels, 0 through 9. A level 0 dump represents a full dump. Levels 1 through 9 are the *incremental* dumps that represent file system changes against the previous less-than or equal-to dump level.

| | |
|---|---|
| Level 0 | Full dump |
| Level 1–9 | Incremental dumps |

### 24.2.5 Backup schedules and rotation

There are many strategies you can use to rotate between full and incremental dumps to optimize media utilization and dump wall clock time. The tradeoff here is media utilization and complexity. On the simple side, a weekly level 0 full dump can be followed by daily level 1 dumps. When a restore operation is requested, the level 0 is consulted, followed by the most recent level 1. Simple, but not very elegant.

To optimize media utilization and dump time, one of the more complex rotation strategies like the *Towers of Hanoi* sequence may be used. I must admit, I have always hated the Towers of Hanoi sequence after having to sweat over the algorithm in Computer Science 101. Nevertheless, it provides a very good rotation mechanism, and it saves on tapes.

The Towers of Hanoi sequence involves a new level 0 dump for each file system, followed by five sequences of level 1 through 9. Four sets of level one tapes are used for each file system. Tapes for levels 2 through 9 are reused and it is assumed that levels 2 through 9 will fit on one tape.

*Towers of Hanoi dump level sequence:*

| Dump type | Dump level number sequence |
|---|---|
| Full | 1 |
| Incremental | 3 2 5 4 7 6 9 8 |

Complex dump sequences can be tracked through the use of the `/etc/dumpdates` file. The `dumpdates` file records the file system, dump level, and time stamp. The -u flag provided by the backup and rdump commands will update the time stamp each time a backup is run.

/etc/dumpdates:

```
/dev/rhd1        1 Mon Aug 30 02:10:56 1993
/dev/rhd2        1 Mon Aug 30 02:04:25 1993
/dev/rhd1        0 Tue Aug 3 03:25:15  1993
/dev/rhd2        0 Sun Aug 1 03:23:12  1993
/dev/rhd4        0 Fri Aug 20 02:00:04 1993
/dev/rhd9var     0 Sat Aug 21 02:30:59 1993
/dev/rhd4        1 Mon Aug 30 02:00:04 1993
/dev/rhd9var     1 Mon Aug 30 02:09:33 1993
/dev/rlv00       0 Sun Aug 1 04:24:41  1993
/dev/rlv00       1 Mon Aug 30 02:17:25 1993
```

The sequence of dump levels can be automated using cron.

*Backup-level crontab:*

```
0 2 * * 1 /etc/backup -0 -uf/dev/rmt0.1 /home
0 2 * * 2 /etc/backup -3 -uf/dev/rmt0.1 /home
0 2 * * 3 /etc/backup -2 -uf/dev/rmt0.1 /home
0 2 * * 4 /etc/backup -5 -uf/dev/rmt0.1 /home
0 2 * * 5 /etc/backup -4 -uf/dev/rmt0.1 /home
0 2 * * 6 /etc/backup -7 -uf/dev/rmt0.1 /home
0 2 * * 7 /etc/backup -6 -uf/dev/rmt0.1 /home
```

### 24.2.6 Disaster recovery and validation

It follows that while you are safeguarding your file systems, you will also want to safeguard the backups themselves. First and foremost, you should periodically test your backup sets by performing a restore operation. Verify that the backup media is good and that the data is valid. This will eliminate the problem of backing up bad data.

Periodically rotate a full set of backup media off-site. Disasters can range from the file level to the building and city level.

Regularly cycle the media through a physical cleaning and validation check. This will include periodic maintenance and cleaning of the backup devices.

### 24.2.7 Backup media

Choose backup media that fit your environment. I think we all agree that it doesn't make much sense to back up 500 MB of file system space using diskettes. Careful consideration must be given, weighing media cost, transfer rate, and storage capacity. Larger shops might opt for optical storage or robotic jukeboxes. See Chap. 7 for information on the various tape media characteristics.

## 24.3 Backing Up a File System

The AIX backup/restore commands are very similar to their BSD dump/restore counterparts. backup can be used to dump entire file systems, as well as to support a backup by name for dumping subdirectory trees. The following examples demonstrate a file system full dump and backing up a subdirectory tree by name:

```
# backup -0 -u -f /dev/rmt0.1 /usr
# find /usr/local -print | backup -i -f /dev/rmt0.1
```

## 24.4 Restoring Files and File Systems

The `restore` command options are similar to those used by `backup`. If you have problems remembering the path name of a particular file you wish to restore, you can use the `-t` flag to output an index of the files on the tape. You can also use the `-i` flag to run `restore` in an interactive mode for file system inode dumps. This allows you to move around the directories stored on the tape similar to the way you would with directories on a disk.

| | |
|---|---|
| `# restore -T -f/dev/rmt0.1` | Display media index |
| `# restore -r -f/dev/rmt0.1` | Restore full file system |
| `# restore -f/dev/rmt0.1 -xdv bin` | Restore file in bin directory |
| `# restore -i -f/dev/rmt0.1` | Start interactive restore |

## 24.5 Other Dump Utilities

The `tar` and `cpio` utilities can be used when portability is an issue. Both `tar` and `cpio` will allow you to copy files and directory trees between systems, preserving uids and permissions. In some cases, `tar` will not span multiple volumes. Use `cpio` on SYSV UNIX machines where `tar` is not available.

| | |
|---|---|
| `# tar -cvf /dev/rmt0.1 ./source` | Copy to tape |
| `# tar -xvf /dev/rmt0.1` | Restore `tar` archive |
| `# find . -print \| cpio -ov > /dev/rmt0` | Copy to tape |
| `# cpio -ipdmv < /dev/rmt0.1` | Restore `cpio` archive |

If you have the disk space to spare, you can copy a logical volume using the `cplv` command. This mechanism could be used to create a file system copy for backup, leaving the primary copy on-line.

| | |
|---|---|
| `# cplv -e <ExistingLV> <SourceLV` | Copy a logical volume |

## 24.6 Operating System Dumps

To backup AIX `rootvg` filesystems, consider using the `mksysb` command. `mksysb` creates a `tar` image of root file systems, complete with file system descriptions that can be used to restore from the standalone maintenance system. Invoke the `mkszfile` to create a `.fs.size` table that describes the `rootvg` file systems. Edit `.fs.size` to include only those file systems to be used for restore purposes. Run the mksysb command to create the backup image.

*Create* mksysb *image:*

1. mkszfile
2. Edit .fs.size
3. mksysb /dev/rmt0

A series of documents is available, via anonymous ftp from the University of Virginia, that describe a number of problems encountered when creating rootvg dumps. See pub/rs6000/rootvg.restores on uvaarpa.virginia.edu.

## 24.7 Network Backups

What about using the network to back up remote workstations onto machines equipped with high-capacity tape drives? You can do this by using the rdump and rrestore commands. rdump and rrestore are very similar to the backup and restore commands previously described. They share many of the same flags and parameters. The primary difference is that they use a remote_host:device argument to the -f flag, which designates the host name of the machine equipped with the backup device.

```
# rdump -u -0 -f daffy:/dev/rmt0.1 /home
# rrestore -x -f daffy:/dev/rmt0 /home
```

Another network-based option is to use the remote shell command, rsh, with one of the local backup or copy commands. You can use rsh with pipes and redirection to obtain results similar to rdump and rrestore.

```
tar cvf - ./home | rsh judy "dd of = /dev/rmt0 obs = 1024"
rsh judy "dd if = /dev/rmt0 ibs = 1024" | ( cd /home; tar xvf - )
```

In either of these cases, if you do not wish to be prompted for a password on the remote system, create a .rhosts file in the $HOME directory of the remote user ID being used for the remote shell. On each line of the .rhosts file, enter the name of each machine and user ID that are allowed to connect without providing a password.

## 24.8 The Whole Nine Yards

The preceding information, combined with Chap. 7, describes the traditional tools used to manage UNIX tapes and backups. These are a long way from the features supported by the mature proprietary backup packages available on other operating systems. The vendor community is quickly filling this gap. A number of very good packages are available, complete with features like label validation, multivolume support, and tape librarian interfaces. See "Taming the Backup Beast," *RS/Magazine,* vol. 2, no. 2, Feb. 1993, for details on a number of vendor packages which are supported under AIX.

## 24.9 InfoExplorer Keywords

| | |
|---|---|
| compress | tctl |
| pack | rmt |
| /etc/dumpdates | tar |
| backup | cpio |
| rdump | cplv |
| cron | mksysb |
| restore | mkszfile |
| rrestore | .fs.size |
| find | rsh |
| rmt | .rhosts |
| mt | dd |

## 24.10 QwikInfo

### System backups

*Backup and restore:*

| | |
|---|---|
| /etc/dumpdates | Set file system dump dates and levels |
| backup -<level> -u -f <media> <file-system> | Back up file system |
| where level = 0 | Full dump |
| 1-9 | Incremental dumps |
| find /usr/local -print \| backup -i -f <media> | Back up by name |
| restore -T -f <media> | Display media index |
| restore -r -f <media> | Restore file system |
| restore -f <media> -xdv <file\|dir> | Restore file/directory |
| restore -i -f <media> | Interactive restore |
| tar, cpio | Archive commands |
| cplv -e <ExistingLV> <SourceLV | Copy a logical volume |

rootvg *backup:*

| | |
|---|---|
| mkszfile | Create .fs.size file for mksysb |
| mksysb | rootvg backup |

*Network backup:*

| | |
|---|---|
| rdump -u <level> -f <host>:<media> <file-sys> | Network dump |
| rrestore -x -f <host>:<media> <file-sys> | Network restore |

Chapter

# 25

# System Monitoring and Tuning

## 25.1 Know Your Workload

You've heard the following advice many times. Before you can begin to tune your system or recommend adding resources, you have to know what the workload profile is and what level of response is expected. You have to accurately define the performance goals in order to achieve them!

Begin with a good understanding of how the operating system manages its resources. Document the throughput limits of the physical resources (hardware, peripherals, network). Next, characterize the workload as *single-user workstation, multiuser time sharing,* or *batch/network server.* Identify and prioritize critical applications and the resources they require. Look for areas of contention. It may be that partitioning workloads by shift or by machine will solve particular resource bottlenecks. Now begin monitoring the system under real and modeled workloads. This requires some knowledge of the tools available and their characteristics. Gather and review all the data to determine where adjustments or additional resources are required. Sounds easy doesn't it?

Since it's your workload, applications, resources, and performance expectations, I'll concentrate on AIX OS characteristics and the available tool sets. Hardware characteristics are described in chapters related to the particular devices.

## 25.2 AIX Operating System Characteristics

### 25.2.1 CPU scheduling

A good deal of CPU resources can be saved by painstakingly profiling and tuning application code. Even though you may not have the luxury or source code, the AIX `tprof` profiler can give you a very good idea of where the application is spending its time.

As described in Chap. 16, the AIX scheduler uses a set of 128 run queues to prioritize active processes. Lower-numbered queues are scheduled more often than those with higher numbers; thus, they receive a larger share of CPU resources. Processes in a common priority queue are scheduled round robin. After execution, the process returns to the end of the line.

Process priorities are based on the sum of the short-term CPU usage (0 to + 100), process nice value (0 to 40), and the minimum user process level. At each reschedule time quantum, the short CPU usage is updated and new priorities computed for processes in the *ready-to-run* state. Processes burning higher CPU usage levels will have their priority number increased, dropping their relative priority to other processes. Any process with a priority value greater than 120 will only be run when no other process in the system requires the CPU.

Process rescheduling can occur at every clock tick. Unless a process is preempted, blocked, or terminates, it will consume its CPU quantum (up to 10 ms) and be rescheduled at the next clock interrupt. Processes tend to spend their time in either the `runnable` or `blocked` state.

Because priorities tend to float up and down, the `nice` command doesn't provide an adequate hammer to control process priorities. Some degree of success can be accomplished by implementing a daemon that periodically checks CPU usage and scheduler priority, then `renices` jobs to favor critical applications. AIX also provides a `setpri()` system call that can be used to fix the priority level of a process. This is especially useful for real-time applications. Care must be taken in multiuser workloads that fixing a process priority above 60 (lower number) does not adversely effect interactive response.

### 25.2.2 Virtual memory management

The *virtual memory manager*'s (VMM) job is to allocate memory for process active working sets and recover stale or unused memory pages. The latter requires that some process pages be moved from memory to secondary storage (paging space). Even in well-tuned systems, some amount of paging activity will usually be taking place.

The VMM in AIX 3.2 has been enhanced with the addition of process swap support. AIX 3.2 uses a *lazy swapping* technique that keeps the system from swapping processes when memory is not constrained. If a thrashing situation is detected, AIX suspends the processes that are responsible. The offending process pages become stale and are paged out. If thrashing continues, new processes are suspended as well. When the memory becomes available, the suspended processes are reactivated.

The AIX 3.2 VMM enhancements also include the differentiation of *computational memory* and *file memory.* As you would expect, computational memory defines those pages that belong to a program's working set, and file memory makes up the rest. The VMM maintains a *repage fault history* for each of these memory types, which is then used to determine if a thrashing condition exists. A *repage fault* represents a recently read page from disk that has been referenced and is not found in memory. The VMM looks at the computational and file repage rates to determine which type of page should be stolen in a constrained situation.

You may tune the following set of memory load parameters to represent your workload's computational and file memory requirements. An example application for tuning these parameters called `schedtune` is available in `/usr/lpp/bos/examples`. Care must be taken when modifying these parameters. Use `schedtune` in conjunction with `rmss` to model memory loading. The `rmss` command allows you to simulate real memory configurations on the running system.

h—Memory commitment high water mark

w—Wait time before reactivating suspended procs

p—Process memory high water mark

m—Minimum active processes

e—Time exempt from suspension

Memory is overcommitted when:

$$\frac{\text{\# page writes in last second 1}}{\text{\# page steals in last second}} > \frac{1}{h}$$

A process is considered to be thrashing when:

$$\frac{\text{\# repages in last second}}{\text{\# page faults in last second}} > \frac{1}{p}$$

Make sure you have adequate paging space available. The actual amount required is going to depend on your workload. I generally use a 3-to-1 ratio of paging space to real memory. Paging space should be distributed across multiple volumes if possible.

### 25.2.3 Disk I/O

You may recognize the situation on many UNIX systems when a process creating large write queues holds up processes attempting to read. These large write queues can exhaust the file system free lists and hold up the reads required to replenish the free list, making the problem worse. AIX 3.2 provides a facility to control file output queue contention through the use of high and low water marks, `maxpout`, and `minpout`. When a process writing to a file hits its high water mark, that process is suspended until the queue drops to or below the low water mark. This facility is called *I/O pacing*. I/O pacing will allow you to manage the tradeoff between interactive response and I/O throughput. The default `maxpout` and `minpout` values of "0" disable I/O pacing. You can set these parameters using the SMIT `chgsys` fast path. (See Fig. 25.1).

```
# smit chgsys
```

The AIX *asynchronous I/O* facility can be used to improve I/O performance for applications that are heavily I/O bound. Asynchronous I/O routines must be added to the application source code and the application rebuilt. These routines allow the application to continue processing rather than being blocked during I/O operations. Notification of I/O completion is posted as an event back to the process. The application can poll for these events to keep track of data written to disk.

### 25.2.4 Network performance

If you have spent any time administering large networked multiuser or application server systems, then you have experienced the dead-end situation of `no more mbufs`. mbuf structures are used to store

```
= = = = = = = = = = = = = = = = = = = = = = = = = = = = = = = = = = = = = = = = =
                    Change / Show Characteristics of Operating System

Type or select values in entry fields.
Press Enter AFTER making all desired changes.

Maximum number of PROCESSES allowed per user                    [40]            +#
Maximum number of pages in block I/O BUFFER CACHE               [20]            +#
Maximum Kbytes of real memory allowed for MBUFS                 [2048]           #
Automatically REBOOT system after a crash                       false            +
Continuously maintain DISK I/O history                          true             +
HIGH water mark for pending write I/Os per file                 [33]            +#
LOW water mark for pending write I/Os per file                  [16]            +#
Enable memory SCRUBBING                                         false            +
Amount of usable physical memory in Kbytes                      524288
Primary dump device                                             /dev/hd7
Secondary dump device                                           /dev/sysdumpnull
Error log file size                                             1048576
State of system keylock at boot time                            normal
Size of data cache in bytes                                     64K
Size of instruction cache in bytes                              32K
[BOTTOM]

F1 = Help            F2 = Refresh          F3 = Cancel        F4 = List
Esc + 5 = Undo       Esc + 6 = Command     Esc + 7 = Edit     Esc + 8 = Image
Esc + 9 = Shell      Esc + 0 = Exit        Enter = Do
= = = = = = = = = = = = = = = = = = = = = = = = = = = = = = = = = = = = = = = = =
```

**Figure 25.1** SMIT operating system parameters panel.

data moving between the network and the operating system. In most cases, when you hit the mbuf wall, you had to increase the kernel parameter for mbufs and/or mbclusters, rebuild the kernel, and reboot. This is real bad news for your up-time statistics.

AIX provides an mbuf management facility that dynamically controls the allocation and use of mbufs and mbclusters. The default allocation is based on a low to medium packet rate and is somewhat dependent on the number of adapters. The mbuf management facility *netm* uses a set of parameters to control the minimum and maximum available free space in the pools, and the maximum amount of memory that may be used for the pools. Note that the mbuf and mbcluster pools are pinned in memory. netm increases the pool sizes as network load increases. The mbcluster pool is reduced as load decreases; however, the mbuf pool is never decreased. Each mbuf is 256 bytes in size and each mbcluster is 4096 bytes.

You don't want netm to be dispatched unnecessarily, and you don't want to overcommit memory to mbuf pools. What you need to do is monitor your packet rates under normal loads and adjust the mbuf parameters at boot time to pin as much memory as you will need and no more. You can modify the following mbuf parameters with the `no` command. Build a script which is run at boot time to set the parameters and execute a packet spray program or `ping` in a loop to generate enough network traffic to pin the memory required.

| | |
|---|---|
| `lowmbuf` | Free mbuf low water mark |
| `lowclust` | Free mbcluster low water mark |
| `mb_cl_hiwat` | Max number of free clusters |
| `thewall` | Max memory available mbufs and clusters |

Some network environments require modification of other kernel network parameters like *time to live* and *keep alive* values. The `no` command can be used to display and set a number of these kernel network parameters.

```
# no -a

          dog_ticks = 60
           lowclust = 48
            lowmbuf = 176
            thewall = 2048
        mb_cl_hiwat = 96
          compat_43 = 1
             sb_max = 65536
       detach_route = 1
   subnetsarelocal = 1
             maxttl = 255
          ipfragttl = 60
    ipsendredirects = 1
       ipforwarding = 1
            udp_ttl = 30
            tcp_ttl = 60
         arpt_killc = 20
```

```
  tcp_sendspace = 16384
  tcp_recvspace = 16384
  udp_sendspace = 9216
  udp_recvspace = 41600
 loop_check_sum = 1
 rfc1122addrchk = 0
 nonlocsrcroute = 1
  tcp_keepintvl = 150
   tcp_keepidle = 14400
      ipqmaxlen = 50
```

## 25.3 AIX Monitoring and Tuning Tools

### 25.3.1 Traditional UNIX tools

| | |
|---|---|
| uptime<br>rup | uptime and rup provide system load averages and the current number of users. These are quick, one-stop commands to get a brief picture of system activity. |
| ps | ps displays process table statistics. Don't underestimate the information you can get from ps. AIX supports both SYSV and BSD options. You can easily set up shell aliases with ps to get quick information on the top CPU and storage users on your system. Use it to check for *defunct* processes which may be tying up memory. |
| sar | sar is the *system activity recorder*. Along with sadc, sa1, and sa2, it can be used to snapshot system activity for all or specific system resources at specified intervals. Use cron to regularly execute sar at specific times based on your workload profile, and the sa1, sa1 scripts to maintain a report history of system usage. |
| vmstat | vmstat provides statistics on process queues, memory, paging, interrupts, and CPU usage. You can run vmstat at specified intervals and repetitions to take a quick look at memory and CPU usage. |
| iostat | iostat is similar to vmstat in that it can be run for specified intervals and a number of repetitions. It provides usage statistics on CPU, and the I/O subsystem. Using the -d flag will display a snapshot of disk I/O activity. |
| pstat | pstat is similar to crash in that it allows you to display the contents of various systems tables. It is not interactive. |
| netstat | netstat provides various information on network activity. The -m flag can be used to review mbuf allocation. There are options to display routing tables and current connections statistics. |
| nfsstat | nfsstat displays information concerning NFS and RPC interfaces. You may distinguish between client and server information, and between NFS and RPC traffic. |
| acctcom<br>acctcms | acctcom and acctcms process and display system accounting information from the /usr/adm/pacct file. acctcom provides a detailed process chronology by user. acctcms combines identical process information to give you overall system totals. |
| gprof<br>time<br>timex | If you have tracked down resource untilization problems to a specific application, these tools provide a means of profiling and tuning the code. time and timex can be used to snapshot the user, system, and wall clock execution times. gprof will provide CPU usage by subroutine and a call graph profile of the application. Note that you must compile the code with the -pg option. |

### 25.3.2 AIX 3.2 tools

| | |
|---|---|
| `trace` `trcrpt` | `trace` and `trcrpt` allow you to record and report on system events at a finer granularity than any of the other performance tools in this set. System events are time stamped such that the sequence and context of execution is maintained. The `trace` facility does not cause significant additional overhead to the running system. System tracing is started and stopped using the `trcon` and `trcstop` commands. |
| `rmap` | `rmap` is run against the log data produced by `trace` and `trcrpt` to extend the analysis of processes and I/O activity. `rmap` requires a customized configuration file that specifies the input data and report options. |
| `filemon` | `filemon` is also run against trace data to provide statistics on file system performance. It provides detailed information on the most active files, logical volumes, and physical volumes in the system. |
| `fileplace` | `fileplace` maps the placement of file blocks within logical and physical volumes. It indicates the level of fragmentation for files in a file system. |
| `rmss` | `rmss` is a tool that will allow you to simulate reductions in available real memory on the RS/6000. This tool is quite useful when monitoring the behavior of an application in a memory-constrained situation. |
| `svmon` | `svmon` displays a snapshot of virtual memory. Note that it is not entirely accurate because it is run in user state with interrupts enabled. |
| `netpmon` | `netpmon` also uses trace data to monitor network activity. `netpmon` is a new version of what was formally known as `netmon` in older versions of AIX. It gathers statistics on CPU usage, device driver queue lengths and utilization, socket calls, and NFS I/O calls. |
| `lslv` `lvmake` `lvedit` `lvextend` `reorgvg` | `lslv`, `lvmake`, `lvedit`, `lvextend`, and `reorgvg` provide finer-grained control over the definition and allocation of logical and physical volumes in the system. They are quite useful when tuning the placement of databases. |
| `tprof` | `tprof`, like its predecessor `gprof`, is used to profile CPU usage by subroutine in an application. `tprof` does not require that the application be recompiled, but will provide additional information if the application is compiled with the `-qlist` option. |

### 25.3.3 Performance Tool Box/6000 and Performance Aide/6000

To augment the base AIX tuning and monitoring tools, *Performance Tool Box / 6000* (PTX/6000) and *Performance Aide / 6000* (PAIDE/6000) can be installed on the RS/6000. The PTX/6000 Motif GUI is used to adjust and graphically display monitor data provided by PTX/6000 tools, AIX tuning and monitoring commands, PAIDE/6000 data, and SNMP data. PTX/6000 can be used to tune a networked cluster of machines through a real-time 3-D graphical display of configuration and performance data.

PAIDE/6000 is a prerequisite product to PTX/6000 that provides additional local performance data, filters, alerts threshold management, and an API for retrieving raw system statistics. PAIDE/6000 can also be configured as an SNMP subagent in a networked environment.

### 25.3.4 AIX Capacity Planner—BEST/1 for UNIX

The *AIX Capacity Planner,* based on the BGS System's *BEST/1 for UNIX* product, can be used to collect and partition performance data for capacity planning purposes. The tool can be used to collect statistics from networked systems, analyze the performance and workload information, then model and predict growth trends. Like PTX/6000, the BEST/1 product uses a Motif-based GUI to configure and display data collection and results. It provides an excellent facility for developing and testing *what-if* scenarios. BEST/1 is also available for AS/400 environments.

### 25.3.5 Public domain monitor package

If you're on a budget, take a look at the public domain *monitor* package written by Jussi Maki. The package provides pseudo-real-time statistics on CPU, memory, and I/O utilization and rates. An ASCII-based interface allows it to be used with most display types. The monitor system may be downloaded via anonymous ftp from `aix-pdslib.seas.ucla.edu`. (See Fig. 25.2.)

```
# monitor
```

```
= = = = = = = = = = = = = = = = = = = = = = = = = = = = = = = = = = = = = = = = =
System monitor v1.06.1: daffy                           Tue Sep 14 10:35:53 1993
                                                        Refresh: 10.06 s

Sys 31.3% Wait 0.1% User 6.8% Idle 61.8%
0%                25%                50%                75%                100%
= = = = = = = = = = = >>>> ..........................................

Runnable processes 1.49 load average: 4.07, 0.65, 0.21
Swap-in processes  0.00

                                         Paging (4kB)   Process events    File/TTY-IO
Memory       Real          Virtual       4.3 pgfaults    213 pswitch      3 iget
free          1.6 MB       202.6 MB      0.0 pgin       1680 syscall      1 namei
total       128.0 MB       480.0 MB      0.2 pgout        43 read         0 dirblk

                                              0.0 pgsin    34 write     1297 readch
DiskIO       read      write       busy       0.0 pgsout    0 fork      4520 writech
hdisk0       0.0       0.8 kB/s    0% 0                     exec           5 ttyrawch
hdisk1       0.0       0.0 kB/s    0% 0                     rcvint         0 ttycanch
hdisk2       0.0       0.0 kB/s    0% 0                     xmtint       379 ttyoutch
                                                            0 mdmint

                                                            Netw      read      write
                                                            lo0       0.0       0.0 kB/s
                                                            en0       11.2      0.0 kB/s
= = = = = = = = = = = = = = = = = = = = = = = = = = = = = = = = = = = = = = = = =
```

**Figure 25.2** Monitor panel.

## 25.4 Additional Help and Documentation

Take a look at the AIX 3.2 *Performance Monitoring and Tuning Guide,* SC23-2365. This document contains a wealth of information and examples. Your IBM SE can also assist in tuning and capacity planning activities.

## 25.5 InfoExplorer Keywords

| | | |
|---|---|---|
| tprof | ps | timex |
| nice | sar | trace |
| renice | sadc | trcrpt |
| setpri | sa1 | rmap |
| schedtune | sa2 | filemon |
| rmss | vmstat | fileplace |
| maxpout | iostat | svmon |
| minpout | pstat | netpmon |
| chgsys | netstat | lslv |
| no | nfsstat | lvmake |
| ping | acctcom | lvedit |
| mbuf | acctcms | lvextend |
| uptime | gprof | reorgvg |
| rup | time | repage |

## 25.6 QwikInfo

**System monitoring and tuning**

*Kernel parameters:*

| | |
|---|---|
| `/usr/lpp/bos/examples/schedtune` | Sample program to set kernel parameters |
| `getpri(), setpri()` | Set/query process queue priority |
| `rmss` | Simulate real memory |
| `maxpout/maxpin` | Limit I/O pacing levels for writes |
| `smit chgsys` | Set kernel parameters |
| `no` | Display/set kernel network paramters |

More tools—see Sec. 25.3.1.

Chapter

# 26

# Problem Analysis and Recovery

## 26.1 When Things Go Bump in the Night

Do you ever wonder if there isn't a little gremlin lurking just behind the front cover of your RS/6000? From time to time you just catch a glimpse of two beady little eyes peering out of the diskette slot. You do a double take, and nothing is blinking except one of the tape or diskette lights. With a nervous shrug, you go ahead and fire up that high-priority application you have put off until the very last minute. Just at the critical point in your time line you notice an eerie flickering in the room. With a sinking feeling in your stomach, you look at the front panel and there it is, the dreaded flashing `888`. Fingers trembling, you press the reset button and stare at the play of glowing numbers after each touch. Your luck continues to fail as the dump LED reads `0c5 System dump attempted and failed`. You power down, pause to wipe the sweat off your brow and power cycle back up. The numbers dance across the LED window. Is that a malevolent giggling you hear? It can't be. You tell yourself that it's only too many hours of overtime or one too many *lattes*. With bloodshot eyes you wince at the glare from the LEDs and they pound into your head, `888, 888, 888...`

Gruesome, isn't it? The only thing missing is "It was a dark and stormy night." Don't get me wrong, I'm not insinuating that system failures and panics are particularly commonplace on the RS/6000. As a matter of fact, we have been using a model 530 on a 7-by-24 schedule with very few outages for nearly four years. System failures do happen, however, and they usually occur at the most inopportune times. The trick is to make sure that you have your system logging and recovery homework done before the gremlins begin playing with your sanity.

## 26.2 Backups and Bootable Media

Backups—If you don't have them, then none of the rest of this information is going to do you much good. It's surprising how many calls I get from users who are hoping for a miracle, one that will recover a bad disk because they never took the time to do backups. See Chap. 24 for details on system backups.

Next, make sure you have multiple copies of stand-alone bootable media that reflect your systems maintenance level. Notice I said *multiple copies.* I must admit that I have been bitten more than once by having only a single copy of some crucial bit of data. Let's start with the *BOSboot diskettes.* If you carefully read the *AIX Installation Guide,* SC23-2341-05, there is a chapter on creating boot diskettes. Note that the procedure is version-dependent, so make sure you have the right documentation in hand. Basically you will create a set of diskettes that contain a small bootable kernel, code to set your console display type, and the AIX installation/maintenance code.

| | |
|---|---|
| Boot diskette | `bosboot -a -d fd0` |
| Display diskette | `mkdispdskt` |
| Display extension diskette | `mkextdskt` |
| BOS install/maint diskette | `mkinstdskt` |

Make certain that you test the diskettes after creating them. It will bring you peace of mind and familiarize you with the stand-alone boot procedure.

*Stand-alone Boot Procedure*

1. Insert the boot diskette/tape and power on/reset.
2. At LED `c07`, insert the display diskette.
3. When prompted, select the console display.
4. Insert the BOS install/maint diskette and press ENTER.
5. Select `Maintenance` option from the menu.
6. Select `Standalone Maintenance` option from the menu.
7. Access the root volume group: `getrootfs hdisk0`.

You can also create a bootable tape that contains a tar'd copy of your `rootvg` with the `mksysb` command. The tape can be used to recover from a disk failure or it can be used to install other machines. Begin by using the `mkszfile` command to create a `/.fs.size` file which contains descriptive information about the file systems in the `rootvg`. You may edit this file so that it contains only those file systems you wish to recover. Next, run `mksysb` *device* to create the bootable tape. When booting from the stand-alone tape, the AIX install/maint menus are displayed. These will guide you through restoring the `rootvg` file systems.

| | |
|---|---|
| Create `rootvg` description | `mkszfile` |
| Boot tape and `rootvg` | `mksysb /dev/rmt0` |

## 26.3 LED Status

The story always begins with the dreaded flashing `888` on the LED front panel. Before deciding to punt and hitting the power switch, press the reset button to cycle through the set of four halt status numbers. These numbers indicate the current system state, reason for the halt, and the dump state. Write them down. You're going to need them later in the analysis processes.

*LED halt status sequence:*

```
888 - bbb - eee - ddd
```

The first number following "888" on the LED display, represented by `bbb` in the example, indicates the hardware *built-in self-test* (BIST) status. In most cases the BIST status will read 102, which indicates that BIST has started following a system reset. Other values may indicate a hardware problem. The next number, represented by `eee`, indicates the cause of the system halt. See Table 26.1. The last number in the sequence indicates the status of any dump associated with the failure. (See Table 26.2.)

When a system fault occurs, an automatic dump of selected kernel address regions are recorded on the dump device as defined in the *master dump table.* The *primary* dump device is a dedicated storage area for holding dumps. A shared *secondary* device may be defined, which requires operator intervention. The default primary dump device is `/dev/hd7` and the secondary device is `sysdumpnull`. Dump devices are defined and managed using the `sysdumpdev` command.

**TABLE 26.1 LED Halt Reason Code**

| | |
|---|---|
| 20x | Machine checks |
| 300 | Storage interrupt: processor |
| 32x | Storage interrupt: I/O channel controller |
| 38x | Storage interrupt: serial link adapter |
| 400 | Storage interrupt: instruction |
| 500 | External interrupt: DMA, bus error |
| 52x | External interrupt: IOCC checks/timeout |
| 53x | External interrupt: IOCC timeout |
| 700 | Program interrupt |
| 800 | Floating point unavailable |

**TABLE 26.2 LED Dump Status Codes**

| | |
|---|---|
| 0C0 | Dump successful |
| 0C2 | User dump in progress |
| 0C4 | Partial dump successful |
| 0C5 | Dump device not accessible |
| 0C6 | Prompt for secondary dump device |
| 0C7 | Remote dump in progress |
| 0C8 | No dump device defined |
| 0C9 | Dump in progress |

Make certain that your dump device is assigned and is large enough to contain at least one full dump.

| | |
|---|---|
| `# sysdumpdev -L` | List current dump status |
| `# sysdumpdev -l` | List primary dump device location |
| `# sysdumpdev -P` | Assign dump device |

Although it is acceptable to interrogate kernel dumps residing in the primary dump area, it's a good idea to copy them onto an AIX file system or removable media type. This will secure the data and free up the dump area for problems lurking in your future. Use `dd` to read from the raw dump device, or mount the dump device and use `cp` or `backup` to copy the dump to alternate storage.

```
# dd if = /dev/rhd7 of = /dev/rmt0.1
# mkdir/tmp/dumpdev
# mount /dev/hd7 /tmp/dumpdev
# cp /tmp/dump-dev/dump-name /tmp/dump-name
# ls /tmp/dumpdev | backup -ifv
```

You can force a system panic dump by using the `sysdumpstart` command or by turning the key to the *service* position and pressing the *left-cntrl + alt + 1* keys simultaneously.

## 26.4 System Logs

Now that your disaster recovery media is in place, it's always nice to be able to determine why you crashed in the first place. Start by looking at the system error log. The error log file, `/var/adm/ras/errlog`, is updated by `/usr/lib/errdemon`, which is exec'd at system start-up. The error daemon reads system exception data from `/dev/error` and creates entries in the log file based on templates from `/var/adm/ras/errtmplt` and the message catalog `/usr/lpp/msg/$LANG/codepoint.cat`. You can produce a report of entries in the error log by running the `errpt` command or via `smit errpt`. Make sure that you save and clean out error log data periodically so that problem information doesn't get lost in the noise. You can accomplish both of these tasks by having cron regularly back-up the error log, and then clearing out old information using the `errclear` command. There are also commands that allow you to add your own error templates and messages to the system for custom applications.

| | |
|---|---|
| Create error log report | `errpt` |
| Clear error log | `errclear` |
| Stop errdemon | `errstop` |
| Update templates | `errupdate` |
| Add/display msg catalog | `errmsg` |
| Modify msg catalog | `errinstall` |

Individual events in the error log report are identified by error type labels. The labels are listed in the *AIX Problem Solving Guide and Reference,* SC23-2204. Each error event is time stamped and contains summary information by type. For example, suppose the LED halt reason code was "700," indicating that a *program interrupt* caused the crash. The error log should contain an entry labeled `PROGRAM_INT`, time stamped with the date and time of the failure. The associated detail data lists the segment, status, and state registers (SRRs) entries that point to the subroutine and instruction involved in the failure. This information will be used when analyzing the dump.

*Example error log entry:*

```
ERROR LABEL:          PROGRAM_INT
ERROR ID:             DD11B4AF

Date/Time:            Wed Dec 8  11:46:08
Sequence Number:      484128
Machine Id:           000015086600
Node Id:              mead
Class:                S
Type:                 PERM
Resource Name:        SYSPROC

Error Description
Program Interrupt

Probable Causes
SOFTWARE PROGRAM

Failure Causes
SOFTWARE PROGRAM

   Recommended Actions
   IF PROBLEM PERSISTS THEN DO THE FOLLOWING
   CONTACT APPROPRIATE SERVICE REPRESENTATIVE

Detail Data
Segment Register, SEGREG
0000 0000
Machine Status Save/Restore Register 0
0005 3AC4
Machine Status Save/Restore Register 1
0002 0000
Machine State Register, MSR
0002 90B0
```

The next place to look is at messages created by `syslogd`. The `syslogd` daemon receives messages via datagram sockets created by applications which use the `syslog` subroutine. `syslogd` directs the incoming messages to files or other systems as described by entries in the `/etc/syslog.conf` file. This file is read each time `syslogd` is started or receives a `HUP` signal. Due to the application-specific nature of `syslogd`, AIX provides an example `/etc/syslog.conf` template which must be configured to your application requirements. Each line in `/etc/syslog.conf` contains message selectors separated by semicolons, followed by a field indicating where the message is to be sent. Incoming messages specify a facility code that represents one of the selectors. See `/usr/include/sys/syslog.h` for a list of codes and selectors. In the following example, mail messages are sent to a central repository on another system called `daffy`, all debug messages to `/var/adm/debug.log`, kernel-critical and emergency messages to `/var/adm/kernel.log`, and alert messages are sent to the `ops` user ID.

```
/*********** Example /etc/sys.log.conf *************/
mail                        @daffy
*.debug                     /var/adm/debug.log
kern.crit;kern.emerg        /var/adm/kernel.log
*.alert                     ops
```

Remember that for real-time debugging, you can always use the system trace for even finer detail.

| | |
|---|---|
| Start trace | `trcon` |
| Stop trace | `trcstop` |
| Generate trace report | `trcrpt` |

## 26.5 AIX Kernel Structure

With the error log and LED status information in hand, we are ready to examine the dump. First let's lay a little groundwork concerning the characteristics of the AIX kernel. AIX is based on a preemptible kernel. The kernel is divided into pinned and pageable regions. The pinned low region of the kernel contains the interrupt handler, kernel text and data areas, the process table, and page map. Pageable kernel regions include the file table; vnode, gnode, and inode structures, and kernel extensions. It is important to remember that activities and services in the pageable kernel region are synchronous, whereas the pinned region activities are asynchronous. For example, an external I/O interrupt may be serviced by the pinned region long after the process initiating the request has completed its time slice and has been paged out.

Interrupts are divided into processor and external interrupt classes. All I/O type interrupts are multiplexed into one external inter-

**TABLE 26.3 AIX Address Segments**

| | |
|---|---|
| 0 | Kernel segment (data and extensions) |
| 1 | Text segment |
| 2 | Private process segment (data, u-block, and stack) |
| 3-C | Available |
| B | VMM data |
| D | Shared libraries |
| E | Reserved |
| F | I/O support |

rupt. External interrupts include I/O bus and system board devices. External interrupts are the only interrupt class that can be masked. Processor interrupts include system reset, machine check, storage, program, alignment, floating-point, and SVC interrupts.

Memory addresses on the RS/6000 are based on a 32-bit *effective address* and a 24-bit *segment address.* The first four most significant bits of the effective address represent one of 16 segment registers. The remaining 28 bits of the effective address are used along with the 24-bit segment address to indicate a position in virtual memory. See Table 26.3.

Kernel and application address spaces are somewhat similar. For debugging purposes, it is important to understand the general layout of kernel regions. The exact addresses of kernel boundaries will be dependent on the AIX release you are running.

*Kernel symbols and addresses* (*3.2.5*):

| | |
|---|---|
| Beginning of kernel | 0x00000000 |
| End of pinned kernel | pin_obj_end |
| Table of contents | TOC |
| End of kernel | endcomm |
| Kernel extensions | 0x01A00000 |
| Process table offset | 0xe3000000 |

It's a good idea to generate a complete listing of kernel symbols and addresses for use when analyzing a dump. Use the nm command on the kernel object file associated with the dump.

```
# nm -vfx /unix
```

## 26.6 Using crash

crash can be run in interactive or batch mode. Batch mode is useful when you need to send a formatted dump to IBM Support. Use the crash -a option directed to a file to produce a formatted crash dump. For an interactive session, invoke crash, specifying the dump file or device and kernel file as arguments.

| | |
|---|---|
| `# crash /dev/hd7 /unix` | Interactive mode |
| `# crash -a /dev/hd7 /unix > /tmp/crash.MMDD` | Batch mode |

*Useful* `crash` *subcommands:*

| | |
|---|---|
| `p` | Display process blocks of all processes or a particular process. |
| `u` | Display u-block or u-area. If no process ID is given, the running process at the time of the dump is displayed. |
| `ds` | Offset to the nearest kernel symbol. |
| `nm` | Display address of a symbol. |
| `od` | Display hexidecimal dump of memory. |
| `trace` | Display traceback of stack. |
| `dump` | Dump information. |
| `?` | Help. |

Now you are ready to get down to business. Display the *u-area* of the process running at the time of the dump by entering the `u` subcommand without an argument (or nasty comments). A formatted display of the process private u-area is displayed. The first line of the display indicates the process name and process table address. Each process table entry on the RS/6000 is 0x100 bytes in length. Subtract the process table offset, 0xE3000000 from the process slot address. Ignore the lower two digits of the answer, and you have the process slot number of the last running process. The u-block and process table data will provide you with the process state, executing program, open files, locks, controlling TTY, etc.

*Example:*

```
# crash /dev/hd7

Using /unix as the default namelist file.
Reading in Symbols .....................

>u                              Display u-block

        USER AREA FOR xperfmon (ProcTable Address 0xE3001200)

Do the arithmetic ....................

Process slot address           0xE3001200
Process table offset         - 0xE3000000
                             = = = = = =
                                   0x1200
Ignore lower 2 digits                0x12
Decimal Process Slot ID                18

>p - 18                      Display Process Table Entry
```

The `trace`, `nm`, and `ds` subcommands are very helpful when diagnosing kernel problems. The trace subcommand provides a look backwards through the kernel stack. The `nm` and `ds` commands display the address for a symbol or the symbol associated with an address range, respectively. Error log and LED information may be more helpful with kernel problems than the current running process information. For example, in the case of exceptions caused by an interrupt, the process which requested the service related to the interrupt may have been paged out while the request was being serviced.

In the event of a system hang, you may not have error log or LED data to assist. The hang may be the result of a resource deadlock or a looping process. If deadlock is suspected, check the `proc_lock` and `kernel_lock` symbols. Look at the `RW` values displayed by `nm`. A value of "ffffffff" indicates that the lock is free, otherwise the value is the PID of the process holding the lock. If a high-priority process loop is responsible for the hang, then it is likely to be the last process executing (if you're lucky).

For an addressing exception, use `nm` to locate the `vmmerrlog` structure. Check the vmm return code and fault address at offsets 0x20 and 0x1C, respectively. Next, use trace to display the failing routine, followed by `ds` to locate the offset within the failing routine. If the exception was in a kernel extension, you may have to walk the kernel load list, as kernel extensions are pageable.

Running down the culprit in a crash caused by an interrupt can be a bit tricky. As mentioned earlier, the requesting process may have been paged out. If segment register data was logged in the error log, the address in SRR0 will indicate the return address of the routine that caused or is waiting for a program interrupt to be serviced. External interrupt conditions will likely log the IOCC bus number and interrupt level.

## 26.7 Hardware Diagnostics

The RS/6000 is very good about checking its hardware during the built-in self-test (BIST) at power-up time. Keeping track of the LED information during system power up will assist you in debugging hardware problems. If you suspect hardware problems or the system won't boot, use the *RS/6000 Diagnostic Programs* to assist in determining the failure. The diagnostic programs may be run in *stand-alone mode* from diskettes, or in *concurrent mode* with AIX on-line, using the `diag` command. For concurrent mode operation, as superuser, enter the `diag` command and follow the menu instructions. Stand-alone mode is similar to booting from diskette as previously, described. There are two different boot diskettes depending on whether you have 8 MB of memory or greater than 16 MB. There is a console display definition diskette, and several diagnostic diskettes for testing and configuring adapters.

*Diagnostic stand-alone mode:*

1. With the system powered down, turn the key to service.
2. Insert either the 8-MB or 16-MB boot diskette per your config.
3. Turn the power switch on.

4. At each `c07` LED prompt, insert the next diskette #.
5. At the `c31` LED prompt, select the console.
6. Follow the diagnostic instructions displayed on the console.

While loading the diagnostic diskettes, if a `c02` or `c03` LED status is displayed, you have either loaded the diskettes out of sequence or inserted the wrong diskette, respectively.

## 26.8 Calling for Help

Once you have determined that a software or hardware problem exists, collect all the pertinent log, dump, and LED information before contacting IBM Support. You might also want to run the `snap` and `lslpp -hBc > filename` commands to snapshot the maintenance level and configuration of your system. If you have *AIXtra IBMLink* access, review the problem and service information to determine if this is a previously reported and known bug. The more information you gather, the faster your problem is going to be resolved.

You are now ready to contact IBM Support. If you don't like playing telephone tag and have Internet or uucp access, I would suggest you look into using the `aixserv` facility. `aixserv` is a problem-reporting and feedback facility that is based on electronic mail. Initial problem reporting is done via the `aixserv` shell script that comes as part of the facility. The script prompts you for problem description information and then mails the information to AIX Problem Support. If you would like more information on `aixserv`, contact your local IBM Support Engineer. You can also direct questions and comments to:

```
services@austin.ibm.com
```

Those of you with IBM customer numbers can report problems the old-fashioned way by using the telephone.

| | |
|---|---|
| Software support | 1-800-237-5511 |
| Hardware support | 1-800-IBM-SERV |

It's always a good plan of action to read the required texts as part of the homework. Take a look at *RISC System/6000 Diagnostic Programs: Operators Guide,* SA23-2631-05; *RISC System/6000 Problem Solving Guide,* SC23-2204-02; and *AIX Version 3.2 for RISC System/6000 Installation Guide,* SC23-2341-05.

## 26.9 InfoExplorer Keywords

| | | |
|---|---|---|
| bosboot | errpt | trcrpt |
| mkdispdskt | errclear | panic |

| | | |
|---|---|---|
| mkextdskt | errstop | dump |
| mkinstdskt | errupdate | sysdumpstart |
| getrootfs | errmsg | dd |
| mksysb | errinstall | crash |
| mkszfile | syslogd | errdead |
| .fs.size | /etc/syslog.conf | nm |
| errdemon | trcon | diag |
| /var/adm/ras/errlog | trcstop | snap |

## 26.10 QwikInfo

### Problem determination

*Stand-alone boot diskettes:*

| | |
|---|---|
| bosboot -a -d fd0 | Create boot diskette |
| mkdispdskt | Create display diskette |
| mkextdskt | Display extensions |
| mkinstdskt | Install/maint diskette |

Stand-alone boot procedure:

1. Insert the boot diskette/tape and power on/reset.
2. At LED `c07`, insert the display diskette.
3. When prompted, select the console display.
4. Insert the BOS install/maint diskette and press ENTER.
5. Select `Maintenance` option from the menu.
6. Select `Stand-alone Maintenance` option from the menu.
7. Access the root volume group: `getrootfs hdisk0`.

`rootvg` *backup:*

| | |
|---|---|
| mkszfile | Create `.fs.size` file for mksysb |
| mksysb <media> | Back up `rootvg` |

*System error logs:*

| | |
|---|---|
| errdemon | Error daemon |
| errpt | Error log report |
| errclear | Clear error log |
| errstop | Stop error daemon |
| errupdate, errmsg, errinstall | Update error message catalogs and templates |
| /var/adm/ras/errtmplt | Error message templates |
| /usr/lpp/msg/$LANG/codepoint.cat | Error message catalog |

*System trace:*

| | |
|---|---|
| `trcon, trcstop` | Start/stop tracing |
| `trcrpt` | Gererate trace report |

*System dumps:*

| | |
|---|---|
| `sysdumpdev` | Set/display dump device |
| `sysdumpstart` | Force a panic dump |
| `errdead` | Retrieve `/dev/error` |
| `crash` | Format/review a dump |
| `nm` | Display symbol table |

Part

# 8

# Distributed Systems

Chapter

# 27

# Clustering

## 27.1 Cluster Overview

What do you get when you couple a bunch of RS/6000s together? Answer: a network-based multiprocessor capable of supporting batch, parallel, and multiuser workloads at a fraction of the cost of a high-end mainframe. Workstations like the RS/6000 are already exceeding the CPU performance and addressing range of all but the *technoelite* of mainframe engines. Innovations in networking bandwidth are rapidly approaching and surpassing the I/O bandwidth of traditional storage devices. All that's required is the software glue to make the group function under a *single system image.*

Clustering systems is certainly not a new idea. The scientific and research communities have been experimenting with arrays of processors in networked configurations for a number of years. Although much of this work was directed at the needs of specialized parallel applications and pushing the boundaries of computer science, it laid the ground work required to establish practical workstation clusters today (see Fig. 27.1). We still don't have all the big-iron software infrastructure common in the glass-house computing centers. But hey, it's only software! There are already a number of highly polished batch cluster packages available from software vendors and in the public domain.

## 27.2 Single System Image

What defines a single system image? Basically, the cluster of machines should present themselves as a single machine to the user community. Resources available on any individual machine must be accessible, yet hide any notion of locale outside a single cluster domain name. Some level of process queuing must be available to distribute load evenly among the processors. A common view of file system resources must be available from any machine in the cluster. This includes a uniform UID and GID name space, uniform file permis-

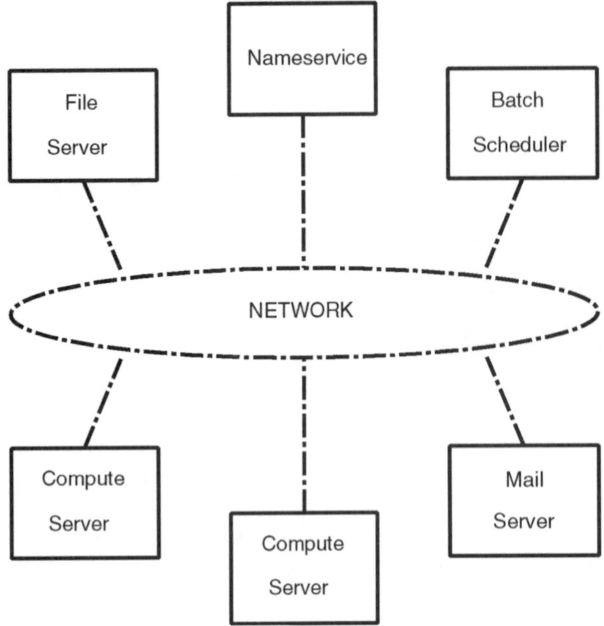


**Figure 27.1** Cluster topology.

sions, and file locking. Lastly, the cluster must support centralized operations and administration. The list goes on, but you get the idea.

### 27.2.1 Cluster domain name

Standard tcp-based services provide the foundation for building the cluster. Name service based on BSD Bind can be modified to respond with any one of a set of IP addresses for a single cluster domain name. A *Time To Live* (TTL) value of 0 is passed back to the querying system with the chosen IP address. If the system making the query does not cache the information, then this IP address will be used for this query only. There is a *feature* in Bind such that any TTL value less than five minutes is reset to five minutes by the resolver. In practice, this five-minute window does not cause significant problems. Without resolver caching, each name service query to resolve the cluster domain name to an IP number will result in a new call to the name service daemon.

The trick is to select an IP number from the available set of machines that maintains some equitable distribution of connections across the cluster. The `groupd` name server developed at UCLA uses a scheme based on a loads database that contains the load average of each machine in the cluster. The `groupd` name server responds to "`A`" record queries with the IP address of the least-loaded machine. The selected machine's load average entry is temporarily incremented to represent the additional load caused by the new connection. Other algorithms use random or round robin mechanisms for selecting an IP number.

### 27.2.2 Common file system

A single view of the cluster file system hierarchy from any machine in the cluster can be realized through the use of *Network File System* (NFS). End-user file systems are exported from a cluster NFS server to each machine. Each machine maintains a local copy of the operating system and application set based on a reference system. This allows each machine to function independently should the NFS server fail. The reliability of the server can be improved through the use of *High-Availability Network File System/6000* (see Chap. 13) If scalability is a problem, then other distributed file systems may be used. For example, the *Andrew File System* (AFS) from Transarc/Carnegie-Mellon.

### 27.2.3 Management

Along with NFS support, *Network Information System* (NIS) can be configured to maintain a uniform UID and GID space, as well as manage common configuration files. The BSD `rdist` command can be used to distribute file sets not managed under NIS. Cluster machines can be cloned from a single reference system `mksysb` image to maintain operating system consistency.

### 27.2.4 Resources

The AIX `qdaemon` and `lpd` daemons can be configured to manage print distribution and queuing both inside and outside the cluster. Electronic mail can be managed by a single `sendmail` daemon for the cluster. Command wrappers based on the BSD *r-commands* (`rsh`, `rdump`, `rmt`, `rlogin`, etc,) can be used to smooth access to distributed resources and assist users in managing distributed processes. The `/etc/hosts.equiv` and `/etc/hosts.lpd` can be used to identify cluster machines, making individual `.rhosts` files unnecessary.

## 27.3 Cluster Batch Queuing

To distribute batch workloads among cluster sites, you could implement a few scripts that take advantage of `at`, `cron`, `rsh`, and the like. However, there are packages available that perform this function with all the bells and whistles we have come to expect from more mature mainframe batch systems.

Most distributed UNIX batch queuing systems are loosely based on the *Network Queuing System* (NQS) model developed for the NASA Ames NPSN complex. A user submits a job to a master scheduler daemon, which in turn hands the job off to local or remote queues for execution. UNIX kernel limits like CPU time, stack and data size, working set size, and file size are used to govern the resources consumed by individual jobs. In most implementations, electronic mail notification of job boundary status is available, as well as distributed spooling of job output.

One of the areas of primary interest and development is in the queuing scheduler. Early systems like NQS had no mechanism to load balance jobs among multiple batch queues. The result is that jobs end up waiting in busy queues while other queues stand empty. Load-balancing schedulers were then introduced that would allocate jobs among queues based on a system load feedback mechanism. Jobs were evenly distributed among machines, but the single scheduler proved to be a single point of failure. The next stage in scheduler development involves redundant schedulers and the ability for schedulers to pass jobs among themselves.

### 27.3.1 Multiple device queuing system

The *Multiple Device Queuing System* (MDQS) is a batch and device queuing system similar to the base NQS model. A central daemon schedules jobs in a round robin or table order algorithm among the individual batch queues. A mapping table identifies routing information, using a vector of `queue`, `device`, `server` data. Queuing is initiated by *enqueuer clients,* which are analogous to UNIX `lpr` and `at` commands. Queued jobs are then dispatched by *dequeuer clients,* analogous to the UNIX `lpd` and `atrun`. MDQS is available from a number of anonymous ftp sites. Use `archie` to find the site nearest you.

### 27.3.2 Network queuing system

The general Network Queuing System (NQS) model was described in the preceding queuing overview. NQS uses a central scheduling daemon to route jobs among any of three queue types: *batch queues* (destinations for job execution) *pipe queues* (route jobs between queues), and *device queues* (destination for hardcopy output). NQS uses a system called *shell strategies* which allow the system administrator to tailor which shell is used for job execution. The *fixed strategy* defines a single default shell. The *free strategy* allows end users to define the shell to be used in their job submission scripts. Finally, the *login strategy* uses the user's login shell as defined in the `/etc/passwd` file.

*Network Queuing System Version 2* (NQS/V2) builds on the Version 1 base by providing an enhanced queuing model called *queue complexes.* Queue complexes provide a mechanism enabling a job to be scheduled on one of a number of queues based on resource limits and availability. NQS V2 also includes device limits. NQS V1 is available from a number of anonymous ftp archives. Use `archie` to find the site nearest you. NQS V2 is available from COSMIC, (706) 542-3265.

### 27.3.3 Monsanto CERN/NQS

Christian Boissat of CERN retrofitted the queue complex capabilities of NQS V2 into NQS V1. A load-based scheduler, as well as a number of other enhancements and bug fixes, are also included. *Monsanto CERN/NQS* is available via anonymous ftp to `wuarchive.wustl.edu` in the `packages/nqs/unix` directory.

### 27.3.4 NQSExec

*NQSExec* is yet another add-on to facilities provided by NQS. The *Exec* option provides a load-based scheduler developed by the Cummings Group called the *Network Computing Executive.* NQSExec is available from Sterling Federal Systems, Inc., (415) 964-9900.

### 27.3.5 Other NQS-based batch systems

There are a number of other NQS-based batch systems implemented by many operating system vendors. Examples include NQS/MVS from IBM, which provides an NQS-like interface to JES, and the Cray UNICOS version of NQS. COSMIC also has an NQS successor called *Portable Batch System* (PBS) in the works. Contact the vendors for more information.

### 27.3.6 Distributed job manager

The Minnesota Super Computer Center has developed a system for their connection machine called *Distributed Job Manager* (DJM). DJM is a drop-in replacement for NQS, supporting the NQS command set. DJM supports a load-balancing scheduler and provides both batch and interactive sessions. Interactive sessions allow disconnect and reconnect capability. DJM also makes use of the connection machine checkpoint/restart facility. DJM licensing is covered by the GNU General Public Licensing. It is available via anonymous ftp to `ec.msc.edu` in directory `pub/LIGHTNING`.

### 27.3.7 Distributed network queuing system

The *Distributed Network Queuing System* (DNQS), originally developed at the Florida State University Supercomputer Computations Research Institute (FSU SCRI), was designed to provide a dynamic mechanism for adding and deleting queues from a distributed batch topology. This capability, along with a mechanism for suspending a local batch queue when keystrokes or mouse interrupts were detected on a workstation, allowed centers to make use of idle cycles on end-user workstations. Users could be enticed into participating in the batch system by allowing them access to the larger cycle base and ensuring that their workstation would be available for their personal use when needed. McGill University and Livermore National Laboratory have enhanced DNQS by implementing improved local administrative controls, multiple queues per workstation, load statistics, and architecture queue classes. DNQS is available via anonymous ftp to `ftp.physics.mcgill.ca`.

### 27.3.8 Distributed queuing system—Codine

The folks at FSU SCRI enhanced their original DNQS design and introduced the *Distributed Queuing System* (DQS). Like DNQS, DQS supports dedicated and nondedicated workstation queues and architecture queue classes. DQS enhancements include a load-based scheduler, PVM support, group queues, NFS/AFS support, user access controls, interactive sessions, and an X11 and Motif GUI.

The SCRI staff have been joined by collaborators from Pittsburgh Super Computer Center and the University of Texas Center for High Performance Computing to continue development of DQS and eventually replace it with the *Scalable Queuing System* (SQS). DQS improvements over the next year will incorporate Kerberos 4.0 and AFS Inter-Cell support, additional parallel toolkits, POSIX 1003.15 compliance, redundant schedulers, and additional resource definitions. The SQS follow-on to DQS is scheduled for 1994 and will be based on OSF technologies. This will include DCE client/server, DME authentication, DFS support, and a multithreaded scheduler. DQS is available via anonymous ftp to `ftp.scri.fsu.edu`.

### 27.3.9 Condor

The University of Wisconsin's *Condor* distributed batch system is designed to reclaim idle cycles on workstations like DQS and DNQS. Condor goes one step further by guaranteeing that once a job enters the Condor queuing system, it will finish. Condor does this by providing a checkpoint/restart and migration capability. Using a custom RPC, Condor ties each batch job to a *shadow process* running on the initiating system. The shadow process maintains a link to the batch job as it moves throughout the queuing system. There are restrictions on the type of job that can be checkpointed. The job cannot fork new processes, cannot use IPC mechanisms, cannot trap or handle signals, and cannot have concurrent read/write access to open files. Condor supports a load-based scheduling system that also takes into account the job priority and date queued.

Future enhancements for Condor include support for PVM 3.0, variable node parallel sessions, and access to remote Condor pools called *flocking*. Portability streamlining of the checkpoint/restart code and an implementation in C++ are also in the works. You can obtain Condor via anonymous ftp to `ftp.cs.wisc.edu`.

### 27.3.10 LoadLeveler

IBM, working with the University of Wisconsin, has enhanced the Condor base system to include support for redundant schedulers. The IBM *LoadLeveler* implementation allows configuration of abstract resource types. A Motif-based GUI and AFS support are also available. LoadLeveler may be used with the *9076 POWER Parallel System* (SP1) to distribute work between nodes in the system. A statement of direction to support LoadLeveler on other UNIX architectures has also been announced.

### 27.3.11 Load-sharing facility—Utopia

Platform Computing Systems and the University of Toronto have developed a distributed queuing system for both batch and interactive work. The system is being marketed by Platform Computing Systems under the name *Utopia.* Utopia uses a load-based scheduling algorithm that goes far beyond the standard kernel load average used more commonly by other systems. Utopia's load daemons track CPU queue lengths, memory utilization, paging rate, block I/O rate, number of logins, system idle time, `/tmp` utilization, and network packet rates in determining system load aggregates. Utopia supports redundant schedulers and abstract resource types. A distributed API library is available for developing your own applications. Utopia is claimed to be scalable to thousands of nodes.

### 27.3.12 There's still more

If this doesn't seem like enough, there are still a few systems I'd like to mention before closing. The *Vienna Queuing System* (VQS), developed at University of Vienna, Austria, is a queuing system similar to DNQS that provides a fair-share scheduler to balance the load among users. VQS also tracks the aggregate resource usage among multiprocess jobs. The Fermilab *Cooperative Process Farm* is built from a scheduling system and API library for developing distributed and parallel applications. The *Hewlett-Packard Task Broker* uses a unique algorithm, where nodes in the batch system bid for additional work. Finally, the Cummings Group have a number of products to facilitate distributed applications. These include *NCE, NCLOGIN, NCADMIN,* and *NCCACHE.*

### 27.3.13 POSIX 1003.15 Batch Standard

With all these batch systems in the works, what is the chance that they will support some level of interoperability? Most of the product development plans listed include compliance with the POSIX 1003.15 Batch Standard. The scope of the 1003.15 standard includes the definition of distributed batch terminology, concepts, and variables. It will identify application environments, define command syntax, and incorporate rationale for external interfaces. Draft 12 of this standard will have been voted on by the time this book is in your hands. Future work will define a network protocol, administration commands, a programming interface, and resource controls. The 1003.15 group is not addressing issues like security, directory services, authentication, account mapping, and network administration, as these are under the auspices of other groups.

If you are interested in the work being done by the POSIX batch committee or any of the other committees, please make it a point to get involved. You can contact the IEEE at the following address, or access their no-charge dial-up bulletin board. The bbs supports speeds up to 2400 bps, no-parity, 8 data bits, and 1 stop bit. Download the *bbsguide.txt Users Guide* for more information.

IEEE Standard Office
P.O. Box 1331
Piscataway, NJ 08855-1331
Telephone (908) 562-3809
Fax: (908) 562-1571
IEEE bbs: (908) 981-0290

## 27.4 Cluster Futures

With the OSF technologies just around the corner, tools like DCE (Distributed Computing Environment), DME (Distributed Management Environment), and ANDF (Architecture Neutral Distribution Format) promise to extend the capabilities of workstation clusters. X.500 directory services will provide enhanced access to users, applications, and services. POSIX is actively working on a standard for distributed batch systems. The result of all this is a unified and standard mechanism for supporting distributed resources vs. resorting to piecing together the odds and ends listed this chapter.

Chapter

# 28

# Network Archiving

## 28.1 Storage Management

It seems like every time I want to build a new software package, I spend most of the time trying to reclaim sufficient disk space to perform the build. I do make a half-hearted attempt to keep things cleaned up. I keep telling myself that I'm going to need those old test programs and e-mail messages someday. Let's not forget all those X11 background images I've collected and just have to keep on-line. One gigabyte of disk space just doesn't seem to go as far as it used to. I remember when I got my first IBM PC/XT and thought that 10 MB was disk heaven. *Sigh!*

Does this sound familiar? Even the glass-house computer centers with large operations staffs are finding that they are spending nearly all their time running system backups. Exponential growth in CPU and network bandwidth, along with expanding connectivity, are resulting in mountains of data looking for a home. You can't keep throwing cheap disks at the problem and hope it will go away. How much of this data really needs to be saved? Many centers find that 80 percent of their backup data is never accessed again. Some applications require more immediate access to data than human-managed tape restore allows.

What is needed is a software-controlled hierarchical storage management system. This system would automatically move inactive files onto lower-cost storage media, yet present a single view of the data to the end user regardless of where it resides in the physical hierarchy. Users must be able to interact with the system to control where data resides in the hierarchy to meet their access requirements. The system must also be able to manage the physical storage devices to ensure free space and availability.

## 28.2 IEEE Mass Storage Reference Model

The IEEE Mass Storage Systems Technology Committee (MSSTC) has been working for over 15 years to define a standard storage reference model. The model describes a modular system for small-to-large, stand-alone, and distributed heterogeneous environments. Although parts of the model are still being formulated, it provides an excellent foundation for implementation of software to meet the needs described here. The user interface hides the storage architecture and hierarchy from the users, yet allows them to control what data requires archiving, for how long, the number of copies, versions, and access security. It recommends a separation of data and control message paths, but does not define a particular network protocol to ensure open connectivity. Rather than dictate a single access method for interacting with data storage, it describes three options which may be used to develop clients: operating system traps (similar to NFS trapping of I/O system calls), application level processes (for example, ftp), or a callable program library of routines. It also provides an open interface to support various storage media.

### 28.2.1 Components

In a nutshell, the components and interaction of the reference model are as shown in Fig. 28.1. Files are called *bitfiles* and are represented

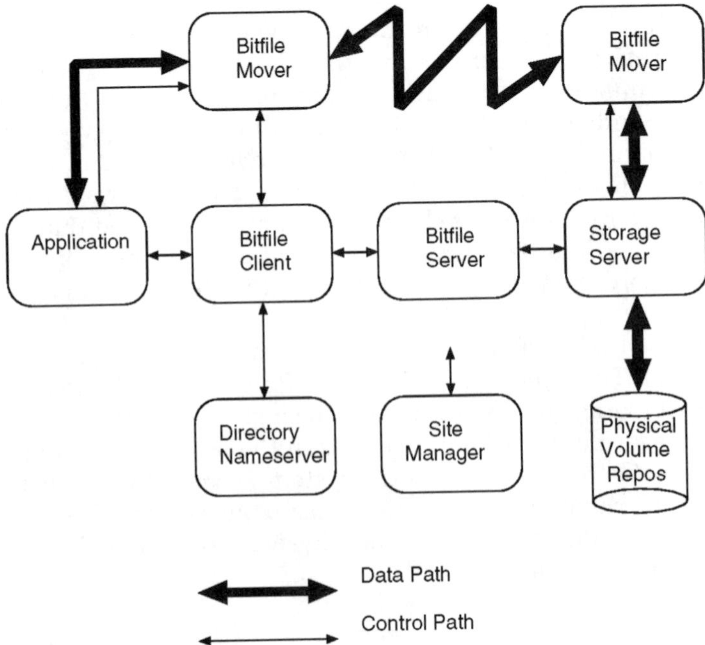


**Figure 28.1** IEEE mass storage reference model.

as bitstreams with an associated unique *bitfile ID* and header. There is no modification of the data itself. A *name server* maps the operating-system-dependent file names to the unique bitfile IDs. *Bitfile servers* manage bitfile attributes maintained in the headers. This includes things like file size, access control information, logical location, etc. *Bitfile movers* are used to transfer bitfiles between client systems and the storage servers. The *storage servers* track the location of bitfiles on the *physical volume repositories.* There is also a *migration manager* that is responsible for maintaining free space on the storage media by migrating bitfiles between devices as needed. The modular nature of this model provides flexibility in distributing and replicating functions among many nodes in a network environment.

### 28.2.2 Development history

You may be familiar with a number of mass storage implementations that may or may not follow the IEEE reference model. Examples are IBM's MVS System Managed Storage (DFSMS), and VM Workstation Data Save Facility (WDSF). The MVS-based *Common File System,* developed by Los Alamos National Laboratory, has been in production for over 13 years and is now marketed by the DISCOS division of General Atomics under the name *DataTree.* Lawrence Livermore National Laboratory developed a UNIX-based mass storage system called *LINCS* and it has been in production there since 1988. The Livermore Lab is a test bed for software and hardware integration under the IEEE reference model. The LINCS system is now marketed by many vendors as a product called *Unitree.* The Livermore National Storage Laboratory has since developed an enhanced version of Unitree called *NSL-Unitree.* NSL-Unitree moves further into the realm of distributed storage servers and storage hierarchies. Unitree has been ported to AIX, and is conformal to the IEEE mass storage reference model. For the sake of this discussion, I'll focus on Unitree, since it is representative of the IEEE reference model and is the most commonly known implementation.

## 28.3 Unitree Central File Manager

The Unitree Central File Manager (UCFM) provides a hierarchical data storage facility in single-system or distributed computer environments. In its most common incarnation, Unitree uses a two-tier storage hierarchy consisting of disk as a first-level archival staging area, and tape as the second level. Users move files into and out of the storage system via NFS, FTP, or Unitree provided DFTP clients. A migration process in the central server copies files from the disk staging area to tape after aging or to maintain free space. Eventually, the disk copy of the file may be purged. When a user accesses a particular file, Unitree will retrieve the data from the current level of storage on which it resides transparent to the user. This is where a robotic tape system comes in handy for files that have been migrated to tape. You can easily run your operations staff ragged in a fairly active system without the use of some kind of robot.

### 28.3.1 File system view

The user's view of the archive system is what appears to be a standard UNIX file system. Under NFS, you may operate on files in your archive directory with standard UNIX commands just as if they were located in your home directory. Remember that if a file has been migrated to tape, that `tar` or `make` you just issued might take a little longer than you expect. I should note that Unitree replaces the NFS and FTP code on the central file server, so it may be advantageous to make the central server a dedicated system. Since Unitree isolates data from control messages, you can move some of the logical operations onto lower-cost computers.

### 28.3.2 Client access

To enable some of the NFS file management capabilities in the FTP environment, Unitree provides some additional commands that can be quoted using standard FTP client access. The `GTRSH` and `STRSH` commands allow you to display and set the trashcan timeout interval. Trashcans are a safety feature that allow you to recover files you have inadvertently deleted. The `NMDUP` command lets you control how many copies of a file may be stored in the system. Standard UNIX file access commands `chgrp`, `chown`, `chmod`, `umask`, and `ln` are supported. You can use the `stage` and `wait` commands to control waiting for a file you wish to retrieve that has been migrated to tape. Finally, there is a byte-size option to the standard FTP `hash` command. Unitree also offers its own file transfer protocol called *dftp*. dftp is used just like ftp, but it offers better performance and contains a superset of ftp commands. You must install the dftp client code on your local machine.

### 28.3.3 Media architecture

There are few architectural limits in the Unitree system. There are no maximum limits in the code for number of files, number of directories, file size, or file names. Granted, there may be limits imposed by the operating system. A single file may span multiple physical volumes. Thus, terabyte files and file systems may be configured. At Livermore National Laboratory, Unitree is tracking over 50,000 3480 cartridges of data in StorageTek silos. Unitree also operates in raw mode on the media assigned to it. Raw access allows for moving very large blocks of data, making the most of interface bandwidth and optimizing use of devices like raid disk arrays. Compression and encryption routines can also assist in making the most use of system interfaces and media, and provide an additional level of data security. As your space requirements grow, you can dynamically add new media into the system.

Appendix

# e-mail Lists and ftp Sites

There are some fringe benefits available to the UNIX user community that are a direct result of the openness and growth of UNIX over the years. These are the collections and archives of public domain software, and the public help and discussion lists available on the international networks. Here is a wealth of software, "hard knocks" stories, shoulders to cry on, and general information that can make life with UNIX much easier. But before you can take advantage of these benefits, you have to know where they exist, and how you access them. I'll address these issues with emphasis on archives and lists of interest to the AIX community, and (here comes the pitch) the OPEN SYSTEMS GROUP.

## Electronic Mail Lists

Probably the first and easiest of these facilities to try to use are the electronic mail lists. If you are familiar with using e-mail facilities, and have some type of network access to the Internet, then interacting with the discussion lists will be little different than sending mail to a colleague. To begin using a list, you must first subscribe. Most e-mail discussion lists are either managed by real humans, or are automated to support commands like subscription requests. With the former, once you know the list name and address, you can send mail to:

```
listname-request@somehost.domain.address
```

You replace "listname" with the appropriate name and the host address in "somehost.domain.address." In the mail body text, simply ask to be added as a subscriber. Then, to participate in the discussions, address your mail to:

```
listname@somehost.domain.address
```

In the case of automated servers, you send your subscription request to the servers' e-mail address, supplying specific commands to activate your subscription. To subscribe to the following lists, address your mail to:

```
listserv@vm.its.rpi.edu
listserv@uwavm.u.washington.edu
listserv@uga.bitnet
```

In the mail body text type the command:

```
SUBSCRIBE listname Your Full Name
```

where "listname" is one of those listed as follows, and "Your Full Name" is your given name. listserv will locate your e-mail address in the mail header it receives with the request. Make sure you do not make this command a part of the "Subject:" line, as it will be ignored by the server. If at some time in the future you wish to unsubscribe, use the command:

```
UNSUBSCRIBE listname
```

e-mail lists of interest via listserv:

| *List name* | *Discussion topic* |
|---|---|
| AIXESA-L | AIX/ESA on large systems |
| AIX370-L | AIX V1.2 on large systems |
| POWER-L | RISC System 6000 AIX V3 |
| AIX-L | General AIX topics |
| DQS-L | Distributed Queuing System—Batch |
| LL-L | Load Leveler discussion |
| SP1-L | Power Parallel SP1 discussion |
| POWER-PC | Power Personal PC discussion |
| UNIX-WIZ | UNIX Wizards Usenet redistribution |
| SHARENIX | SHARE UNIX group information |

Once you have received notification that you have been added to the list of subscribers, you may then participate in list discussions by sending mail to the list name and address. For example, mail to:

```
AIXESA-L@vm.its.rpi.edu
```

will be distributed to all subscribers of AIXESA-L.

## Usenet News

Another discussion list facility is Usenet News. This is somewhat similar to e-mail, but requires access to a site which acts as a server and receives news feeds from other sites on the network. Usenet News is accessible by a number of user interface programs, one of the more popular of which is "rn." Discussions are divided into *newsgroups* with a limited classification hierarchy that groups topics of interest. To participate in a newsgroup, you must first subscribe. Here I will point you to the man page for the particular interface program you use. Like most mail systems, there are facilities to browse, save, reply, subscribe, and post to newsgroups. Newsgroups of interest include:

| *Newsgroup* | *Topic* |
|---|---|
| comp.unix.aix | General AIX, leans to AIX V3 |
| bit.listserv.aix-l | Redistribution of AIX-L |
| comp.unix | General UNIX topics |
| comp.unix.wizards | UNIX sys admin, internals, etc. |
| comp.unix.internals | UNIX internals, programming |
| comp.archives | Software via anonymous ftp |
| comp.sources.wanted | Requests for software all OS |

There is also a newsgroup being formed for the AIX users group. Watch for it at a news feed near you.

## Anonymous FTP Archives

A number of sites on the network provide public access to software archives via anonymous ftp. Instead of requiring that you have an account on the given site, you may log in in as user ID "anonymous," and supply a password that is either your user ID or e-mail address. This allows these sites to keep track of who is using their service. After logging in, you are free to browse the directories and download anything that may be of use to you.

*FTP sites:*

```
aixpdslib.seas.ucla.edu     AIX/6000 public domain software
ibminet.awdpa.ibm.com       IBM announcements, OEM hardware list
ftp.egr.duke.edu            AIX archive
straylight.acs.ncsu.edu     AIX archive
alpha.gnu.ai.mit.edu        AIX archive
ftp.ans.net                 wais stuff
wuarchive.wustl.edu         Public Internet archive site
```

## Anonymous FTP by e-mail

If you don't have ftp access, but do have e-mail access, you may obtain access to anonymous ftp archives via a server at Princeton. The server will retrieve files for you via e-mail. You may request access by sending mail to:

```
bitftp@pucc.princeton.edu
```

On your first attempt to use the server, include the commands HELP and FTPLIST on separate lines in the mail text. These will prompt the server to send you a help file and anonymous ftp site list. There is also information on encoding techniques supported for transferring files to you via e-mail.

Appendix

# B

# Sample Code

The following set of sample code is provided for illustration purposes only. No warranties or guarantees are implied. These are just a few tools I use from time to time that you might find useful. I'm not going to try to defend my coding practices, so please don't write!

*Set RTS on a TTY Port:*

```
/* Set RTS on a TTY line and don't block. */

#include <stdio.h>
#include <fcntl.h>
#include <termios.h>
#include <sys/ioctl.h>

main(argc,argv)
int argc;
char *argv[];
{
   int fd;
   union txname ttytx;

   if (argc < 2)
       fprintf(stderr,"Usage: %s /dev/tty?",argv[0]);

   if ((fd = open(argv[1],O_NONBLOCK)) < 0) {
       fprintf(stderr,"Can't open device %s\n",argv[1]);
       exit(1);
   }

   strcpy(ttytx.tx_name, "rts");
   if(ioctl(fd,TXADDCD,&ttytx) < 0) {
       fprintf(stderr,"Add rts failed %s\n",argv[1]);
       perror(argv[1]);
       exit(1);
   }

   exit(0);
}
```

*Clean corrupted UTMP file:*

```
/*
** Clean dead proces from UTMP file.
*/
```

```
#include <sys/types.h>
#include <utmp.h>
#include <fcntl.h>

main ()
{
   int fd;
   struct utmp utmp;

   if ((fd = open ("/etc/utmp", O_RDWR)) < 0)
   exit (1);

   while (read (fd, &utmp, sizeof utmp) = = sizeof utmp) {
       if (utmp.ut_type = = USER_PROCESS && kill(utmp.ut_pid, 0) != 0) {
           lseek (fd, - (long) sizeof utmp, 1);
           utmp.ut_type = DEAD_PROCESS;
           write (fd, &utmp, sizeof utmp);
       }
   }
   close (fd);
   printf("UTMP clean complete\n");
   exit (0);
}
```

*Open a PTY master/slave pair:*

```
/*
** Open a master/slave pty pair on AIX and print the names. */
*/

#include <stdio.h>

main (argc, argv)
int argc;
char *argv[];
{

   char *ptsname;
   int number;
   int fd;

   if ((fd = open ("/dev/ptc", 0)) < 0) {
       perror ("/dev/ptc");
       exit (1);
   }

   ptsname = ttyname(fd);

   printf("Slave: %s\n",ptsname);
   sscanf(ptsname,"/dev/pts/%d",&number);
   printf("Master: /dev/ptc/%d\n",number);

   exit(0);
}
```

*Get and set process queue priority:*

```
/*
** getpri: Get process queue priority.
*/

#include <stdio.h>
#include <sys/types.h>
#include <sys/pri.h>
#include <sys/errno.h>
```

```
main(argc,argv)
int argc;
char *argv[];
{
   int pid;
   int pri;

   if ( argc <= 1 ) {
       printf("Usage: getpri pid\n");
       exit(1);
   }

   pid = atoi(argv[1]);
   pri = getpri(pid);
   if (pri == -1) {
       perror("Getpri failed");
       exit(1);
   }
   printf("Priority for pid: %d --> %d\n",pid,pri);
}


/*
** setpri: Set process queue priority.
*/
#include <stdio.h>
#include <sys/types.h>
#include <sys/pri.h>
#include <sys/sched.h>
#include <sys/errno.h>

main(argc,argv)
int argc;
char *argv[];
{
   int pid;
   int opri,npri;
   if ( argc != 3 ) {
       printf("Usage: setpri pid priority\n");
       printf("        priority = %d (high) thru %d (low)\n",
                       PRIORITY_MIN, PRIORITY_MAX);
       exit(1);
   }

   pid = atoi(argv[1]);
   npri = atoi(argv[2]);
   if (npri < PRIORITY_MIN | npri > PRIORITY_MAX) {
       printf("Priority %d out of range!\n",npri);
       printf("Usage: setpri pid priority\n");
       printf("        priority = %d (high) thru %d (low)\n",
                       PRIORITY_MIN, PRIORITY_MAX);
       exit(1);
   }
   printf("set priority for pid: %d \n",pid);
   opri = setpri(pid,npri);
   if (opri == -1) {
       perror("setpri() failed");
       exit(1);
   }
   printf(" old %d new %d\n",opri,npri);
}
```

*Attempt to reset a hung tape drive:*

```
/*
**rmtreset - Clear hung tape device.
```

```
**
** Use openx() call to force a Bus Device Reset (BDR) regardless of
** device reservation by another initiator. See InfoExplorer rmt
** SCSI Device Driver for more information.
*/

#include <stdio.h>
#include <sys/devinfo.h>
#include <sys/scsi.h>
#include <sys/tape.h>
#include <fcntl.h>

int main(argc, argv)
int argc;
char *argv[];
{

   if (argc ! = 2) {
       fprintf(stderr, "Usage: rmtreset /dev/<rmt?>\n");
       exit(1);
   }

   if (openx(argv[1], O_RDONLY, 0, SC_FORCED_OPEN) < 0) {
       perror("openx() failed:");
       exit(1);
   }
   exit(0);
}
```

# Bibliography


*AIX for RISC System/6000 Installation Guide,* SC23-2341.

*AIX Version 3 for RISC System/6000 Communication Concepts and Procedures, Volumes 1 and 2,* GC23-2203.

"AIX Version 3.1 Additional Authorization: An Example," *IBM International Technical Support Centers Redbook.* GG24-3750.

*AIX Version 3.2 Problem Solving Guide and Reference,* SC23-2204.

*AIX Version 3.2 System Management Guide,* SC23-2457.

*AIX Version 3.2 System User's Guide,* GC23-2377.

Andleigh, Prabhat K., *UNIX System Architecture,* Prentice Hall, Englewood Cliffs, N.J., 1990.

Cox, Daniel, "High Availability Cluster Multi-Processing/6000," */AIXtra* **3**(3) (May/June 1993).

Darwin, Ian, "PC-NFS," *SunExpert* **3**(11) (November 1992).

DeRoest, Jim, "AIX and DOS—A Marriage Made for the RS/6000," *RS/Magazine* **1**(5) (May 1992).

DeRoest, Jim, "AIX and DOS—A Marriage Made for the RS/6000," *RS/Magazine* **1**(6) (June 1993).

DeRoest, Jim, "AIX V3 tty and Modem Support," *RS/Magazine* charter issue, Fall 1991.

DeRoest, Jim, "Bump in the Night: AIX Debugging and Recovery," *RS/Magazine* **1**(12) (December 1992).

DeRoest, Jim, "Down on the Farm," *RS/Magazine* **1**(1) (January 1992).

DeRoest, Jim, "Everything in its Place—UNIX Archiving," *RS/Magazine* **1**(8) (August 1992).

DeRoest, Jim, "Glass Menageries of X: IBM Xstations," *RS/Magazine* **2**(4) (April 1993).

DeRoest, Jim, "Highly Available UNIX," *RS/Magazine* **1**(10) (October 1992).

DeRoest, Jim, "Highways and Byways," *RS/Magazine* **1**(9) (September 1992).

DeRoest, Jim, "Home Away from Home," *RS/Magazine* **2**(2) (February 1993).

DeRoest, Jim, "Orthodox Window Managers," *RS/Magazine* **1**(6) (June 1992).

DeRoest, Jim, "Red Hot Chili Servers," *RS/Magazine* **2**(5) (May 1993).

DeRoest, Jim, "Share and Share Alike—UNIX Batch Processing," *RS/Magazine* **1**(7) (July 1992).

DeRoest, Jim, "Taming the Beast—AIX Tuning," *RS/Magazine* **1**(11) (November 1992).

DeRoest, Jim, "UNIX Batch Queuing Revisited," *RS/Magazine* **1**(7) (July 1993).

DeRoest, Jim, "Who Did You Say You Are?—AIX Alternate Authentication," *RS/Magazine* **1**(8) (August 1993).

Dowd, Kevin, "Programming in Parallel," *RS/Magazine* **2**(3) (March 1993).

Eargle, John, *Handbook of Recording Engineering,* Van Nostrand Reinhold, New York, 1986.

Frisch, Aeleen, "Boosting Performance on the RS/6000," *RS/Magazine* **2**(5) (May 1993).

Frisch, Aeleen, *Essential System Administration,* O'Reilly & Associates, Inc.

Frisch, Aeleen, "Writing it Down," *RS/Magazine* **2**(6) (June 1993).

Gibbs, G. Benton, "Demystifying the Object Data Manager—Part 1," */AIXtra* **2**(2) (April 1992).

Gibbs, G. Benton, "Demystifying the Object Data Manager—Part 2," */AIXtra* **2**(3) (July 1992).

Gibbs, G. Benton, "Demystifying the Object Data Manager—Part 3," */AIXtra* **2**(4) (October 1992).

Heise, Russel A., "Performance Tuning: A Continuing Series—The vmstat Tool," */AIXtra* **3**(5) (September/October 1993).
"IBM RISC System/6000 Processor," *IBM Journal of Research and Development* **34**(1) (January 1990).
*IBM RISC System/6000 Technology,* SA23-2619.
Lewis, Elizabeth "Performance Tuning: Theory and Practice," */AIXtra* **3**(2) (March/April 1993).
Linthicum, David S., "NFS Explained," *RS/Magazine* **2**(4) (April 1993).
Linthicum, David S., "Using UUCP: The Basics," *RS/Magazine* **1**(7) (July 1993).
Loukides, Mike, "System Performance Tuning," O'Reilly & Associates, Inc., Sebastopol, Calif., 1990.
Majkiewicz, Jane, "Taming the Backup Beast," *RS/Magazine* **2**(2) (February 1993).
Martin, Paul, and Dinah McNutt, "Customizing SMIT," *RS/Magazine* **1**(5) (May 1992).
Mullender, Sape, *Distributed Systems,* ACM Press, Addison-Wesley, Reading, Mass., 1993.
Nemeth, Evi, Garth Snyder, and Scott SeeBass, *UNIX System Administration Handbook,* Prentice Hall Software Series, Englewood Cliffs, N.J., 1989.
Onic, Elmer, "Setting Up OSIMF/6000," */AIXtra* **2**(3) (July 1992).
Peek, Jerry, Mike Loukides, and Tim O'Reilly, *UNIX Power Tools,* Bantam Books, Sebastopol, Calif., 1990..
*POWERstation and POWERserver Common Diagnostics and Service Guide,* SA23-2687.
"Printing for Fun and Profit Under AIX V3," *IBM International Technical Support Centers Red Book,* GG24-3570.
Stevens, W. Richard, *Advanced Programming in the UNIX Environment,* Addison-Wesley, Reading, Mass., 1992.
Stevens, W. Richard, *UNIX Network Programming,* Prentice Hall Software Series, Englewood Cliffs, N.J., 1990.
Stoessel, Doris, "The IBM 7051 POWER Network Dataserver," */AIXtra* **3**(5) (September/October 1993).
Stokes, Dawn C., "A Comparison of DCE DFS and AFS," */AIXtra* **2**(4) (October 1992).
Tanenbaum, Andrew S., *Computer Networks,* Prentice-Hall, Englewood Cliffs, N.J., 1981.
"TCP/IP Tutorial and Technical Overview," *IBM International Technical Support Centers Red Book,* GG24-3376.
Wise, Mary Vicknair, "High Availability for Network File System," */AIXtra* **3**(1) (January 1993).

# Index

## ABOUT THE AUTHOR

James W. DeRoest manages the Advanced Systems Technology Group at the University of Washington. He writes the monthly "AIXtensions" column for *RS/Magazine* on technical applications for the RS/6000, and is also past AIX project manager for SHARE Inc., IBM User Group. He has been involved in IBM AIX development for more than eight years.